SECOND EDITION

WOMEN, POLITICS, AND POWER

For our mothers

SECOND EDITION

WOMEN, POLITICS, AND POWER

A Global Perspective

◆

PAMELA PAXTON

The University of Texas at Austin

MELANIE M. HUGHES

University of Pittsburgh

Los Angeles | London | New Delhi
Singapore | Washington DC

Los Angeles | London | New Delhi
Singapore | Washington DC

FOR INFORMATION:

SAGE Publications, Inc.
2455 Teller Road
Thousand Oaks, California 91320
E-mail: order@sagepub.com

SAGE Publications Ltd.
1 Oliver's Yard
55 City Road
London EC1Y 1SP
United Kingdom

SAGE Publications India Pvt. Ltd.
B 1/I 1 Mohan Cooperative Industrial Area
Mathura Road, New Delhi 110 044
India

SAGE Publications Asia-Pacific Pte. Ltd.
3 Church Street
#10-04 Samsung Hub
Singapore 049483

Printed in the United States of America

Library of Congress Cataloging-in-Publication Data

Paxton, Pamela Marie.

Women, politics, and power: a global perspective / Pamela Paxton, The University of Texas at Austin, Melanie M. Hughes, University of Pittsburgh. — Second Edition.

pages cm
Includes bibliographical references and index.

ISBN 978-1-4129-9866-6 (alk. paper)

1. Women—Political activity. 2. Women—Political activity—Cross-cultural studies. 3. Representative government and representation. I. Hughes, Melanie M. II. Title.

HQ1236.P39 2013
324.082—dc23   2013007396

This book is printed on acid-free paper.

Acquisitions Editor: David Repetto
Editorial Assistant: Lauren Johnson
Production Editor: Libby Larson
Copy Editor: Megan Markanich
Typesetter: C&M Digitals (P) Ltd
Proofreader: Kate Peterson
Indexer: Jeanne Busemeyer
Cover Designer: Karine Hovsepian
Marketing Manager: Erica DeLuca

11 12 13 14 15 10 9 8 7 6 5 4 3 2 1

Contents

List of Figures, Tables, and Maps

Figures

Tables

Maps

About the Authors

Pamela Paxton is professor of sociology and government and the Christine and Stanley E. Adams, Jr. Centennial Professor in the Liberal Arts at The University of Texas at Austin. She received her undergraduate degree from the University of Michigan in economics and sociology and her PhD in sociology from the University of North Carolina at Chapel Hill. She has consulted for the U.S. Agency for International Development (USAID) and the National Academies. She is the author of numerous scholarly articles on women in politics, which focus on statistical models of women's parliamentary representation. Her research has appeared in a variety of journals, including *American Sociological Review, American Journal of Sociology, Social Forces, Comparative Politics, British Journal of Political Science,* and *Studies in International Comparative Development.* She is also an author of *Nonrecursive Models: Endogeneity, Reciprocal Relationships, and Feedback Loops* (2011).

Melanie M. Hughes is assistant professor of sociology at The University of Pittsburgh. Born in Milwaukee, Wisconsin, she graduated from the University of Texas at Austin in 2001 with a degree in sociology and government and earned her PhD from The Ohio State University in 2008. She is affiliated with the Department of Political Science, the European Union Center of Excellence, Global Studies, and Women's Studies. She is author of several articles on women in politics, and she specializes in political representation of women from marginalized groups. Her research has appeared in journals such as *American Sociological Review, American Political Science Review, Social Forces, Politics & Gender, European Journal of Political Research, Social Problems,* and *Legislative Studies Quarterly.* Her current work investigates the legislative representation of women from Muslim origins across Europe.

Preface

I magine that your country has 100% women in its parliament or national legislature. How does this make you feel? Are you concerned that men are not being well represented or served by the government? Now add 5% men back into the legislature. Do you feel better about a 95%–5% split? What about 10% men? Are you comfortable yet?

Most readers might feel uncomfortable with a parliament made up entirely of women. But the reverse—the complete dominance of legislatures by men—is actually a reality in some countries. And where men do not completely dominate, they still hold over 90% of parliamentary seats in a wide range of countries. This book documents and explains the forces that contribute to such gender inequality in politics. But the story of women's exclusion from politics is changing. Increasingly, women are holding political positions around the world, and in some countries, women's political power has increased dramatically in recent years. Thus, in addition to exploring barriers to women's political access, this expanded second edition devotes even more attention to where and how women have been gaining ground.

We open the second edition of our book by outlining the theoretical and practical reasons to incorporate women in politics formally, descriptively, and substantively. In the early chapters of the book, we track the growth in women's political participation over time beginning with the fight for women's suffrage (Chapter 2) and moving through women's parliamentary representation and ascendance to leadership positions as heads of state or cabinet ministers (Chapter 3). In order to describe different patterns of growth in women's representation over time, we introduce five basic historical paths to power: (1) Flat, (2) Increasing, (3) Big Jump, (4) Low Increasing, and (5) Plateau. One point we make in these early chapters is that the West did not necessarily lead the world historically in women's political power and is not currently in the forefront of women's representation.

In Chapters 4, 5, 6, and 7, we explore why women have succeeded in gaining political representation in some places and not in others. We distinguish between two broad sets of factors that produce different levels of representation for women across the world: supply-side factors and demand-side factors. Supply factors are those that increase the pool of women with the will and experience to compete against men for political office (see Chapter 5). Demand factors, on the other hand, are characteristics of countries, electoral systems, or political parties that make it more likely that women will be pulled into office from the supply of willing candidates (see Chapter 6). Other factors, such as culture and international pressure, cross both supply and demand (see Chapters 4 and 7). In the second edition, we have expanded coverage of influences such as the media and quotas and added new sections that consider the importance of role model effects, informal networks, and natural resources, among others. The central message of these four chapters is that if we are to understand how women can gain political power, we must simultaneously understand cultural beliefs about women's place, the social structural position of women, the political environment in which women operate, and key international pressures on states to change.

But do women make a difference? Do women in positions of power change anything? Have women changed the style of politics? Chapter 8 attempts to answer these questions by assessing not only women's numbers but their impact on policy, agenda setting, and legislative style. We argue that understanding women's influence is critical but that we face a variety of challenges in attempting to demonstrate the impact of women. We highlight additional possible sites of influence such as women's movements, raise concerns about whether a "critical mass" (30%) of women is necessary for impact, and point out that many questions about minority women's impact remain.

With this second edition of the book, we more clearly acknowledge differences among women both within countries and across geographic regions. Chapter 9 discusses the political participation and representation of women from marginalized groups. We discuss some of the multiple barriers faced by racial, ethnic, and religious minority women, but we also discuss some of the circumstances under which such women are politically successful. The chapter also includes sections on indigenous women and sexual minorities— lesbian, bisexual, and transgender women.

Chapters 10 through 15 focus on women in politics in six geographic regions of the world, drawing out key issues and trends in each region. In Chapter 10, on Western industrialized countries, we focus on North America, Western Europe, Australia, and New Zealand. We highlight how the political culture of Scandinavia has enabled women to make impressive advances in politics, and we discuss where the United States falls in global rankings of women in politics, and why. Then, turning to Eastern Europe, we consider topics such as the history and fall of the Soviet Union and its implications for women (Chapter 11). In both Chapters 10 and 11, we look at women's political representation in the European Union (EU). Women's activism in movements for democracy, gender quotas, and the Catholic Church are emphasized in Chapter 12, on Latin America. Then, in Chapter 13, we turn to the Middle East and North Africa, exploring women's informal political activity and the relationship women have to the Arab Spring. In Chapter 14, on Asia and the Pacific, we discuss a wide range of issues from Confucianism to modernization, and we consider specific challenges faced by women in particular countries or subregions, including Afghanistan and the Pacific Islands. We end our regional exploration with sub-Saharan Africa, where women have made some of the most dramatic gains in political representation in recent years (Chapter 15).

The concluding chapter asks where we are going and how we can get there. It introduces our updated Women Power Index—a way to measure women's political power. We assess lessons learned and list a number of web resources for further reading. We also consider what the world would look like if we lived in a truly 50/50 world—that is, if neither sex dominated political positions.

It is our purpose with this book to explore the experiences of women in politics in countries around the globe. We focus largely on women's participation and representation in formal political positions. But throughout the text, we also emphasize the importance and power of women's informal political activities, such as participation in social movements. Although much of the book focuses on national-level politics, the second edition includes expanded coverage of women in local governance (see Chapter 6, in particular).

Of course, this book—both in its first iteration and this revised edition—would not have been possible without the support of a wide range of people and institutions. We thank Kira Sanbonmatsu, Clarissa Hayward, Mona Lena Krook, Evan Schofer, Anne Jolliff, Jennifer Green, Josh Dubrow, Sheri Kunovich, Colin Odden, Judy Wu, John Gerring, Nicholas Reith, Megan Neely, Pamela Neumann, Philip Cantu, and Letisha Brown for helpful suggestions, comments, and/or advice at various points in the project.

We also thank our reviewers who provided invaluable suggestions for revision. For the first edition, we benefited from the advice of Hannah Britton (Departments of Political Science and Women's Studies at the University of Kansas), Dianne Bystrom (Carrie Chapman Catt Center for Women and Politics at Iowa State University), Deirdre Condit (Departments of Women's Studies and Political Science at Virginia Commonwealth University), Valentine Moghadam (Department of Sociology and International

Affairs Program, Northeastern University), Barbara Ryan (Departments of Sociology and Women's Studies at Widener University), and Kathleen Staudt (Department of Political Science at The University of Texas at El Paso). For the second edition, we thank anonymous reviewers from Bethel University, Kalamazoo Valley Community College, Mississippi State University, Aurora University, Bemidji State University, the University of Alberta Augustana, San Francisco State University, Southern Illinois University, the University of Detroit-Mercy, and the College of Saint Rose. These reviewers helped us invaluably as we made decisions about the new edition.

Special thanks go to Vinnie Roscigno and David Repetto, who shepherded our first and second editions through to their completion. We are also grateful to series editors Joya Misra, Gay Seidman, and York Bradshaw, and to Jerry Westby, Ben Penner, Camille Herrera, Elise Smith, Maggie Stanley, and Lauren Johnson at SAGE Publications. We also thank the National Science Foundation, the Mershon Center for International Security at The Ohio State University, the Coca-Cola Critical Difference for Women Program, and the Departments of Sociology at The University of Texas at Austin, University of Pittsburgh, and The Ohio State University for their support of this project.

We are grateful to our partners, Paul and Britton, as well as our friends, family members, and colleagues for their encouragement and support. Finally, we thank the female politicians of the world for inspiring us to write this book.

1

Introduction to Women in Politics

W omen are underrepresented in politics. Simply turning on the television to a summit of world leaders, a debate in the British Parliament, or a UN Security Council meeting reveals few female faces. Women make up half of the population of every country in the world. But the worldwide average percentage of women in national parliaments is only 20%. Of the more than 190 countries in the world, a woman is the head of government (president or a prime minister) in only 13. Women are 15% of ambassadors to the United Nations and 17% of the world's cabinet ministers.

But women's participation in politics has increased dramatically over the past 100 years. In 1890, women did not have the right to vote anywhere in the world. Today, no country in the world denies only women the right to vote. In 1907, Finland became the first country to elect a female member of **parliament.** Currently, women make up over 50% of the **national legislature** in two countries. The first country to reach 10% women in its national legislature was the Union of Soviet Socialist Republics (USSR), in 1946. Today, 75% of countries have at least 10% women in their national legislatures. Although women still are substantially underrepresented in politics in most countries of the world, women's representation in politics is increasing quickly. In the 10 years between 2000 and 2010, the average number of women in parliaments nearly doubled, from 11.7% to 19.4%. The growth in women's political power is one of the most important trends of the past 100 years.

There is also significant variation in women's political representation across countries. In some countries, such as Sweden, Argentina, and Rwanda, women have made remarkable progress in their political representation. Unfortunately, in many other countries, the struggle for equal representation proceeds slowly. And some populations, religions, and governments remain openly hostile to the notion of women in politics.

For years, Sweden reigned as the country with the highest percentage of women in its parliament. In 2003, however, Sweden was dethroned by Rwanda, which reached 48.8% women in its legislature. And in 2008, Rwanda became the first country in the world to breach the 50% barrier by electing 56% women to its parliament. The two countries could not be more different. Sweden is a developed Western nation, has been at peace for almost two centuries, and governs through a parliament first established more than 500 years ago (Kelber 1994). In Sweden, women's increasing participation in politics was a long, slow process. Beginning with reforms in the 1920s, Sweden broke the 10% mark for women's legislative representation in 1952, boasted the first female acting prime minister in 1958, and then passed the 20% mark for female legislative presence in 1973 and the 30% mark in 1985.

In contrast, in 2003 Rwanda had just begun to recover from a brutal genocide during which more than 1 million people lost their lives. Rwanda is a poor nation in Africa that ranks 166th out of 187 countries in its level of "human development" (United Nations Development Programme [UNDP]

Figure 1.1   Finding the Eight Female World Leaders Among Those Gathered for the United Nations 60th Anniversary Is a Challenge

Source: UN/DPI Photo. Reprinted with permission.

2011). The 2003 election was the inaugural election of a new constitution, which guaranteed women at least 30% of the National Assembly seats. Before that time, women had been less of a presence, never hitting 20% of the parliament before the transition to an interim government in 1994. But even with a guaranteed 30%, voters chose even more women—19% more in 2003 and 26% more in 2008. The promotion of women by international organizations, the influence of local women's organizations, and the sheer number of men killed during or imprisoned after the genocide help to explain the sudden rise of women to substantial political power (Longman 2006).

That Rwanda and Sweden both rank so highly in women's legislative presence suggests that one cannot assume that women do better in Western, industrialized nations. Indeed, there is substantial variation across regions of the world, and many highly developed Western countries fall far behind developing countries in their representation of women as political leaders (Inter-Parliamentary Union [IPU] 2012b). For example, as of December 2011, the United States ranked 95th of 188 countries in percentage of women, falling behind Bosnia and Herzegovina, Ecuador, and Mozambique. Britain ranked 59th and is behind Mexico, Namibia, and Vietnam. France, Italy, and the United States have never had a female president, whereas Sri Lanka, the Philippines, and Indonesia have. It is also important to recognize that Sweden and Rwanda are two of only a handful of stories of extraordinary success for women's presence in politics. Today, of all countries, nearly 60% of countries have less than 20% women in their national legislatures. And six countries have no women at all.

The story of women, politics, and power is therefore different than that of women in education or women in the labor force. Although women have made remarkable inroads into both higher education and traditionally male occupations, the political sphere remains an area where, despite the progress they have made, women still have far to go.

Arguments for Women's Representation in Politics

Why should we care about a lack of women in politics? First, politics is an important arena for decision making. Individuals who hold official positions in government get to decide how to allocate scarce resources such as tax revenues. Politicians make decisions that may help some people at the expense of others. Decisions by politicians even affect people's individual choices by encouraging some behaviors and outlawing others. Second, political power is a valuable good. Politicians hold power over other social institutions, such as the family or education, and are able to codify particular practices into law (Martin 2004). Politicians have the power to enforce their decisions, sometimes with force. Third, to hold a political position is to hold a position of authority. Looking at the makeup of political figures in a country highlights who is legitimated to make society-wide decisions in that society.

But does it matter if all political decision makers are male? In principle, the answer could be no. But in practice the answer is often yes. In principle, most laws are gender neutral, and elected representatives pay attention to all of their constituents equally. In practice, however, **feminist** political theorists have argued that the appearance of neutrality toward gender or equality between men and women in government actually hides substantial gender inequality. If gender-neutral language is used in principle but in practice only men appear in politics, then women are not equal but rather invisible. Theorists such as Carole Pateman (1988, 1989), Anne Phillips (1991, 1995), and Iris Young (1990) have shown that abstract terms used in political theory, such as *individual* or *citizen*, though having the appearance of being gender neutral, actually signify White males. Even more forceful arguments say that the state was structured from its inception to benefit men and that it has a continuing interest in the maintenance of male domination, both in Western countries (Lerner 1986; MacKinnon 1989) and in non-Western countries (Charrad 2001).

Without women, the state, being populated only by men, could legislate in the male interest. That is, if women are not around when decisions are made, their interests may not be served. Golda Meir was an Israeli cabinet minister before she became prime minister of Israel. She related the following story:

> Once in the Cabinet we had to deal with the fact that there had been an outbreak of assaults on women at night. One minister (a member of an extreme religious party) suggested a curfew. Women should stay at home after dark. I said: "but it's the men attacking the women. If there's to be a curfew, let the men stay at home, not the women."

Golda Meir's presence on the cabinet allowed her to point out the unfairness of making women stay home rather than men. If she had not been there, who would have pointed this out?

In general, male lawmakers are less likely to initiate and pass laws that serve women's and children's interests (Berkman and O'Connor 1993; Bratton and Haynie 1999; Childs and Withey 2004; Taylor-Robinson and Heath 2003). Men less often think about rape, domestic violence, women's health, and child care. Women, in turn, have demonstrably different policy priorities than men (Chattopadhyay and Duflo 2004; Gerrity, Osborn, and Mendez 2007; Schwindt-Bayer 2006; Swers 1998). In democracies, the points of view of all groups need to be taken into account. Therefore, the views and opinions of women as well as men must be incorporated into political decision making.

These arguments are interesting in theory but what about in practice? What might it mean to women around the world to be underrepresented in politics?

The Story of Mukhtaran Bibi: Village Council Justice

In June 2002, in Meerwala, a remote village in Pakistan, Mukhtaran Bibi's 12-year-old brother was accused of having an affair with a woman of a higher caste. The village council ruled that her brother had committed a crime and sentenced Mukhtaran Bibi to be gang-raped by four men as punishment. The four men stripped her naked and took turns raping her. She then had to walk home almost naked in front of several hundred people (Kristof 2004, 2005; Kristof and WuDunn 2009).

The expectation was that now Mukhtaran Bibi would commit suicide. Indeed, because they are now considered deeply dishonored and stigmatized, this is the typical path taken by the hundreds of Pakistani girls gang-raped every year due to family or tribal rivalries. Instead, Ms. Mukhtaran defied tradition by testifying against her attackers, resulting in six convictions. Government investigators now say that the accusation against her brother was false. Instead, members of the higher caste tribe actually sexually abused Mukhtaran Bibi's brother and tried to cover it up by falsely accusing him of the affair.

Mukhtaran Bibi's story has a mostly happy ending. She received compensation money from Pakistani president Pervez Musharraf and used it to start two schools in her village—one for boys and the other for girls. When the government detained her for planning to visit the United States in June 2005, international attention and outcry forced her release. Her autobiography was a best seller in France, and she has received an honorary doctorate from a university in Canada. Although her attackers' convictions were overturned by a high court in March 2005 and the acquittal was upheld in 2011 by the Supreme Court, she receives public police protection to ensure the safety of her family.

The stories of many other young girls in Pakistan do not have such happy endings. They are beaten for not producing sons, raped, disfigured for trying to choose a husband for themselves, or killed as a matter of family honor. Under the 1979 Hudood Ordinances, courts could view a woman's charge of rape as an admission of illegal sex unless she could prove that the intercourse was nonconsensual. Although the 2006 Protection of Women law reformed the way Pakistan prosecutes rapists, marital rape remains unrecognized, and the effects of the ordinances are still felt: Some estimates suggest that three quarters of women in Pakistan's jails today are rape victims (*The Economist* 2002).

Wife Beating in Nigeria— Legal Under the Penal Code

In December 2001, Rosalynn Isimeto-Osibuamhe of Lagos, Nigeria, wanted to visit her parents. Her husband, Emmanuel, told her she had to stay home. Their argument ended when Emmanuel beat Rosalynn unconscious and left her lying in the street outside their apartment. This was hardly the first time she'd been beaten. During the course of their 4-year marriage, Emmanuel beat her more than 60 times (LaFraniere 2005).

This story is not an unusual one in Africa, where domestic violence is endemic. Chronic underreporting, cultural acceptance, and women's shame make it difficult to provide hard-and-fast numbers on the extent of wife beating in Africa. But a recent study suggests that one half of Zambian women report being physically abused by a male partner. An earlier Nigerian survey explains that 81% of married women reported being verbally or physically abused by husbands. Domestic and international advocacy groups have increasingly put pressure on African governments to address high rates of violence against women (Burrill, Roberts, and Thornberry 2010; Htun and Weldon 2012). But many African countries still do not have domestic violence laws on the books (Kishor and Johnson 2004; LaFraniere 2005; Odunjinrin 1993).

What could Rosalynn Isimeto-Osibuamhe do? Domestic violence is entrenched in Nigerian law. Section 56 of the Nigerian Penal Code allows husbands to use physical means to chastise their wives, as long as the husbands do not inflict grievous harm, where grievous harm is defined as loss of sight, hearing, power of speech, facial disfigurement, or other life-threatening injuries. Nigeria, a country of 350,000 square miles, has only two shelters for battered women. Police do not pursue domestic violence as assault, and Rosalynn's pastor told her not to make her husband angry and to submit to him. Indeed, many of Isimeto-Osibuamhe's female neighbors believe that husbands have a right to beat wives who argue, burn dinner, or come home late (LaFraniere 2005).

Rosalynn Isimeto-Osibuamhe is unusual in that she was able to leave her husband. She is university educated and the founder of a French school. And she did find a shelter and stayed there for weeks. Many other women in Africa, unable to leave their husbands, are not so lucky.

Delaying the Clarence Thomas Vote— Female Representatives Speak Out

For many people in 1991, the television image of 16 White men interrogating Anita Hill during Senate Judiciary Committee hearings epitomized the lack of women's presence in American politics. But that hearing might not have taken place at all if not for the swift and decisive actions of a small group of female congresswomen.

In the fall of 1991, Clarence Thomas was close to being confirmed as a U.S. Supreme Court justice. But on October 6th, two days before the Senate was scheduled to vote on his nomination, a distinguished law professor, Anita Hill, accused Thomas of sexually harassing her in 1981. The story exploded in the media, and various groups began calling for a delay on the confirmation vote until the charges of sexual harassment could be fully investigated.

But on Tuesday morning, the 8th of October, it looked as though the Senate vote on Thomas would go forward as planned. The men of the Senate (at the time the Senate had 98 men and two women) did not plan to investigate the charges of sexual harassment and appeared ready to confirm Thomas's nomination to the Supreme Court. This continued a monthlong pattern, as Hill had told the Senate Judiciary Committee about her allegations in early September, but the committee had not pursued it. The male senators seemed ready to take Judge Thomas's word over Professor Hill's without formal or detailed examination of the evidence.

Because 98% of the Senate was male, congresswomen were concerned that women's perspectives on sexual harassment were not being fully considered. Therefore, a number of congresswomen decided to take action. They began by speaking on the floor of the House of Representatives, reminding their colleagues that justice required that Hill's allegations be taken seriously. Barbara Boxer argued the following:

Mr. Speaker, imagine yourself dependent on another human being for your livelihood. Imagine the power that person holds over you. Imagine that person making suggestive comments to you, and beyond that, telling you in detail about pornographic materials he had seen. Would you be intimidated? Yes, especially if you are in your 20s and you are a woman in a man's field. . . . And, which court is that final protection of women from this kind of harassment? . . . The Supreme Court of the United States of America.

When procedural rules were used to stop these speeches, the congresswomen decided to go further and take their concerns directly to the Senate. In a march immortalized in photographs, seven congresswomen left Congress and strode over to the Senate side of the Capitol to speak with Senate Democrats during their regular Tuesday caucus meeting. High heels clicking as they advanced up the steps of the Capitol, these elected representatives were determined to emphasize that the women's point of view might be very different from the view of these male senators (see Figure 1.2). To them, these charges were serious and worthy of genuine consideration.

Figure 1.2   Congresswomen March to U.S. Senate

Source: Paul Hosefros/*The New York Times.*

The congresswomen were turned away from the closed-door caucus meeting, despite repeated pleas to be allowed in. The Senate majority leader ultimately agreed to meet with the women separately, and they stated their case. That night, facing mounting public pressure, he announced that a confirmation vote on Thomas would be delayed so hearings on Anita Hill's charges could be held.

Thus, seven elected female congresswomen, Patricia Schroeder of Colorado, Barbara Boxer of California, Louise Slaughter of New York, Jolene Unsoeld of Washington, Patsy Mink of Hawaii, Nita Lowey of New York, and Barbara Kennelly of Connecticut, as well as delegate Eleanor Holmes Norton of the District of Columbia, played a critical role in helping America and the Senate understand that women's concerns were important in the halls of power.

This story also has a mostly happy ending. Although many felt that the Anita Hill hearings were ultimately a farce, public resentment of that farce helped to send Barbara Boxer, one of the marchers, and three other women to the Senate the following year—a Senate that would not have a women's bathroom until 1993. The Anita Hill hearings also helped increase awareness of sexual harassment of women in the workplace, which was only incorporated into the guidelines set by the Equal Opportunity Commission (the body responsible for adjudicating sexual harassment claims) in 1980 (Boxer 1994; Dowd 1991; Winess 1991).

Ultimately all of these situations lead to this question: If a government chronically underrepresents women, are we positive the rules of the game are fair?

Justice Arguments for Women's Representation

Women make up half of the population of every country in the world. A simple justice argument would therefore suggest that women and men should be equally represented in politics. But what does equal representation mean? Arguments for women's equal representation in politics fall into one of three types—each with a different conception of representation. These types of representation are formal, descriptive, and substantive.

The earliest and most basic formulation of equal representation is **formal representation**, meaning that women have the legal right to participate in politics on an equal basis with men. Formal representation requires that any barriers to women's participation in decision making be removed. Women must have the right to vote and the right to stand for office. Discrimination against women in the arena of politics must be eradicated. Men and women must be equal before the law. In short, women must have the same opportunity as men to participate in politics.

This may sound straightforward to people who have voted their whole life, but the fight for the formal representation of women in politics was long, difficult, and occasionally bloody. In the early part of the 20th century, as women fought for the right to vote, it was not always clear that they would get it. Furthermore, this struggle continues into the present: Multiple votes were taken before women got the vote in Kuwait in 2005, proof of education is required for a woman to vote in Lebanon, and women have just been granted the right to vote in local elections (in 2015) in Saudi Arabia.

Kuwait, Lebanon, and Saudi Arabia are anomalies in the present day. The idea that women require formal representation in politics has become nearly universally accepted over the last 100 years. Women's political rights are now seen as human rights, and statements about women's political participation are set out in the resolutions, codes, and formal conventions of most international bodies as well as in the law of many individual countries. The United Nations (1946) adopted the first of a number of resolutions dealing with women's political rights in 1946 when, during its first session, the UN General Assembly recommended that all member states fulfill the aims of its charter "granting to women the same political rights as men" (Resolution 56 [1]). At the time, only about 50% of UN member states allowed women the vote.

Today, women can formally participate in politics almost everywhere, and resolution statements are much stronger, taking for granted the notion that women can and should participate. For example, at the fourth UN World Conference on Women held in Beijing in 1995, 189 countries agreed to a platform for action stating, "No government can claim to be democratic until women are guaranteed the right to equal representation" (United Nations 1995). Ultimately, these arguments for formal representation are about equal opportunity for women. The goal of formal representation is the absence of direct and overt discrimination against women in politics.

But observation suggests that formal representation does not necessarily result in substantial numbers of women in positions of political power. Even though most countries of the world grant women the equal opportunity to vote and to participate in politics, women remain substantially underrepresented in positions of political decision making. More than 99% of countries in the world have granted women the formal right to vote and the formal right to stand for election. But as noted earlier, fewer countries have more than 20% women in their legislative bodies. Equal opportunity through formal representation does not appear to automatically produce large numbers of women in politics.

For this reason, in the last decades of the 20th century, feminist political theorists began to argue that a different conception of equal representation was needed. Equal representation can also require **descriptive representation**—that there must be descriptive similarity between representatives and constituents. If women make up 50% of the population, they should also make up roughly 50% of legislative and executive bodies.

Arguments for descriptive representation suggest that it is not enough to have formal political equality in politics. This is because simply extending the legal right to pursue public office to women does not ensure that they will. Rights alone do not remedy the substantial social and economic inequalities that prevent women from taking advantage of their political opportunities. Instead, their past and continued exclusion from elites reinforces the idea of women's inferiority in the political arena (Phillips 1995).

Advocates of descriptive representation therefore view formal political equality as only the first step in achieving equal representation for women. In principle, laws can ensure that women have an equal opportunity to vote and to pursue political careers. In practice, however, women may not come to the starting line with the same resources or skills as men, and this can result in differences in outcomes, even without differences in opportunity.

In discussing the limits of equal opportunity, an analogy to a foot race is often used. Perhaps the most famous example is President Lyndon Johnson's 1965 speech to the graduating class of Howard University:

> You do not take a man who for years has been hobbled by chains, liberate him, bring him to the starting line of a race, saying, "you are free to compete with all the others," and still justly believe you have been completely fair.

It is easy to substitute *woman* for *man* in this speech and understand the critique of simple formal representation. The present effects of past discrimination can prevent laws ensuring equal opportunity from translating into equal outcomes.

Instead, something more is required: "Those who have been traditionally subordinated, marginalized, or silenced need the security of a guaranteed voice and . . . democracies must act to redress the imbalance that centuries of oppression have wrought" (Phillips 1991:7). Further action must be taken—electoral laws changed, gender quotas introduced—to ensure that women are represented in politics in numbers more proportionately similar to their presence in the population.

Arguments for descriptive representation hinge on the notion that racial, ethnic, and gender groups are uniquely suited to represent *themselves* in democracies. Social groups have different interests due to varied economic circumstances, histories of oppression, and cultural or ideological barriers they continue to face. In principle, democratic ideals suggest that elected representatives will serve the interests of the entire community and be able to transcend any specific interests based on their own characteristics, such as sex, race, or age. But in practice, "while we may all be capable of that imaginative leap that takes us beyond our own situation, history indicates that we do this very partially, if at all" (Phillips 1991:65). Although elections make representatives accountable to their constituents, they are sporadic enough to allow representatives to pursue private preferences or party loyalties.

If groups cannot be well represented by other groups, they need to be represented themselves among political elites (Williams 1998). In the case of women, the argument is that due to different socialization and life experiences, women are different from men. Thus, "women bring to politics a different set of values, experiences and expertise" (Phillips 1995:6). Women have different interests than men do, and those interests cannot be represented by men; therefore, women must be present themselves in the political arena. When asked why there should be more women in politics, Sirimavo Bandaranaike, the world's first female prime minister, replied with the following:

> Because they are not considered. Women's problems are not considered now . . . women have to work very hard, not necessarily at a desk in an office . . . they have . . . family problems that are different than what the men have. (Liswood 1995:109)

Arguments for descriptive representation are not essentialist (Phillips 1995:55–56; Williams 1998:5–6). They do not assume that, by definition, all women share an essential identity with the same interests and concerns. Instead, these feminist writers make it clear that women have a common interest because of their social position. Because of women's historically marginalized position, their general relegation to certain economic roles, and their primary responsibility for child and elder care, women have shared experiences and therefore common interests. And because women can best represent themselves, the argument continues, they need to be numerically represented in politics, not simply formally represented. Descriptive representation requires that women have a legislative presence (Williams 1998).

Arguments for descriptive representation are becoming more common in international statements on women's political position. For example, the

1995 Beijing Platform for Action stated, "Women's equal participation in decision making is not only a demand for simple justice or democracy but can also be seen as a necessary condition for women's interests to be taken into account" (United Nations 1995, paragraph 181). In 2000, the Women's Environment and Development Organization (WEDO) launched its 50/50 Campaign with the goal of increasing women's representation in governments around the world to 50%.

Even if we accept that women have different interests than men and therefore cannot be represented by men, a question remains: Can women represent women? This question leads to a third type of equal representation: **substantive representation,** which means that women's interests must be advocated in the political arena. Substantive representation requires that politicians speak for and act to support women's issues.

Going even further than the numerical representation of women outlined in descriptive representation arguments, advocates of substantive representation point out that *standing for* is not the same as *acting for* (Pitkin 1972). Getting higher numbers of women involved in politics is only a necessary but not sufficient condition for women's interests to be served. Instead, for women's interests to be represented in politics, female politicians have to be willing to and able to represent those interests.

But what does it mean to represent women's interests, needs, or concerns? There are a variety of answers to that question:

- Female politicians could state that they view women as a distinct part of their constituencies or that they feel a special responsibility to women (Childs 2002; Reingold 1992).
- Female politicians could draft or support legislation that directly attempts to promote social, educational, or economic equity for women. Examples include the U.S. Equal Pay Act of 1963, which worked to end the pay differential between men and women, and Mozambique's 2003 new Family Law that allows wives to work without the permission of their husband (Disney 2006).
- Female politicians could prioritize, support, or vote for "women's issues"— issues of particular interest and concern to women. These issues may be directly and obviously related to women—for example, Namibia's 2003 Combating of Domestic Violence Act, which supports victims of domestic violence and aids the prosecution of crimes against women (Bauer 2006). Or women's issues may be indirectly related to women through their greater responsibility for child and elder care. Examples include the Canadian 2001 Employment Standards Act, which extended parental leave from 10 weeks to 35 weeks. Or women's issues may not even seem like "women's issues" on the surface. For example, stemming from a gendered division of labor in rural India, women are more interested in digging wells to increase access to clean

water while men are more interested in building roads to travel to work (Chattopadhyay and Duflo 2004).

• Female politicians may also prioritize, support, or vote for policies of particular interest to feminists, such as abortion or contraception (Molyneux 1985b; Tremblay and Pelletier 2000). For example, a female politician in South Africa may have supported the Choice on the Termination of Pregnancy Act of 1996, which allows abortion for all women on demand (Britton 2006).

Talking about substantive representation raises three distinct issues. First, female politicians may not have the desire to act "for women." Second, even if they want to, female politicians may not be able to act "for women." Finally, female politicians of a particular race, ethnicity, class, or caste may not desire to or be able to act "for all women."

To begin, women who reach positions of political power may not have any desire to act for women in one or all of the ways described earlier. Women vary in their interest in advancing equality for women or in their commitment to feminist concerns such as access to abortion. Not all women feel moved to devote special attention to the interests of women, children, and families. For example, Margaret Thatcher, prime minister of Britain from 1979 to 1990, was famously antifeminist and pursued policies that many deemed detrimental to the women and children of England and Scotland.

Even if they want to act in the interests of women, female politicians may not be able to. Simply being a politician does not mean that one's interests can be effectively pursued. There are a number of reasons why female politicians may be unable to initiate or support legislation related to women's interests. First, as Joni Lovenduski (1993) warned, institutions may change women before women can change institutions. Female legislators are embedded in political institutions where male behavior—for example, forcefulness, detachment, and impersonality—is considered the norm. Thus, women may need to change or adapt to conform to those norms. Consider what a female legislator from Southern Europe had to say: "Politics may change women because, in order to survive politically, women may copy the men in their methods and behavior" (IPU 2000:23).

Even if women do not change their behavior, they may be sanctioned if they act in the interests of women. Relating the experience of members of parliament (MPs) from the Labour Party in Great Britain, Childs (2002) explained the following:

The most common perception is that women who seek to act for women act *only* for women. This results in a tension between a woman MP's parliamentary career and acting for women. If an MP desires promotion, she cannot afford to be regarded as acting for women too often or too forcefully. (p. 151, emphasis added)

If women act for women, they may be relegated to "female" committees such as health or social services. A desire to break out of these roles and gain more prestigious "masculine" committee assignments can lead to the disavowal of gender ("I'm a politician not a woman") (Sawer 2000:374).

Finally, as members of political parties, female politicians are beholden to party stances on various issues. Indeed, for many issues relevant to women, party differences may be greater than differences between men and women. Many studies of male and female legislators have demonstrated that women tend toward the **political Left,** prioritize women's issues more highly, and espouse feminist ideals more often than men do. But much of the difference between men and women disappears if political party in taken into account. So, for example, women may tend to support women's issues such as public funding for day care or equality between the sexes more than the men of their own party. However, the men of left-wing parties may espouse more support for such issues than the women of parties on the **political Right** (Burrell 1994:160–161; Dolan 1997; Swers 1998, 2002a; Tremblay 1993).

Still, having more women in politics unquestionably makes the government more receptive to the interests of most women. Advocates of substantive representation therefore argue that not only must the numbers of women in politics increase but those women must also receive support when they attempt to act for women's interests. For example, women's caucuses can help achieve substantive representation by supporting women and providing them with resources. As an example, the bipartisan U.S. Congressional Caucus for Women's Issues adopts legislative priorities, plans strategies to move women's issues forward, and links like-minded congressional members to each other and to outside groups. Some advocates of substantive representation argue that rather than simply electing women to political office, voters should elect feminists—either women or men—who are more likely to be directly supportive of women's interests (Tremblay and Pelletier 2000).

But can female politicians represent all women? Women are not just women—they are women of a particular race, ethnicity, religion, class, sexual orientation, or linguistic group. Although women's unique relationship to reproduction and the family cuts across all other social categories, women are not a monolithic group. The interests of a woman from a lower class may be different from those of a woman from an upper class. The problem arises when the women who attain political power are of only certain classes, races, or ethnicities—when they are elite women. For example, Costa Rican female legislators argued against an 8-hour workday for domestic workers, saying that they could not participate in politics if their domestic workers did not work extended hours (Sagot 2010:31). Or consider recent laws limiting Muslim women's right to wear Islamic headscarves and/or face veils, which have been passed by legislatures that lack any women representatives that wear traditional Islamic dress (Hughes and Tienes 2011). Therefore, it is vital to ask whether these female politicians can represent all women, or whether they can represent only rich, or White, or Western interests (Smooth 2011).

Utility Arguments for Women's Representation

Arguments for why women should be represented in politics are not restricted to justice arguments. Other arguments focus on the utility, or usefulness, of having women represented in politics. These arguments can be divided into two types: arguments that increasing women's participation improves the quality of deliberation and arguments that visible women in politics act as role models for younger women.

Including women in politics can increase the quality of political decision making. When women are included among potential politicians, it doubles the pool of talent and ability from which leaders can be drawn. When women are not included, valuable human resources are wasted (Norderval 1985:84). Without women's full participation in politics, political decision making will be of lower quality than it could be or should be.

The quality of political decision making should also increase with greater inclusion of women because including women increases the overall diversity of ideas, values, priorities, and political styles. Introducing women to the political realm should introduce new ideas because women have different interests. In his philosophical work, John Stuart Mill (1859, 1861) argued that allowing diverse and competing views in the marketplace of ideas helps societies determine what is true and what is not true. If certain ideas are not allowed in the marketplace, then they cannot be proven right and used to change policy, or proven wrong and used to bolster existing ideas.

Diversity is certainly good in and of itself, but it should also make political decision making more flexible and capable of change. The analogy here is to diversity of species in ecological niches. Biologists know that ecological niches dominated by a single species are more vulnerable to changes in the environment than niches with a diversity of species. In a similar manner, having only the ideas and perspectives of men represented in a country's polity could make a country less flexible to changes in its internal or international environment.

A final utility argument is that female political leaders act as role models for young girls and women. Having a visible presence of women in positions of leadership helps to raise the aspirations of other women (Burrell 1994:173; Campbell and Wolbrecht 2006; Mansbridge 1999; Wolbrecht and Campbell 2007). For example, High-Pippert and Comer (1998) found that women in the United States who were represented by a woman reported more interest in politics than did women who were represented by a man. In Uganda, following the implementation of a law requiring that women make up at least 30% of local councils, women also began participating more in community events (Johnson 2003). Alternatively, if groups are excluded from politics, this creates the perception that persons in these groups are "not fit to rule" (Mansbridge 1999:649). Without the presence of women in politics, there are no role models to inspire the next generation.

A female legislator from Central Europe put it well:

> Because of cultural differences women often have different experiences and different views on certain issues. That means that as women move into previously male-dominated positions, new perspective and new competence are added. . . . The presence of women in parliament means new skills and different styles in politics. . . . It also brings a new vision, which ultimately leads to revision of laws in order to improve existing ones. Most of all, they [women] serve as role models for future generations. (IPU 2000:41)

But women can hardly affect dominant political values if their numbers are small. If there are only a few women in a country's national legislature, they will be under pressure to behave like men. With only a few other women for support, any efforts by a woman legislator to raise a "women's issue" are likely to be denigrated, and the woman who raises them is likely to be marginalized. Women need to be at least a large minority to have an impact (Kanter 1977). In fact, the United Nations has stated that to make a difference, women need to have a **critical mass** of at least 30% of a legislature. When women are at least a large minority, then women's issues get more support (Sawer 1990:10). We discuss critical mass and the impact of women in greater detail in Chapter 8.

Consider the view of a female politician from North Africa:

> The central committee of the RCD [Constitutional Democratic Rally] has included 21.3 percent women. The change is tangible. In meetings, when a woman speaks in favor of a proposal which concerns women, the applause is louder and more sustained, at least from her female colleagues. They can have a decisive influence during debates and on decisions. A significant percentage can sway a vote. (IPU 2000:68)

A Brief Overview
of Women's Participation in Politics

Women's modern-day participation in politics began with the acquisition of voting rights (suffrage). The first country to fully enfranchise women, and the only country to give women suffrage in the 19th century, was New Zealand in 1893. In 1902, Australia was the second country to give women suffrage and was followed by a variety of Western and Eastern European states. By 1945, 46% of the world's countries allowed women to vote. We discuss the fight for women's suffrage in detail in Chapter 2.

Today, the average percentage of women in national legislatures around the world is 20% (IPU 2012b). There is substantial variation across nations, however. Table 1.1 presents a sample of countries and their world rank in female representation in parliament at the end of 2011. As discussed earlier, Rwanda currently has the highest percentage of women in its national legislature, followed by tiny Andorra in the second position. These are the only two countries with 50% women in their national legislatures. Cuba is next at third in the world (45%), followed closely by Sweden and Seychelles. Afghanistan, under its new constitution, is ranked 36th in the world in women's representation with 27.7%. The United Kingdom and the United States are in the middle of the world rankings, 59th and 95th respectively. Toward the bottom, we find Japan and Brazil, with 10.8% and 8.6% women in their legislatures, and Lebanon, ranked 173rd with 3.1% women. Saudi Arabia and Micronesia are among the countries tied in 183rd position for having no women in their national legislatures.

Table 1.1   World Rankings for Women in Parliament
for Select Countries, 2011

Rank	Country	% Women
1	Rwanda	56.3
2	Andorra	50.0
3	Cuba	45.2
4	Sweden	44.7
5	Seychelles	43.8
6	Finland	42.5
7	South Africa	42.3
8	Netherlands	40.7
9	Nicaragua	40.2

Rank	Country	% Women
10	Iceland	39.7
11	Norway	39.6
15	Angola	38.2
21	Nepal	33.2
28	Guyana	31.3
35	Ethiopia	27.8
36	Afghanistan	27.7
39	Mexico	26.2
52	Poland	23.7
59	United Kingdom	22.3
69	China	21.3
74	Israel	20.0
95	United States	16.8
111	Russian Federation	13.6
133	India	11.0
134	Japan	10.8
149	Brazil	8.6
161	Nigeria	6.8
165	Georgia	6.6
168	Haiti	4.2
173	Lebanon	3.1
177	Egypt	2.0
183	Saudi Arabia	0.0
183	Micronesia	0.0

The sampling of rankings in Table 1.1 demonstrates that highly ranked countries can come from any region. For example, the top 10 countries come from Africa, Europe, and Latin America. But regional difference in women's representation, on average, is still a reality. Table 1.2 shows how the percentage of seats held by women in national legislatures (in the **lower house** and **upper house**) varies by region. As would be expected from the rankings, Scandinavia has the highest average rates of female participation, followed by the Americas (which includes the United States) and Europe. Other regions have averages below the worldwide average—for example, Asia and countries in the Pacific. The Middle East has the lowest levels of women's participation of any region.

Currently, seven countries have no women in their national legislature. Three of these countries are in the Middle East—Saudi Arabia, Qatar, and Kuwait. It would not be expected that women would be well represented in

Table 1.2   Regional Percentages of Women in Parliament, 2011

Region	Single House or Lower House	Upper House or Senate	Both Houses Combined
Scandinavia	42.0	—	42.0
Americas	22.7	23.3	22.8
Europe	20.9	21.1	20.9
Asia	18.8	14.1	18.2
Sub-Saharan Africa	19.8	19.0	19.7
Pacific	12.4	34.8	14.9
Arab States	11.7	6.4	10.6

these countries, as women only recently received the vote in Saudi Arabia (for 2015) and only gained the vote in Bahrain in 2002 and Kuwait in 2005. The other countries without women in their national legislature are all small Asian-Pacific island nations—the Solomon Islands, Micronesia, Nauru, and Palau. Of these, Micronesia and Palau have never had women represented in their national legislatures.

Women are less well represented as heads of government or in high-level appointed offices such as cabinet ministers. There are currently 12 female heads of government around the world: Sheikh Hasina Wajed, prime minister of Bangladesh; Angela Merkel, chancellor of Germany; Ellen Johnson Sirleaf, president of Liberia; Cristina Fernández de Kirchner, president of Argentina; Jóhanna Sigurðardóttir, prime minister of Iceland; Laura Chinchilla Miranda, president of Costa Rica; Julia Gillard, prime minister of Australia; Kamla Persad-Bissessar, prime minister of Trinidad and Tobago; Dilma Rousseff, president of Brazil; Yingluck Shinawatra, prime minister of Thailand; Helle Thorning-Schmidt, prime minister of Denmark; and Joyce Banda, president of Malawi. We return to the issue of women in leadership positions, as well as women in parliaments, in Chapter 3.

Orienting Theories

Before continuing with our exploration of women in politics around the world, it is important to first introduce a number of key concepts and theories that we use throughout this volume. To understand women in politics, we must understand power, gender, and the interaction between the two.

Power

Sociologists often use a classic definition of power developed by Max Weber: the ability to impose one's will on others, even in the face of opposition. Specifically, Weber (1978) argued that "'power' is the probability that one actor within a social relationship will be in a position to carry out his own will despite resistance, regardless of the basis on which this probability rests" (p. 53). According to this definition, power is a valued resource that cannot be held by all. If one person has power, another does not. Power is overt—applied directly and visibly.

However, theorists do not agree on the proper way to define or conceptualize power, and scholars such as Michel Foucault, Antonio Gramsci, C. Wright Mills, and Talcott Parsons have debated the nature of power for decades. Although we do not discuss the various definitions and debates here, we do suggest that in the field of women in politics, it may be especially important to conceptualize power in a way that accounts for ways of exercising power that are less visible or overt. Thus, we employ a threefold definition of power developed by Stephen Lukes (1974), who is also especially useful because his work specifically addresses primarily political (rather than economic) components of power. In short, Lukes's definition includes three dimensions:

- Dimension 1: prevailing in a conflict over overt political preferences
- Dimension 2: preventing the preferences of others from reaching the agenda
- Dimension 3: shaping the preferences of others to match yours

First, Lukes (1974) agreed with Weber that in some cases, power is explicit and direct. But he distinguished a particular form of direct power often termed the *pluralist* view, which follows the work of theorists such as Robert A. Dahl and Nelson Polsby. This first, one-dimensional view of power focuses on actual and observable behavior, decision making, and conflict. We can evaluate the first dimension of political power by looking at the policy preferences, and political participation of legislators or other actors, how they behave, and who prevails (p. 15).

The second dimension of power involves preventing the preferences of others from even reaching the agenda. This dimension is developed partly as a critique of the first dimension's focus on observable decisions, arguing that, alternatively, power can be exercised by setting limits on the scope of decision making to include only certain issues. According to this perspective, demands for change can sometimes be "suffocated before they are even voiced; or kept covert; or killed before they gain access to the relevant decision making arena; or, failing all these things, maimed or destroyed in the decision-implementing stage of the policy process" (Bachrach and Baratz 1970:44, cited in Lukes 1974:19). This dimension of power can include a variety of mechanisms for controlling the agenda, including agenda setting, influence, authority, and manipulation.

Finally, Lukes (1974) introduced a third dimension of power that supplements both of the first two dimensions. The third dimension, unlike the first two, recognizes that one person may exercise power over another not only by getting the person to do what he or she does not want to do but also by influencing or shaping what the person even wants. The mechanisms of this process include the control of information, mass media, and socialization. This dimension allows us to recognize that perhaps "the most effective and insidious use of power is to prevent conflict from arising in the first place" (p. 23). Lukes acknowledged that this dimension is the hardest to study, but in the case of women's political power it is especially important to try to understand.

Before we finish our discussion of power, it is important to go beyond Lukes's dimensions, which compare the power of one actor or group over another, to considering the social structure in which individuals and groups operate. Structural theorists argue that power does not come just from an individual's or group's intrinsic qualities but from the roles and social relationships that structure power relations. For example, in schools, the structure of the education system creates an uneven distribution of power between teachers and students who each have a different set of social powers (Isaac 1987, cited in Hayward 2000). Other structural theorists have pointed to the importance of individuals or norms outside of the immediate relationship that contribute to the power of one side (e.g., Wartenberg 1990, 1992). For example, the teacher–student power relation is affected by parents, university admissions officers, and companies that take cues from the teacher. The teacher's power is thus reinforced by these other actors. A teacher's power is also reinforced by social norms—for example, expectations that he or she will be addressed formally, with the title Mr. or Ms. Similarly, when thinking about women in politics, one must think about how women's power relations are affected by political parties, pressure groups, cultural beliefs, and even global forces.

Addressing gendered power directly, feminist theorists further emphasize the process of personal transformation as a form of power—power within rather than power over. That is, when women—or men—come to better understand themselves and their position in an unequal world, they can be inspired to challenge gender inequality (Kabeer 1994; Rowlands 1997). And feminist theorists stress the ability to work collectively with others as another form of power—power with others to bring about political change (Kabeer 1994; Parpart, Rai, and Staudt 2002). A useful example of the dimensions of power and how they relate to gender appears in the following example.

The Dimensions of Power: An Example

To further understand the dimensions and structure of power, we discuss this simple example. Suppose there are two young siblings named John and Jane. Every week their mother allows them to pick one breakfast cereal at the grocery store that the two will then eat on weekday mornings before going to school. The first week, John decides that he wants the frosted cereal, but Jane prefers the rice squares. While in the cereal aisle, John stands over Jane and tells her that because he is bigger he should get what he wants. Even though Jane still wants the rice squares, she agrees, and the family goes home with the frosted cereal. In this example, John has one-dimensional power over Jane.

Before the family's next trip to the store, however, John begins to worry that his sister may put up a fight the next week to get the rice squares. But while eating his frosted cereal the following morning, John finds a solution—a coupon on his frosted cereal box for $1 off wheat flakes, chocolate grahams, or frosted cereal. He clips the coupon off of the box and takes it to his mother. When the family goes to the store, the mother sends John and Jane down the cereal aisle with the coupon. Faced with the choice of only three cereals, Jane cannot get her rice squares so she again acquiesces to her brother's will, and the family goes home with the frosted cereal. In this case John has exercised two-dimensional power, preventing rice squares from even entering the realm of decision making.

Later that day, John is very nervous. He looked at the frosted cereal box, and this time there is no coupon. He is sure that after 2 weeks of frosted cereal, Jane might finally get her way. So John devises a plan. Over the next week while watching television with his sister, every time the commercial for frosted cereal comes on the TV, he mentions how delicious the cereal looks. And every morning as he walks to school with his sister, he hums the song from the frosted cereal commercial. The next week at the grocery store standing in the cereal aisle, John begins to hum the song from the frosted cereal's commercial. "That frosted cereal sure is good," he says. Jane replies, "Hmm. Let's get frosted cereal again. It's delicious!" In this example, John exercised three-dimensional power over his sister Jane.

Faced with this example, structural theorists would likely argue that it is not just the interaction between John and Jane that is important for understanding power. One must consider their roles within the larger social structure that is their family. For example, as the older brother, John may believe that he knows what is best for his sister, and Jane is used to looking to her older brother for advice and guidance. Thus, the power is not just a function of John's forceful or scheming ways but also is grounded in the older brother–younger sister relationship of John and Jane.

Finally, it is important to consider why this situation did not play out differently. When threatened by her brother the first week at the grocery store, why did Jane not put up a fight? Why did Jane not pick up a box of breakfast bars and throw them at John, demanding that the family buy the rice squares? To understand this question, we have to consider who John and Jane are and how they were raised. What messages have they received from their parents, their teachers, and the outside environment about how to behave properly? To understand John and Jane, we must talk about gender.

Gender and Gender Stratification

Any discussion of gender usually begins by distinguishing sex and gender. *Sex* typically refers to biological differences between men and women, whereas *gender* refers to socially constructed differences between men and women. Why do we prefer to talk about gender instead of sex? Because sex is typically not socially interesting. Gender is. Think about comparing Hillary Clinton to Barack Obama in the Democratic presidential primary in 2008. What difference did it make that Hillary Clinton was a woman? Answering the question by pointing to obvious physiological differences between Clinton and Obama will not get one very far (D'Amico and Beckman 1995). What interests us is Hillary Clinton's socially constructed gender: Does her gendered upbringing lead her to have different attitudes than male politicians? Will she adhere to or break out of the roles and behaviors expected of her? What stereotypes will other politicians, or the public, bring to bear in evaluating her?

So what is gender? To begin, gender is difference. Even though human beings are among the least sexually dimorphous of species, most cultures actively work to distinguish men and women through dress, ornamentation, and exaggeration of physiological differences (Lorber 2003). Similarly, gender character traits are often defined in opposition so that if a particular trait, such as aggressiveness, is attributed to one gender, it is typically determined to be lacking in the other. Men and women are polar opposite sexes. In Western cultures, we often find male–female pairings, such as rational–emotional, aggressive–passive, competitive–cooperative, or assertive–compliant (D'Amico and Beckman 1995:3).

Gender is created. Gender characteristics are cultural creations that get passed on from generation to generation through socialization. From birth, individuals are taught their gender. For example, today in the United States, infant girls are dressed in pink and described as cute or adorable, whereas male infants are dressed in blue and described as big or strong. Children begin to refer to themselves as members of their gender as soon as they learn to speak (Lorber 2003). When moving from infancy to childhood, toddlers are encouraged to move from baby to either big boy or a big girl. Researchers point out that these categories mean different things—in the United States, boys are taught to manipulate their surrounding environment using strength, whereas little girls learn the importance of physical appearance (Cahill 1986; West and Zimmerman 1987). And during playtime in the Philippines, girls enact mother–child scenarios and play house (*bahay-bahayan*) but are cautioned against boys' games, such as ball games (*larong bola*) and wandering about (*paggala-gala*) (Sobritchea 1990). Throughout childhood, parents and other authority figures often interact with children differently based on sex, encouraging appropriate gendered behavior while discouraging transgressive behavior. As Simone de Beauvoir (1952) said, "One is not born, but rather becomes, a woman; it is civilization as a whole that produces this creature which is described as feminine" (p. 267 cited in Lorber 2003).

Gender is recreated. We "do gender" by constantly creating and recreating it in our interactions with each other (West and Zimmerman 1987). We behave like a man or a woman, thereby practicing being a man or a woman every day. Thus, gender is not complete when a young person is fully socialized; instead it must be practiced on a daily basis. Grown individuals are not socialized robots. They are active agents who choose to display, perform, and assert their gender in any given interaction (Martin 2004). But choice is constrained—if someone chooses not to "do" gender appropriately, then he or she will likely be sanctioned (West and Zimmerman 1987:146). The sum of countless individual displays of gender across social interactions creates an overarching gendered social landscape and helps to maintain a conception of gender difference as normal and natural.

But gender is not fixed. Gender varies across countries and over time and even within a single woman's lifetime. The characteristics or behaviors expected of women in one country may be very different from those expected of women in another (Costa, Terracciano, and McCrae 2001). What it means to be a man or woman has also changed over time (Connell

1987:64). Hansen (1994) demonstrated that in the 19th century men as well as women made quilts and wrote passionate letters to each other. A century ago, women were not meant to participate in politics, whereas today they are presidents and prime ministers. The meaning of gender can even change dramatically within a single person's lifetime. Over a 50-year period in the United States, men began to take care of children and even stay at home. Women have succeeded in occupations that were considered inappropriate to their nature 75 years ago.

Gender can be hard to notice. Because people are socialized to perform gender since infancy and because they recreate gender on a daily basis, people often take gender for granted (Lorber 2003). Gender is a part of everything people do. But because gender is internalized, people often do not notice its impact on their perceptions or actions. Therefore, gender can be a powerful background identity that colors people's judgments about one another in very subtle ways (Ridgeway 2001). Because gender is in the background, people may consciously focus on more obvious characteristics of a person's personality or actions without noticing that, unconsciously, they are bringing gender assumptions into their evaluations. Thinking back to the previous section and our discussion of three-dimensional power, it is important to consider forces that may shape a person's perceptions, actions, and desires without the person's knowledge.

Gender is an institution. Like other institutions, gender is a persistent and pervasive social form that orders human activity (Acker 1992; Martin 2004). It is an overarching system of social practices for making men and women different in socially significant ways (Ridgeway and Smith-Lovin 1999). A set of social positions is defined by gender and are characterized by rules for conduct and procedures for interactions. Gender has a legitimating ideology that constrains and facilitates behavior on the part of individuals. Gender is tightly linked to other institutions such as the family, the economy, and education. Conceiving of gender as an institution helps to highlight power and the unequal allocation of resources, privilege, and opportunities (Acker 1992; Martin 2004; Risman 2004).

Gender is ranked. Gender is a socially constructed relationship of inequality where the gender categories of male and female are linked to unequal prestige and power (D'Amico and Beckman 1995). The gender differences created and maintained through socialization, everyday performance, and social practice are not neutral but instead create unequal power relationships and ultimately translate into omnipresent gender hierarchy. Gender as rank crosscuts all other social categories—wealthy, powerful women are disadvantaged compared to wealthy, powerful men.

Gender and Power Concepts: Patriarchy, Public Versus Private, and Intersectionality

So far, we have discussed how gender is both institutionalized and ranked. The combination of these factors means that, worldwide, women have less power than men do. Women's lower levels of power and status can be described in many ways, but common terms include gender stratification, gender inequality, female disadvantage, sexism, and **patriarchy** (Chafetz 1990). Patriarchy is a term used to describe the social system of male domination over females, where male domination is built into the social, political, and economic institutions of society. Patriarchal societies are characterized by male control of economic resources, male domination of political processes and positions of authority, and male entitlement to sexual services. According to the feminist perspective, though some societies are more patriarchal than others, all modern societies have a patriarchal structure.

Women's power relative to men varies not only across cultures but within societies as well. Specifically, under patriarchy women almost always have more power in the home than in political or economic environments outside of family life. To distinguish between these domains, we use the terms **public sphere** and **private sphere**. Throughout history and in many societies in the modern world, it is considered natural or proper for women's concerns to be in the home, or the private sphere. Women may still lack control over important decisions regarding how resources should be allocated within the home, but the private sphere is generally considered a female domain. According to this perspective, women should be focused on their family and children and making their husbands happy.

One form of this belief, the Cult of True Womanhood, was present in the United States during the 1800s. According to this ideal, women's proper behavior involved four virtues: piety, purity, submissiveness, and domesticity. Clearly none of these virtues suggested that women should engage in public political participation or try to run for office. Instead, women were encouraged to assist the church, a task that did not threaten to take women away from their proper sphere or make women less domestic or submissive. If any woman wanted more than the four virtues, she was thought to be tampering with society, undermining civilization, and unwomanly. For example, early women's activists such as Mary Wollstonecraft, Francis Wright, and Harriet Martineau were considered "semi-women" or "mental hermaphrodites" (Welter 1966).

Although it is clear that women have been oppressed throughout history, some people may think patriarchy is an outdated concept. Over the past few decades, women across a wide range of societies have made remarkable gains in literacy, life expectancy, education, the labor force, and control over reproduction. For instance, in the United States women were once excluded from the most prestigious universities but now often outnumber men. Around the world, professional and managerial classes are now composed of both men and women. And in some countries, men are taking on more responsibilities in the home. So do men really still dominate, oppress, and exploit women?

Michael Mann (1986) argued that though gender inequality still exists, patriarchy is an outdated concept. Mann's reasoning is that patriarchy is fundamentally based on a male-dominated household. And as gender roles have changed over time, public and private boundaries between men and women have dissolved. But feminist theorists have countered that patriarchy is not just about public/private distinctions. The concept of patriarchy posits that there is "systematically structured gender inequality" (Walby 1996:28). And as the household form of patriarchy diminishes, other forms of patriarchy arise (Walby 1996). Although women may now work alongside men, in the United States they still earn 77 cents to every male dollar, and this figure has not changed in 10 years (National Committee on Pay Equity 2013). And in relation to the state and policy, politics is not only historically a male institution, but it also continues to be "dominated by men and symbolically interpreted from the standpoint of men in leading positions" (Acker 1992:567).

The public/private distinction has also received criticism from researchers focusing on non-Western countries. In many African countries, for example, women engage in economic activities outside of the home, such as trade; women and men often both have control over household finances; and women form collectives with one another for mutual benefit (Staudt 1986). Many of the public/private distinctions that do exist in these African countries came about during colonialism when Western powers engaged in trade solely with men, undercutting female influence. Thus, although women across the world have less power than men do in the public realm, there are still important cultural distinctions to keep in mind.

When talking about women in Africa and other countries of the **global south** (formerly known as the Third World), feminists often point out that these women must manage multiple forms of disadvantage or oppression. Not only do they suffer the universal subordination shared by women across the world but also they must contend with living in poorer or less developed countries. Therefore, to reiterate the discussion in the earlier section on women's substantive representation, it is important to realize that although women may share a common identity grounded in reproduction or status, they are not a monolithic group. Women have differential amounts of power based on factors such as region, class, religion, race, and ethnicity.

When talking about these multiple sources of power or disadvantage, feminists use the term **intersectionality** (Crenshaw 1991; hooks 2000). The idea of intersecting disadvantage is useful because it is difficult to average or add up the situation of being a racial, ethnic, or religious minority and the situation of being a woman to equal the experience of being a minority woman. Nor can you privilege either gender or minority status as the defining category for identity (Hancock 2005). Intersectionality research asks one to consider that women who are also poor, minority, or from the global south face multiple sources of oppression that may not combine in simple ways.

Earlier in this chapter, we introduced the work of feminist political theorists who argue that gender-neutral terms such as *individual* or *citizen* actually signify White males. Similarly, intersectionality researchers find that statements about women as citizens, activists, or politicians are often truly statements about White women, whereas research on minorities focuses on minority men. But as Kimberlé Crenshaw (1994) articulated, "[W]omen of color experience racism in ways not always the same as those experienced by men of color, and sexism in ways not always parallel to experiences of white women" (p. 99). And politically, women may be situated in multiple groups that pursue conflicting agendas (Crenshaw 1994). Without focusing on the intersections of disadvantage, the unique obstacles faced by minority women seeking rights, opportunities, or representation may simply be ignored altogether. We discuss intersectionality and the experience of women from marginalized groups in Chapter 9.

Overview of the Book

The rest of the book is divided into two sections. The first half of the book is general and thematic. We begin in Chapters 2 and 3 by providing a descriptive and historical account of women's struggle for the right to vote and of women's political participation and representation globally. Four chapters (4–7) follow that provide overarching explanations for women's representation in politics: culture, social structure, politics, and international factors. The final chapter in this section of the book (Chapter 8) considers substantive representation and whether women make a difference when they appear in politics.

The second half of the book acknowledges differences among women, both within countries and across geographic regions. Chapter 9 discusses intersectionality and heterogeneity among women. Chapters 10 through 15 break the world into six regions—(1) the West and the United States, (2) Eastern Europe and Central Asia, (3) Latin America and the Caribbean, (4) the Middle East and North Africa, (5) Asia and the Pacific, and (6) sub-Saharan Africa—and introduce important themes for women in politics within each region. Altogether, the second half of the book articulates the different paths women may take to political power in different parts of the world and within countries when accounting for marginalized identities. We conclude the book by taking stock and speculating about the possibilities for women's empowerment in the future.

2

Women Struggle for the Vote

The History of Women's Suffrage

*It requires philosophy and heroism to rise above the opinion of
the wise men of all nations and races.*

—Elizabeth Cady Stanton

Today in the United States, women vote in federal, state, and local elections more often than their male counterparts. For example, according
to the U.S. Census Bureau, 9.7 million more women than men voted in the
2008 presidential election. During campaigns, nonpartisan organizations
seek to increase women's registration and turnout; political pundits talk
about the influential vote of groups such as "soccer moms," "security
moms," and unmarried women; and candidates and political parties develop
strategies designed to address women's interests. Women's importance as a
group of voters is also not unique to the United States. Countries such as
Barbados, Chile, Finland, Malta, and the United Kingdom all have witnessed
women turning out in higher numbers than men in recent elections
(International Institute for Democracy and Electoral Assistance [IDEA]
2005). In other countries, women have been an influential force since they
began voting. In the first election after women in New Zealand were granted
the right to vote in 1893, 78% of women voted compared with 69% of men
(Catt 1918).

Today, people often take for granted that women have the right to vote, but this was not the case across the globe just a century ago. Since the time of the world's first democracy in ancient Greece through the mid-1800s, political thinkers excluded women from notions of citizenship and male lawmakers from extensions of democratic rights. Politics was the domain of men, and women were thought to lack the qualities and capabilities necessary for equal citizenship. Furthermore, religious doctrine or practice and cultural traditions regarding women's proper place in society served as barriers to women's political participation (see Chapter 4). It was only following decades of struggle that women in many countries achieved **suffrage**, or the right to vote. The enfranchisement of women was the primary goal of **first-wave feminism**, which generally covers the time from the late 19th through the early 20th century. The term *first wave* is used to distinguish early women's movements from the women's liberation movements of the 1960s and 1970s. Although women in many countries won the right to vote during **feminism**'s first wave, in parts of the world the struggle continues.

At the beginning of this chapter, we introduce three important theoretical concepts used in research on **social movements** to provide for a better understanding of the struggle for female suffrage. Then, we turn to the exploration of the struggle for women's suffrage with the U.S. case. Because the struggle for female enfranchisement is one of the largest and well documented in the United States, we discuss at some length the progression of the suffrage movement in America. First, we discuss how the American political system evolved from the colonial period to formally exclude women from voting. We then discuss the political activity of women during the Progressive Era, stressing the importance of women's connections to other social movements of the period. We also apply the concepts of social movement theory to understand why state suffrage movements experienced quite different outcomes. Finally, we outline the events leading up to the extension of the franchise to women at the national level through the **19th Amendment** of the U.S. Constitution. Following the detailed discussion of the U.S. case, we address how other suffrage movements around the world compare with those of the United States across a number of dimensions, including movement size, ideology, and tactics. We touch briefly on struggles for suffrage following World War II, and we conclude with a discussion of women as voters today.

Social Movement Concepts

To better understand the struggle for women's suffrage, we borrow a few important concepts from the study of social movements. In recent years, scholars in this field have come to agree that there are at least three interdependent factors that affect the emergence and development of social movements: (1) **resource mobilization,** (2) **framing processes,** and (3) **political opportunities** (McAdam, McCarthy, and Zald 1996). First, resource mobilization refers to the ability of social movement participants to organize and effectively use both financial and human resources to their benefit. Resource mobilization often refers to the organizational structure of the movement, including the number and size of organizations, ties to other social movements, the skill level of leadership, the movement's ability to raise funds, or the varied tactical strategies used by movement actors. Resource mobilization research has shown that disrupting public order can often be a successful tactic for social movements (Gamson 1990; Jenkins 1983; McAdam 1983).

Second, a social movement is often a struggle over meanings and beliefs. Individuals participate in social movements because they are dissatisfied with some aspect of their lives or surroundings and believe that they can promote change through organized group effort. Therefore, one should not ignore the psychological, cognitive, or ideational components of movement participation. To address this area, movement scholars use the concept of framing processes. *Framing* refers to the "conscious strategic efforts by groups of people to fashion shared understandings of the world and of themselves that legitimate and motivate collective action" (McAdam et al. 1996:6). From a strategic standpoint, movement leaders and activists often seek to link their ideals to popular or widely held beliefs to expand the support for their cause.

Finally, the origin, development, and outcome of a social movement are shaped by the wider **context** in which the movement operates. Changes that are favorable for movement advancement or success and occur in the broader environment are termed political opportunities. Looking across regions or countries, different political systems or environments may also be more or less open to social movement activity, resulting in a different **political opportunity structure.** For example, authoritarian governments may be more likely to suppress movement activity than democracies, making it more likely that movements will develop and grow in democratic systems. In addition, how politicians are elected in democratic systems may make them more or less responsive to the pressure exerted by social movements. Although the structure of political opportunities is sometimes defined narrowly in terms of the interaction between social movements and institutionalized politics, it is also often applied more generally. For example, suffrage researchers have argued that changing gender relations can create gendered opportunities (McCammon, Campbell, Granberg, and Mowery 2001). According to movement scholar Doug McAdam (1982), a shift in political opportunities is "*any* event or broad social process that serves to undermine the calculations and assumptions on which the political establishment is structured" (p. 41).

Suffrage in the United States

Female Suffrage and the U.S. Constitution

As Thomas Jefferson penned the famous words, "All men are created equal," the right to vote in most American colonies was not based on sex but on land ownership. Thus, in some colonies, such as Massachusetts and Connecticut, female property holders did have voting privileges. However, the Declaration of Independence enshrined the belief that governing was a male activity, that "governments are instituted among Men, deriving their just powers from the consent of the governed." At the time, there was no organized women's movement in America, and the founding fathers of the United States were able to largely avoid the discussion of women's rights (Kelber 1994).

Despite the overall absence of a women's movement during this period, a small number of prominent women were arguing for women's rights. For example, in March 1776, Abigail Adams wrote to her husband in the Continental Congress in Philadelphia the following:

> In the new code of laws . . . I desire you would remember the ladies, and be more generous and favorable to them than your ancestors. Do not put such unlimited power into the hands of husbands. Remember, all men would be tyrants if they could.

She followed this statement with the first threat of female revolt for the denial of suffrage: "If particular care and attention are not paid to the ladies, we are determined to foment a rebellion, and will not hold ourselves bound to obey any laws in which we have no voice or representation" (Stanton, Anthony, and Gage 1887:32). Unfortunately, however, her pleas went unheeded. Her husband, future U.S. president John Adams, replied, "Depend upon it, we know better than to repeal our Masculine systems" (Kelber 1994:3). Women's struggle for suffrage in the United States had just begun.

Although the Constitution did not extend suffrage to women, it also did not preclude it. Whereas the Declaration of Independence used gendered terms such as *men*, the Constitution was more inclusive, using the term *persons*. After the Constitution was ratified, women's suffrage was still somewhat of an open question. From 1776 to 1807, for example, women had the right to vote under the New Jersey Constitution. But, according to Johnson (1913), New Jersey never intended women to vote. The extension of suffrage to "all inhabitants" with a certain amount of property was an "error in wording" that reflects men's belief at the time that women's non-participation as voters could simply be taken for granted.

Ironically, it was the extension of the vote to former slaves under the 14th and 15th Amendments that first codified women's exclusion from voting in the U.S. Constitution. Although the 14th Amendment established the universality of U.S. citizenship for "all persons born or naturalized in the United States," it then set up penalties against states that denied the right to vote to significant numbers of adult male citizens. Thus, women were considered citizens but denied inclusion in the electorate. When it became clear that the 14th Amendment would be insufficient to force the rebel states of the Confederacy to grant votes to freed slaves, the 15th Amendment was introduced. Ratified in 1869, the 15th Amendment authorized congressional action to guard against disfranchisements by the states on the basis of "race, color or previous condition of servitude." Once again, women were excluded.

Women and Progressive Movements: The Struggle Begins

Although women generally spent their time and energy maintaining their homes and families during the 18th and 19th centuries, women also increasingly worked outside of mainstream channels to influence government. Women participated in crowd actions, circulated petitions, founded reform organizations, and lobbied legislatures. Women often concentrated their efforts on matters connected to the well-being of the home, family, children, women, and the community (Baker 1994). Yet even on these issues, some argued women should abstain from public participation. As one lady's journal stated in 1847, "It is woman's mission. Let her not look away from her own little family circle for the means of producing moral and social reforms, but begin at home" (Arthur 1847:178, cited in Welter 1966:163).

Despite perceptions about women's "proper place," women were active participants in the abolitionist (antislavery) movement. And in the early 20th century, the fight for women's suffrage became aligned with the Progressive movement. The Progressive movement was a response to the dramatic changes that were taking place in American society during the latter half of the 19th century. The frontier had been tamed, cities began to sprawl, and powerful men like Andrew Carnegie and John D. Rockefeller had risen to dominate the business world. Yet not all citizens shared in the country's new wealth and prestige. In response, social activists undertook the reform of working conditions, sought to humanize the treatment of mentally ill people and prisoners, and worked to outlaw the consumption of alcohol, perceived as a central cause of society's problems.

The importance of women's participation in the reform movements of the 19th and 20th centuries for the rise of female suffrage cannot be underestimated. From a resource mobilization perspective, **suffragists** not only gained experience through participating in other movements but they could draw on the financial and organizational resources of other progressive organizations. In Montana, for example, women's suffrage and temperance groups were successful allies in the fight for suffrage (Cole 1990). However, the presumed alliance between women's suffrage and Prohibition movements also caused the suffrage movement to inherit many enemies, including organized liquor interests and retail saloon operators.

Early on, the themes of the antislavery movement led women to draw conclusions about their own status in society. Paradoxically, women's exclusion from full participation in the antislavery movement also served as a wake-up call. In 1840, two founders of the American suffrage movement, Lucretia Mott and Elizabeth Cady Stanton, traveled to London to attend an antislavery convention. After being denied the right to participate in the convention, the women decided that when they returned to America, they would organize a women's rights convention. They followed through in 1848 by organizing the **Seneca Falls Convention** in New York (see Figure 2.1). Three hundred women and men attended, and for the first time, a formal demand was made in the United States for women's right to vote: "It is the duty of the women of this country to secure for themselves their sacred right to the elective franchise" (Stanton 1848).

The Leadership, Organization, and Tactics of the Early Suffrage Movement

The women's suffrage movement in the United States was spearheaded by a number of passionate and influential women. Two especially prominent women in the struggle for suffrage in the United States were Elizabeth Cady Stanton and Susan B. Anthony. Stanton and Anthony met in 1851 and quickly established a lifelong friendship. As the better writer, Stanton crafted many of the pair's speeches whereas Anthony focused on movement organization and tactics.

Stanton and Anthony fought for women's suffrage in a number of ways. In 1866, Elizabeth Cady Stanton tested women's right to stand for election by running for Congress, receiving 24 of 12,000 votes cast. And in 1872,

Figure 2.1 Timeline of the American Women's Suffrage Movement

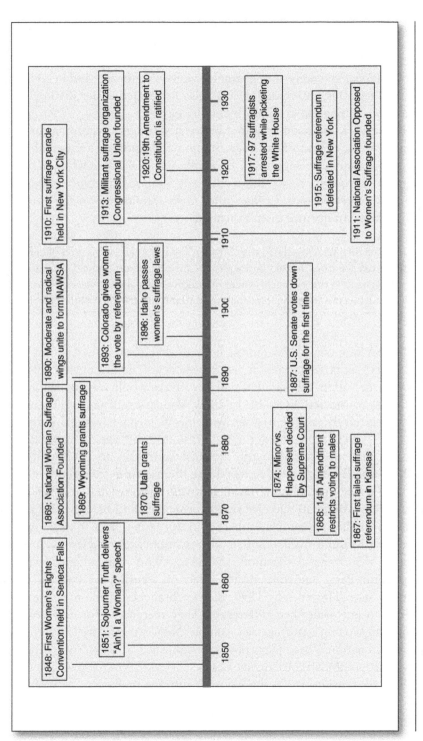

Source: Inter-Parliamentary Union (IPU) (2005b); *Minor v. Happersett* (1835).

Susan B. Anthony was arrested and stood trial for casting a Republican vote in the presidential election. In 1869, Stanton and Anthony founded the National Woman's Suffrage Association (NWSA). NWSA sought a federal constitutional amendment to guarantee women's suffrage, and in addition to advocating votes for women, NWSA also advocated easier divorce and an end to discrimination in employment and pay.

However, a gulf soon appeared between suffragists regarding the extension of voting rights to Black men. Stanton and Anthony accused abolitionist and Republican supporters of emphasizing Black civil rights at the expense of women's rights. Elizabeth Cady Stanton, though herself an abolitionist, expressed outrage that other races should receive the vote while White women remained disenfranchised:

> If Saxon men have legislated thus for their own mothers, wives and daughters, what can we hope for at the hands of Chinese, Indians, and Africans? . . . I protest against the enfranchisement of another man of any race or clime until the daughters of Jefferson, Hancock, and Adams are crowned with their rights. (hooks 1981:127)

NWSA was considered radical because they took on a "by any means necessary" approach, known as **expediency** (Giddings 1996:124–125). Movement leaders believed that female suffrage would cure the nation's ills. So it was considered justifiable to allow women's suffrage organizations to be segregated by race or to align with the Women's Christian Temperance Union (WCTU), even though the WCTU sought suffrage for vastly different reasons than the predominantly feminist suffragists in NWSA. In short, NWSA would stop at nothing to achieve the franchise for women.

But Lucy Stone and other prominent suffragists argued that NWSA tactics were too extreme, and civil rights for women and Blacks could proceed hand in hand. Therefore, later in 1869, Lucy Stone, Julia Ward Howe, and Josephine Ruffin formed a more moderate organization called the American Woman's Suffrage Association (AWSA). AWSA was aligned with the Republican Party and concentrated solely on securing the vote for women state by state. However, by 1890, the two branches of the movement were willing to put aside their differences. They merged to form the National American Woman's Suffrage Association (NAWSA), and in 1900, the organization's national headquarters were established in New York City under the direction of Carrie Chapman Catt.

Still, the tension within the women's suffrage movement between women's and civil rights meant that Black women were often marginalized or excluded from participating in White women's suffrage organizations.

Southern White women were the most vehement in their opposition to Black women joining their organizations, but Northern White women also supported organizational segregation. Black women therefore often formed their own suffrage associations. By the 1900s, Black women suffrage clubs were active in Tuskegee, St. Louis, Los Angeles, Memphis, Boston, Charleston, and New Orleans (Giddings 1996).

Although White women outnumbered Black women in the suffrage movement (Chafetz and Dworkin 1986), a number of prominent Black women were active in the women's suffrage movement and questioned the exclusion of Black women. For instance, in 1851, Sojourner Truth gave a now famous speech titled "Ain't I a Woman?" (see the next section). Abolitionists such as Harriet Tubman and Frances Ellen Harper were active in the movement, addressing women's suffrage meetings. And Ida Wells-Barnett, an anti-lynching crusader and journalist, challenged segregation in the women's movement. In a massive 1913 suffrage march, Wells-Barnett refused to march separately from White Chicago delegates (Giddings 1996).

It is also important to note that Black women were actually more likely to support universal suffrage following the Civil War than were White women (Giddings 1996). Black women viewed suffrage as the vehicle through which to gain influence with school boards and improve education. And because the majority of Black women worked, voting rights could allow Black women to seek labor protection legislation (Giddings 1996).

Ain't I a Woman? By Sojourner Truth, 1851

Sojourner Truth was born Isabella Baumfree, one of 13 children of slave parents. When she was 29 years old, she ran away with her infant son after her third master reneged on a promise to free her. Seventeen years later, Isabella experienced a spiritual revelation, and changing her name to Sojourner Truth, she began walking through Long Island and Connecticut preaching about God. Later, she began speaking about abolitionism and women's suffrage, drawing on her life experiences as a slave. In 1851, at the age of 54, she gave a now legendary speech at a women's convention in Akron, Ohio:

> Well, children, where there is so much racket there must be something out of kilter. I think that 'twixt the negroes of the South and the women at the North, all talking about rights, the white men will be in a fix pretty soon. But what's all this here talking about?
>
> That man over there says that women need to be helped into carriages, and lifted over ditches, and to have the best place everywhere. Nobody ever helps me into carriages, or over mud-puddles, or gives me any best place! And ain't

I a woman? Look at me! Look at my arm! I have ploughed and planted, and gathered into barns, and no man could head me! And ain't I a woman? I could work as much and eat as much as a man—when I could get it—and bear the lash as well! And ain't I a woman? I have borne thirteen children, and seen most all sold off to slavery, and when I cried out with my mother's grief, none but Jesus heard me! And ain't I a woman?

Then they talk about this thing in the head; what's this they call it? [member of audience whispers, "intellect"] That's it, honey. What's that got to do with women's rights or negroes' rights? If my cup won't hold but a pint, and yours holds a quart, wouldn't you be mean not to let me have my little half measure full?

Then that little man in black there, he says women can't have as much rights as men, 'cause Christ wasn't a woman! Where did your Christ come from? Where did your Christ come from? From God and a woman! Man had nothing to do with Him.

If the first woman God ever made was strong enough to turn the world upside down all alone, these women together ought to be able to turn it back, and get it right side up again! And now they is asking to do it, the men better let them.

Obliged to you for hearing me, and now old Sojourner ain't got nothing more to say. (Truth 1851; cited in Halsall 1997)

The State Suffrage Movement: Why the West Was Best

In December 1869, Wyoming territory became the first modern legislative body to grant suffrage to women. There was no active suffrage movement in Wyoming at the time (McCammon 2001, 2003), so some might wonder why suffrage came first to Wyoming. In the early days, it was often said that the passage of female suffrage in Wyoming was a joke. Edward M. Lee, secretary of the Territory in 1869, wrote the following:

Once, during the session, amid the greatest hilarity, and after the presentation of various funny amendments and in the full expectation of a gubernatorial veto, an act was passed enfranchising the Women of Wyoming. The bill, however, was approved, became a law, and the youngest territory placed in the van of progress. . . . How strange that a movement destined to purify the muddy pool of politics . . . should have originated in a joke. (printed in Cheyenne's *Wyoming Tribune*, October 8, 1870; cited in Larson 1965:58)

Although it is unlikely that women's suffrage passed only as a joke, Lee's quote does suggest another reason—legislators wanted Wyoming to appear modern (Larson 1965). Research also suggests that the legislators wanted to publicize the territory to the rest of the country and that the heavily male population may have wanted to attract more women. In 1890, when Wyoming was admitted to the Union, it also became the first state in America to allow women to vote. Congress wanted to refuse statehood to Wyoming as long as it allowed women to vote, but the legislature wired back to Washington: "We'll stay out a thousand years rather than come in without our women." To this day, Wyoming's leadership on female suffrage is a part of its identity, calling itself the Equality State.

Although Wyoming was first, other western states soon followed suit, granting women the right to vote. Utah was right on Wyoming's tails, passing female suffrage only 2 months later, and the Dakota Territorial Legislature failed by one vote to pass female suffrage in January of that year (Larson 1965). Furthermore, by 1920, most western states had passed bills allowing female suffrage, whereas most nonwestern states had not. See Map 2.1 for a map of state **ratification** of women's suffrage.

As evident in Map 2.1, suffrage movements were much more successful in western states. Except for Michigan and Kansas, midwestern states were willing only to offer women the vote for presidential elections. Of the southern and eastern states, only Oklahoma and New York granted full female suffrage. Explanations for the regional differences in the success of suffrage movements are numerous. For example, in 1967, Alan P. Grimes advanced the Puritan ethos hypothesis, asserting that the White male voters of the West were reacting to the social instabilities of frontier culture. The men thought women voters could bring order to public life.

In a series of studies researching the American women's suffrage movement, however, Holly J. McCammon and her colleague Karen Campbell (2001) were able to dismiss Grimes's claim, along with a number of other possible explanations for why state suffrage movements were so much more successful in the West. For example, suffrage organizations in the West were no larger or more numerous than those in other parts of the country. By collecting and analyzing more than 650 secondary accounts of suffrage movements in 48 states, McCammon and Campbell found that the success of women's suffrage movements in the West was likely a product of political opportunities, resource mobilization, and framing processes.

First, societies in the West were newly formed and constantly changing, allowing women more opportunities than they could have in eastern states. Women in the West had higher educational enrollments, and the region had more women in law and medicine. There were also a good number of female homesteaders—women who owned property. Where the separate spheres of men and women became blurred, it may have been perceived as more justifiable for women to participate in government (McCammon and

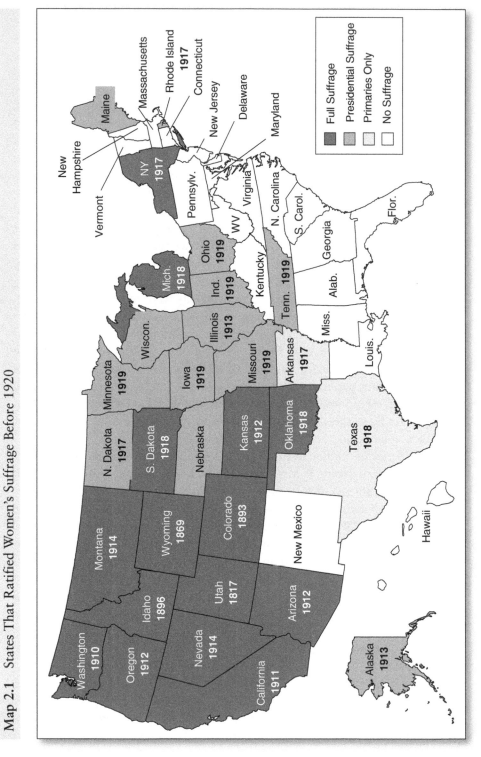

Map 2.1 States That Ratified Women's Suffrage Before 1920

Legend:
- Full Suffrage
- Presidential Suffrage
- Primaries Only
- No Suffrage

Maine

Massachusetts
Rhode Island **1917**
Connecticut
New Jersey
Delaware
Maryland

New Hampshire
Vermont

NY **1917**

Pennsylv.
Virginia
WV
N. Carolina
S. Carol.
Georgia
Flor.

Ohio **1919**
Mich. **1918**
Ind. **1919**
Kentucky
Tenn. **1919**
Alab.

Wiscon.
Illinois **1913**
Missouri **1919**
Arkansas **1917**
Miss.
Louis.

Minnesota **1919**
Iowa **1919**

N. Dakota **1917**
S. Dakota **1918**
Nebraska
Kansas **1912**
Oklahoma **1918**
Texas **1918**

Montana **1914**
Wyoming **1869**
Colorado **1893**
New Mexico

Washington **1910**
Oregon **1912**
Idaho **1896**
Nevada **1914**
Utah **1817**
Arizona **1912**
California **1911**

Hawaii

Alaska **1913**

Campbell 2001). Therefore, in social movement terms, the changing definition of proper female behavior in the West created political opportunities for the women's suffrage movement. Though evident first in the West, research suggests that the increase in female labor force participation likely helped lead to the suffrage movement's eventual overall success (Cornwall, Dahlin, and King 2005).

Second, the women's suffrage movement also pursued different tactical strategies in the West. Across the country, suffragists used both outsider tactics—parades, fair booths, leaflet distribution, canvassing, attempting to vote—and insider tactics such as legislative lobbying and candidate campaigning (King and Cornwall 2004). In the West, suffragists often avoided visible outsider tactics, such as large public demonstrations (McCammon and Campbell 2001). For example, Abigail Scott Duniway, an activist in the Northwest, coined the term *still hunt,* which meant that she sought to persuade influential voters, not the public at large (McCammon 2003). This technique may have succeeded in part because it did not inspire as much opposition.

Although large, vocal movements were not more successful in the state ratification movement, public tactics became more frequent as state ratification lagged. Movement scholars note that suffragists were more likely to use these outsider tactics after suffering setbacks, such as a loss in a state referendum (King and Cornwall 2004; McCammon 2003). Women stood on soapboxes or on the backs of open cars, and after 1908, women began marching in parades. Given that women's proper place was still considered the home, parades were very controversial. Some women even chose to quit the movement rather than marching in public (Blatch and Lutz 1940).

In addition to differences in movement strategies, female activists in different regions framed the goal of female suffrage differently. McCammon and Campbell (2001) distinguished two approaches used by state suffrage movements: justice and expediency. **Justice frames** suggest that it is a woman's right to vote. According to these arguments, women should not be treated differently from men, and women's political participation is better for women and women's interests. Voting privileges allow women both to influence the passage of favorable legislation and to pressure for the removal of laws that are unjust. Because these frames challenged the public versus private distinction and asserted gender equality, they were often met with fierce resistance.

On the other hand, **expediency frames** suggest that women are different and bring special skills to the political arena (Fischer 1994; McCammon and Campbell 2001). (Expediency frames are distinguishable from the strategy of expediency, discussed earlier in this chapter.) Because women were perceived as less corrupt, female suffrage could make it harder to elect notoriously bad candidates. Because women were perceived as law abiding and moral, women's participation in the political process could remediate social problems, leading to more moral, educational, and humane legislation and laws that would protect children. McCammon and Campbell (2001) found that expediency frames were used more frequently as time marched on, were used more often in western states, and more often led to movement success.

Opposition to Female Suffrage

Although suffrage movements in western states were more successful prior to 1920, female suffrage never proceeded unopposed. For example, in Wyoming in 1871, women's suffrage was challenged. Due to accounts that women more often voted for Republicans in the previous election, Democrats in the legislature voted to repeal the vote for women. Although Governor Campbell vetoed the bill, the legislature responded by attempting to override his veto. Ultimately, the veto failed by only one vote (Larson 1965).

Although less common in the West, anti-suffragists formed several organizations to advance their cause. As early as 1882, women took the lead in establishing the Boston Committee of Remonstrance to oppose women's suffrage in Massachusetts. There was also a Women's Anti-Suffrage Association, founded by the wives of two popular Civil War commanders. They declared, "If women gain the vote, it upsets the natural order and sows 'division and discord' in the family unit and in the country" (Clift 2003:65). Anti-suffrage organizing by both men and women grew as time passed and as the suffrage movement made gains. After the vote was won in California in 1911, numerous anti-suffragist organizations joined forces to form the National Association Opposed to Woman Suffrage (see Figure 2.2).

Many opponents of suffrage grounded their arguments in the ideas of separate male and female spheres. Anti-suffragists predicted that family life would collapse if women were allowed out of their preordained sphere of house and home. In 1889, there were 104 women who published "An Appeal Against Female Suffrage," claiming that men were developing a "new spirit of justice and sympathy" that had caused them already to address the "principal injustices of the law toward women . . . by means of the existing constitutional machinery" (Ward et al. 1889:413, cited in Thomas 2003:49). With men sympathetically taking care of women's

Figure 2.2   National Association Opposed to Woman Suffrage

Source: Courtesy of the Library of Congress, Prints and Photographs Division.

interests, there was no reason for women to subvert their proper role in society as wives, mothers, and guardians of the home.

Suffrage movements in the West, however, did not have to contend with some of the major oppositional forces of female suffrage. In big cities, for example, the belief that women were reformers often led political machines to oppose their enfranchisement. Researchers also suggest that textile and manufacturing interests often opposed female suffrage because they wanted to keep women as a source of cheap labor (McDonagh and Price 1985). Railroad magnates and meatpackers supported anti-suffragist organizations through financial contributions (Barber 1997). Finally, suffrage was largely opposed in the South, where the expansion of voting rights was hindered by opposition to suffrage for Black women.

Women Gain the Vote: The Events
Leading to the Passage of the 19th Amendment

Although the radical and moderate branches of the American women's suffrage movement had joined forces under NAWSA in 1890, a new militant group called the Congressional Union, known later as the National Woman's Party (NWP), was organized in 1913 by Alice Paul and Lucy Burns. Scholars often credit this more militant wing with carrying the movement forward during a period when the mainstream movement was suffering after a number of major setbacks in state referenda (Flexner 1975). Social movement researchers often find that radical wings are beneficial to social movements through what they call **radical flank effects.** The presence of radical or extremist groups operating within the same movement as more moderate social movement organizations tends to strengthen the bargaining position of moderate groups politically and to increase their funding as a way of undercutting radical influence (McAdam et al. 1996).

The first radical move by Alice Paul and her militant suffrage organization was to organize a parade of 5,000 on the day before Woodrow Wilson's inauguration. One newspaper account recounted the event:

> The women had to fight their way from the start and took more than one hour in making the first ten blocks. Many of the women were in tears under the jibes and insults of those who lined the route. . . . It was where Sixth Street crosses the avenue that police protection gave way entirely and the two solid masses of spectators on either side came so close together that three women could not march abreast. (*Baltimore Sun,* March 4, 1913, cited in Flexner 1975:273)

Although difficult for the suffragists, the event received much coverage in the press and brought national attention to the cause.

The NWP sought a constitutional amendment, believing that the state suffrage movement had gone as far as it could. To force the adoption of a suffrage amendment in Congress, Alice Paul and the NWP held the Democrats, the controlling party in Congress and the party of the president, responsible for enacting change. Beginning in 1914, the group began campaigning against Democratic candidates for Congress, regardless of their position on suffrage (Flexner 1975). In 1914, women's suffrage came to the floor of the Senate, failing to pass by a vote of 34 to 35. The following year, the measure was also defeated in the House of Representatives, 204 to 174. The struggle for women's suffrage continued.

In 1917, Alice Paul and the NWP staged the first political protest ever to picket the White House. Known as Silent Sentinels, the pickets marked the first nonviolent civil disobedience campaign in the United States. Following months of protest, the picketers were arrested on charges of obstructing traffic. Many, including Alice Paul, were convicted and incarcerated. Viewing themselves as political prisoners, the women began a hunger strike to protest the conditions at the prison. Paul, along with several of the women, were moved to the psychiatric ward and fed forcibly through tubes in their noses. News of the forced feedings, along with the continuing demonstrations and attendant press coverage, kept pressure on the Wilson administration to grant women the vote.

As relations with Germany were deteriorating and the possibility of war loomed greater, suffragists were uncertain about how the war would influence the movement. Although suffrage was still the organization's primary concern, Catt committed the services of NAWSA to the Wilson administration in the event of war. Women were brought out of their homes into new spheres of action. Women rushed into industrial work and public service, sharply altering their standing in the community and proving their competence to assume political responsibility (Flexner 1975). In January 1918, the president announced that women's suffrage was urgently needed as a war measure. Thus, World War I provided an important shift in the political opportunity structure of the women's suffrage movement.

The passage of the 19th Amendment, called the Anthony Amendment in honor of Susan B. Anthony, was scheduled in the House of Representatives for January 10, 1918. Despite the call by the president for the passage of the amendment, his party was divided almost evenly, and the vote would be close. Knowing this, Representative Hicks from New York followed what would have been the wishes of his wife, a devoted suffragist, who had just passed away. He left her deathbed to go to Washington for the vote, returning afterward for her funeral (Flexner 1975). The amendment passed with exactly the two-thirds majority required.

After another fight in the Senate, on June 4, 1919, the U.S. Congress voted to amend the Constitution with the following words: "The right of citizens of the United States to vote shall not be denied or abridged by the United States or by any State on account of sex. Congress shall have power to enforce this article by appropriate legislation." In both the House and Senate, most of "nay" votes came from representatives of the South, making it a surprise, therefore, that the suffrage movement reached its final success in that region.

Before the amendment could become law, it required ratification by 36 states. Alabama was the first state to defeat the measure, quickly followed by Georgia. But 11 states ratified the amendment within 1 month and 22 within 6 months. After 35 states ratified the amendment, the issue came before the Tennessee State Legislature in August 1920.

Suffragists knew the battle would be a tough one. The notion that Black women would also get the vote under the amendment was enough to inspire opposition by both men and women. Carrie Chapman Catt, the president of NAWSA at the time, stated the following:

> We now have 35½ states. We are up to the last half of the last state. . . . The opposition of every sort is here fighting with no scruple, desperately. Women . . . are here, appealing to Negrophobia and every other cave man's prejudice. (Flexner 1975:335)

Anti-suffragists had good reason to hope that if Tennessee failed to pass the 19th Amendment, the amendment would never become law. Catt joined forces with movement leaders in Tennessee to organize a vigorous fight for the cause. Tennessee women from different social classes and races worked together in writing letters, making speeches, and lobbying legislators (Hiers 2004).

The battle that ensued would come to be remembered as the War of the Roses. Proponents of the suffrage amendment united under the symbol of the yellow rose, and anti-suffragists adopted the red rose. Even the legislators displayed their intentions by wearing roses on their lapels. By counting the number of red roses worn by legislators, the suffragists knew they were in trouble for the vote on August 18. It looked as though the amendment would be defeated: 47 for and 49 against. In the first roll call, however, one representative came over to the suffragist's side and the vote was 48–48. The second roll was taken, and the vote remained deadlocked. During the third roll call, with a red rose pinned to his jacket, Harry Burn—the youngest member of the legislature—suddenly broke the tie (Hiers 2004).

Burn was asked by journalists to explain his yellow-rose vote. He replied that although he was wearing a red rose, his breast pocket contained a telegram from his mother in East Tennessee, which read, "Vote for suffrage, and don't keep them in doubt. . . . Don't forget to be a good boy and help Mrs. Catt put the Rat in ratification!" (*Baltimore Sun,* August 22, 1920, cited in Flexner 1975:336). Burn stated, "I changed my vote in favor of ratification because a mother's advice is always safest for her boy to follow, and the opportunity was mine to free millions of people from political bondage" (Braun 2003). Women had finally won their struggle.

On August 18, 1920, the 19th Amendment was ratified, and women won the right to vote. After decades of organizing, the women's movement no longer had a unifying goal and quickly declined. Although women had achieved suffrage, they did not initially move forward to demand large-scale political representation, and at the time, women were no more willing to vote for female candidates than men were. The struggle for female political representation was still to come.

Suffrage Movements Outside the United States

Although the movement for female suffrage in the United States has much to teach, it is important to remember that battles for female suffrage occurred across the globe. During the 1800s, women's exclusion from political participation was seen as "natural" and was often taken for granted worldwide. Indeed, similarly to what happened with the New Jersey Constitution, countries like Chile and France initially did not mention sex as a qualification for voting—not because they wanted women to vote but because they did not see women as equal citizens (Przeworski 2009). It was only when women registered to vote that Chilean legislators and French courts clarified that the laws were never intended to grant women suffrage.

But taking a step back and looking broadly across time, we can also see that women's voting rights changed fairly rapidly during the first decade of the 1900s. New Zealand became the first country to give women suffrage in 1893, and only Australia, Finland, and Norway followed suit during the next 20 years. But in the years following World War I, the tide began to turn as a flood of countries began to grant women the right to vote. And by 1948, what was taken for granted was that woman should have the right to vote. We show this pattern of suffrage adoption over time in Figure 2.3.

So how did this sweeping transition occur? Women's movements are an important part of the story. As women were organizing in the United States, women marched, lobbied, and agitated for political rights in many countries, often struggling for years to gain access to the rights men were handed without dispute. But not all countries experienced struggles like those that unfolded in the United States. The size of the American suffrage movement, for example, was only rivaled by the movement in the United Kingdom. Yet there are also similarities between the suffrage movements in the United States and movements in other countries, such as the education and social class of movement members. In the following sections, we focus on five ways women's suffrage movements varied around the world: (1) time period; (2) movement size, composition, and alliances; (3) goals and ideology; (4) oppositional forces; and (5) level of militancy.

Figure 2.3   The Worldwide Progression of Female Suffrage

—1893	New Zealand
—1902	Australia*
—1906	Finland
—1913	Norway
—1915	Denmark, Iceland
—1917	Canada*
—1918	Austria, Estonia, Georgia, Germany, Ireland*, Kyrgyzstan, Latvia, Poland, Russia, United Kingdom*
—1919	Belgium*, Belarus, Kenya*, Luxembourg, Netherlands, Sweden, Ukraine
—1920	Albania, Czech Republic, Slovakia, United States
—1921	Armenia, Azerbaijan, Lithuania
—1924	Kazakhstan, Mongolia, St. Lucia, Tajikistan
—1927	Turkmenistan
—1928	Ireland**, United Kingdom**
—1929	Ecuador, Romania*
—1930	South Africa*, Turkey
—1931	Portugal*, Spain. Sri Lanka,
—1932	Maldives, Thailand, Uruguay
—1934	Brazil, Cuba
—1935	Myanmar
—1937	Philippines
—1938	Bolivia*, Uzbekistan
—1939	El Salvador
—1941	Panama*
—1942	Dominican Republic
—1944	Bulgaria, France, Jamaica
—1945	Croatia, Indonesia, Italy, Japan, Senegal, Slovenia, Togo
—1946	Cameroon, Djibouti, Guatemala, Liberia, Macedonia, North Korea, Panama**, Romania**, Trinidad & Tobago, Venezuela, Vietnam, Yugoslavia
—1947	Argentina, Malta, Mexico, Pakistan, Singapore
—1948	Belgium**, Israel, Niger, Seychelles, South Korea, Suriname
—1949	Bosnia and Herzegovina, Chile, China, Costa Rica, Syria*
—1950	Barbados, Haiti, India
—1951	Antigua and Barbuda, Dominica, Grenada, Nepal, St. Kitts and Nevis, St. Vincent & the Grenadines
—1952	Bolivia**, Cote d'Ivoire, Greece, Lebanon
—1953	Bhutan, Guyana, Hungary, Syria**
—1954	Belize, Colombia, Ghana
—1955	Cambodia, Ethiopia, Eritrea, Honduras, Nicaragua, Peru
—1956	Benin, Comoros, Egypt, Gabon, Mali, Mauritius, Somalia

—1957	Malaysia, Zimbabwe
—1958	Burkina Faso, Chad, Guinea, Laos, Nigeria
—1959	Madagascar, San Marino, Tunisia, United Republic of Tanzania
—1960	Canada**, Cyprus, Gambia, Tonga
—1961	Bahamas, Burundi, Malawi, Mauritania, Paraguay, Rwanda, Sierra Leone
—1962	Algeria, Australia**, Monaco, Uganda, Zambia
—1963	Congo, Equatorial Guinea, Fiji, Iran, Kenya**, Morocco
—1964	Libya, Papua New Guinea, Sudan
—1965	Afghanistan, Botswana, Lesotho
—1967	Democratic People's Republic of Yemen, Democratic Republic of the Congo, Kiribati, Tuvalu
—1968	Nauru, Swaziland
—1970	Andorra, Yemen Arab Republic
—1971	Switzerland
—1972	Bangladesh
—1974	Jordan, Solomon Islands
—1975	Angola, Cape Verde, Mozambique, Sao Tome and Principe, Vanuatu
—1976	Portugal**
—1977	Guinea-Bissau
—1978	Republic of Moldova
—1979	Micronesia, Marshall Islands, Palau
—1980	Iraq
—1984	Liechtenstein
—1986	Central African Republic
—1989	Namibia
—1990	Samoa
—1994	South Africa**
—1999	Qatar
—2002	Bahrain
—2003	Oman
—2005	Kuwait
—2006	United Arab Emirates
—2011	Saudi Arabia

Suffrage was sometimes granted to women with restrictions; for example, only women of a certain racial or ethnic group could vote. When women's enfranchisement proceeded in stages, a single asterisk (*) denotes the *first* time women in a country were allowed to vote nationally, while two asterisks (**) signify *universal* suffrage.

Source: Updated from Paxton, Green, and Hughes (2008).

Time Period

The United States and United Kingdom were the locations for the first women's movements. Around the time that Elizabeth Cady Stanton and Lucretia Mott were planning a women's convention to advance female suffrage, the women's movement was beginning in the United Kingdom. In 1847, Ann Knight, a Quaker, produced the first recognizable women's suffrage pamphlet, and the first British suffrage organization was formed 4 years later in 1851. The first wave of the women's movement in France and Germany began during the 1860s and developed slightly later in the Nordic countries (1870s and 1880s). Women's movements in Asia, Latin America, and the Middle East often lagged slightly behind, developing movements in the first decades of the 20th century. The development of first-wave women's movements was inhibited by forces such as political authoritarianism, Catholicism, or both (Randall 1987:211).

Movement Size, Composition, and Alliances

Most countries had only small or incipient first-wave women's movements. Others, such as Canada, Cuba, France, Holland, and Mexico, reached an intermediate size, and some were slightly larger—Denmark, Germany, Iceland, Japan, and Sweden (Chafetz and Dworkin 1986). The United States and the United Kingdom were the only countries to reach the mass movement level. Yet cases like New Zealand, where the movement was not particularly large, again suggest that movement size was not necessarily related to women's success. Even where movements were small, women were often involved in some form of protest about their exclusion, making it hard to ignore them completely (Hannam, Auchterlonie, and Holden 2000). A smaller number of active women may also have the advantage of failing to inspire widespread opposition, and tactics like the still hunt could have been effective with movements of any size.

One of the most striking similarities between suffrage movements before World War II is the education and social status of those involved. Across the world, the leaders and rank-and-file members of suffrage organizations were largely educated, urban, middle-class women. Such women had the resources to organize, lead, and participate in social action. Furthermore, suffrage leaders frequently had links with Europe through birth and education. For example, Sarojini Naidu, an Indian nationalist and vocal supporter of women's education and suffrage rights, was from a Brahmin (a Hindu priestly caste) family, was educated at Cambridge, and married a doctor.

Women's education was a key factor in the struggle for suffrage. Where literacy rates were high, women often organized first to fight for higher educational opportunities (Hannam et al. 2000). In Latin America, Asia, and the Middle East, Westernized males usually first raised the issue of basic education, followed by small groups of women who were often the first to be educated (Chafetz and Dworkin 1986). As women struggled for the right to education and challenged their relegation to the home, they recognized the importance of the vote in the ability to secure their demands and further women's status in their societies. Indeed, it was only when substantial portions of middle- and upper-class women started to find work outside of the household that suffrage appeared on the political agenda in many countries (Lloyd 1971).

First-wave feminist movements were often also composed mainly of middle- or upper-class women. For example, Bertha Lutz, the president of the Brazilian Federation for the Progress of Women, was the daughter of a pioneer of tropical medicine. In Egypt, women formed a federation in 1923 to defend the right of women to education and advocate for reforms such as women's suffrage; however, according to Morgan (1984), the federation consisted of exclusively upper-class women and had no links to the working classes. In Sri Lanka, middle-class women fought for education, suffrage, and equal political rights, and the working women of the country struggled for material gains, equal wages for men and women, and more humane conditions at work (Chafetz and Dworkin 1986). This does not mean that working-class women did not take part in suffrage movements. Schoolteachers and journalists were important, often serving as a bridge between upper and working classes. Working-class participation also increased when suffrage organizations developed closer ties to the labor movement (DuBois 1998).

Goals and Ideology

Both between and within countries, movements also disagreed regarding their primary goal. Although women in many countries demanded universal suffrage, some countries still placed education or property restrictions on male suffrage. In these nations, therefore, women often demanded rights on the same terms as men. In some instances where men did have universal suffrage, movements still carefully weighed whether imposing voting restrictions on women would aid their cause. In Norway, for example, Gina Krog supported a limited franchise for women even after men had achieved adult suffrage because she believed that gradualism would be a more effective policy. In the United States, some suffrage movement leaders wanted to restrict the vote to educated women, and similarly in 19th-century Britain there were disagreements within the movement over whether the demand for the vote should include married women.

For former colonies, suffrage often came later for indigenous women than for White women living in the colonies. For example, in Kenya, a British colony, a legislative council was established in 1907. European women were given the vote in 1919, and Asian men and women were granted suffrage in 1923. Black African voters had to wait until 1957 when a wide franchise was introduced—one still restricted by property and educational qualifications. Still excluded, Arab women from Mombasa protested that the legislation had denied them the franchise. Finally, upon independence in 1963, universal adult suffrage was introduced. This phenomenon was not unique to British colonies or to sub-Saharan Africa. In Indonesia, for example, Dutch women, but not local women, were given municipal voting rights in 1941.

Arguments that suffrage should be limited to educated or propertied women were labeled by socialists as bourgeois suffrage and contributed early on to a split between suffrage movements and socialist women. *Bourgeois* is a term used to refer to wealthy or propertied social classes in a capitalist society. The split between socialist and bourgeois women was actively promoted by socialists as "anti-collaborationism" (DuBois 1998:263). Yet in some cases, such as Puerto Rico and Austria, socialist and working-class women took the lead in the suffrage campaign (Azize-Vargas 2002). Alliances were also sometimes made between bourgeois and socialist working-class women. In Mexico in the 1930s, for example, an umbrella suffrage organization, Frente Único Pro-Derechos de la Mujer, recruited at its height 50,000 members from a wide array of backgrounds.

Despite the separation of many socialist women from Western suffrage movements, the adoption of Marxist ideas by governments was often quickly followed by female suffrage. As we discuss in Chapters 3 and 11, communist governments espoused an ideal of a genderless state. And women were expected to participate in all areas of social, political, and economic life. Thus, several countries, such as China and Democratic Yemen, adopted suffrage in their first year of Communist rule. And Yugoslavia, though independent in 1918, did not adopt female suffrage until 1946 after declaring itself a socialist state (Paxton, Hughes, and Green 2006). Socialist women also played important roles in organizing for women's rights. German political activist Clara Zetkin, for example, organized the First International Conference of Socialist Women in 1907, and she proposed March 8 as International Women's Day in 1911.

Still, because of the prominence of women's movements in the West, Marxists and nationalists worldwide denounced feminism as Western imperialism, and suffragists in non-Western countries sometimes faced opposition on these grounds. Thus, women in these countries developed indigenous feminist forms. Although the women's suffrage movement is often considered a Western phenomenon, movements for women's emancipation in China, India, and other parts of Asia can be traced back to the 19th century. Women "participated in social and political movements, in nationalist and patriotic struggles, in working-class agitations and peasant rebellions" and formed autonomous women's organizations (Jayawardena 1986:254).

Movement Opposition

Perhaps the most obvious similarity between the United States and other social movements is that no matter where they were, proponents of female suffrage faced opposition. Women around the world confronted the belief that they lacked the necessary qualities or capabilities to participate in politics. In the Third World, these beliefs were often reinforced by European Colonialism, which carried notions of separate spheres backed by political philosophers of the Enlightenment. Women themselves were not unified in their belief that women should be voting. Queen Victoria, who ruled the United Kingdom from 1837 to 1901, staunchly opposed women's suffrage. And around the world, women feared that changing the status quo would disrupt the family and lead to the loss of male economic and social protection.

Oppositional groups were stronger in some countries than in others. In countries with strong suffrage movements like the United Kingdom, anti-suffrage organizations were formed, while in countries like Australia and New Zealand, women faced much less opposition. Women in many countries also faced opposition from both sides of the political spectrum. In France, for example, republicans feared women would vote according to Catholic lines, and conservatives thought women were more likely to support progressive reform interests like temperance.

Women often faced unique obstacles grounded in distinctive cultural, political, or religious circumstances. In Latin America, for example, traditional values and machismo served to hinder women's progress (Lavrin 1994). In Uruguay, one opponent to suffrage invented a new term, *machonismo,* to describe the desire to copy men and divert women from their natural path (Hannam et al. 2000). Authoritarian regimes and conservative parties tended to oppose democratization and the extension of voting rights. For example,

Japan had a small women's movement that emerged in the 1880s, but it was silenced by the government until the 1920s (Chafetz and Dworkin 1986). Direct government suppression of independent women's organizations occurred at various times in France, Russia, China, Japan, Indonesia, Iran, Brazil, and Peru (Randall 1987).

In addition to traditional values or political authoritarianism, a country's dominant religion often influenced the development and success of first-wave women's movements. Specifically, Catholic countries are often seen as more resistant to suffrage than Protestant countries. For example, Ehrick (1998) argued that a liberal-feminist movement developed in Uruguay in part because the Catholic Church was not as strong as in Chile, where the suffrage movement was less successful. None of the first six countries to enfranchise women were predominantly Catholic, and of 14 nations, which may have had suffrage movements beyond an incipient, or beginning level, 10 were predominantly Protestant (Chafetz and Dworkin 1986:160).

Scholars do not all agree, however, on why Catholicism presented a barrier to women's suffrage. One argument is that the Catholic Church often discouraged women from involvement in public affairs, while Goode (1963) suggested that feminism is the logical, philosophical extension of Protestant notions about the rights and responsibilities of the individual (p. 56, cited in Randall 1987:213). But the official position of the Church changed to a pro-suffrage one in 1919, thirty years before most majority-Catholic countries granted women suffrage. Chafetz and Dworkin (1986) argued that the religion effect is not direct but indirect through education: Protestantism emphasizes education more than other religions. They point out that the Quakers, a religious group that emphasized education and individualism for both sexes, were influential in the early American and British movements. Furthermore, many of the women's movement leaders in Asian countries were educated in Christian schools, their education serving as the catalyst for future mobilization.

Others scholars argue that it comes down to politics—specifically, perceptions about how women would cast their votes. In France, activists feared female suffrage would lead to political Catholicism and a return to monarchy; some argued that women needed a secular education first that would liberate them from the church. The same pattern is evident in Belgium, where socialists and liberals dropped suffrage due to fear of religious fanaticism. The negative "Catholic effect" was partially fueled by women's rights activists themselves, who feared that women would vote Catholic (Hannam et al. 2000). Overall, the argument goes that left-wing parties in Catholic countries tended to procrastinate extending the vote to women because they believed Catholic women would not support them (Przeworski 2009).

Tactics and Level of Militancy

Another factor that varied both within and across suffrage movements is women's use of militant tactics. The term *militancy* was first applied to the activities of the Women's Social and Political Union (WSPU), a suffrage organization in the United Kingdom, to distinguish them from more constitutional methods, including lobbying, petitioning, and letter writing. The term is associated with a wide range of tactics including the disruption of meetings, tax resistance, refusing to fill in census forms, breaking windows, arson attacks on public buildings, other forms of property destruction, imprisonment, hunger striking, and forcible feeding.

The WSPU in Britain is the most well-known of militant suffrage organizations. Just as women's protests in the United States grew more public over time, the WSPU's tactics changed as well. The first act of militancy occurred in October 1905, when WSPU leaders Christabel Pankhurst and Annie Kenney interrupted an election meeting by standing up and shouting, "Votes for women!" They were subsequently arrested when Christabel spat at a policeman. After 1908, the militancy of the WSPU escalated to include symbolic acts, such as women chaining themselves to the Ladies Gallery in Parliament and threats to public order, such as groups of women rushing the House of Commons and destroying property. For example, in early March 1912, **suffragettes** launched two window-breaking campaigns. The first, on March 1, involved women making coordinated raids throwing stones to break windows throughout London at 15-minute intervals.

The second incident, 3 days later, involved more than 100 women smashing all panes of glass along a street in Knightsbridge (Jorgensen-Earp 1999). By the summer of 1912, 102 British suffragettes were in prison, and 90 were being forcibly fed. While the idea of militant, stone-throwing suffragettes may be shocking, it is also important to note the use of violence by the government and individual men. It is simultaneously important to recognize the reluctance of some women to use these militant tactics. The following story, related by Cheryl Jorgensen-Earp (1999), illustrates both these points:

Despite its symbolic beginning, stone throwing was quickly adopted by WSPU members as a practical response to meet the second exigency often encountered during suffrage protests. Before they would arrest suffrage speakers or members of suffrage deputations, the police would subject women to a period of "buffeting." Buffeting was a term used at the time to describe a delay of arrest during which time the suffragettes would be pummeled and manhandled by police and angry male crowds. Injuries to Union members were inevitable, and it was clearly the hope of the government and police that the threat of such injury would dissuade suffrage activism. Then, too, the practice of buffeting allowed the police to inflict maximum physical punishment while simultaneously claiming that they arrested the suffragettes only when absolutely necessary. Quickly, Union members discovered that if they threw a stone (even if it did not reach its target) or committed simple assault (dry "spitting" or slapping a policeman), they would be arrested in short order and not subjected to as much physical damage. This initial step into illegal action caused such mental anguish for many of the suffragettes that they swaddled the stones in heavy paper and even took the precaution of tying long strings from stone to wrist, thus avoiding injury to bystanders. Despite their scruples, union members came to agree with Sylvia Pankhurst's assertion, "Since we must go to prison to obtain the vote, let it be the windows of the government, not the bodies of women, which shall be broken" (p. 101).

The actions of the WSPU often inspired women in other movements. Alice Paul, for example, spent several years in the WSPU before leading women in militancy in the United States. In the United Kingdom, however, militancy was used earlier and was more widespread. Figure 2.4 depicts the perceived contrast in tactics between the two movements.

Figure 2.4   Political Cartoon Depicting British and American Suffragists

Source: Utica Saturday Globe, March 1913. Courtesy of BoondocksNet.com.

Although militancy is most well known in the United Kingdom, women in other countries also organized demonstrations and stormed legislatures (Jayawardena 1986; Randall 1987). For example, in 1911, Tang Junying founded the Chinese Suffragette Society in Beijing and led women to the first meetings of the National Assembly. When they were refused the vote, the women launched an attack, and by the third day, the assembly had to send for troops for protection. Similarly, in Guangdong, the provisional government promised women the vote but retracted it, and women invaded the legislature (Hannam et al. 2000; Morgan 1984). Women also used militancy in Japan (1924), Egypt (1924), Iran (1917), and Sri Lanka (1927).

On the other hand, women in some countries were very reluctant to use militant tactics. In Europe, many women shied away from street demonstrations, and in South America, many movements distanced themselves from militancy to avoid being called unwomanly or too radical. Women also may have been reluctant because militancy was not necessarily perceived as more successful. Many movements, such as those in New Zealand, Canada, and Scandinavia, were successful in achieving suffrage before the United Kingdom without using militant tactics. Figure 2.5 satirizes this point in a political cartoon, showing women in the Netherlands gaining suffrage before their more militant English counterparts.

The International Women's Movement

In addition to the struggles that took place at the national level in countries across the world, women also organized at the international level. In 1878, the first international women's congress convened in Paris, attended by 11 foreign countries and 16 organizations (Moses 1984; Rupp and Taylor 1999). The better-known first International Council of Women (ICW) was founded a decade later by Susan B. Anthony, May Wright Sewell, and Frances Willard and held its first convention in Washington. The convention was attended by representatives of Canada, Denmark, Finland, France, Great Britain, India, and Norway. Though the congress's primary goal was the advancement of women, it initially did not demand female suffrage so as not to alienate its more conservative members. The early international conferences were extensively covered by the press, especially the 1899 meeting in which Anthony met Queen Victoria.

Early years of organizing at the international level also included Latin America. In 1910, the first International Feminist Congress was held in Buenos Aires, and in 1916, the International Conference of Women convened in the Yucatán. Often these events in the international movement had

Figure 2.5   Political Cartoon Depicting Women in the Netherlands
Gaining the Vote Before the More Militant British

Source: Minneapolis Journal, November 1913. Courtesy of BoondocksNet.com.

profound implications for women active in local movements. For example, according to Morgan (1984), the International Feminist Congress was a watershed moment for Argentina's suffrage movement, inspiring women across the country.

Despite the varied geography of international meetings, the international movement was composed of mostly Western, upper-class, educated, White women. Groups such as the International Woman Suffrage Alliance (IWSA) sought to convert non-Western women to the suffrage campaign (Hannam et al. 2000). Yet, as discussed earlier, women were engaged in indigenous women's movements across the globe. IWSA president Carrie Chapman Catt expressed surprise when, as a result of her travels in 1911 and 1912, she found that woman in Asia already had a movement of considerable strength. Socialist women participated in the international movement with the International Socialist Women's Conference in 1907 and the International Communist Conference of Working Women in 1920.

Besides encouraging national-level women's movements, as the international women's movement grew in strength it actively began to pressure international organizations such as the League of Nations and the United Nations. Berkovitch (1999) argued that the League of Nations and the International Labor Organization (ILO) "opened a new arena for women's mobilization by offering a central world focal point that theretofore had been lacking" (p. 109). In 1931, ten of the largest women's organizations joined forces to form the Liaison Committee of Women's International Organisations, which in 1937 lobbied the League of Nations to collect data on women's legal status around the world (Berkovitch 1999). These international women's groups successfully placed a women's rights issue, the nationality of married women, on the agenda of the ILO. In 1946, the General Assembly of the United Nations recommended that all member states fulfill the aims of its charter "granting to women the same political rights as men" (Resolution 56 ([1]). As discussed in the next section, the international women's movement helped to make women's suffrage, once considered unacceptable by both politicians and the public, a taken-for-granted requirement of a modern country. See also Chapter 7 for a longer discussion of the international women's movement and its impact.

Women's Suffrage After 1945

Up to this point, we have focused on women's struggle to be recognized as men's political equals. In some countries, this struggle took decades; in some, women were even willing to destroy property and endure prison, hunger strikes, and forced feedings. Women were fighting against the belief held for centuries that they lacked the capacity to participate politically. They worried that simply by voting they might damage the institution of the family and the very fabric of their society. Despite these challenges, women won the vote in New Zealand and in the United States, Sweden, Spain, Chile, and Myanmar. And as increasing numbers of countries increasingly granted women suffrage, the pressure on surrounding countries that had not yet extended rights to women mounted.

With the end of World War II, the world landscape changed. France, Italy, Romania, Yugoslavia, and China immediately granted women the right to vote, and others soon followed. As empires began to dismantle and colonies around the world struggled for independence, new countries began to enter the world system. With only a few exceptions, these new countries granted both men and women the right to vote in their constitutions. Varying national debates about women's rights gave way to an internationally recognized universal belief in women's enfranchisement. The gendered definition of political citizenship had changed (Paxton et al. 2006; Ramirez, Soysal, and Shanahan 1997).

Interestingly, it was sometimes countries with longer histories of democratic principles that held out, continuing to deny women rights. In Switzerland, which has a **direct democracy**, women in Zurich began to demand the vote in 1886, but a majority of men voted against women's suffrage in six national referendums (Geschichte-Schweiz 2004). Anti-suffrage campaigns made it clear that only "mannish" women even wanted to vote and that children would be neglected if women began participating in politics (Slater 2011). The first victory came in 1957, when Basel City voted to allow women to vote in local elections. But it wasn't until 1971 that a referendum passed granting women the right to vote in federal elections. Even then, two conservative half-cantons in eastern Switzerland refused to let women vote in local elections based on an interpretation of the word *citizen* as male only. It took an act by the Federal Supreme Court in 1990 to declare that women, too, were citizens and impose universal female suffrage countrywide (Geschichte-Schweiz 2004).

Another group of holdout countries resided in the Gulf region of the Middle East (for more on this region, see Chapter 13). Yet these countries often had not extended political rights to men or women. Whether women would be allowed to vote when democracy was first instituted was a question that remained to be answered. In 1999, women secured voting rights in the country of Qatar, followed by Bahrain in 2002. Political reform in Bahrain was driven by King Hamad, who worked to advance women's rights despite ambivalence even of women in Bahrain, of which 60% opposed female suffrage in 2001 (Janardhan 2005). But the extension of voting rights to women in Bahrain encouraged activists elsewhere in the region to step up demands for women's suffrage. Oman passed women's suffrage in 2003 and Kuwait in 2005. We profile women's struggle for suffrage in Kuwait in Chapter 13.

The last holdout was Saudi Arabia, where women were excluded from participating in the country's first municipal elections in February 2005. In the run-up to the elections, the head of the election committee, Prince Mutaib bin Abdulaziz, said, "I expect women to participate in elections in future stages, after conducting studies to assess whether it is useful or not" (Amnesty International 2004). But, in 2011, King Abdullah made a bold move, announcing that women in Saudi Arabia will be able to vote and run in future municipal elections. Some hope the move will provide space for broader debates about women's rights in Saudi Arabia, where women were arrested in the months before the suffrage announcement for defying the ban on women driving. It is also important to remember that women have not yet voted in Saudi Arabia, and in the past, suffrage promises by national leaders have sometimes lacked follow-through. Nothing is certain until women cast ballots on Election Day in 2015.

Today, political rights are not fully equal everywhere. In Lebanon, proof of education is required for a woman to vote whereas a man is not subject to any education restrictions. Women's vote is optional, whereas men are required to vote by law. And in Bhutan, only one vote per family is allowed at the village level, meaning that oftentimes women are excluded. But there is no country where only women are barred from voting.

Women Exercising Their Vote

After suffrage struggles were won, women immediately began exercising their new rights. But women rarely started voting on par with men right out of the gates. Voting is an act we learn to do early in life and generally continue to do out of habit (Franklin, Lyons, and Marsh 2004). Yet women had been socialized that voting was for men. And these attitudes had long-lasting effects. One study based in the United States shows that women who grew up before the passage of the 19th Amendment continued to vote less frequently over their lifetime than women born later an socialized to believe that women were voters too (Firebaugh and Chen 1995). In short, disenfranchisement had long-lasting effects.

Yet, over time, women in many countries have closed the gap and even started voting more often than men. Although we do not have complete data on women as voters, International IDEA has compiled information about the **gender gap** in turnout after 1945 across eight democracies: Barbados, Finland, Germany, Iceland, India, Malta, New Zealand, and Sweden (Pintor and Gratschew 2002). In two of these countries, Barbados and Sweden, women have been voting more often than men since even the 1950s. In countries such as Germany, Finland, and Iceland, women voted less often than men in modest numbers during the 1950s and 1960s. In all of these countries except for India, women closed the voting gap or reversed it.

Information on men's and women's voting behavior in the 1990s is available for 19 countries across the world. The group of countries includes not only Western industrialized countries but also a small number of countries in Latin America, Asia, and Central and Eastern Europe. In most countries, men's and women's participation was close to even. In only one of the countries did women participate at significantly higher rates than men—Sweden. Women reported lower rates of turnout in the newer democracies of Poland, Hungary, and Romania by a margin of 4% to 7% (Pintor and Gratschew 2002).

But even in places where women lagged behind in the 1990s, women are closing gaps in voter turnout. Women now vote on par with men in Poland (Kunovich 2012). And even in India, where women long voted in numbers substantially lower than men (Chari 2011; Pintor and Gratschew 2002), changes are afoot. In 2012, the numbers of women voters surged unexpectedly, and women voted at higher rates than men in all five states that had elections (Thirani 2012).

Of course, these statistics all focus on likelihood of voting among men and women. Unpacking these groups shows that the gap in voter turnout between men and women varies across groups. In the United States, for example, Black, Hispanic, and White women have all voted in higher numbers than Black, Hispanic, and White men for the last six presidential elections. The greatest gender difference in voter turnout is among Blacks, in which 64% of women voted in 2008 compared with 56% of men (Center for American Women and Politics [CAWP] 2011a). For Asians and Pacific Islanders, the first year in which data for both gender and race are available is 2000, and though men were found to have slightly higher turnout than women in that year, Asian and Pacific Islander women voted in slightly higher numbers than men in 2004 and 2008 (CAWP 2011a). Research based outside the United States similarly finds that women from different racial, ethnic and religious minority groups vote at different rates (Bird 2010).

Another important question to ask is "For whom do women vote?" Remember that debates about which parties and issues women would support figured prominently into struggles for suffrage. Suffragists and anti-suffragists alike argued that allowing women to vote would radically change politics. But for the most part, such expectations never materialized. Speaking about women's experiences as voters some 20 years after the 19th

Amendment was ratified in the United States, First Lady Eleanor Roosevelt said it well, "I think it is fairly obvious that women...are influenced by their environment and their experience and background, just as men are" (1940:45; cited in Corder and Wolbrecht 2006).

Still, broadly speaking, there have been differences in the way men and women have voted. Historically, women across the world were more conservative than men (Goot and Reid 1975; Inglehart and Norris 2000; Klausen 2001). In 1960, Seymour Martin Lipset (1960) found that "practically every country for which we have data . . . women tend to support the conservative parties more than do men" (p. 221). Similarly, Pulzer (1967:107) argued that in the United Kingdom, "there is overwhelming evidence that women are more conservatively inclined than men."

Over time, however, women's party preferences in many countries began to shift. In the 1970s, younger women, in particular, began to align with the more liberal, or leftist, parties, whereas older women continued to vote more conservatively (Klausen 2001). And by the post–1990 period, women's tendency to vote more conservatively had reversed in many advanced industrial societies, such that women had moved to the left of men (Inglehart and Norris 2000). But women continued to be more conservative than men in post-Communist countries and in the developing world.

Today, when one heads to the polls, men and women are seen casting ballots alongside each other to choose a leader. Whether women today are voting more or less often—or more or less conservatively than men—it is important not to forget history. Women's right to vote came only after decades of struggle by thousands of brave men and women. In the next chapter, we move beyond the vote to begin thinking of women's roles in other parts of the electoral process.

3

Women Struggle for Representation

Accessing Positions of Power

Once women had the vote, they had a voice in politics for the first time. They were formally represented in power, having the legal right to participate in politics on an equal basis with men. But as discussed in Chapter 1, formal political equality is only the first step in achieving equal representation. Women now needed to fight for descriptive representation in the traditional halls of power. Slowly, over the course of the 20th century, women began to make inroads into areas of power typically held by men: Pioneering women became the first to hold political office, others led the way as presidents and prime ministers, and women began to fill **cabinet** positions and advise leaders on public policy.

But though women successfully stormed the male political castle in some countries, they remained encamped on the outside in others. In some countries, women became commonplace as members of parliament (MPs), reaching 20%, 30%, and even 50% of legislatures. In many other countries, however, the struggle for descriptive representation has proceeded slowly, and women remain barely visible in political life. Still other countries demonstrate that women can lose political power even after they have gained it. The pace of women's access to positions of power was also very different from country to country. In some countries women were appearing in politics in substantial numbers by the 1970s whereas in others it would take until the 1990s to gain political clout. And women are still waiting for minimal levels of descriptive representation in some countries.

This chapter provides an overview of women's struggle to access a variety of positions of political power. It begins with a brief look at the vanguard group of women who first held elected office. It then turns to a historical overview of the growth of women's participation in national legislatures. Then female world leaders and female cabinet members are discussed.

First Female Members of Parliament

In Chapter 2, we described how New Zealand led the world to become the first country to grant women suffrage; however, New Zealand did not capture all "firsts" for women in politics. In 1907, Finland became the first country to elect a female MP. Although this was a truly historic event, we cannot tell you the story of the first female parliamentarian because there was not one woman elected in 1907 to Finland's new unicameral parliament, nor were there two women. In the world's first election to allow women to contest seats alongside men, 19 women were elected.

During the 1907 Finnish election, advertisements directed at women stressed the importance and historical significance of the general elections. Organizations affiliated with the women's movement urged every Finnish woman to ensure that a sufficient number of women were elected into office, using the argument that women are best at interpreting women's wishes. In a historic moment for both the country and the world, 19 women (9.5%) were elected to the new legislative body. Nine of the women members were socialists, and 10 represented bourgeois parties. However, the majority of women cast ballots for men candidates.

During the first parliament, 26 bills were presented by women members. The legislation covered topics such as the legal rights of married women, maternity insurance, women's property rights, female employment, and funding for schoolchildren. However, women from the suffrage movement still expressed disappointment that female MPs appeared more loyal to their parties than to a common women's cause. After the 1907 election, Finland would not elect so many women to its parliament until 1954. Women candidates fared worst in the general election of 1930, when women's representation fell to less than 6%. The number of female MPs began rising in 1966, when women's share of seats exceeded 15% for the first time ("Finnish Women" 1911; Gronlund 2003; Manninen 2004).

The ability of women to run for political office went hand in hand with female suffrage in the vast majority of countries. Typically, when women were granted the vote, they were also granted the right to run for political office and be elected. Yet voting and obtaining initial representation were sometimes separate struggles. For example, though women in New Zealand could vote in 1893, they did not receive the right to stand for election until 1919 and could not sit in the upper house until 1941. In Djibouti, women could vote in 1946, prior to the country's 1977 independence, but women were not able to run for office until 1986. Often the gap was shorter such as in Turkey (4 years) and Mexico (5 years).

In some countries, the opposite was true: Women were allowed to hold political office before they could vote. For example, women were elected to legislatures before they could officially vote in Brazil, Hungary, the Netherlands, and Yugoslavia (Inter-Parliamentary Union [IPU] 1995). In the United States, women could in theory run for office from the ratification of the Constitution in the late 1700s. However, it took almost 100 years for a woman to test the theory that she could run for political office. In 1866, Elizabeth Cady Stanton did run for Congress—although she only received 24 votes. America's first female MP was Jeannette Rankin, elected to the U.S. House of Representatives from Montana in 1917, three years before the passage of the 19th Amendment.

Jeannette Rankin was a native of Missoula, Montana; a suffragist; and a lifelong pacifist (see Figure 3.1). She was active in the suffrage movement and in 1914 helped women win the right to vote in Montana—6 years before the 19th Amendment was passed. After winning the vote, Rankin promptly ran for the House of Representatives on the Republican ticket. Thus, alone among her fellow suffragists, she was able to declare, "The first time I voted . . . in 1916 . . . I voted for myself" (Hoff 1985).

Rankin won the election and entered the House of Representatives on April 2, 1917, to cheers and applause. Only a few days later, on April 6, 1917, following her pacifist beliefs, she along with only 50 representatives voted against U.S. entry into World War I. Despite receiving harsh criticism, she was adamant that women and peace were inseparable, saying, "The first time the first woman had a chance to say no against war she should say it" (Jeannette Rankin Peace Center 2006). Probably as a result, she lost her reelection bid in 1918. But before leaving office she amended a bill to secure equal employment for women, helped reform working hours for women in the Bureau of Printing and Engraving, and worked for a federal constitutional amendment to give women the right to vote. After leaving office, she remained active in pacifist issues.

Rankin ran for Congress again in 1940, winning a second term. But in 1941, she stood alone as the sole vote against U.S. entry into World War II, a vote that drew immediate hostility. On the way back to her office, she had to take refuge in a phone booth to escape an angry crowd. The vote ended

Figure 3.1   Jeannette Rankin Planting a Montana Fir Tree,
Arbor Day 1917

Source: Montana Historical Society Archives.

her political career. Throughout the rest of her life, she was active in the peace movement and today is remembered as the only member of Congress to oppose U.S. entrance into both world wars (Jeannette Rankin Peace Center 2006; Josephson 1974).

Once women had the vote and the right to run for public office, public opinion was still hard to change. Citizens were sometimes not ready to elect women, and often women were no more willing to vote for female candidates than were men. Women were still considered inferior and viewed as belonging in the home. In New Zealand, after women won the right to run for political office, three women contested seats, but none was successful in getting elected. The first female MP in New Zealand was not elected until 1933, when the Labour Party's Elizabeth McCombs was chosen by the electorate to fill the seat of her deceased husband, James McCombs, in a by-election. Because of continuing concern about women's abilities and qualifications, less than 30% of the world's countries actually elected a woman to parliament in the election following female enfranchisement.

Not all women had to run as candidates to achieve political office. The appointment process allowed some women to gain entry to legislative bodies before they were perceived as viable candidates by the electorate. For example, in Jordan, women first voted in parliamentary elections in 1989. Of the 10 women who presented their candidature in these elections, none won a seat, but 1 woman was appointed to the Senate (Abou-Zeid 1998; Lane 2001). According to the IPU (1995), about 12% of countries appointed a woman to their parliament before one was elected.

Women Access Parliaments: Patterns of Representation

Once the first woman was elected to political office, others typically followed. When did women achieve other milestones of descriptive representation? When did women reach 10% of parliaments or 20%? The answer is "it depends." Some countries experienced steady growth in the number of women in parliaments over time. Others had no growth at all. Some countries have only recently encountered women in politics in large numbers. Other countries had higher levels of female participation in the past than in the present.

To provide an overview of women's growth and decline in descriptive representation across countries, we have divided country parliamentary histories into five basic paths: (1) Flat, (2) Increasing, (3) Big Jump, (4) Low Increasing, and (5) Plateau. In this section, we describe each of these historical paths, which run from 1945 to 2010. We present a general picture of each type of path, discuss some of the countries that follow each pattern, and provide a brief explanation of the path.

Flat Countries: Women's Representation Does Not Change Over Time

The first category, Flat, includes a diverse array of countries whose numbers of women are fairly stable or constant across time. Some of the countries in this grouping never elected a significant number of women to their parliament, hovering at less than 5%. This group of countries is indicated by the dotted line in Figure 3.2 with examples of the countries in this group listed next. Many of these countries are in the Middle East and North Africa, including Egypt, Jordan, Kuwait, Lebanon, and Yemen.

The concentration of countries that have never incorporated women into politics in a few regions of the world suggests that there is something in these regions that acts as a barrier to women's political representation. Research suggests that this barrier is culture. As discussed in Chapter 4,

Figure 3.2   Patterns of Representation: Flat

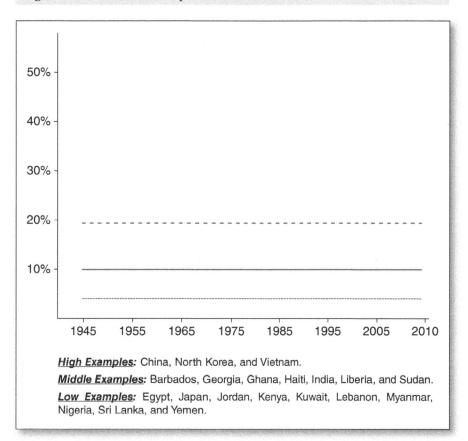

High Examples: China, North Korea, and Vietnam.

Middle Examples: Barbados, Georgia, Ghana, Haiti, India, Liberia, and Sudan.

Low Examples: Egypt, Japan, Jordan, Kenya, Kuwait, Lebanon, Myanmar, Nigeria, Sri Lanka, and Yemen.

Note: These are generalized examples of country histories. Individual countries may have slight variations away from the general trend. Also ignored are periods of crisis or war when a parliament was dissolved, and, for countries independent after 1945, we considered the percentage of women in parliament following the country's independence. Each graph includes three lines that demonstrate variations of the same basic configuration: The best-performing group is indicated by a dashed line, the middle group by a solid line, and the lowest-performing group is marked with a dotted line. Examples of countries in each group are recorded below the figure in each instance.

negative cultural beliefs toward women are based in either religious traditions or cultural attitudes that suggest that women should not participate in the political realm.

The second group of Flat countries, marked by the solid line, also elects a fairly constant number of women to parliament over time, but the number of women is higher: around 5% to 10%. A good example of this trajectory is Georgia, which elected 7.1% women to its first parliament in 1991 and continued to hover within a few percentage points of that number for the next 20 years.

Finally, three of the world's remaining Communist countries—China, North Korea, and Vietnam—appear together in the High Flat group and are indicated by the dashed line. This group has high and very steady levels of women's participation in parliaments. For the 35 years between 1975 and 2010, for example, China held steady around 21% women in their parliament, deviating from that number by less than 2% in either direction. The extent to which women have real power in Communist countries is in question, however, as we will discuss in Chapter 11.

Increasing Countries: Women Make Steady Gains in Representation

We label the next general pattern that countries follow Increasing. Many countries in the West fall into this category along with a few from Latin America and Africa. Looking at Figure 3.3, it becomes clear that countries with generally increasing trajectories vary across two main dimensions: (1) the height of the curve (what percent of the parliament women eventually attain) and (2) where the increase started (the time period when women started making substantial gains). The main classifying dimension is height, or the largest percentage women in parliament the country reached. For example, the High Increasing category includes some of the countries with the highest female parliamentary representation in the world in 2010: Sweden (45%), the Netherlands (40.7%), Finland (40%), Norway (39.6%), and Denmark (38%). The Middle Increasing category includes countries that reached between 25% and 35%, and countries in the Low Increasing category end up between around 18% and 24%. Countries with increases that did not reach 18% are often in the Low Increasing category, which is discussed later.

The second dimension for classifying countries in the Increasing category is when women began making gains in descriptive representation—the point in time where the graph's curve begins to increase. Among this group of countries, the timing of women's gains in political power goes hand in hand with what percentage of the legislature they ultimately attained. That is, of the countries that follow a general increasing pattern, higher performing countries often had an earlier inflection point—beginning to make significant gains earlier in time than countries in the lower performing groups. Figure 3.3 shows that countries in the High Increasing group often started their steep incline in the late 1970s and early 1980s. Finland and Sweden

Figure 3.3   Patterns of Representation: Increasing

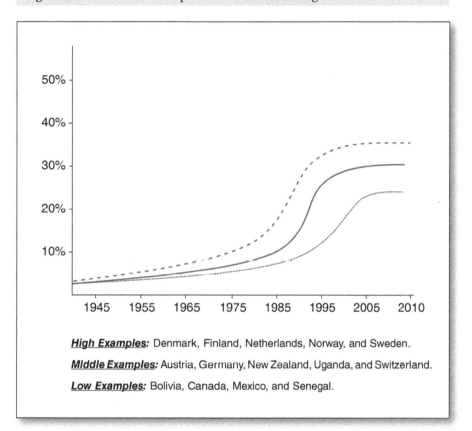

High Examples: Denmark, Finland, Netherlands, Norway, and Sweden.

Middle Examples: Austria, Germany, New Zealand, Uganda, and Switzerland.

Low Examples: Bolivia, Canada, Mexico, and Senegal.

follow this trajectory, both crossing the 30% women in parliament threshold by 1985. Middle Increasing countries, marked by the solid line, often began their incline a little bit later. For example, Austria did not make significant gains until the early 1990s. Several countries in the Low Increasing group, such as Bolivia, did not cross the threshold of 10% women in parliament until the mid-to-late 1990s.

Why did women do so well in these countries? First, many countries in the High Increasing category are Scandinavian countries, and this reaffirms the importance of regional differences, and culture, in women's representation. Heckscher (1984:172) noted the following:

It is no exaggeration to say that the fundamental principle of equality between men and women is more widely accepted in Scandinavia than in most other countries of the world; this is seen in legislation, in the apparent attitudes of the public, and in actual practice.

But more is going on than simply a culture of equality. All of the High Increasing countries, and many of the Middle Increasing countries also have a proportional representation (PR) system. PR systems are different from the **majoritarian electoral systems** found in the United States and Britain. The importance of PR electoral systems, and other political factors, is discussed in Chapter 6.

Big Jumps: Women Make Sudden Gains

The third historical pattern of women's parliamentary representation is the "Big Jump." Countries in this group experience extremely large gains in women's representation in short periods of time—often a single election cycle. Countries vary substantially in the timing and extent of their jump in women's representation, so in Figure 3.4, we provide three examples of Big Jump countries. In each case, the country significantly increased its representation of women in a single electoral cycle and then either leveled off or continued to grow beyond that point. We use thresholds similar to the Increasing category described earlier and delineate by the percentage of women in parliament at the end of the jump. The High Jump country, Rwanda, finished its jump above 35% women in parliament; the Middle Jump country, South Africa, only reached between 25% and 35% women at the time of its jump; and the Low Jump country, the United Kingdom, achieved between 16% and 24%.

But doesn't where a country starts make a difference for how high it can jump? Yes. There are two kinds of jumps a country can make: absolute jumps and relative jumps. Absolute jumps are the simple percentage increase in women's parliamentary representation. Rwanda's representation, for example, jumped from 25.7% to 48.8% in 2003, an absolute gain of 23.1% in a single year. No matter where a country starts in its level of female representation—be it 2% women or 30% women—large absolute gains create significant changes to the gender composition of a parliament.

Relative gains, on the other hand, take into consideration where a country started. Big relative jumps are seen when a country starts with few women in its parliament. It is easier for a country with 2% women in its legislature to double women's numbers to 4% than it is for a country to double 20% women to 40%. Relative jumps also signify important changes to parliamentary composition. If the number of women in parliament doubles or triples, this represents a significant change to the status quo, even if it does not represent an especially large absolute gain or bring the number of women to

Figure 3.4   Patterns of Representation: Big Jump

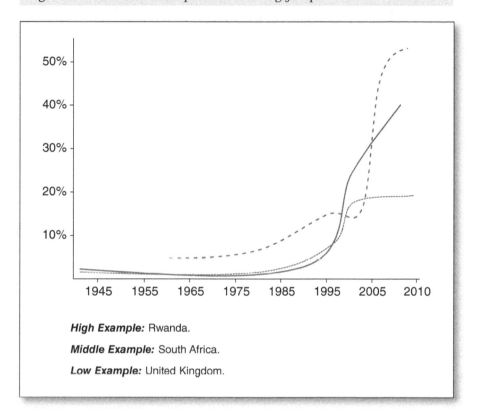

High Example: Rwanda.

Middle Example: South Africa.

Low Example: United Kingdom.

a particularly high level. Relative gains are easier to make if the prior percentage of women in parliament was low, so they often identify when women made their first significant gains in representation.

To illustrate the difference, let's return to the case of Rwanda. Before the 23.1% gain in 2003, Rwanda experienced its first big jump in 1997, from 4.3% to 17.1%, almost quadrupling the percentage of women in parliament. Thus, in an absolute sense, the 2003 gain was much larger, but in a relative sense, the 1997 gain is more significant.

Table 3.1 presents the absolute and relative jumps in women's parliamentary representation in select Big Jump countries. Countries with the largest absolute gains appear at the top of the list. Notice that countries can appear multiple times in the table.

Notice that the countries in Table 3.1 often experienced their big jump from the mid-1990s through the early 21st century. This is no coincidence. During that period, countries around the world began to implement gender

Table 3.1   Absolute and Relative Gains in the Percentage
of Women in Parliament of Select Big Jump Countries

Country	Start Percentage	End Percentage	Absolute Percentage	Relative Percentage	Years
Kyrgyzstan	0.0	25.6	25.6	—	2006–2007
Iraq	7.6	31.6	24.0	4.2	2003–2005
South Africa	1.2	25.0	23.8	20.8	1994–1995
Rwanda	25.7	48.8	23.1	1.9	2002–2003
Algeria	8.0	31.4	23.4	2.9	2011–2012
Belarus	10.3	29.4	19.1	2.9	2003–2004
Pakistan	2.3	21.1	18.8	9.2	1999–2002
Argentina	5.8	21.8	16.0	3.8	1992–1995
Costa Rica	19.3	35.1	15.8	1.8	2001–2002
Spain	21.6	36.0	14.4	1.7	1999–2004
Andorra	14.3	28.6	14.3	2.0	2004–2005
Ecuador	3.7	17.4	13.7	4.7	1997–1998
Turkmenistan	4.6	18.0	13.4	3.9	1993–1994
Australia	8.8	21.6	12.8	2.5	1995–1998
Rwanda	4.3	17.1	12.8	4.0	1996–1997
Croatia	7.9	20.5	12.6	2.6	1999–2000
Belgium	23.3	35.3	12.0	1.5	2002–2003
Laos	9.4	21.2	11.8	2.3	1996–1997
Singapore	4.3	16.0	11.7	3.7	2000–2001
Tunisia	11.5	22.8	11.3	2.0	2003–2004
Namibia	6.9	18.1	11.2	2.6	1993–1994
Belgium	12.7	23.3	10.6	1.8	1998–1999
Macedonia	7.5	17.5	10.0	2.3	2001–2002
Bosnia and Herzegovina	7.1	16.7	9.6	2.4	2001–2002
United Kingdom	9.5	18.2	8.7	1.9	1996–1997

quotas in which individual parties or country constitutions mandate a certain percentage of female candidates or parliamentarians. In fact, the vast majority of countries on this list introduced gender quotas into law just before large gains were made. For example, South Africa, the country with the largest relative gain, achieved these results via a gender quota. After the major political party in South Africa, the African National Congress (ANC), adopted a 30% quota for women, women's share of parliamentary seats rose by 23.8%, increasing by more than 20 times. Similar is the Iraq case, whose 2004 interim constitution introduced a quota requiring that one quarter of parliamentary seats be filled by women. The 25% quota in Iraq led to the largest absolute increase in women's parliamentary representation ever seen until Kyrgyzstan jumped 25.6% in 2007. We explore the different types of gender quotas and their effects in Chapter 6.

Low Increasing: Women Catching Up?

The fourth pattern of women's representation over time is the Low Increasing pattern, shown in Figure 3.5. In these countries, women truly remain just a "blip on the male political landscape" (Reynolds 1999:547). Unlike the Flat category, Low Increasing countries experience change over time. But they did not experience either the steady increases or big jumps that resulted in a substantial percentage of female parliamentarians. Percentages of women remain relatively small in these countries, and women's gains came comparatively late.

Because these countries have not experienced large gains, the Low Increasing category only has two subsets: low and middle. Low countries have come close to but not yet achieved 10% women in parliament. In fact, many of these countries could be placed in the Low Flat category if not for recent evidence that women's participation in politics is on the rise. Bhutan, for example, did not elect more than 2% women to its parliament for most of the country's history, but in 2000, the country reached 9.3%. Countries in the Middle category have typically reached between 10% and 15%. Ireland and the United States fall into this category—as neither has enough women in power as of 2010 to be placed in the Increasing group.

Plateaus: Women Fall Back

Women can also lose the power they have gained over time. The countries classified as Plateau demonstrate this pattern (see Figure 3.6). Countries in

Figure 3.5   Patterns of Representation: Low Increasing

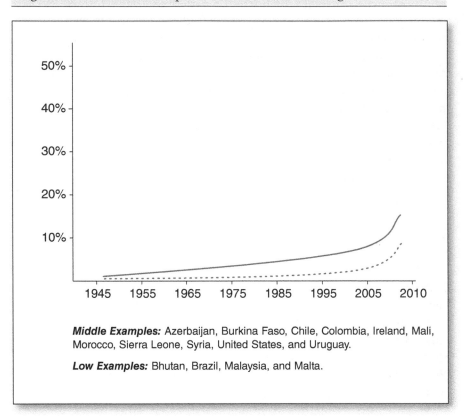

Middle Examples: Azerbaijan, Burkina Faso, Chile, Colombia, Ireland, Mali, Morocco, Sierra Leone, Syria, United States, and Uruguay.

Low Examples: Bhutan, Brazil, Malaysia, and Malta.

the Plateau category often experience an early jump in women's parliamentary representation followed by a period of general stability and then a sharp decline. Of the five general patterns, this is the only one associated with a major decline in the percentage of women in parliament.

Most of the Plateau countries are formerly Communist countries, including Albania, Cambodia, Bulgaria, Czechoslovakia, Hungary, Mongolia, Poland, Romania, and the Soviet Union. During their Communist period, these countries espoused the same ideology as the Communist countries (China, North Korea, and Vietnam) discussed earlier. But female politicians in these Plateau countries were not in truly powerful positions. When these countries transitioned to democracy around 1990, their legislatures became politically powerful for the first time, and women's participation dropped sharply. For example, Hungary had between 20% and 30% women in its legislature between 1979 and 1989. As in other Communist countries, this legislature was not the seat

Figure 3.6   Patterns of Representation: Plateau

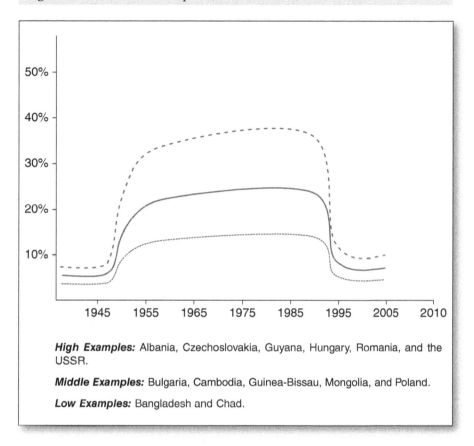

High Examples: Albania, Czechoslovakia, Guyana, Hungary, Romania, and the USSR.

Middle Examples: Bulgaria, Cambodia, Guinea-Bissau, Mongolia, and Poland.

Low Examples: Bangladesh and Chad.

of ultimate authority. When Hungary transitioned to democracy in 1990, thirteen parties fought for seats in the newly powerful legislature. After those elections, women's participation in politics dropped to 7%. The unique history of women's representation in Eastern Europe and the former Soviet Union is covered in more detail in Chapter 11.

The other Plateau countries have similar stories. Some of the Plateau countries, such as Guyana and Guinea-Bissau, were not formally communist but did have leftist authoritarian governments. Like the Communist countries, these governments kept the number of women in politics artificially high. Once free and fair democratic elections were held, the percentage of women in parliament declined sharply.

The Plateaus in Figure 3.6 vary in several important ways. First, like the other patterns, they differ by height. High Plateaus (the dashed line) peaked at around 30% to 35%, Middle Plateaus ranged at their highest point from about 20% to 25%, and Low Plateaus reached around 10% to 15%. Second, within High, Middle, and Low Plateaus, individual countries differ by the length of time spent at the peak of the plateau. Chad, for example, spent only 4 years at 16.4% women in parliament before dropping down to 2.4%. On the other end of the spectrum, Bulgaria crossed 15% women in parliament in 1949 and gradually increased for a full 40 years (to 21%) until 1990, when it dropped to 8.5%.

A final way that Plateaus vary is that some countries have rebounded in women's representation since their sharp declines (e.g., Bulgaria and Poland) whereas others have not (e.g., Hungary and Romania). Figure 3.6 deliberately does not extend the time lines past the end of the Plateau to indicate the diversity of paths these countries took in the post-Communist period.

Women in Top Leadership Positions

Women's representation in legislative bodies is only one of the many ways that women can access power. Women can also ascend to the highest levels of politics as the primary national leader of their country—such as president Corazón Aquino of the Philippines or prime minister Margaret Thatcher of Britain. But a female in the top leadership position of a country is an extremely rare creature. In 1980, Jean Blondel estimated that 5 out of the 1,000 leaders in the contemporary world were women (Blondel 1980:116). Today, a few more female leaders have appeared on the world stage, but numbers are still small. Since 1960, when Sirimavo Bandaranaike became the first female to lead a modern country, only 48 women have become the top political executive of their country.

Table 3.2 lists these 48 female political executives over the last 50 years. Although it might seem simple, it is not an easy matter to determine who is a political leader of a country and who is not. National leaders may be called a head of state, a **head of government,** or both—and a title in one country means something very different in another. For example, in some countries the head of state is a very powerful position. Barack Obama is the head of state of the United States of America. In other countries, the head of state is a purely ceremonial position—for example, Elizabeth II, the queen of Great Britain and Northern Ireland.

Looking down the list of leaders, some have held the title "prime minister," and others have held the title "president." In all cases, these women are the leaders of their respective countries; what differs is the form of government of their country. In a parliamentary system, the top political leader is often called a prime minister. In a presidential system, that person is usually known as a president. Understanding the distinction is important

Table 3.2   Female National Leaders

	Title	Country	Dates of Rule	Relationship to Previous Executive Leader?	Global North or South
Sirimavo Bandaranaike	prime minister	Sri Lanka	1960–65, 1970–77	Yes, husband	South
Indira Gandhi	prime minister	India	1966–77, 1980–84	Yes, father	South
Golda Meir	prime minister	Israel	1969–74	No	North
Isabel Peron	president	Argentina	1974–76	Yes, husband	South
Margaret Thatcher	prime minister	UK	1979–90	No	North
Lydia Gueiler Tejada	president[t]	Bolivia	1979–80	No	South
Eugenia Charles	prime minister	Dominica	1980–95	No	South
Gro Harlem Brundtland	prime minister	Norway	1981, 1986–89, 1990–96	No	North
Corazón Aquino	president[t]	Philippines	1986–92	Yes, husband	South
Milka Planinc	prime minister	Yugoslavia	1982–86	No	North
Benazir Bhutto	prime minister	Pakistan	1988–90, 1993–96	Yes, father	South
Violeta Chamorro	president	Nicaragua	1990–96	Yes, husband	South
Ertha Pascal-Trouillot	president[t]	Haiti	1990–91	No	South
Khaleda Zia	prime minister	Bangladesh	1991–96, 2001–06	Yes, husband	South
Kim Campbell	prime minister[t]	Canada	1993	No	North
Silvie Kinigi	president[t]	Burundi	1993–94	No	South
Tansu Çiller	prime minister	Turkey	1993–96	No	South
Reneta Indzhova	prime minister	Bulgaria	1994–95	No	North
Chandrika Kumaratunga	president	Sri Lanka	1994–2005	Yes, mother and father	South
Ruth Perry	president	Liberia	1996–97	No	South
Sheikh Hasina Wajed	prime minister	Bangladesh	1996–2001, 2009–present	Yes, father	South
Jenny Shipley	prime minister	New Zealand	1997–99	No	North
Janet Jagan	president	Guyana	1997–99	Yes, husband	South
Mireya Moscoso de Arias	president	Panama	1999–2004	Yes, husband	South
Helen Clark	prime minister	New Zealand	1999–2008	No	North
Megawati Sukarnoputri	president	Indonesia	2001–04	Yes, father	South
Gloria Macapagal-Arroyo	president	Philippines	2001–10	Yes, father	South

(Continued)

(Continued)

Title	Country	Dates of Rule	Relationship to Previous Executive Leader?	Global North or South
Anneli Jäätteenmäki	prime minister	Finland	2003	No	North
Nino Burdzhanadze	president[t]	Georgia	2003–04, 2007–08	No	South
Radmila Sekerinska	prime minister[t]	Macedonia	2004	No	South
Angela Merkel	chancellor	Germany	2005–present	No	North
Ellen Johnson-Sirleaf	president	Liberia	2005–present	No	South
Michelle Bachelet	president	Chile	2006–10	No	South
Portia Simpson-Miller	prime minister	Jamaica	2006–07, 2012–present	No	South
Cristina Fernández de Kirchner	president	Argentina	2007–present	Yes, husband	South
Zinaida Grecianîi	prime minister	Moldova	2008–09	No	South
Jóhanna Sigurðardóttir	prime minister	Iceland	2009–present	No	North
Jadranka Kosor	prime minister	Croatia	2009–11	No	North
Roza Otunbayeva	presidentt	Kyrgyzstan	2010–11	No	South
Laura Chinchilla	president	Costa Rica	2010–present	No	South
Mari Kiviniemi	prime minister	Finland	2010–11	No	North
Julia Gillard	prime minister	Australia	2010–present	No	North
Kamla Persad-Bissessar	prime minister	Trinidad and Tobago	2010–present	No	South
Iveta Radičová	prime minister	Slovakia	2010–12	No	North
Dilma Rousseff	president	Brazil	2011–present	No	South
Yingluck Shinawatra	prime minister	Thailand	2011–present	Yes, brother	South
Helle Thorning-Schmidt	prime minister	Denmark	2011–present	No	North
Joyce Banda	president	Malawi	2012–present	No	South

Notes
t = interim or acting
Ruth Dreifuss (1999), Micheline Calmy Rey (2007, 2011), Doris Leuthard (2010), and Eveline Widmer-Schlumpf (2012) served as president of Switzerland and as part of a seven-member chief executive with a rotating chair.
Relationship to a previous executive leader does not include leaders related to politicians who did not hold executive office. For example, Kyrgyz Interim President Rosa Otunbayeva's father served on the Supreme Court. Helle Thorning-Schmidt, Prime Minister of Denmark, is the daughter-in-law of Neil Kinnock, the former leader of the British Labour Party and candidate for British prime minister.

because it can help us to distinguish women who truly hold positions of power from those who hold largely ceremonial roles. "It is clear that one wants to define leaders by their real activities, not by a title which they possess" (Blondel 1980:11). A person holding the title of president in a parliamentary system is *not* the leader of the country but holds a position that is typically ceremonial and boasts little power. A person holding the title "prime minister" in a presidential system at best shares power with the president.

To understand the distinctions, consider three different female prime ministers:

Gro Harlem Brundtland was prime minister in a parliamentary democracy. In the Norwegian government, the prime minister acts as both the executive and legislative head of the government. He or she holds the most powerful political position in the country. While in office Brundtland pursued strong economic and foreign policy agendas and will be remembered for bringing environmental issues to the top of the nation's political agenda.

Edith Cresson was the prime minister of France from 1990 to 1992. France has a mixed political system with a strong president and a potentially powerful prime minister. The prime minister is chosen by the president from the dominant party in the parliament. If the dominant party in the parliament is different from the party of the president, then the prime minister can be a very strong political figure (this is called cohabitation). However, if the dominant party is the *same* as the president's party, then the prime minister is generally viewed as subservient to the president and holds little independent power. Edith Cresson was of the same party as Francois Mitterrand, a strong President. Indeed, as Cresson herself explains: " . . . you are not entirely free to choose [your] ministers (far from it). As far as I [was] concerned, my freedom was certainly limited" (Liswood 1995:122). In a list of leaders of France in the twentieth century, Francois Mitterrand would appear from 1990 to 1992, but not Edith Cresson.

Elisabeth Domitien held the position of prime minister of the Central African Republic from 1975 to 1976. She was appointed to the position by the dictator Jean-Bédel Bokassa when he formed a new government and decided to include a prime minister. But when Bokassa began discussing making the country a monarchy and crowning himself emperor (which he ultimately did), Domitien publicly spoke out against his plans and was promptly fired. Domitien cannot be considered to have had any substantial political power: she "was only a puppet" (Opfell 1993:65).

Changing political systems and mother–daughter succession can make titles even more interesting. In Sri Lanka, the title indicating the most powerful position in the country has changed over time. If you look at Table 3.2, you see two women from Sri Lanka on the list of powerful women—a mother, who was prime minister, and her daughter, who was president. When

Sirimavo Bandaranaike became prime minister of Sri Lanka in 1960, Sri Lanka's political system was a Westminster-style parliamentary system with a powerful prime minister. Thus, Sirimavo Bandaranaike was a powerful leader in Sri Lanka from 1960 to 1965 and again from 1970 to 1977. But in 1978, Sri Lanka's president was given much greater power. Thus, Bandaranaike's daughter, Chandrika Kumaratunga, was *also* a powerful leader because she held the title "president" from 1994 to the present. In a further twist, Chandrika Kumaratunga appointed her mother as prime minister from 1994 to 2000. But because Bandaranaike now held the position of prime minister in a presidential system, she could not be classified as the leader of the country. Her daughter held that honor. Notably, although Sri Lanka was the first country to have two women leaders at the same time, New Zealand became the first country to have women lead all of the top governing bodies of the land. Between March 2005 and August 2006, Prime Minister Helen Clark and Speaker of the House Margaret Wilson led the government, Queen Elizabeth II and Governor-General Silvia Cartwright served as heads of state, and Chief Justice Dame Sian Elias presided over the judiciary.

Another important group of female leaders are not the top executive in their country but can be viewed as holding a type of dual leadership role. As discussed in the case of Edith Cresson, in some political systems, a president holds much of the power but the prime minister is an important leader in government, especially if she is from the opposition party. Table 3.3 lists all female prime ministers who have served in such systems.

Table 3.2 contains only those women who have held truly top political positions, either as prime minister in a parliamentary system or president in a presidential system. Table 3.3 contains women who have shared power in a dual leadership system. This means that there are some famous female leaders who do not appear on either list. For example, Ireland is often highlighted as exemplary in having had two female presidents in a row. But neither Mary Robinson, president of the Ireland from 1990 to 1997, nor Mary McAleese, the president of Ireland from 1997 to 2011, were allowed to suggest legislation or even make partisan statements. Similarly, Vigdis Finnbogadottir of Iceland held a largely ceremonial position as president from 1980 to 1996. Table 3.4 contains female leaders who only held ceremonial, or symbolic, power. All of the prime ministers featured in this list hold office in dual executive structures with a dominant president (Jalalzai 2008). In these systems, the president appoints the prime minister and has the power to remove them. Élisabeth Domitién of the Central African Republic and Beatriz Merino of Peru were removed within a year of entering office.

Table 3.3   Female Prime Ministers in Presidential Systems

	Country	Dates of Rule
Maria de Lourdes Pintasilgo	Portugal	1979–80
Edith Cresson	France	1991–92
Hanna Suchocka	Poland	1992–93
Sirimavo Bandaranaike	Sri Lanka	1994–2000
Claudette Werleigh	Haiti	1995–96
Tarja Halonen[a]	Finland	2000–12
Madoir Boye	Senegal	2001–02
Maria das Neves Ceita Batista de Sousa	Sao Tome and Principe	2002–04
Luísa Días Diogo	Mozambique	2004–10
Yuliya Tymoshenko	Ukraine	2005, 2007–10
Maria do Carmo Silveira	Sao Tome and Principe	2005–06
Han Myung-Sook	South Korea	2006–07
Michèle Pierre-Louis	Haiti	2008–09
Cissé Mariam Kaïdama Sidibé	Mali	2011–12

a. Halonen is the president of Finland but shares power with the prime minister.

Symbolic power, however, does not necessarily mean that the leader is not influential in world politics. For example, Dalia Grybauskaitė of Lithuania has minimal executive powers, but she holds primary powers in handling foreign policy (Office of the President of the Republic of Lithuania 2011). Her responsibilities include signing treaties and appointing diplomats. Many of the women in Table 3.4 held prominent leadership positions on the international stage.

As noted earlier, the tables also do not include hereditary heads of state, such as Queen Elizabeth II of Great Britain and Northern Ireland or Queen Beatrix of the Netherlands. In most countries today, such positions are entirely ceremonial.

How Women Attain Top Leadership Positions

What paths to power do women take to gain top political office? Let's begin by considering the world's first female prime minister, Sirimavo

Table 3.4 Female National Leaders Holding Mainly Symbolic Power

	Title	Country	Dates of Rule
Élisabeth Domitién	prime minister	Central African Republic	1975-76
Vigdís Finnbogadóttir	president	Iceland	1980-96
Agatha Barbara	president	Malta	1982-87
Sabine Bergmann-Pohl	president	Germany (Dem Rep)	1990
Mary Robinson	president	Ireland	1990-97
Agathe Uwilingiyimana	prime minister	Rwanda	1993-94
Mary McAleese	president	Ireland	1997-2011
Vaira Vīķe-Freiberga	president	Latvia	1999-2007
Beatriz Merino	prime minister	Peru	2003
Pratibha Patil	president	India	2007-present
Dalia Grybauskaitė	president	Lithuania	2009-present
Atifete Jahjaga	president	Kosovo	2011-present
Rosario Fernández	prime minister	Peru	2011

Note: Tables 3.2–3.4 do not include female leaders of states that are not recognized as independent. For example, Pamela Gordon, premier of Bermuda (a British territory), in 1997–1998 is not included. Neither is Kazimiera Prunskiene, prime minister of Lithuania during the transition to independence.

Bandaranaike of Sri Lanka (called Ceylon at that time). Sirimavo Bandaranaike was the wife of the sitting prime minister when, in 1959, he was assassinated. She proceeded to campaign on behalf of his party and became the head of the party soon thereafter. When her party won a majority of the seats in the next election, Sirimavo Bandaranaike was appointed prime minister. She immediately began to follow through on some of her husband's policy priorities.

The story of Sirimavo Bandaranaike's rise to political prominence introduces our first important theme. As would many of the female leaders who followed her, the world's first female prime minister gained power originally as a surrogate for her husband. This was not uncommon for the earliest women who became national leaders. Forty-two percent of the women elected before 1995 in Table 3.2 had famous husbands or fathers who preceded them in political life. To name just a few, Indira Gandhi's father was

India's founding prime minister, Corazón Aquino's husband was viewed as a national martyr, and in Bangladesh, the widow of a former president replaced the daughter of a former prime minister. The phenomenon of daughters or wives standing as surrogates for their fathers or husbands was particularly apparent in regions of the world where women in leadership positions would be least expected (Jalalzai 2004). For example, before 1995, Asia had relatively low levels of female participation in other areas of politics but accounted for 32% of female national leaders. However, every woman who held high political office in Asia before 1995 was part of a political dynasty. In fact, apart from Yingluck Shinawatra (whose brother held high office before her), every woman who has ever held high political office in Asia had a husband or father who preceded her in office.

D'Amico (1995:18) labeled this the "widow's walk to power," and Burn (2005:234) explained that the surrogate route to power may have been most common where attitudes toward women are especially traditional. In places where women were seen as helpmates to their husbands, it is easy to visualize them as stand-ins for their husbands. The husband or father may have been assassinated, hanged, or have spent a great deal of time in prison, thereby making him a martyr in the eyes of the public and the surrogate wife or daughter a symbol of the continuing struggle.

There is nothing subtle about women's surrogacy. During campaigns, references to the husband or father are repeated time and again with the spoken or unspoken implication that the female candidate would simply continue his legacy. Benazir Bhutto referred often to her father in speeches and made sure his picture was in the background of her official portraits (Anderson 1993:52). During her campaign, Violeta Chamorro repeatedly invoked her assassinated husband, who was viewed as a national martyr: "I am not a politician, but I believe this is my destiny. I am doing this for Pedro and for my country" (Boudreaux 1991, quoted in Saint-Germain 1993). On hearing of Indira Gandhi's election in 1966, the crowds cried out not only "long live Indira" but also "long live Jawaharalal" [her father] (Moraes 1980:127, quoted in Everett 1993).

But family dynasties in politics are hardly restricted to women who achieve high office. Men also often follow their famous fathers into politics. Asia, in particular, has a strong legacy of family politics, so women's use of familial ties to achieve power is not unusual in the region. In Asia, we now see some men who have followed their famous mothers or wives into politics. For example, in India, Indira Gandhi's son followed her into politics, cementing a Gandhi–Nehru dynasty lasting for most of the last half of the 20th century. And Asif Ali Zardari, the current president of Pakistan, is the widower of Benazir Bhutto and used his connection to her in achieving political office. Men from political families have also come to power in Nicaragua and Sri Lanka.

Turning to the second female leader, Indira Gandhi, introduces another theme in women's path to power—that women have done better gaining high-level positions of power in nations of the global south than in the global north. Until 1979, when Margaret Thatcher ascended to the top political position in Britain as prime minister of the House of Commons, the only women to have achieved leadership positions were in the global south. Looking at all of the women who have ever held the highest political positions of a country, 67% of them are from the developing world. The global north does not lead the world in elevating women to highest political office (see Bauer and Tremblay 2011).

The third woman to ever hold the highest political office, Golda Meir of Israel, exemplifies how women can climb through the ranks of political systems to achieve high office (D'Amico 1995). From 1928 to 1968, Golda moved up the ranks into the political elite of Israel, acting as fund-raiser, signer of the proclamation of the State of Israel in 1948, ambassador, and ultimately both minister of labor and foreign minister. In 1968, at age 70, she officially retired from politics—a retirement that was to last only a little over a year. In 1970, Israel's prime minister suffered a fatal heart attack, and Golda was asked to return to politics, first as interim prime minister and then as the nationally elected prime minister. She served until 1975 and during her term contended with economic problems, terrorism, and the Yom Kippur war with Egypt and Syria.

Other women have followed a similar path. Margaret Thatcher, the fifth woman to hold office, worked her way through Britain's Conservative Party ranks, was elected to the House of Commons in 1959, was elected leader of the Conservative Party in 1975, and finally became prime minister in 1979. Kim Campbell of Canada also took this route, as did Eugenia Charles of Dominica, Portia Simpson-Miller of Jamaica, Julia Gillard of Australia, and Helle Thorning-Schmidt of Denmark.

The last female to lead a country before 1980 illustrates how women have risen to positions of prominence in situations of social or political instability (Genovese 1993). Often, in this case, their time in office is very short. Lidia Gueiler Tejada of Bolivia exemplifies this path to power. The years between 1978 and 1980 were very unstable in Bolivia, with multiple elections, coups, counter-coups, and caretaker governments. In 1979, Wálter Guevara Arze was elected president but was almost immediately overthrown in a military coup. However, the leader of the coup also stepped down because he was not accepted by the military, civilians, or the United States. Thus, Lidia Gueiler was appointed interim president to arrange fresh elections. Before these elections were finalized, however, Bolivia's first female president was overthrown by General Luis García Meza. She had not been president for even a year. Looking at all the female national leaders from 1960 to 2007, Farida Jalalzai (2008) showed that 10 women entered during periods of transition, 23 came to power in countries with a recent history of instability, and 21 after a military takeover.

As suggested by reviewing the biographies of the first female leaders, there are many similarities among the women in Table 3.2. But there is great diversity among them as well. Sirimavo Bandaranaike and Indira Gandhi were from wealthy and privileged backgrounds, whereas Golda Meir and Margaret Thatcher were not. Benazir Bhutto entered office at 35 years old, whereas Janet Jagen of Guyana first entered office at 77 (Jalalzai 2004). Some of the women who have held the highest political office of a country had less than a high school education, whereas others held PhDs. Some were in office less than a year, whereas Margaret Thatcher was Britain's longest serving prime minister of the 20th century. Some are married, others divorced, and Jóhanna Sigurðardóttir of Iceland is the world's first openly lesbian head of government.

Of the women who have served in the most powerful political positions in their country, none fit the most stringent definition of a racial, ethnic, or religious minority: a person whose parents are both members of a historically subordinate group. However, roughly a third of these women could be classified as minorities on some grounds. Perhaps the most straightforward case of electing a woman from a marginalized group is recent elect Jadranka Kosor, prime minister of Croatia, who is half-Serbian.

Many female heads of state have immigrant ancestors. President Dilma Rousseff of Brazil was born to a Bulgarian immigrant father. Former Filipino president Corazón Aquino, the first female president in Asia, has ancestral roots in China. And, President Christian Kirchner of Argentina has a mother with German heritage. Janet Jagan, president of Guyana from 1997 to 1999, is herself an immigrant, born to Jewish-American parents.

Difficulties Faced by Female Leaders

Regardless of gender, leaders are expected to behave in certain ways. Traditionally, effective leadership is associated with aggression, competitiveness, dominance, and decisiveness. As discussed in Chapter 1, people also have expectations of women and men. Male stereotypes suggest that men are assertive, aggressive, dominant, independent, and competitive. Women, on the other hand, are stereotyped as nurturing, helpful, likeable, gentle, and polite.

The match between stereotypes of men and leaders is much better than the match between women and leaders. For this reason, women face prejudice as leaders because people tend to assume that leadership is a masculine trait (Eagly and Karau 2002). Further, because women have traditionally been in a subordinate position to men, cultural beliefs lead people to assume that men are more competent and legitimate as leaders than are women (Ridgeway 2001). This prejudice is even more likely to emerge when the leadership position in question is typically male, as in the case of military leaders or political leaders.

Female leaders in highly visible leadership positions therefore must live with assumptions that they are less competent than their male counterparts. They may be held to higher standards than men to obtain and retain their leadership position. Maria Liberia-Peters, prime minister of the Netherlands Antilles (a British protectorate), explained the following:

> . . . and you had to put all into it, and everybody expected you to put everything into it, because nobody questions the [preparedness] of a man over [a] female . . . when you're a woman, you hear, oh, she's a kindergarten teacher, she's this, she's that and she's the other, and suddenly you are being questioned, so you have to put 100 percent, 200 percent in your work. (quoted in Liswood 1995:68)

But female national leaders are not less competent then men. Considering the educational backgrounds and political experience of female national leaders compared to their male predecessors, Jalalzai (2009) showed that the women are very comparable to the men. In fact, women attain higher levels of education than their male predecessors.

One indication of the public's comfort with female national leaders is to compare the number of women who have served as prime ministers and as presidents (Jalalzai 2008). A woman prime minister must share power with her party and can be removed from office, whereas woman presidents exercise independent power without the possibility of removal until the next election. Female prime ministers are also likely to have been appointed by their party, rather than independently elected by a public.

Ellen Johnson Sirleaf of Liberia and Michelle Bachelet of Chile became presidents through popular elections, which makes them different from other women leaders. Only nine women have been elected to the presidency through popular votes. Johnson Sirleaf and Bachelet entered office after unpopular regimes. In their campaigns, both women used gender to differentiate themselves from previous leaders, while also demonstrating their experience in fields dominated by men (Thomas and Adams 2010). For example, campaign slogans for Johnson Sirleaf read as follows: "Ellen, she's our man" and "All the men have failed Liberia—Let's try a woman" (Thomas and Adams 2010).

In addition to being popularly elected less often, if women are viewed as less competent as leaders then they may also appear more often in leadership positions that are shared or otherwise constrained. Jalalzai (2008) showed that 63% of the female national leaders in power from 1960 to 2007 shared power with other executives rather than exercising independent power.

Female leaders face an additional problem because they must serve two roles: their role as a leader and their role as a woman. The two sets of expectations can be very different and, in fact, conflict with each other. This puts a female leader in a difficult position. Should she act the way people expect her to act as a woman? Should she be nurturing, supportive, and gentle? Or should she act the way people expect a leader to act? This may require exhibiting "masculine" behavior, such as aggressiveness and dominance. If female leaders choose the second path, research demonstrates that they will be negatively evaluated. In a review of research, Eagly, Makhijani, and Klonsky (1992) found that people evaluate autocratic behavior by women more negatively than the same behavior by men. Women who act assertively violate the expectations of those around them and subsequently get penalized for this behavior (Ridgeway 2001). For example, Margaret Thatcher, a very assertive and aggressive politician, was called Attila the Hen. This puts female leaders in a real catch-22: "Conforming to their gender role can produce a failure to meet the requirements of their leader role, and conforming to the leader role can produce a failure to meet the requirements of their gender role" (Eagly and Johannesen-Schmidt 2001:786).

Consider how Corazón Aquino's early socialization led her into a conflict between her role as a woman in Philippine society and her role as president:

Aquino: In school you're always taught to be polite, and you always ask—you don't command or you don't order. So, I remember, I guess in the first few months of my presidency, I would call in a cabinet member, or maybe a general or somebody working under me, and I would say, well, I would like to ask you to do this. And then, of course, I'm sure they were very shocked. And then, later on, one of my advisers pointed out to me, he said, "Look, perhaps that was all right when you were not president, you know, to be polite and to ask instead of ordering." . . . I guess, as president, you're not expected to be polite, or you're not expected to be too concerned about good manners, etc. . . . You don't ask, you order. And so, well, I certainly learned that fast enough. But in the beginning . . . I guess from the time I went to school, and during my time, there was always what I would refer to as an etiquette class. . . . There was this lady would come to us, and the class was called Lessons in Charm and Good Manners, or something like that. We were taught how to sit and what to do in social engagements, which is, of course, so very different from what it is when you are president.

Interviewer: They didn't teach you how to order generals?

Aquino: No, they did not. (from Liswood 1995:91–92)

Women may also have to overcome social expectations about a women's proper place. Golda Meir ultimately separated from her husband, at least partly due to her choice of career. She also struggled with her role as mother: "At work, you think of the children you've left at home. At home, you think of the work you've left unfinished. Such a struggle is unleashed within yourself, your heart is rent."

Benazir Bhutto, a female politician in a conservative Muslim country, had to marry to pursue her political career:

I was under so much scrutiny. If my name had been linked with a man, it would have destroyed my political career. Actually, I had reconciled myself to a life without marriage or children for the sake of my career. And then my brothers got married. I realized I didn't even have a home, but in the future I couldn't do politics when I had to ask for permission from their wives as to whether I could use the dining room or the telephone. I couldn't rent a home because a woman living on her own can be suspected of all kinds of scandalous associations. So keeping in mind that many people in Pakistan looked to me, I decided to make a personal sacrifice in what I thought would be, more or less, a loveless marriage, a marriage of convenience. (quoted in Liswood 1995:70)

Bhutto was able to turn her need to marry into political advantage. Her opponents claimed that she was too Western. So she agreed to an arranged marriage, the accepted norm her society, to emphasize her identity as an Asian woman (Anderson 1993:58). Her opponent countered by timing elections to coincide with the birth of her first child. It was "the first election to be timed for gynaecological considerations" (Singh 1988, quoted in Anderson 1993:59).

Bhutto's use of her need to marry for political advantage suggests that women can use cultural expectations about masculinity and femininity to their advantage. Margaret Thatcher is an example of a female leader who was very aware of the impact of her femininity on the men around her. She dressed attractively and would coax, cajole, and flatter to get her way (Genovese 1993:207). But she also adopted traditionally masculine behavior in a way that men found difficult to counter. Thatcher was aggressive, tough, ruthless, and rude—behavior that men did not expect from a woman. Harris (1995:62) related an interview with a member of Thatcher's first cabinet:

> If any male Prime Minister had said things to me in cabinet in the terms and tone that she often adopted, I would have gone to him privately afterwards, given him a blasting, and told him that if he did that again I'd resign. But you can't treat a woman like that.

Similarly, because of unwritten but rigorous codes of chivalry, Poland's male-led parties were hesitant to intrigue against Hanna Suchocka, their female prime minister (Liswood 1995). And Ellen Johnson Sirleaf of Liberia, ran on a gendered platform, claiming that she was free of corruption and would "'bring a motherly sensitivity and emotion to the presidency' as a way of healing the wounds of war" (BBC News 2005a).

Whether or not they can use gender to their advantage, the fact remains that there have been very few female leaders in history. Simone de Beauvoir put it well: "Perseus, Hercules, David, Achilles, Lancelot, the French warriors Du Geslin and Bayard, Napoleon—so many men for one Joan of Arc." Young men growing up today have plenty of heroes to emulate. But who can women look up to? Luckily for today's young woman, there are more examples of powerful female leaders for them to follow. Female national leaders act as prominent exceptions to the rule that "men govern." Today's young women can look to today's leaders as examples, just as Gro Harlem Bruntland looked to Golda Meir (Liswood 1995:99) and Margaret Thatcher looked to Indira Gandhi.

Women in Cabinet Positions

Women can also fill the appointed positions that advise government leaders. Typically called the cabinet, members of these executive positions are responsible for generally running a country. Examples of cabinet officials include John Kerry, the U.S. secretary of state; Chuck Hagel, the U.S. secretary of defense; and Theresa May, the UK secretary of state for home affairs. Descended from the groups of advisors surrounding kings and emperors, "cabinet positions are some of the most powerful political positions in the world" (Davis 1997:12).

As in other areas of politics, women hold only a low percentage of cabinet positions. In 2010, women's share of ministerial positions was only 15.7% (Adams and Scherpereel 2010). But their numbers are increasing over time. Women's share of ministerial positions grew from 11.4% in 2003 to 15.7% in 2010, and the number of countries without any female ministers simultaneously declined from 48 to 18—a 62.5% drop over the same time period (Adams and Scherpereel 2010). In fact, a few recent cabinets have achieved parity—50% women—including Michelle Bachelet's 2006 cabinet and the cabinet of Spanish prime minister José Luis Rodríguez Zapatero in 2008. Further, it is now understood internationally that cabinets *should* contain women and presidents have been criticized when they neglect to appoint women to their cabinets (Escobar-Lemmon and Taylor-Robinson 2009; Htun and Jones 2002).

There is substantial regional variation in women's representation as cabinet officials. In Western Europe, almost 30% of cabinet officials are women, compared with only 4% in the Middle East and North Africa. Table 3.5 compares the percentage of cabinet officials who are women across the major regions of the world. Women are also better represented as cabinet officials in countries that are predominantly Christian (Catholic, Protestant, or Orthodox) compared with countries with other religions, such as Buddhism or Hinduism (Reynolds 1999).

Even within regions, there are significant differences across countries in women's representation in these important committees. It was explained by Adams and Scherpereel, in 2010:

[Sixty percent] of Finland's ministers were women. This contrasts with Burma and Saudi Arabia (0%), but it also contrasts with neighboring Estonia (7.7%). Poland and Hungary, despite their similarities, also found themselves in much different positions (29.4% and 0%, respectively), and there are interesting contrasts between Argentina (23.1%), Uruguay (16.7%), and Brazil (0%). (p. 2)

Table 3.5 Percentage of Women in Cabinets by Region, 2007

Western Europe	27.8
Sub-Saharan Africa	23.9
North America	22
Latin America and the Caribbean	20.5
Eastern Europe	10.5
Asia and the Pacific	6.9
North Africa	4
Total	16.5

Source: Women's Environment and Development Organization (WEDO) (2007).

In most countries, each cabinet official is given responsibility for a specific government department, such as labor or foreign policy. These departments, and the officials that lead them, are not necessarily equal. The prime minister or the president, at the center of the circle of advisors, may have a core group of trusted advisors around him or her. This core usually includes cabinet officials covering finance and foreign affairs (Davis 1997:12–13). Other cabinet officials, farther out in the circle of advisors, may play less of a role in creating and implementing policy.

Women are highly overrepresented in some cabinet positions and underrepresented in others. Female cabinet ministers tend to be given positions in softer areas—health, family, education—that are less prestigious and less likely to be in the core of advisors (Blondel 1988). Table 3.6 lists the percentage of female cabinet officials holding different types of cabinet positions in 2012. Of the varied types of departments women could tackle, they are most often in social affairs (9% of the time). Family/children/youth/etc. and women's affairs are the next two most common. In contrast, women are less likely to appear in cabinet positions such as finance, defense, or as a minister of state. In the last two cases, less than 1% of female cabinet officials hold these positions. Unfortunately, it is these more prestigious cabinet positions that can be viewed as stepping-stones to greater power.

Overall, women tend to be overrepresented in "feminine policy domain" cabinet positions such as children and family and underrepresented in

Table 3.6 Percentage of Female Cabinet Ministers
           Holding Types of Cabinet Positions

Type of Cabinet Position	Percentage
Social Affairs	9
Family/Children/Youth/Elderly/Disabled	7
Women's Affairs	7
Education	6
Environment	6
Health	5
Foreign Affairs	4
Justice	4
Finance/Budget	2
Economy/Development	2
Defense and Veteran Affairs	<1
Ministers of State	<1

Source: United Nations Women (2012).

"masculine policy domain" positions like finance or defense (Escobar-Lemmon and Taylor-Robinson 2009).

But things are changing here too. For example, three of the last five secretaries of state in the United States, a very powerful and visible cabinet position, have been women: Madeleine Albright, Condoleezza Rice, and Hillary Clinton. Although women may traditionally be underrepresented as defense ministers, more women are appearing in that position. In fact, Carmen Chacón, the first female defense minister of Spain, drew international attention for pictures of her reviewing troops while in the last term of her pregnancy (see Figure 3.7).

There are also regional differences in the types of cabinet positions women achieve. If we consider cabinet positions by women's numbers as well as the power of the position, Western Europe appears to do better than other regions. Mona Krook and Diana O'Brien (2011) developed a "cabinet gender power score" that differentially weights cabinet positions based on both women's numbers and the prestige of their ministries for 117 countries. The top 10 cabinet gender power scoring countries are Finland, Norway, Spain, Switzerland, Sweden, Denmark, South Africa, Chile, Argentina, and Rwanda.

Figure 3.7   Spain's Pregnant Defense Minister
Carmen Chacón Reviews an Honor Guard

Source: Mohammed Zaatari, AP Images.

Why do we see low numbers of women in cabinet positions? One important explanation is the lack of women in legislative positions. In parliamentary systems, cabinet ministers are almost always drawn from among parliamentarians (Blondel 1991). Loyal party members come to the attention of prime ministers and get choice cabinet appointments as a reward. This means that when there are few women in a country's parliament, there are few women available for potential appointment to the cabinet. Around the world, higher percentages of females in parliament are related to higher percentages of females in cabinet positions (Davis 1997; Krook and O'Brien 2011; Reynolds 1999; Whitford, Wilkins, and Ball 2007). Also, governments controlled by leftist parties are more likely to appoint women (Davis 1997; Escobar-Lemmon and Taylor-Robinson 2005; Reynolds 1999).

Finally, women are better represented in ministerial positions in presidential systems than in parliamentary systems (Krook and O'Brien 2011; Whitford et al. 2007). Presidents have a greater ability to choose their own ministerial appointees. For example, after calling for increasing women's political involvement in their campaigns, Ellen Johnson Sirleaf of Liberia and Michele Bachelet of Chile followed through on this commitment while holding office. Johnson Sirleaf appointed women to leadership positions, which included justice minister, commerce minister, finance minister, and chief of police (Hunt 2007). Bachelet instituted gender parity in her cabinet by appointing 10 women and 10 men to cabinet positions (Hunt 2007). Johnson Sirleaf and Bachelet demonstrated how women leaders can improve descriptive representative for women by promoting other women to executive positions. Alternatively, Margaret Thatcher, who famously appointed cabinets that were almost exclusively male, shows the constraints placed on prime ministers when choosing cabinets (ministers in the United Kingdom are customarily parliamentarians); she also shows that the promotion of women by women is far from a political certainty.

Why are women overrepresented in the softer cabinet positions? The explanation may again start with their experience as legislators. National legislatures often divide their work into **legislative committees** to prepare or review legislation in a particular area. There are also committees that serve very specific functions, such as the rules committee, which does not focus on a particular policy arena but instead makes decisions about how the legislation submitted by other committees will be debated on the house floor. Subsets of legislators belong to legislative committees of different types—defense, finance, and so on. And committee members often have significant influence over the legislation proposed in their committee's area.

As previously noted, female legislators are more likely to be assigned to "women's issues" committees and social issues committees. Women are less often assigned to the so-called power committees like treasury, budget, or foreign relations (Heath, Schwindt-Bayer, and Taylor-Robinson 2005). It is by serving on these power committees that legislators get the important experience that helps channel them to top cabinet posts. Because women serve on power committees at lower rates than men do, women get channeled to power cabinet posts at lower rates (Krook and O'Brien 2011).

And why are women getting assigned to social issues committees instead of power committees? As relative newcomers to politics, these women pose a serious threat to traditional male power on these committees (Duverger

1955). In most legislative bodies, it is a small number of people who make committee assignments (e.g., the party leaders). If male party leaders can, therefore, they will sideline women into unimportant committees to preserve their own power (Heath et al. 2005). Other explanations for low numbers of women in cabinet positions include the supply of qualified candidates and the different demand for women across political parties. These explanations are discussed in Chapters 4 and 5.

4

Explaining the Political Representation of Women— Culture

T he previous two chapters outlined women's struggle to participate as equals in political decision making. Why has it been such a struggle? And why have women succeeded in gaining political power in some places and not in others? In the next four chapters of the book, we address four broad explanations for differences in women's participation—(1) culture, (2) social structure, (3) politics, and (4) international influences—and consider how they interact to impact women's chances.

Gender and politics researchers often distinguish between two sets of factors that produce different levels of political representation for women across the world: supply-side factors and demand-side factors (Norris 1993; Paxton 1997; Randall 1987). **Supply factors** are those that increase the pool of women with the will and experience to compete against men for political office. **Demand factors,** on the other hand, are characteristics of countries, electoral systems, or political parties that make it more likely that women will be pulled into office from the supply of willing candidates. Although it is not cut-and-dried, you can begin by thinking of **culture** and the social structure as creating a supply of women and political systems as creating a demand. Of course, in reality this distinction is not so simple and these factors combine and interact to influence women's chances.

To understand the overall picture of women's political representation, it is useful to begin with the **political recruitment model**—a model of how individual citizens become politicians. Figure 4.1 presents the political recruitment model developed by Pippa Norris and refined by Richard Matland (Matland 2002; Norris 1993, 1997). As Richard Matland explained, women need to pass three critical barriers to attain elected office. First, they need to decide to run for elected office. Second, they have to get selected as a candidate by a party. Finally, they need to be chosen by the voters. As women pass through those barriers, they move from simply being eligible to run for office (eligibles), to aspiring to hold political office (aspirants), to being selected by a party to run for office (candidates), and then to finally being elected by voters (legislators).

Figure 4.1   The Political Recruitment Model

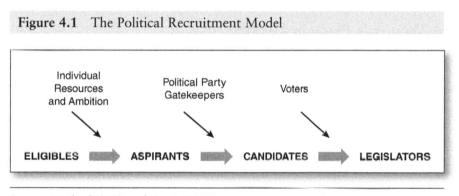

Sources: Matland (2002) and Norris (1993).

In this chapter, we begin by thinking of one important supply-side factor that influences the pool of both eligible women and political aspirants. Cultural traditions influence women's decisions to run for political office. If cultural traditions suggest that women are not mentally or emotionally capable of handling politics, or that a woman's place is at home, then women are unlikely to have the personal ambition to run for political office. Similarly, if a society's social structure limits women's attainment of personal financial and educational resources, there will not be many women who can run for office.

But once women do decide that they would like to run for office, they must also pass the other two barriers. Political parties may work to recruit or nominate different levels of female candidates, and voters may or may not support those female candidates. In Chapter 6, we discuss the political demand for female aspirants, candidates, and legislators.

What people think about women and a woman's place matters for women's ability to attain political power. If women are considered irrational, apolitical, or incapable of acting apart from a male, they will not be taken seriously as contenders for power. If societal norms suggest that women should stay at home, then women acting in the public sphere may be perceived as rebels harming their families and perhaps even the very fabric of society. If women are told they are incompetent, then they may choose to avoid public life and defer to their fathers and husbands for guidance. Overall, culture can help explain women's complete exclusion from politics in the past and their difficulty in attaining power in the present. We begin by examining the arguments that have been used to justify women's exclusion from politics for centuries. These arguments continue to resonate through the present and affect women as they attempt to gain power.

A Women's Place in History: Women in Political Philosophy

Women have been barred from the political process throughout much of human history, and arguments against women's political participation have been remarkably similar across both time and place. Generally, there are two sets of reasons offered for women's political exclusion: assumptions about women's inherent nature or capabilities and beliefs regarding women's proper place in society. Each of these reasons was deeply embedded in the cultures of past societies and was likely used by ordinary people to justify women's lack of power. But each set of reasons was also codified in the political philosophy written by men throughout the ages, helping to legitimize women's exclusion from political power.

The first set of arguments against women in politics asserts that women naturally do not have the temperament or capabilities necessary for political participation. According to this perspective, women's biological difference is thought to extend to differences across moral, intellectual, and emotional dimensions. Aristotle is credited with offering the first comprehensive theoretical account of the superiority of men's virtues, reason, and status (Gardner 2006). Aristotle's theory that women were deformed or inferior versions of men influenced thinkers around the world (Ahmed 1992:29; Okin 1979). Ideas about women's inferiority carried through the Middle Ages, a period that transmitted an image of woman as "lacking judgment and reason; as vain, duplicitous, capricious, seductive, weak-minded, generally inferior and, often, as downright evil" (Coole 1988:70).

In the 18th and 19th centuries, as philosophy began again to tackle questions of man's natural rights, women were still perceived to lack man's rationality.

In 18th-century England, for example, Sir William Blackstone grouped women with lunatics, idiots, minors, aliens, perjurers, and criminals as people that should not be allowed to vote (Kelber 1994). Political philosophers of the Enlightenment, such as Hegel, Rousseau, and Schopenhauer, viewed women as lacking the reason and judgment necessary to participate as citizens. For example, in 1762, Jean-Jacques Rousseau argued, "By the law of nature herself, women, as much for themselves as for their children, are at the mercy of men's judgment" and "opinion is the tomb of man's virtue and the throne of woman's." Similarly, in 1821, German philosopher Georg Hegel ([1821] 1977) wrote, "If women were to control the government, the state would be in danger, for they do not act according to the dictates of universality, but are influenced by accidental inclinations and opinions" (p. 167). Thus, even as ideas about politics, ethics, and natural rights were advanced and debated during the Enlightenment, women remained conceptualized as inferior.

Philosophical arguments about women's inferior nature were not restricted to Western philosophy (Giele and Smock 1977: chap. 2, 3). In non-Western philosophy too, women were portrayed as inferior in reasoning and intellect. For example, Walda Heywat, an Ethiopian teacher writing in the 17th century, cautioned, "O man, remember that a woman is weak by nature and less intelligent than man" (Bonevac, Boon, and Phillips 1992). On another continent and in a different century, Avicenna, an Islamic metaphysician, stated, "For in reality [woman] is not very rational and is quick to follow passion and anger' (Avicenna [~1000] 1963). Nizamu'l-Mulk Tusi (1977), writing around the same time, warned his king not to allow women influence because women are by nature inferior to men in the field of politics and administration.

A second set of arguments against female political power stress that politics is simply out of women's proper sphere or domain. Women's concerns are properly in the home, and women should be focused on the family—caring for their children, and making their husbands happy. Thus, even if women could be accorded equality in intellect or reason, they must remain narrowly relegated to the private sphere, their wishes and desires supposedly known and acted on by the male head of the family.

As discussed in Chapter 1, the distinction between the public and private sphere is a crucial one for women's power (Pateman 1989). In Western philosophical and political thought, the public sphere is the place where laws are contested, contracts honored, and political principles debated. The private sphere, in contrast, is the family, the home, and the site where the daily needs of life are met. The male, the head of the family, is the traditional public political subject, and his wife, daughter, mother, and sister are responsible for providing comfort, support, and training for the next generation.

For Aristotle and the philosophers who followed him, man belonged to the *polis,* the public sphere, whereas woman belonged to the private (Coole 1988; Okin 1979).

Although the vast majority of early political philosophy asserted that women lacked the qualities necessary for political participation, there have of course been exceptions, often voiced by women. In 1792, Mary Wollstonecraft (1999) published *A Vindication of the Rights of Woman,* the first systematic treatise on the rights of women. She argued the following:

> Let an enlightened nation then try allowing them [women] to share the advantages of education and government with man, see whether they will become better, as they grow wiser and become free. They cannot be injured by the experiment; for it is not in the power of man to render them more insignificant than they are at present. (p. 42)

There have also been men that stood for women. In 1792, the same year that Mary Wollstonecraft (1999) published her treatise, Theodor Gottlieb von Hippel published *On Improving the Status of Women.* Speaking to men, von Hippel argued the following:

> Even less should women be forbidden to take part in the inner workings of the state, since at present they are entrusted with the management of their entire household, and their performance at these duties, even in the judgment of us men, is commendable. (p. 156)

John Stuart Mill and Frederick Douglass also famously supported women's political rights. The views of John Stuart Mill were influenced by his wife, Harriet Taylor. In 1869, he published *The Subjection of Women,* which attacked the legal and social position of women and argued there was no reason that women should not have equal suffrage. Outside of the Western world, Vladimir Lenin, one of the founding fathers of Communism, often wrote and spoke about the women's emancipation (Krupskaya 1938) and encouraged men to support women's participation in politics.

But overall, most political philosophy, from the beginning of written records through the early 20th century, articulated serious obstacles to the political participation of women. These obstacles stemmed from problems within women—their inferior intellect, rationality, and so on. And women's "natural" unfitness for public life helped justify their relegation to the private sphere. Worse yet, most of this was not explicit. Historically, political actors were assumed to be men, and women were simply ignored (Coole 1988; Okin 1979). When political philosophers spoke of the principles of equality in nature, they were speaking of equality among men. Recently, however, feminist political theorists have demonstrated that although the language of political philosophy was technically gender neutral, women's absence was critical (MacKinnon 1989; Phillips 1995). One reason is because the family was considered the basic political unit in that men's participation in the public was predicated on women's labor in the private sphere (Coole 1988; Okin 1979). If women manage the family and home, men are freed to come together to decide the workings of the community.

A Woman's Place Today: The Continuing Power of Culture

Political philosophy reflected and shaped prevailing ideas about women's nature and place throughout history. But cultural arguments against women's participation in politics continue to powerfully affect women's chances of attaining political power through the present. In a recent worldwide survey of female politicians, 76% of those interviewed claimed that prevailing values about gender roles limit the participation of women in politics (Inter-Parliamentary Union [IPU] 2000). And even after women have gained office, cultural norms can limit their effectiveness when dealing with their male counterparts. For example, harassment of women was commonplace in Uganda's Parliament (Tamale 1999), and in Bangladesh Islamic fundamentalists turn their backs during speeches by female political leaders (Commonwealth Secretariat 1999:35).

Regional Differences

What cultural features of a society matter for women in politics? Research has attempted to measure culture in a number of ways. First, studies that break countries into regions find more women in power in some regions, and these regional differences are at least partially attributed to ideological differences (Kenworthy and Malami 1999; Paxton 1997). For example, Scandinavian countries, which are considered to have a pervasive ethic of equality, were among the first countries to grant women the right to vote and experienced higher numbers of women in parliament at earlier times than most other countries of the world (Bystydzienski 1995; Rule 1987). But regional differences are broad and signify much more than ideology. So researchers also consider more specific cultural differences across countries.

Religion

Religion is an important source of cultural messages in most countries. The ideological influence of religion on women in politics can range from subtle suggestions that women should stay at home to overt use of particular interpretations of religious texts to maintain male domination of politics. Arguments about women's inferiority to men are present across all dominant religions, and religion has long been used to exclude women from aspects of social, political, or religious life across the world. Susan Moller Okin (1999) described how across myths and religious stories, women's importance is undermined or denied:

> The founding myths of Greek and Roman antiquity, and of Judaism, Christianity, and Islam . . . consist of a combination of denials of women's role in reproduction, appropriations by men of the power to reproduce themselves, characterizations of women as overly emotional, untrustworthy, evil, or sexually dangerous, and refusals to acknowledge mothers' rights over the disposition of their children. (p. 11)

Examples of religious teachings that contradict women's political participation can be found in Christianity, Judaism, Islam, Hinduism, and Buddhism. Among the most recent examples of the direct use of religious doctrine to oppose women's political power took place in both Kuwait and Saudi Arabia, where anti-suffragists used the *shari'a*, the Islamic law or code of conduct, to combat women's agitation for political rights. When religion is used to justify male power, the ideological message is particularly powerful as it makes women's subordination appear divinely approved.

Of course, it is important to recognize that dominant religions have many branches or sects that disagree over women's status under God. The same passage can be interpreted quite differently by proponents and opponents of women's rights. For example, in Islam, Qur'an (also spelled Koran) 2:228 states, "And women shall have rights similar to the rights against them, according to what is equitable; but men have a degree (of advantage) over them." While the first part of the passage ascribes rights to women, the second asserts women's lower status compared to men. Many Muslim women hear and read sacred texts as egalitarian (Ahmed 1992:66). And many modern Islamic scholars view the Qur'an as extending political equality to women. In fact, during the time of Prophet Muhammad, women actively participated in the equivalent of voting, known as *baya*, a way of endorsing political leadership. More recently, some countries have taken strides to advance Muslim women as leaders. For example, in 2006, Morocco broke with tradition by educating women for the first time to be religious guides, or *murchidate*s. One of the roles of the murchidates is to help women understand their rights and protections under Islam.

Unfortunately, despite the possibility of alternative interpretations, religion is often used as a tool of those in power to justify or maintain the status quo. The Qur'an and Hadith, the main sources of Islam, have mainly been interpreted by men. Indeed, although women were important contributors to the early (verbal) texts of Islam, male censoring of the Hadith appears to have begun even as men wrote down the sayings and philosophy of Muhammad as articulated by his wives and daughter (Ahmed 1992:47–57). When women are prevented from learning to read or write, as was the case in Afghanistan under the Taliban, they are unable to challenge patriarchal interpretations of religious texts (Afghani 2005; Sorush 2005).

Similarly, the exclusion of women from most positions of power and authority in the Catholic Church meant that the major interpretations of the Bible were from a male perspective. In recent years, feminist scholars have also criticized the Apostle Paul's passages in the New Testament, arguing that Jesus originally taught an egalitarian view of gender relations. They argue that it was Paul who imposed a patriarchal interpretation of Christianity that taught that women are inferior, primarily culpable for sin and the fall of humanity and excluded from the ordained ministry. Across most religions, however, passages that promote women's equality have not received as much attention as passages that can be interpreted as justifying men's superiority (Burn 2005:205–207).

An important additional trend in religion is the rise of fundamentalist movements in many of the world's major religions (Almond, Appleby, and Sivan 2003). Fundamentalist movements are typically exemplified by a rigid adherence to religious tradition and the literal interpretation of sacred texts and have important consequences for women. Fundamentalists see an assault on the religious foundation of the social order from a secular modern world (Gerami and Lehnerer 2001; Zubaida 1987). The increasingly secular world is seen as responsible for society's moral degradation. Thus, an affirmation of religious authority and tradition is the appropriate, indeed essential, response. In America, Protestant fundamentalists want to correct modern deviations from a stronger Christian past (Coalition on Revival 1999). In non-Western countries and among Islamic fundamentalists, this rejection of the modern world is often linked to an explicit rejection of the West.

Recent fundamentalist movements have worked to reiterate women's subordinate place (French 1992). Part of the modern world rejected by fundamentalists is the gains made by women in the public sphere. Fundamentalist movements have opposed women in positions of power in church—as ordained ministers, for example—because they fear that the natural order would be upset if women were given authority over men. Similarly, fundamentalist movements typically reaffirm a family power structure where women are subordinate. Fundamentalist movements see the family as a critical locale where morality is sheltered and safeguarded for the next generation. Moral decay in the family can quickly spread to other social institutions and result in universal moral ruin (Gerami 1996:31). Thus, keeping women private and protected in the family, with males as gatekeepers to the rest of the world, is essential to the protection of religious and moral values, not only for one's own family but for the entire society (Coalition on Revival 1999). For example, fundamentalist Islamic scholars in Saudi Arabia have issued religious edicts that women driving cars is sinful. This was explained by Sheikh Ayed Al-Qarni, an Islamic scholar:

> I do not see women driving cars in our country because of the consequences that would spring from it such as the spread of corruption, women uncovering their hair and faces, mingling between the sexes, men being alone with women and the destruction of the family and society in whole. (Qusti 2004)

Some religious doctrines are explicitly grounded in ideas of egalitarianism. For example, the Quakers, a religious community founded in England in the 17th century, follow the teachings of Christ and believe in spiritual equality between the sexes. They grant men and women equal authority to speak in meetings for worship. The Quakers were influential in early suffrage movements in both the United Kingdom and the United States. Sikhism, a religion that emerged in the Punjab region of India in the 15th century, employs religious texts that explicitly call for the equal treatment of women (Burn 2005). When 140 apostles were trained to manage the expansion of the religion in the 1500s, 52 of them were women.

Despite that women are typically subordinated in all religions, the major religions of the world are differentially conservative or patriarchal in their views about the place of women, both in the church hierarchy and in society. Scholars expect Muslim and Catholic countries to have fewer women in power because those countries are likely to hold more conservative gender ideologies. Countries with many Islamic adherents may resist women's acquisition of political power since Islamic law is typically interpreted in a manner that constrains the activities of women (Ahmed 1992; Caldwell 1986:175–176; Glaser and Possony 1979). As explained by the 2003 Nobel laureate Shirin Ebadi, "Many people use Islam to justify the unequal position of women" (Associated Press 2004). Scholars also expect Catholic countries, and especially Orthodox countries, to have fewer women in power than Protestant countries because women have traditionally been denied positions of power within the Catholic Church hierarchy. In contrast, scholars have highlighted how predominantly Protestant countries facilitate the education of women, stress individual (men and women) interaction with religious texts, promote nonhierarchical religious practices, and more readily accept women as religious leaders.

Researchers looking at women in politics have compared the percentage of women in politics across countries with different dominant religions (e.g., Paxton 1997; Paxton and Kunovich 2003; Reynolds 1999). These statistical studies of women's participation in national legislatures have consistently found an impact of religion, across many countries and time periods. These studies show that predominantly Muslim and Catholic countries have lower levels of women in parliament than countries that are predominantly Protestant.

You can see evidence of the influence of religion in Table 4.1, which presents the percentage of women in parliament across countries with different dominant religions. Table 4.1 shows that majority Protestant countries have tended to have higher percentages of women in parliament than majority Catholic countries do. And both Protestant and Catholic countries have more women in parliament than Orthodox or Muslim countries do. Countries with mixed religions (no dominant religion) have tended to fall in the middle.

Table 4.1   Average Percentage of Women in Parliament, by Country's Dominant Religion

	1970	1980	1990	2000	2010
Protestant	5	9	12	17	20
Catholic	4	9	9	13	20
Orthodox	11	18	5	8	17
Muslim	4	6	5	5	13
Mixed	3	6	10	16	19

Note: A country is coded as mixed if no one religion is dominant—that is, if at least 50% of its population does not adhere to a single religion. The table does not include countries classified as having indigenous or other religions such as Judaism, Hinduism, or Buddhism.

In all time periods, Muslim countries have the fewest number of women in their parliaments. This is not entirely surprising considering that historical and contemporary interpretations of Islamic texts emphasize women's place in the private sphere. Although more liberal interpretations of these texts exist (Afghani 2005), they are not often visible in public discussion. But it is also important to note that Islam is not an obstacle to women's political power in all countries and across all types of political positions. Women have risen to national political leadership in Muslim-majority countries like Pakistan and Indonesia. And as discussed in Chapter 15, Muslim women have successfully reached nontrivial levels of legislative representation in several Muslim-majority countries in Africa.

Finally, the substantial trend toward equality in 2010 in Table 4.1 suggests that the influence of religion is being mitigated by other factors in many countries today. Gender quotas, to be discussed in Chapter 6, are one reason why countries of different religions show more similarly today in their numbers of women in parliament than in the past.

Cultural Attitudes

Do societies really differ in their attitudes about women? Yes. The World Values Survey (World Values Survey Association 2005) surveyed attitudes toward women in politics in a large number of countries. A random sample of individuals was drawn in each country, and each person was asked how much he or she agreed with the following six statements:

1. On the whole, men make better political leaders than women do.

2. A university education is more important for a boy than for a girl.

3. When jobs are scarce, men should have more right to a job than women.

4. On the whole, men make better business executives than women do.

5. It is always justifiable for a man to beat his wife.

6. Women having the same rights as men is not an essential characteristic of democracy.

Table 4.2 presents the average answer to each question across 51 countries. The first column gives the average answer to a direct question asking individuals whether they thought men made better political leaders than women. Looking down the table, it is apparent that there are differences in the average number of people in each country agreeing that men are better leaders. As would be expected, the Scandinavian countries, with their long tradition of egalitarianism, score lower than other countries. The average answer in Scandinavia is between strongly disagreeing and disagreeing with that statement. In other Western countries, the average answer tends toward just "disagree." But looking at some of the countries in Eastern Europe, Latin America, Asia,

Table 4.2 World Values Survey Questions on Women's Place, as of 2005

	Averages (higher values = more negative ideology)					
	men make better political leaders[1]	university education more imp. for boys[1]	men have more right to a job[2]	men make better business execs[1]	justifiable for a man to beat his wife[3]	democracy: women have the same rights as men[4]
Western Industrialized						
Australia	2.09	1.69	1.93	1.92	1.35	1.79
Canada	1.92	1.64	2.06	1.79	1.16	1.86
France	1.80	1.35	2.11	1.62	1.27	2.38
Germany	1.85	1.71	2.04	1.76	1.76	1.87
Italy	2.04	1.82	2.03	1.97	1.18	—
Netherlands	1.88	1.58	2.07	1.83	1.24	1.94
New Zealand	2.01	1.67	1.89	—	—	—
Spain	1.76	1.60	2.11	1.67	1.52	2.09
Switzerland	1.80	1.56	2.06	1.70	1.38	1.73
Great Britain	2.07	1.78	2.08	1.98	1.33	1.95
United States	2.14	1.77	1.81	1.92	1.40	2.42
Scandinavia						
Finland	1.97	1.71	2.01	1.95	1.27	1.83
Norway	1.55	1.18	2.01	1.63	1.25	1.64
Sweden	1.69	1.46	1.98	1.61	1.19	1.16
Africa						
Burkina Faso	2.80	2.32	2.39	2.95	3.62	2.66
Ethiopia	1.94	1.69	1.98	1.90	1.57	1.95
Ghana	3.10	1.94	2.45	2.91	2.44	2.51
Mali	3.19	2.69	2.48	3.27	4.82	3.12

(Continued)

Averages (higher values = more negative ideology)

	men make better political leaders[1]	university education more imp. for boys[1]	men have more right to a job[2]	men make better business execs[1]	justifiable for a man to beat his wife[3]	democracy: women have the same rights as men[4]
Rwanda	2.58	2.23	2.15	2.58	2.47	3.20
South Africa	2.50	1.81	2.21	2.34	2.38	2.91
Zambia	2.54	1.98	2.19	2.48	4.35	3.28
Asia						
China	2.61	2.13	2.17	2.37	1.68	1.96
India	2.77	2.47	2.23	2.82	—	—
Indonesia	2.74	2.03	2.47	2.44	1.35	2.91
Japan	2.44	2.15	1.72	2.29	1.63	2.73
Republic of Korea	2.56	2.04	1.96	2.42	1.69	2.73
Malaysia	2.88	2.50	2.13	2.63	3.07	4.27
Thailand	2.52	2.16	2.05	2.45	2.53	3.42
Vietnam	2.59	1.99	2.19	2.36	1.62	1.68
Eastern Europe						
Bulgaria	2.48	1.76	2.01	2.03	1.75	2.31
Poland	2.46	1.96	2.13	2.22	1.24	1.98
Romania	2.51	1.74	2.11	2.39	1.64	1.65
Russian Federation	2.80	2.21	2.16	2.60	1.56	1.81
Serbia	2.36	1.82	1.88	2.20	4.81	2.39
Slovenia	2.18	1.75	2.01	1.98	1.51	2.11
Ukraine	2.60	2.23	2.11	2.52	1.94	2.65

	men make better political leaders[1]	university education more imp. for boys[1]	men have more right to a job[2]	men make better business execs[1]	justifiable for a man to beat his wife[3]	democracy: women have the same rights as men[4]
Latin America and the Caribbean						
Argentina	2.17	1.81	2.14	1.98	1.17	1.53
Brazil	2.21	1.85	2.09	2.15	1.56	2.56
Chile	2.42	2.11	2.05	2.13	1.35	2.46
Colombia	2.24	1.89	—	2.09	1.24	—
Guatemala	2.14	1.90	2.11	—	—	2.77
Mexico	2.19	2.12	2.18	2.09	2.02	2.07
Peru	2.08	2.00	2.08	2.01	—	2.15
Trinidad and Tobago	2.07	1.64	2.17	1.92	1.82	2.31
Uruguay	2.05	1.83	2.13	2.01	1.81	
Middle East and North Africa						
Egypt	3.62	2.27	2.81	3.44	—	3.15
Iran	2.98	2.55	2.55	2.94	1.79	3.42
Iraq	3.57	2.47	2.84	—	—	4.63
Jordan	3.29	2.14	2.84	3.07	1.53	3.29
Morocco	2.72	2.09	2.35	2.69	2.28	3.39
Turkey	2.67	1.77	2.37	2.49	1.48	2.23

Averages (higher values = more negative ideology)

1. Questions could be answered on a 1 through 4 scale indicating strong disagreement, disagreement, agreement, and strong agreement.

2. Question answered on a 1 through 3 scale indicating disagreement, neither, or agreement.

3. Question answered on a 1 through 10 scale indicating it is never, sometimes, or always justifiable for a man to beat his wife.

4. Question answered on a 1 through 10 scale indicating that gender equality is essential, somewhat essential, or not essential to democracy.

Source: From the World Values Survey, Wave 5 (World Values Survey Association, 2005).

Africa, and the Middle East, average answers are higher, suggesting that a larger percentage of people agree with the statement that men make better leaders. In Ghana and Mali, for example, the average answer is "agree" (note also Mali's greater acceptance of wife beating). And take the Middle East as the most extreme case: The average answer on the "men make better political leaders" question in Egypt, Iraq, and Jordan is between "agree" and "strongly agree." The first column of Table 4.2 therefore demonstrates that countries differ in their cultural values about women in politics. The other columns ask different questions about gender ideology but produce similar conclusions.

Women can hold negative attitudes about women as well as men. A pervasive cultural ideology suggesting women are inferior is exactly that—pervasive. For example, a United Nations Population Fund (2005b) report found that in Egypt 94% of women thought it was acceptable to be beaten, as did 91% in Zambia. But the women surveyed in the World Values Survey hold slightly more positive attitudes about women than men. For example, on average, across all countries, women's average response to "men are better in politics" was 2.4, whereas men's was 2.6 (remember higher numbers indicate more negative attitudes about women). Men are also more likely to say that men make better business executives (average of 2.2 vs. 2.5) and that a university education is more important for boys (men = 2.1, women = 1.9). Women are less likely than men to agree that men are justified in beating their wives (1.7 vs. 2.0) and less likely to agree that gender equality is not essential for a democracy (2.4 vs. 2.6). Individual countries show big differences across men and women as well. In South Africa, men's average answer to men as better in politics is 2.7, between agree and disagree. Women in the country differ, giving an average answer of 2.3.

Culture and Women's Representation in Politics

But do these differences in cultural attitudes really matter for women's political power? Yes. Some research has explicitly considered how attitudes about women affect women's political power. Until recently, there were few **cross-national** surveys of attitudes about women so researchers relied entirely on region and religion to look for the effects of ideology on women's political participation. But recent worldwide surveys of individuals' attitudes about women in politics show whether countries differ in their cultural attitudes about women.

Pam Paxton and Sheri Kunovich (2003) used the questions discussed earlier to predict women's levels of participation in national legislatures. Their article demonstrated that culture, when measured with direct questions, mattered more than other explanations, such as women's labor force participation, in predicting differences in women's political representation. Cultural beliefs were by far the strongest predictor of women's political power and were stable across many statistical models. Figure 4.2 reproduces a central figure from that article. The figure is a type of scatterplot that plots a country's percentage of women in parliament against its average agreement with the item "men are better in politics." (The scatterplot also statistically accounts for [controls] other explanations of women's political power.) The plot demonstrates a clear, strong, negative relationship between "men are better in

Figure 4.2 Relationship Between Attitudes About Women in Politics and Percentage of Women in National Legislatures

Source: From Pamela Paxton and Sheri Kunovich, "Women's Political Representation: The Importance of Ideology." *Social Forces,* © 2003 The University of North Carolina Press. Used by permission of the publisher.

politics" and the percentage of women in parliament. As negative attitudes about women increase, the percentage of women in parliaments decreases.

To summarize, individuals, groups, and entire societies hold particular views about women's abilities and their place in society. These ideas matter for women's acquisition of political power.

Ambition

How does culture produce lower levels of women in politics? Recent scholarship in the United States argues that cultural beliefs produce differences in political ambition between men and women. Jennifer Lawless and Richard Fox (2010) began with this question: Are equally well-qualified men and women equally interested in and willing to run for political office? To answer this question, they surveyed individuals who could run for political office. That is, they surveyed men and women in the four professions most likely to yield political candidates in the United States—law, business, education, and politics. Looking just at this group of men and women (who share the same professional credentials), they found that women are much less likely to aspire to political office. And even when they do aspire to political office, they are less likely to actually run. As Figure 4.3 shows, when you begin with a 50/50 pool of men and women who could run for political office, 59% of the men will consider running for office compared with only 43% of the women. And of those who consider running for office, 20% of men will actually run, compared with only 15% of women. But Figure 4.3 finally demonstrates that of those men and women who decide to run, there is no gender difference in who actually wins office.

Differences in ambition can also be seen in Lawless and Fox's (2010:44) interviews:

> "If I'm angry about something that the government has done, I write letters and I sign petitions. I'm very interested in politics. I read the paper and I listen to National Public Radio. It would just never occur to me to be part of the fray. Running for office is something I'd just never think to do." Melissa Stevens-Jones, 51, attorney, New Mexico

> "Sure, I've considered running, I'm not interested in it right now, but who knows? Maybe in 10 years I'll want a career change. Maybe I'll want to be a mayor . . . or an astronaut." Charles Bartelson, 44, business owner, Missouri

Even when women do express interest in running for office, Lawless and Fox (2010) found that they express interest in lower-level positions than

Figure 4.3   Male and Female Candidates Emerge
From a Pool of Possible Candidates

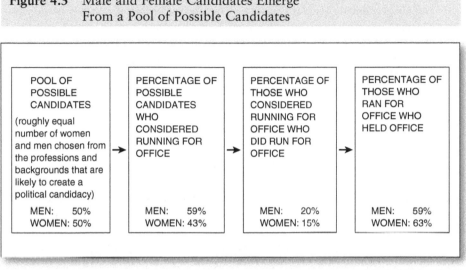

Source: Fox and Lawless (2004).

men. For example, an equal percentage of men and women say they would seek a position on a town or city council, but a significantly lower percentage of women than men say they would seek a position as mayor (11% compared to 17%), state legislator (27% compared to 36%), governor (6% compared to 13%), or a senator (12% compared to 21%).

According to Lawless and Fox (2010), these observed differences in ambition stem from traditional sex-role socialization where girls are encouraged to focus on private, intrafamilial affairs and boys are encouraged to focus on public, extrafamilial affairs (Conover and Gray 1983:2–3). For example, 35% of women report that their parents suggested they run for office compared to 43% of men (Fox and Lawless 2010:66). Early **political socialization** means that politics may seem a reasonable career path to men, while "not even appearing on the radar screen" for many women and girls (Lawless and Fox 2010:12).

Lawless and Fox also reported that when asked about their low levels of political ambition, women say that they "aren't qualified" for political office. Twenty-eight percent of their female respondents claimed that they were "not at all qualified" to run for office compared to 12% of the male respondents (see also Fox and Lawless 2011). As an example, consider the following story.

Alexander Casey, an active member of the Sacramento County Taxpayers' League, recounted . . . his attempts to encourage Judy Morton, a lawyer friend, to run for the state legislature: "She is an All-American athlete, Phi Beta Kappa, Rhodes Scholar finalist, Harvard Law grad, and advisor to President Bush. I met with her for dinner the other night and basically begged her to run for office. She told me she doesn't think she's qualified. Who the hell is qualified if she isn't? I don't get it." (Lawless and Fox 2010:114)

Men and women agree on the skills and emotional traits necessary as qualifications for public office—for example, knowledge of issues, being a good public speaker, or having a thick skin (Fox and Lawless 2011). But women are much less likely than men to feel that they have those qualifications. Remembering that Fox and Lawless were interviewing a sample of equally qualified men and women, it is striking that 46% of women rated themselves as knowledgeable about policy issues compared to 59% of men. Similarly, 57% percent of women stated that they were a good public speaker, compared to 66% of men. Since the men and women come from the same set of professions, it is even more striking that there is an 8% difference (66% to 74%) in women's assessment of their professional qualifications for political office compared to men's (Fox and Lawless 2011).

Part of the concern about qualifications stems from women's assessment of their personality characteristics. Lawless and Fox (2010) found that women more often reported that they lacked certain personality characteristics, such as "gumption" or an "ability to deal with criticism" that were needed for politics. In follow-up research, Fox and Lawless (2011) showed that only 52% of women believe they have a "thick enough skin" to participate in politics, compared to 71% of men. Such views are not restricted to the United States, either. Hunt (2007) explained that women in places like Kyrgyzstan view politics as a dirty game and that they want to stay away from it.

Of course, these gender differences are not restricted to political ambition. Research has shown that men are more likely than women to express overconfidence in the skills they possess (Kling, Hyde, Showers, and Buswell 1999), overestimate their intelligence (Furnham and Rawles 1995), and to be generally more "self-congratulatory" than women (Wigfield, Eccles, and Pintrich 1996). When asked questions about political knowledge, men are more likely than women to guess, rather than say "I don't know" (Mondak and Anderson 2004).

To end our discussion of political ambition on a positive note, if women do feel that they need to be more qualified to run for achieve political office, then perhaps the women who do run will be more successful politicians. Indeed, in the U.S. Congress, Anzia and Berry (2011) showed that congresswomen bring 9% more federal money to their districts than congressmen do and that congresswomen sponsor and cosponsor more bills.

Role Model Effects

Before leaving the topics of political ambition and early gender socialization, consider recent research on the power of female role models for young girls. David Campbell and Christina Wolbrecht (2006) pointed out that the presence of female role models should influence the socialization of young women and girls. Having women in prominent political positions could challenge messages girls might receive about whether politics is a suitable occupation for women. It could also encourage girls to pay more attention to politics and discuss it more with other girls and adults. Campbell and Wolbrecht found that adolescent girls' intention to be politically active spiked at two points between 1976 and 2001. The first time was when Geraldine Ferraro ran as the vice-presidential candidate in 1984 and the second was in 1992 during the "year of the woman" when the press highlighted the unprecedented number of women running for Congress. They found other evidence for a role model effect on young girls and showed that the effect works largely through political discussion.

> Visible female candidates trigger conversations about politics between parents and their adolescent daughters, familiarizing girls with the political world and leading them to envision themselves as participants in politics. (Campbell and Wolbrecht 2006:244)

In follow-up work, Wolbrecht and Campbell (2007) showed that the role model effect holds across Europe. Across 22 countries, the percentage of women in a nation's legislature positively influences the amount that adolescent girls (and adult women) discuss politics but not the amount that boys or men do. Increasing numbers of women in a nation's legislature also increases the political activity of adult women and the anticipated political activity of adolescent girls. And in Rwanda, Burnet (2011) found that the rapid increase in the percentage of women in the parliament enhanced women's political participation not just at the national level but at the local level and has "helped legitimate them as political agents in the popular imagination of rural people" (p. 317).

Media

Finally, what about the role of the media? The news media plays a key role in election campaigns (Scammell and Semetko 2000). The media can certainly play a powerful role in politics by shaping what citizens know and even what they think is important. Gender differences in news coverage could exacerbate existing stereotypes about female candidates or even create new ones. There is some evidence that portrayals of men and women in the press are equal in the amount of coverage devoted to the candidates (Bystrom, Banwart, Kaid, and Robertson 2004; Jalalzai 2006; Smith 1997). But male and female candidates can still be portrayed differently by the media (Gidengil and Everitt 2003). Kim Fridkin Kahn studied how the news media responds to male and female candidates for statewide offices. In both U.S. Senate campaigns and gubernatorial campaigns, the press was more responsive to the campaign messages of male candidates. Rather than simply relating the issues discussed by female candidates, the press instead either focused on women's negative chances in Senate races or on women's personality characteristics in races for Governor. Kahn (1996) concluded that "the media's misrepresentation of women candidates' campaign messages limits the effectiveness of women's campaigns" (p. 133).

Of course, a media bias against female candidates can also be incredibly direct. Consider the following story related by Whitney (2000:53):

> In 1990, when Dianne Feinstein and Pete Wilson were engaged in a hotly contested race for governor of California, they faced off in a televised debate. The next day, the Los Angeles Times declared the debate to be a virtual tie. However, the paper gave Wilson a slight edge because he 'looked' more like a governor. (p. 53)

Something about Dianne Feinstein's appearance, despite her equal performance in the debate, made her seem the less viable candidate to the journalists at the *Los Angeles Times*. That editorial opinion was then transmitted to countless subscribers.

In other countries, too, male and female candidates are portrayed with reference to gender stereotypes. By comparing newspaper coverage of male and female candidates during the 2004 and 2006 electoral campaigns in Australia, Canada, and the United States, Kittilson and Fridkin (2008) showed that candidates are often portrayed in terms of long-standing gender stereotypes. They consider whether female candidates are linked more often in the media to stereotypically "female issues" such as education or health, and linked less often to stereotypically "male issues" such as foreign policy and the economy. In all three countries, a greater percentage of male issues were linked to male candidates than to female candidates and a greater number of female issues were linked to female candidates than to male ones. Similarly "male" traits such as strong, effective, aggressive, tough, and intelligent were more often linked to male candidates by the media in all three countries while "female" traits such as gentle, emotional, and dependent were more often linked to the female candidates. Table 4.3 replicates their findings on traits for the three countries.

Table 4.3   Percentage of Male and Female Traits Linked to Candidates by the Media

	"Male" traits, e.g., hardworking, untrustworthy, strong, vital, competitive, effective, tough, intelligent, aggressive, knowledgeable, independent, ambitious	"Female" Traits, e.g., gentle, honest, weak, attractive, passive, emotional, compassionate, noncompetitive, dependent
Canada		
male candidates	84	16
female candidates	60	40
Australia		
male candidates	83	17
female candidates	66	34
United States		
male candidates	88	12
female candidates	43	56

Source: Kittilson and Fridkin (2008). © 2008 Cambridge University Press. Reprinted with permission.

The high-profile race for the U.S. Democratic presidential nomination between Hillary Clinton and Barack Obama in 2008 affords a unique opportunity to consider differential media coverage. Melissa Miller, Jeffrey Peake, and Brittany Boulton (2010) examined 6,600 news articles and editorials during the 2008 run-up to Super Tuesday. Interestingly, while they found no difference in the amount of coverage between Clinton and her rivals (in fact, Clinton enjoyed an advantage in raw coverage compared to the other potential nominees), portrayals of Clinton by the media were profoundly and significantly more negative than portrayals of her rivals, especially portrayals of Barack Obama.

In terms of coverage, Hillary Clinton was mentioned more often than her male rivals, was the primary subject of articles or editorials more often than her rivals, had more sentences written about her, and was mentioned in the headline more often than her rivals (Miller et al. 2010:177). Raw attention by the news media was not a problem for Hillary Clinton in 2008.

Likewise, traditional issues of attention to dress or appearance were not a problem for Clinton. Only 2.4% of articles mentioning Clinton referenced her clothing or her appearance; a similar amount of articles mentioned the clothing or appearance of John Edwards or Bill Richardson. On the surface, the balance of coverage of Clinton on personality, policy positions, and standing in the race was also positive; 18% of articles referenced positive traits and 17% referenced negative traits. Similarly, headlines about Clinton were balanced across the positive and negative. But the "balanced" portrayal that Clinton experienced was swamped by the positive-to-negative skews enjoyed by other candidates—13% more positive for John Edwards, 14% more positive for Barack Obama, and 24% more positive for Bill Richardson. In short, while we can describe newspaper coverage of Clinton as "balanced," it was highly positively skewed for the other candidates (Miller et al. 2010).

Of critical importance, the negative coverage of Clinton was markedly different than the negative coverage of Obama as was explained by Miller and colleagues (2010):

> The tone of her negative coverage was also markedly personal. Her negative trait references were much more likely to include character oriented terms, such as "polarizing," "unlikable," and "deceptive." Such personal, negative trait references were nearly twice as common as job related, negative trait references for Clinton. Newspapers' negative portrayal of Obama, meanwhile, focused largely on his relative lack of experience. Whereas she was "cold," "secretive," and "divisive"—arguably gender-based stereotypes—Obama was "inexperienced." The latter is certainly a serious negative charge against anyone running for president, but is clearly job-related and unlikely to be construed as a damaging character flaw. (p. 192)

In summary, as we discussed in Chapter 1, three-dimensional power is exerted by influencing the beliefs or wants of others, even without their knowledge (Lukes 1974). If cultural values, traditions, socialization, and the media imply that men—not women—are the better political actors, then women may come to assume that their political participation is not appropriate. Culture is therefore one important way to explain a lack of supply of females in the political process.

5

Explaining the Political Representation of Women—Social Structure

I t is clear from the previous chapter that ideas, beliefs, and attitudes toward women in politics may constrain the number of women who run for public office. However, it is also important to consider how a country's **social structure** affects women's political participation and the supply of potential female politicians. It seems logical that when the structures of a society treat men and women more equally, women will be more able to compete against men for power. According to structural perspectives, the family, education system, labor force, and other societal structures can be configured in ways that prevent women from gaining the skills necessary to participate in politics or compete against men for public office. Instead of focusing on why men or women may not want women to run for political office, structural arguments often center on why women cannot run for political office.

In gender and politics research, several theoretical traditions have contributed to structural arguments about the supply of women. One variant of the structural perspective, developed in political science, is the **resource model of political participation.** The resource model argues that differences in men's and women's political participation are the result of individual-level inequalities in certain prerequisites to participation such as money, free time, and civic skills (Schlozman, Burns, and Verba 1994).

A second group of theorists, elite theorists, link these factors explicitly to political decision-making positions, noting that political elites are often well connected and highly educated and hold professional jobs in certain fields such as law (Putnam 1976). The elite perspective also compares and contrasts the paths to office by male and female politicians to evaluate which factors can help or hinder women's political participation. A third group, gender stratification theorists, focuses on societal-level inequalities in male and female **economic power**. This standpoint holds that greater female economic control must come before female political influence. We discuss each of these perspectives, focusing on seven structural factors that are thought to influence the women's political participation and the supply of female candidates: (1) money, (2) time, (3) civic skills and community participation, (4) education, (5) work, (6) economic power, and (7) informal networks.

Also relevant are the larger structural forces that shape institutions like the economy. In the last section of the chapter, we will discuss a recent and controversial argument by Michael Ross (2008) that oil and other valuable minerals are indirectly to blame for women's low levels of political participation in some parts of the world.

Money

When it comes to politics, it should be no surprise that money matters. As Herbert E. Alexander (2001) aptly summarized, "People, not dollars, vote. But money helps to shape both voter behaviour and governmental decisions" (p. 198). And in recent years, politics has become a more expensive endeavor. Driven by a decline in loyalty to political parties around the globe, campaign ideologies are shifting to the political center, resulting in "expensive, personality-driven television and direct-mail campaigns" (Bussey 2000:77). Many countries, especially in the West, do not have any limits on private political donations, advantaging the wealthy and well connected (Casas-Zamora 2005). In the United States, for example, there is no shortage of examples of wealthy businesspeople who have bankrolled their own multimillion-dollar campaigns. And in central and Eastern Europe, powerful business interests even form their own political party systems (Walecki 2005). Consider also the example of Cameroon, where constituents are often paid to vote by the rich, so "power is literally purchased by those who can afford it" (Noftsinger 2010). Overall, one study of campaign finance regulations in 104 countries found that 59% of countries had no limits on campaign spending, and 72% had no limits on financial contributions by individuals, groups, or businesses

(Pinto-Duschinsky 2002). With rising campaign costs and no caps on spending or contributions, money has become an ever more important political commodity.

In a world where money matters, women have less of it. On average, women are less likely to work full-time than their male counterparts, and even when they do, women earn less money than men. In the United States, women working full-time, year-round make 78 cents on the male dollar. And female British workers earn 27% less than their male colleagues (BBC News 2005b). Across 63 countries of the world, the International Trade Union Confederation finds that women make 16.5% less than men do and that higher education of women does not necessarily lead to a smaller pay gap (Chubb, Melis, Potter, and Storry 2008). Adriana Munoz, a Chilean parliamentarian, explains the problem of money:

> Being a candidate is difficult for a woman because you need to have a lot of money. We have little help economically. Men have access to circles or networks where money is lent—they are friends with bank managers. But we are not supported this way. For us, it's pretty complicated, this arena of power and money. (quoted in Franceschet 2001:216)

And Maria Anonieta Saa elaborated "men will take risks, they will sell the family house . . . but a woman is not going to put her family at risk" (quotes in Franceschet 2005:89). Ransford and Thomson (2011:34) showed this process at work in municipal government in New England, where some women felt unable to obtain financial resources from the business sector.

In sum, women may less able than men to contribute to campaigns, finance their own candidacy, or take on temporary or poorly paid positions in local or regional governments.

However, there are sources of hope for women office-seekers. In some countries such as Spain, a larger role is played by public financing of elections (Pinto-Duschinsky and Postnikov 1999). More than 80 countries offer candidates free political broadcasts, and more than 60 provide direct public subsidies for political campaigns (Pinto-Duschinsky 2002; see also Ohman 2011). And in some countries, women's political organizations have emerged that focus explicitly on financing women's political efforts. For example, EMILY's List, founded in 1985 in the United States, is a political network dedicated to providing early financial support to progressive female candidates. In the 1990s, the organization spread to Australia and the United Kingdom, aiding the successful election of more than 100 women to parliament in those nations (EMILY's List Australia 2005). At the end of 2004, the group was the largest single source of donations to candidates in the United

States, directing nearly $11 million to pro-abortion–rights female candidates (Cillizza 2005; but see Hannagan, Pimlott, and Littvay 2010). Perhaps because of such efforts, recent research has found that in the United States, men and women are equally well funded in political campaigns, with even a slight advantage for women (Hogan 2001). And as discussed in Chapter 10, a woman recently broke the record for the most personal funds spent in a single U.S. campaign.

Time

Another important political resource is time. As Schlozman and colleagues (1994) explained, "Most forms of political involvement—working in a campaign, taking part in a community activity, attending a protest—require an investment of at least some time" (p. 974). But women's responsibility for the overwhelming share of child care and housework may deprive them of the free time required to participate in politics (Phillips 1991:99–100). Even women who participate in the labor force still perform the lion's share of domestic tasks such as cooking and cleaning, a phenomenon sociologist Arlie Hochschild coined the **second shift** (Burns, Schlozman, and Verba 2001; Calasanti and Bailey 1991; Hochschild 1989; Shelton 1990). Furthermore, running for and serving in public office is extremely demanding in terms of both time and energy. Women may fear that if they pursue political careers, they must do so at the expense of their families (Kirkpatrick 1974). Golda Meir, prime minister of Israel from 1969 to 1974, articulated this fear: "At work, you think of the children you've left at home. At home, you think of the work you've left unfinished. Such a struggle is unleashed within yourself, your heart is rent."

In their survey of potential candidates, Lawless and Fox (2010:73) found that 42% of women say they are responsible for the majority of child care, while only 4% of the men report the same. Similarly, only 6% of women report that their spouse or partner is responsible for the majority of child care while 46% of men do. There are generational differences in gendered responsibility for domestic tasks; a higher percentage of women over 60 report that they are responsible for the majority of household tasks. But 31% of women under 40 still report being largely responsible for household chores. Research on women in political elites indicates that women tend to begin their political careers at an older age than men do (Dubeck 1976), are less likely to be married and have children than men in political elites (Black and Erickson 2000; Dodson 1997; Franceschet and Piscopo forthcoming; Saint-Germain 1993; Sapiro 1982), and are also less likely to be married and have children compared to women in the general population (Saint-Germain and Chávez Metoyer 2008). These differences suggest that the combination of women's family or domestic roles and the substantial time required to campaign for and to serve in public office place substantial limitations on the pool of female candidates (Lawless and Fox 2010).

There are also significant differences in the amount of free time that women have in the global north compared with women in the global south. As we discuss later, development frees up time for individuals to pursue additional activities, including political activities. To illustrate the constraints on time faced by women in developing societies, let's consider the free time of a woman living in a developing country—Sierra Leone (Table 5.1).

Table 5.1   A Typical Day's Work for a Woman in Sierra Leone

4:00 A.M. to 5:30 A.M.	Fish in local pond.
6:00 A.M. to 8:00 A.M.	Heat water, make breakfast, wash dishes, sweep floors.
8:00 A.M. to 11:00 A.M.	Work in rice fields while watching 4-year-old son and carrying baby on back.
11:00 A.M. to 12:00 P.M.	Gather berries and fuel for the fire while hauling water from a distant well.
12:00 P.M. to 2:00 P.M.	Process and prepare food, make lunch, wash dishes.
2:00 P.M. to 3:00 P.M.	Wash clothes, clean and smoke fish.
3:00 P.M. to 5:00 P.M.	Work in local gardens.
5:00 P.M. to 6:00 P.M.	Fish in local pond.
6:00 P.M. to 8:00 P.M.	Process and prepare food, make dinner.
8:00 P.M. to 9:00 P.M.	Wash dishes, care for children.
9:00 P.M. to 11:00 P.M.	Chat around the fire while making fishnets.
11:00 P.M. to 4:00 A.M.	Sleep.

Source: Food and Agriculture Organization (2003), cited in Burn (2005).

This example makes it clear that the average woman in Sierra Leone would find it difficult to begin a life in politics. Even when women do have spare time, cultural norms may require them to spend that time in nonpolitical activities (Yarr 1996). Across democratic countries, research indicates that levels of women's political representation have been consistently higher in the industrialized world (Matland 1998).

Civic Skills and Community Participation

Participating in the political realm and running for office also require civic skills. Civic skills are the "communication and organizational abilities that allow citizens to use time and money effectively in political life" (Schlozman et al. 1994:974). Civic skills include the ability to speak in public, run a meeting, read a budget, or navigate through parliamentary procedure. These skills can be developed during the formative years through the family and educational systems but are solidified later in life through employment and activity in nonpolitical organizations and churches.

Women worldwide have fewer civic skills than men do. Women are less educated, and on average, men are more likely to hold more highly skilled jobs (see later discussion). Because women may have less access to civic skills in the workplace, their voluntary association memberships (e.g., in church or a bird-watching group) may be particularly important. Research in the United States supports this idea, finding that although men and women are equally likely to be affiliated with a voluntary nonpolitical organization, it affects men and women differently. Organizational activity does not affect men's political participation, but it significantly increases women's participation in politics (Schlozman et al. 1994).

Community action provides women with the motivation, connections, and civic skills to run for office. In her classic study of female legislators in the United States, Kirkpatrick (1974) argued that the motives that lead a woman to volunteer in her community are often the same motives that lead her to run for office. For example, one female state legislator recounted, "After years of working with the Urban League and civil rights groups, I just knew something more had to be done" (Kirkpatrick 1974:62). Participation in voluntary associations may also foster networking and impart the civic skills necessary for political success. Legislators are often drawn from careers that foster connections to the public, and membership or leadership in community affairs may also cultivate these connections. Further, "a woman active in a civic organization learns how to run a meeting, how to plan one, how to develop an agenda and recruit support for a position. She learns how to operate in a public context . . ." (p. 64).

Although the nature and form of women's community participation differ across countries and regions of the world, research suggests that the value of organizational activity to women is widespread. In Canada, 64% of female members of the House of Commons in 1993 were members of women's associations. And in interviews with minority female members of parliament in Canada, Jerome Black (2000) found that many voiced that their extensive experience with volunteer organizations had made them more well known to constituents. The impact of women's civic participation is also well documented across southern Africa. For example, Longman (2006) found that in Rwanda since the 1980s, women's growing participation in civil society provided them with a route to politics. In fact, some Rwandans complain that the best women in civil society keep being drawn into government, named to commissions or ministries or the parliament (Longman 2006:138). In Tanzania and Uganda, women's organizations impart valuable skills to women, prepare them for office, and actively lobby for women's incorporation (Tripp 1994). And in her research on South Africa, Britton (2005:97) identified many women who pursued political careers after years of community activism (see also Hunt 2007).

Even though community activism may currently provide an important path to power for women across the world, scholars suggest that in some national legislatures, this path may become less traveled. In Australia, Mexico, and South Africa, the professionalization of politics has decreased the number of women with community backgrounds who run for national office (Britton 2005; Camp 1998; Sawer 2000). The professionalization of politics means that party activities take precedence over other types of associations, so individuals with backgrounds in law and paid party work are more likely to populate parliaments (Sawer 2000). (See Chapter 10 for a discussion of professionalization in the United States.)

Education

Elite theorists point out that political elites are often highly educated (Putnam 1976). Thus, in countries where women have access to educational opportunities, one expects that they will be more likely to participate in politics. Basic education may be an especially important resource because it bestows political knowledge that may be essential for participation in the political realm (Verba, Burns, and Schlozman 1997). However, in nations of the global north, researchers often focus on graduate or professional education. Education at elite institutions may also provide individuals with important connections or access to elite networks.

In the developing world, education means basic skills like literacy or language. International development organizations share the consensus that education is crucial to improving the quality of women's citizenship and leadership (Knight 2004). It is therefore encouraging that significant progress in female education has been made in recent years. For example, although education for women was outlawed under the Taliban in Afghanistan, since the 2001 U.S. invasion, the new government has opened hundreds of schools for women and girls. Unfortunately, however, women and girls are still less educated and more likely to be illiterate than men in many countries (United Nations Educational, Scientific, and Cultural Organization [UNESCO] 2005). Across the developing world, 83% of men are literate compared with only 69% of women. As a specific example, in China, 95% of men are literate compared with 87% of women. In Pakistan, fewer people are literate, but gender differences remain strong—53% of men and 29% of women are literate (UNESCO 2005).

A more critical perspective argues that in developing countries, women's presence in schools can actually be "economically dysfunctional" (Robertson 1986:92). Because education encourages women's removal from the labor force, it may promote their dependence on men, reinforcing their subordinate roles. In sum, instead of presenting women with a path to greater autonomy and power, in the developing context education may actually function "as an instrument of oppression" (Robertson 1986:92).

However, few researchers or policy makers agree with this position. They argue that in some situations, education may provide a path to political power for women when other resources (such as wealth) are unavailable to them. In Uganda, for example, a woman was elected to the position of vice-chairperson in part because she had been through 7 years of schooling and could speak English. On the other hand, the chairman of the same council, a wealthy businessman in the village, did not have any formal education or English-language skills (Johnson 2003). An increasing number of studies are also finding that female politicians have superior education credentials than their male counterparts, supporting the notion that education may provide a vital resource for women (Black and Erickson 2000; Escobar-Lemmon and Taylor-Robinson 2008; Verge 2011).

Work

Just as elites are often highly educated, they are also usually successful businesspersons or come from professional occupations such as law (Putnam 1976). Thus, the argument follows that where women do not regularly obtain prestigious or highly skilled positions in the labor force, they will fail to be represented politically. Kira Sanbonmatsu (2002b) found that in the

United States a greater percentage of women working in a state (including women executives and women in the legal field) increases the number of women in the state legislature. But while women's overall participation in the labor force is increasing worldwide, women are still concentrated in low-paying and low prestige jobs (Bielby and Baron 1986; England, Chassie, and McCormack 1982; Reskin and Hartmann 1986; Reskin and Roos 1993; Wright, Baxter, and Birkelund 1995). And, as noted before, even for jobs requiring the same level of education, women make 16.5% less than men do around the world (Chubb et al. 2008).

Furthermore, women still face limited economic rights and unchecked economic discrimination in several countries of the world. David Cingranelli and David Richards (2004b) developed a scheme for classifying countries into four ranked categories according to the economic rights they afforded women. Economic rights include equal pay for equal work, choice of employment without a male relative's consent, freedom from sexual harassment, and the right to work at night. A country in the highest category not only guarantees women's economic rights in law but the government fully and vigorously enforces the law. In 2003, however, only eight countries achieved this feat: Australia, Belgium, Canada, Iceland, Netherlands, the Republic of Moldova, Sweden, and Tunisia. In these countries, the government tolerates no or almost no discrimination against women.

Many more countries fell into the middle-high or middle-low categories where there is at best a degree of tolerance for low levels of discrimination against women and at worst a lack of government enforcement of the laws protecting women's economic rights and the toleration of a moderate level of discrimination against women. In these countries, "women are rarely compensated equally with men, are more likely than men to be laid off, and frequently hold lower paying, low-status jobs" (Cingranelli and Richards (2004a:37). This is the most common classification for countries in 2003. Although most countries in this group are still developing economically (e.g., Ethiopia, India, Mexico, North Korea), this category also includes industrialized countries such as Japan, South Africa, and Spain.

Finally, in 2003, twelve countries fell into the lowest group, where there are no economic rights for women under law. In fact, systematic discrimination based on sex may be built into the law.

> Employers often openly discriminate against women (e.g. pregnancy and marriage bars, discriminatory hiring practices, pay differentials, etc . . .) and the government tolerates these practices. The Civil and Penal Codes contain discriminatory regulations against women, such as law allowing the husband to oppose his wife's right to work or to own a business. (Cingranelli and Richards 2004a:37)

Countries in this category are located in Asia (Afghanistan and Pakistan), Africa (Cameroon, Central African Republic, Chad, Guinea-Bissau, Lesotho, Liberia, and Togo), and the Middle East (Saudi Arabia and Yemen).

Talking about women's "labor force participation" in general does not capture how certain jobs are conduits to political power. Without information on the types of jobs in which women work, it is unclear whether women are gaining politically relevant human capital from their job or whether they are simply working too many hours to find the time to participate politically. But obtaining accurate information about women's share of professional or managerial occupations is a difficult task. The general lack of quality data on a worldwide basis has prevented important questions about the connections between women's professional and political lives from being answered. Labor force arguments about the supply of female politicians are further complicated by research that demonstrates that women may follow different career paths to politics. Women may pursue political office after careers in fields such as education (Jalalzai 2004:99). Therefore, women's occupational resources may be different from those of men. Critics of the labor force supply argument also contend that models based upon female labor force statistics or women's share of positions in the professional occupations are based on Western models of women's incorporation into politics (Hughes 2004; Staudt 1986).

Participation in the paid labor force may have additional benefits for women besides simply providing skills or a conduit to political office. Women who work outside the home have access to organizational networks such as labor unions or professional associations that may politicize them (Norris 1987:122). Women in the labor force are also more likely to discover inequalities between men and women, which can provoke them to increase their political participation and/or demand greater representation (Matland 1998; Togeby 1994). In Bangladesh, poor, young, single female garment workers gain self-confidence, develop networks, and learn negotiation skills (Amin, Diamond, Naved, and Newby 1998; Kabeer and Mahmud 2004). The independent source of income provided by labor force participation also helps women develop more gender egalitarian beliefs (Thornton, Alwin, and Camburn 1983).

Ultimately, Ross (2008) summarized it this way:

> Joining the labor force can boost female political influence through at least three channels: at an individual level, by affecting women's political views and identities; at a social level, by increasing the density of women in the labor force and hence the likelihood they will form politically salient networks; and at an economic level, by boosting their economic importance and hence forcing the government to take their interests into account. (p. 108)

Economic Power

In most societies, women's work has long been overlooked or underestimated. Although many often think that throughout human history men have been the workers while women have been the mothers and wives, anthropological research indicates that among early civilizations, women were the primary labor force in the vast majority of gathering and cultivating societies (Murdock 1967; cited in Blumberg 1984). Even today, statistics on labor tend to ignore the work of poor rural women (Donahoe 1999). Therefore, it is clear that women's labor alone is not sufficient to give them economic power. Specifically, economic power is based in control over the **means of production** and control over the **allocation of surplus.** It is control over surplus (in money, goods, land, or the labor of others) that leads individuals to have the resources to pursue and acquire political power. So though women's level of labor force participation or income may be important, gender stratification theorists argue that it is control over labor or income that matters (Blumberg 1984; Chafetz 1984). For example, Burnet (2011) explained the following:

> Prior to the genocide, Rwandan law had forbidden Rwandan women from engaging in commercial activities, entering into contracts, or seeking paid employment without authorization from their husbands (Human Rights Watch 1996:22). In practice, many husbands (and even most husbands in the cities) allowed and even encouraged their wives to work, but the husbands often controlled the women's salaries or profits from commercial endeavors. In practice and by law, women's businesses were vulnerable to plunder by their husbands or to complete takeover. (p. 312)

Although economic power does not guarantee that women will gain formal political power, gender stratification researchers argue strongly that women's economic power must precede political power. For example, according to Rae Lesser Blumberg (1984), a power hierarchy exists—political power rests at the top, and other types of power, such as economic power, appear below. Achievement of power at the lower levels of power, such as in the labor force, must occur before power can be reached at the next highest level (cited in Paxton 1997). In an ethnographic analysis of 61 preindustrial societies, Blumberg (1984) found only one instance in which women had significant political input without autonomous economic power. (The exceptional example was the Mende of Liberia. Although the women did not do much of the productive labor, they were organized in a secret society and used their clout to influence the political sphere.)

Informal Networks

Thinking about the secret society of Mende women suggests one more structural barrier to women's empowerment—the informal networks that reinforce the political power of historically advantaged groups. Men's structural power is sometimes not easily nailed down in the statistics of labor force participation and representation in elite universities. What those numbers can miss is the informal structures that have and continue to privilege men. For example, informal networks matter in local politics and women have less access to these networks (Briggs 2000; Tremaine 2000). Studies show that institutions can be slow to change—in part because of these informal structures (Mackay, Kenny, and Chappell 2010). In **clientelist systems,** in particular, men's dominance of informal political positions may contribute to their dominance of formal political positions (Bjarnegard 2009; Franceschet and Piscopo forthcoming).

Informal networks can affect women's ascension to office but also their ability to get things done once there. Indeed, as Smooth (2001) found in her study of African American women, it was women's exclusion from informal power circles that affected perceptions of their influence in state legislatures.

Structural Arguments: The Evidence

Arguments about the importance of a supply of qualified women eligible to run for public office are compelling. We begin evaluating their usefulness by comparing countries at different levels of development. As mentioned earlier, developed countries have **industrialized** and gained wealth over time, providing their female citizens with resources like free time, which should allow them to participate more extensively in politics. In Figure 5.1, we classified countries by level of development using the 2004 Human Development Index and show women's parliamentary representation from 1970 to 2005 (United Nations Development Programme [UNDP] 2004). The Human Development Index is a composite measure of indicators of development including education, life expectancy, and gross domestic product (GDP). As Figure 5.1 demonstrates, women do have higher average levels of representation in more developed countries (but see Ross 2008).

But empirical research looking at the components of social structure has found, at best, mixed support for these supply-side effects on women in politics. For example, in a study of 12 states in the midwestern United States, Susan Welch (1978) found that women's representation in the legislature was only one third of what would be predicted by the pool of women with

Figure 5.1   Percentage of Women in Parliament in 173 Countries by Level of Development, 1970–2005

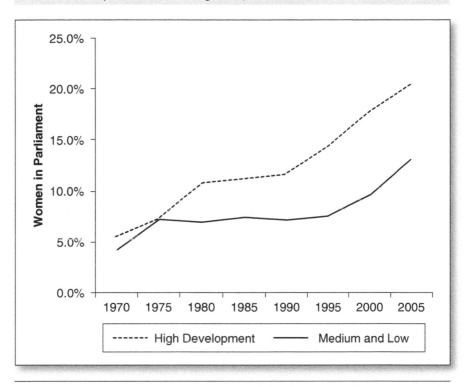

Sources: Inter-Parliamentary Union (1995, 2005a) and United Nations Population Fund (2005b).

the appropriate education, occupational experience, and associational memberships to qualify them to run for office. So structural supply does not fully explain women's low access to power.

Research also suggests that in some contexts, resource differences may not be as great or as important as previously thought. For example, in their investigation of the resource model of political participation in the United States, Schlozman et al. (1994) found only a slight gap between men and women in terms of political participation, and differences in political resources failed to fully explain the gap. Women and men were found to have roughly similar amounts of free time, and once women were politically active, they contributed more hours to political activities than men (Schlozman et al. 1994). This research took place in a Western, developed country, however, where one would expect women to have the greatest amount of free time.

But in statistical analyses performed in many countries around the world, measures of social structure are inconsistent predictors of women's representation in national politics. Generally, the most support has been found for the effects of women's labor force participation (Matland 1998; Moore and Shackman 1996; Paxton and Kunovich 2003; Rule 1981, 1987) or share of professional jobs (Kenworthy and Malami 1999). Still, a few studies contradict this trend, finding no real differences in female parliamentary representation when comparing countries in which women make up a greater part of the labor force to countries in which most women stay at home, once other theoretically important factors were taken into account (Kenworthy and Malami 1999; Paxton 1997). A recent and comprehensive look at 120 countries over 15 years (1995–2010) finds a positive effect of women's labor force participation on women's political representation. The authors find that for every 5% women are able to narrow the gap between their contribution and men's contribution to their country's GDP increases their representation in politics by 1% (Stockemer and Byrne 2011).

When considering education, the opposite is true. Most research finds that women's higher educational attainment does not matter for their representation in national political bodies (Kenworthy and Malami 1999; Matland 1998; Moore and Shackman 1996; Norris 1985; Paxton 1997; Paxton and Kunovich 2003). Some researchers have suggested that this is a problem of development (Hughes 2004). What counts as significant education in one country may be taken for granted for another. For example, in the case of Uganda discussed earlier, 7 years of education was significant enough to allow a woman to gain leadership in a local village council. Yet in many countries, education far beyond 7 years is compulsory for both men and women.

Although evidence for structural arguments is mixed, researchers often point out that this may be due to the limitations of current data. Information on women's position in the social structure, such as their participation in education and the labor force, is often difficult to collect, especially in less developed countries. Specific statistics such as the percentage of women in professional or managerial occupations is often only available in a few countries. In addition, as we noted earlier, what matters for women's access to politics in one country may be different from what matters in another. So it remains unclear whether, overall, structural factors are insignificant for women's political participation. What is clear is that, for women to be represented in politics, women must be willing and able to run for office. Political careers require time, money, and skills, and when it comes to these important resources, women are structurally disadvantaged.

Larger Structural Forces: Oil Extraction and Mineral Production

Traditionally, social structural arguments have focused on differences between women and men in various institutions like the economy, education, or the family. But a recent provocative article by Michael Ross (2008) argued that we need to think more broadly—to the larger structural characteristics of countries that shape institutions like the economy. Specifically, he argued that countries with higher levels of oil production will experience a distorted economy. This distortion in the economy will reduce women's labor force participation and ultimately their political representation.

Briefly, Ross (2008) argued that when countries discover oil, their new wealth tends to change their economy in a number of significant ways (this is called the "Dutch Disease"). Most important for women, there will be a shift in the economy away from the "traded sector" (agriculture and manufacturing) and toward the "nontraded sector" (construction and services). In the global south, women more often participate in the traded sector of the economy, in low-wage jobs in factories and agriculture. In contrast, men more often work in the nontraded sector, in jobs in construction and retail, since these jobs are more likely to entail heavy labor, or to require contact with men outside the family. In short, an increase in oil production will change the economy of a country in a way that squeezes women out of the labor force. Therefore, Ross (2008) explained the following:

> The failure of women to join the nonagricultural labor force has profound social consequences: it leads to higher fertility rates, less education for girls, and less female influence within the family. It also has far-reaching political consequences: when fewer women work outside the home, they are less likely to exchange information and overcome collective action problems; less likely to mobilize politically, and to lobby for expanded rights; and less likely to gain representation in government. (p. 107)

Most controversially, Ross argued that, in the Middle East, it is the structural fact of oil extraction and changes in the economy that produce strong patriarchal cultures and lead to women's lower representation, not Islam.

Ross did find evidence for the "resource curse" of oil in a cross-national, over time analysis. Countries with greater oil extraction and mineral production have lower levels of women in their legislatures and in ministerial positions.

Ross's claims are contentious, and scholars have challenged him on a number of fronts (Charrad 2009; Kang 2009; Norris 2009; Tripp 2009). For example, Charrad (2009) argued that Ross does not adequately account for history in the Middle East, especially the kin-based patriarchal networks that wish to control women and that were present in most of the high oil-producing countries. Kang (2009) demonstrated that if gender quotas are included in his models, it significantly reduces the effect of oil on women's representation. Regardless, Ross challenges us to think about the ways in which larger structural forces might influence women's political participation and representation in sometimes surprising ways.

6

Explaining the Political Representation of Women—Politics

J ust as there is a supply side of women, created by cultural traditions and social structure, there is a demand side. Political parties may have different levels of demand for female candidates and voters may or may not support those female candidates. In this chapter, we discuss various political factors that affect the demand for women as candidates and legislators.

Recall the political recruitment process discussed at the beginning of Chapter 4. Explanations focusing on political demand are concerned with the latter portion of Figure 4.1. Once women decide that they would like to run for office, they must also pass the two barriers at the end of the process: They must be selected as candidates by gatekeepers and elected to office by voters.

The political recruitment process highlights that gatekeepers decide who among political aspirants gets to run as a candidate. Who are these gatekeepers? They are **political parties**. In most countries, the recruitment and selection of political elites occur entirely within political parties (Gallagher and Marsh 1988; Norris 1993). For an individual, man or woman, to run for political office, he or she must be selected and supported by a political party. Sometimes who ends up in public office is affected by who parties ask to run (Fox and Lawless 2010). As explained by Pesonen (1968), "The nomination stage eliminates 99.96% of all the eligible people; the voters choose from only .04%" (p. 348).

Understanding the role of political parties is therefore critical to understanding how women can gain access to politics. And to understand how political parties make their decisions about candidates, one must understand the electoral system under which they operate. A country's electoral system determines how the votes cast in an election get translated into seats won by parties and candidates (Reynolds, Reilly, and Ellis 2005:5). You can think of a country's electoral system as shaping the rules of the game played by various parties as they try to win political power. Electoral systems vary dramatically from country to country. So, although the rules of the game in one country may favor women, the rules of the game in another country may hinder women. Because political parties want to obtain political power, they need to put forward candidates who can win; therefore, they are substantially influenced by their electoral system.

And parties operate in political systems that may be more or less democratic. Democratic systems, with clear, well-detailed, and consistent rules, make it easier for parties and candidates to follow the rules of the game. Nondemocratic systems, in contrast, might be based on the charisma of an individual leader or held via military force, leading to intermittent elections, changing rules, and difficulties in determining how political power can actually be attained. Also, the meaning of *candidate* or *legislator* differs depending on whether a country is a democracy or not. In some countries, women run as candidates in corrupted elections, and in others they are placed into legislatures that act purely as rubber stamps for the policies of a president-for-life.

In this chapter, we begin our discussion of the political demand for women at the broadest level by distinguishing democratic from nondemocratic political systems. We then turn to electoral systems and to a detailed discussion of how political parties make a difference for women. Finally, we address an important new source of demand for women in some countries—gender quotas requiring that a certain percentage of candidates or legislators be women.

Democracy

One of the most basic ways to classify countries' political systems is to determine whether a country operates under a **democracy**, a **semidemocracy**, or an **authoritarian regime**. Whether countries are democratic or not can influence whether women can attain, and how they attain, political power. It also influences how effective women are once they have obtained some power. One can begin by asking whether, theoretically, women *should* do better in democratic systems or in nondemocratic systems. Because women's political equality is often justified on grounds of democratic justice, it may seem logical that women would be more adequately represented in countries where democratic processes are more firmly entrenched. And in democracies, the rules of the political game should be clear and consistent, helping women to see how they can work within the system to attain power. But in nondemocracies, in the absence of true elections, women can be placed into power, even when citizens do not support them.

Large, cross-national statistical studies have shown that more democratic countries have no more women in parliament than less democratic countries (Kenworthy and Malami 1999; Paxton and Kunovich 2003; Reynolds 1999; Stockemer 2009). In fact, some research has even found that women are less represented in democratic systems (Paxton 1997; Tripp and Kang 2008). One reason for this finding is that Communist countries, such as Cuba and China, have high numbers of women in politics due to the continued use of affirmative action strategies by communist party elites (Norris and Inglehart 2001). Authoritarian countries in Africa, such as Rwanda, often reserve large shares of parliamentary seats for women. These cases suggest that some nondemocracies are indeed placing women into power. Yet even excluding communist countries, level of democracy and the number of women in parliament appear to be unrelated.

But democracy is not static. Many countries experience changes—transitions to and away from democracy—that also have consequences for women. Countries that are newly democratizing are often have disappointing gender outcomes, including declines in women's political representation (Waylen 2007a). For example, of 31 countries sub-Saharan Africa countries that transitioned to multiparty democracies during the 1990s, many experienced initial declines in female political representation (Yoon 2001). This pattern has been the same for transitions from Eastern Europe to Latin America. And even if women are very active in pushing for democratic transition, as they were in Latin America, once democracy is established and political parties are formed, women may be pushed aside (Franceschet 2005; Friedman 1998; Htun 2003).

Yet in many countries, such declines and exclusions are only temporary, and women's political representation can bounce back (Fallon, Swiss, and Viterna 2012; Lindberg 2004; Yoon 2001). In fact, many scholars of African politics link democratization to the sweeping gains in women's political representation across the continent in the past two decades (Bauer and Britton 2006; Fallon 2008). And one study recently found that when looking over longer periods of time, expanding civil liberties help explain growth in women's representation (Paxton, Hughes, and Painter 2010). Civil liberties like free speech and a free press may be necessary for women's movements to be able to organize and pressure governments for women's greater inclusion. Overall, then, both democratization and women's increasing political representation can be understood as processes that unfold over time (Fallon et al. 2012).

It is also important to ask whether women's representation in ineffective national legislatures that serve under the thumb of a dictator should be treated the same as women's representation in an elected body that checks the power of the head of state. If the legislature has no real power and instead serves as a "rubber stamp," does women's political representation still matter?

In some ways, women's presence matters regardless of the political system. The position of parliamentarian is visible and carries prestige, having important symbolic effects that may improve women's status in society. Watershed moments, such as the election of the first woman to parliament, were likely just as significant to women in Syria or Kenya as to women in the United States or the United Kingdom. Furthermore, as women's numbers in parliament increase, perceptions of women may change (Norris 1993). When only a few women are present in politics, people perceive that women's political roles are exceptional. But as countries move beyond token membership, it changes perceptions about how a parliamentarian looks and acts.

Yet, in very real ways, women's representation in nondemocratic systems limits their ability to influence legislation or otherwise make an impact. Even if women successfully pass legislation in parliament, a powerful president may simply dispose of the parliamentary reforms. Unlike democratic systems with executive controls, the legislature in an authoritarian state likely has no way to dispute or oppose the president's intervention. For example, in Goetz and Hassim's (2003) study of Uganda and South Africa, women's ability to change the law (not just propose legislation) depended on whether they were in a democracy or a semidemocracy (see also Chapter 15). Of course, women too can override legislatures and otherwise act in nondemocratic ways (Indira Gandhi is one such example).

Because women in authoritarian or semidemocratic systems have limited power, some researchers talk about women in politics solely in democratic regimes (e.g., Matland 1998). Others, feeling that women's symbolic power is important to acknowledge, discuss nondemocracies (e.g., Paxton and Kunovich 2003). Regardless, it is always important to ask whether one is talking about a country where women were elected under fully democratic procedures and have full political power or a country where they have only partial or symbolic power.

Electoral Systems

All countries that hold elections have an electoral system that determines the rules of the game. Electoral systems can be complicated, but they are very important for understanding the political demand for women. Electoral systems are typically divided into three broad families: (1) **plurality–majority systems,** (2) **proportional representation (PR) systems,** and (3) **mixed systems** (Reynolds et al. 2005:28). Plurality–majority systems ask voters to vote for just a single person to represent them. Voters go to the polls, see a slate of candidates (one from every party), and choose just one person. The United States has a plurality–majority electoral system, as does the United Kingdom.

PR systems are different. PR systems typically ask voters to vote for a list of candidates to represent them. Voters go to the polls, see a slate of parties (each of which has a list of candidates), and choose a party to represent them. Voters therefore vote for parties rather than specific candidates. PR systems directly relate the number of seats won by a political party to the number of votes cast for that party. So, if a party wins 30% of the votes, the party receives 30% of the parliamentary seats. Legislators are selected by moving down the party's list, in order, until the party's 30% of seats are filled. A key feature of most PR systems is therefore that they have **multimember districts,** where multiple people represent the voters of a particular electoral district. Put another way, more than one candidate can be elected from a particular district in PR systems. In contrast, plurality–majority systems typically have single-member districts, where the voters in an electoral district have only one person representing them in the legislature.

Mixed systems combine both PR voting and plurality–majority voting, typically running side by side. Under a mixed electoral system, part of the legislature is elected through PR and part through plurality or majority. (Note: This discussion of electoral systems is general and simplified. There are variants on each of these three types of electoral systems that are more complicated than presented here. But 70% of the world's electoral systems fall into the three types as described in this section. *Electoral System Design: The New International IDEA Handbook,* www.idea.int/publications/esd/index.cfm, is an excellent source for more extensive detail on the types of electoral systems around the world.)

It is generally accepted that women do better in gaining political office under PR electoral systems (Kenworthy and Malami 1999; Matland 1998; Norris 1985, 2006; Paxton 1997; Paxton et al. 2010; Rule 1987). For example, Norris (2006:41) looked at more than 180 countries and found the following: "As a simple rule, women proved almost twice as likely to be elected under proportional than under majoritarian electoral systems." Richard Matland (2005:100) produced a table that succinctly demonstrates the difference in women's levels of representation between PR and plurality–majority systems in 24 Western democratic national legislatures. We provide an updated version of his table as Table 6.1.

Mixed systems are particularly interesting places to see the impact of electoral system. Countries with mixed electoral systems elect part of their legislature using plurality–majority methods and part using PR. In countries with both systems, women are elected at much higher rates under the PR system than the alternative plurality–majority system (Henig and Henig 2001; Norris 1993:313; Rule 1987). For example, after Germany's 1990 election, women won 28% of the PR seats and only 12% of the plurality–majority seats. In Australia's 1990 election, women won 25% of PR seats but only 7% of the plurality–majority districts. Similarly, in New Zealand's 2005 election, women won 43% of PR party-list seats but only 20% of the plurality–majority districts.

Why Are Proportional Representation Systems Good for Women?

Why do women do better under PR systems? The key reason is **district magnitude**—how many representatives an electoral district sends to the national legislature. Remember the difference between multimember and single-member electoral districts? Single-member districts have a district magnitude of 1—only one person represents an electoral district. Other countries have much higher district magnitudes, sending 2, 20, or 50 representatives to a legislature. Sometimes the electoral district is the entire country, and individual voters are therefore simultaneously represented by hundreds of legislators.

Higher district magnitudes are better for women because they can get on a party's ballot without displacing a male. In a single-member district, getting on the ballot is a zero-sum process. If one person gets on the ballot, it means another person is not on the ballot. In single-member districts, therefore, parties must make a choice between male and female candidates rather than placing both on the ticket. As relative newcomers to politics, when women compete head-to-head against men to be candidates, the women are disadvantaged. Men have been in politics longer, are entrenched in positions of power, and do not want to give up that power. Further, if women are seen

Table 6.1 Women's Representation in Plurality–Majority Versus Proportional Representation or Mixed Systems

	1945	1950	1960	1970	1980	1990	2000	2010
Plurality–Majority (single member)	3.1	2.1	2.5	2.2	3.4	8.2	19.3	20.9
PR or Mixed (multimember)	2.9	4.7	5.5	5.9	11.9	18.1	24.8	30.3

Plurality–Majority Systems:

Australia, Canada, France (1960–), Japan (–1990), New Zealand (–1990), United Kingdom, United States

PR and Mixed Systems:

Austria, Belgium, Denmark, Finland, France (–1950), Greece, Iceland, Ireland, Israel, Italy, Japan (2000–), Luxembourg, Netherlands, New Zealand (2000–), Norway, Portugal, Spain, Sweden, Switzerland, West Germany/Germany

Note: PR = proportional representation.

Sources: Data for 1945 through 1990 adapted from Matland (2005). Data for 2000 through 2010 collected by the authors.

as worse candidates than men, perhaps due to long-standing cultural traditions against women in politics, it is not in the party's interest to run women.
The party elite wants candidates who they believe can win.

In contrast, PR systems have multimember districts where voters vote for
parties with published lists of candidates. When a party needs to produce a
list of candidates, it is under pressure to **balance** its ticket across interest
groups in society: "Rather than having to look for a single candidate who
can appeal to a broad range of voters, party gatekeepers think in terms of
different candidates appealing to specific sub-sectors of voters" (Matland
2005:101). So a party in a PR system wants to have some women on its list
of candidates so it can attract female voters. As a female legislator from Asia
explained, "There has been recognition over the last 10 years (1988–98) that
it is essential for the credibility of any political party to be seen to be prese-
lecting and electing women to parliament" (Inter-Parliamentary Union [IPU]
2000:57).

Running multiple candidates in the same district also allows parties in PR
systems to appease internal party factions more easily. Like interest groups
in the general population, there are interest groups in parties. Balancing can
be used by party gatekeepers to resolve internal party disputes through compromise (Gallagher and Marsh 1988; Matland 2005). If women in the party
demand to be included as candidates, it is easier for a party operating in a
PR system to accommodate them. The cost is lower because men do not have
to step aside to accommodate women. Instead, men and women can run side
by side on the same party list.

Types of Proportional Representation Systems

But not all PR systems are created equal (for women). There are important differences across PR systems that can also make a big difference for
women getting nominated as candidates. First, even though PR systems
typically have multimember districts, there is variation in actual district
magnitude across countries. Countries may have a district magnitude of 3,
or it may be 20 or higher. The higher the district magnitude, the better for
women (Rule 1987, 1994).

Why? Remember that in PR systems parties get a share of seats in the
legislature based on how many votes they got. Legislators are selected by
moving down the party's list in order. So where are women on the party's
list? Are they in a **safe position**, guaranteed to win a seat in the legislature
based on the party's expected share of the vote? Or are they in a risky list
position or even a hopeless list position? Parties can certainly present the
appearance of balance between the genders but have men at the top of the

list and women at the bottom (Kunovich 2003). Indeed, the party leaders (typically male) always hold the top spots on party lists. When women are not at the top of the list, parties have to go further down their list (by winning a higher percentage of the vote) for the women to become legislators. Wilma Rule (1994) put some hard numbers on what is needed: "It is usually essential that the number of representatives per district be five or more for the election of women in meaningful numbers. Ten or fifteen members would enhance greatly the number of women candidates elected" (p. 18).

A similar way for women to benefit is when parties have high party magnitude. Like district magnitude, party magnitude is the number of seats a party tends to win in an electoral district. Parties in systems with high party magnitude go farther down their lists and are therefore likely to pick up more women. Indeed, party magnitude is likely more important than district magnitude because it directly, rather than indirectly, determines how far down a list a party has to go (Matland 1993).

Another important difference is between **closed party lists** and **open party lists**. Under a closed list PR system, parties produce an ordered list of candidates that cannot be changed by voters. In open list systems, voters can influence the order of the candidates. Whether open or closed lists are better for women is disputable. It depends who is more likely to advance women on lists—party gatekeepers or voters (Matland 2005). In closed list systems, it is necessary to convince party gatekeepers to put women in winnable list positions. In open list systems, it is necessary to convince voters not to move men ahead of women on the party's suggested list.

Of course, why couldn't women use open lists to promote women on the list to winnable seats? If women can organize, this is certainly a possibility. But Richard Matland (2005) told an interesting story of how such a strategy ultimately backfired in Norway:

> Norway has an open-list PR in local elections at the municipality level. In the early 1970s, women were able to organize a remarkably effective campaign to promote women. In the 1971 local elections women's representation in several large Norwegian cities rose from being approximately 15–20 per cent of the city council to majorities on the council. This "women's coup" became a source of great surprise and pride at women's abilities to take advantage of the electoral structure. It should be noted, however, that there was a reaction in the following election, when many men who felt that striking male candidates simply because they were men was unfair, went out of their way to strike women candidates. In the following local election and in every local election since, the number of women elected in local elections in Norway has probably been less than it would have been had there been no personal vote. (p. 99)

Are the Same Systems and Rules Good for All Women?

Political parties creating lists face pressure to appeal to all sorts of voter constituencies. And that means including not only women but minority groups as well. Therefore, PR-list systems can also benefit minority women. Many of the countries in which minority women are represented at levels nearing or exceeding their population share—for example, Burundi, Costa Rica, the Netherlands, and Norway—have PR-list systems (Hughes forthcoming). After New Zealand transferred to their mixed system, the representation of Asians, Pacific Islanders, and Maori increased from 8% to 17%. Furthermore, even though 57% of the seats were elected by plurality–majority (including seven reserved seats for Maori) in the 2005 election, 56% of minority men and 70% of minority women in the legislature were elected from the PR portion of the electoral system. In her opening statement to the New Zealand House of Representatives, Asian female representative Pansy Wong (1997) attributed her election to the new mixed system, which enabled her to capitalize on support from "Chinese, Korean, and other ethnic communities throughout the country."

Certainly, electoral systems don't explain everything. There have been exceptional cases where White, rural constituencies elected minority women under the plurality–majority system. In 1999, for example, one such district in New Zealand elected the world's first **transsexual** parliamentarian, Georgina Beyer (2005). Beyer is Maori minority, who lived as a sex worker before undergoing a full sex change in 1984. Before being elected to parliament, Beyer worked as an actress, a broadcaster, an educator, an author, a justice of the peace, and a mayor. A documentary of her life, *Georgie Girl*, was released internationally in 2002. (See Chapter 9 for more on sexual minorities in politics.)

It is also important to remember that not all minority groups are the same, nor are the countries in which they live. PR electoral systems are not an "institutional panacea" for problems of underrepresentation (Moser and Holmsten 2008:25). Substantially sized, geographically concentrated minority groups can benefit from plurality–majority systems, provided that district boundaries are not drawn in ways that carve up the neighborhoods where minorities live. And minority women are increasingly gaining representation under these circumstances. For example, the United Kingdom—which uses a plurality–majority system—elected South Asian women to parliament for the first time in 2010 (118 years after the first South Asian man was elected). The three women, also the first Muslim women to serve in the British parliament, all represent districts with large ethnic minority and Muslim populations.

Similarly, in the United States, 27% of the women elected to Congress in 2012 were women of color, overwhelmingly elected in districts in which minority groups hold a numerical majority, called **majority–minority districts**. These minority congresswomen were elected in districts averaging 29% White, less than half the share of Whites in a typical congressional district (Center for American Women and Politics [CAWP] 2012b; U.S. Census Bureau 2010).

Research on women's political representation in less economically developed countries has also raised the question of whether PR-list systems are really the best electoral system for *all* women. Although global studies consistently find PR-list systems clearly enhance women's representation, studies focusing on less economically developed countries do not find the same effects (Hughes 2009a; Matland 1998). Countries such as Tanzania and Uganda, for example, have around 35% women in their parliaments despite using plurality–majority systems.

Characteristics of Political Parties

Parties play a critical gatekeeping role in political systems and are a critical mediator between women and political power (Caul 1999; Kunovich 2003; Kunovich and Paxton 2005; Sanbonmatsu 2002a). Political parties make decisions about who to recruit, which candidates to field, and how much support to give them (e.g., through placement on party lists). As succinctly explained by a female legislator from Central America, "In order for women to be elected to Parliament, the political parties have the responsibility of trusting in women, encouraging them, and putting them forward in constituencies where they can be certain of electoral success" (IPU 2000:97).

So how do political parties go about picking candidates? Even in the United States, which uses a primary system—giving voters some input on who runs for office—women's underrepresentation in politics has been linked to the parties lesser likelihood of asking women to run (Fox and Lawless 2010). In most other countries, candidate selection is not open for public inspection and participation. Instead, candidate selection is the purview of a small set of party elites (Gallagher and Marsh 1988:2). For example, both the Conservative and Liberal Democratic parties in Britain generate a list of centrally approved candidates that local constituency members use in selecting candidates (BBC News 2001).

Generally, parties of all stripes look for certain features in their political candidates. First, parties want to field candidates who show a proven track record of winning. Thus, **incumbents** are much more attractive than challengers, evidenced by an extremely high rate of incumbent renomination (Matland 2005). Other experience with the party—a history of activism and party participation—is also important, especially for new candidates. Yet lacking high visibility in the party may be overlooked if a candidate has been highly visible in his or her community as a leader of a business or other organization. Because incumbents and community leaders are more often men, women may be less attractive to political parties as potential candidates (Matland 2005).

Political parties may all have the same goal—to attain political power. But parties vary substantially in the number of women they send to parliament (Caul 1999). Consider Table 6.2, which shows the percentage of female legislators in 1975, 1985, 1995, and 2005 by party for five different countries. Note that these are differences across parties within the same electoral system.

Why do some political parties do better than others in promoting women? The first explanation is the political ideology of the party itself—is it a party with a Left agenda, or is it more to the right of the political spectrum? Parties that are further left in their political leanings tend to espouse egalitarian ideals and historically were more likely to put forward female candidates (Caul 1999). Research on parties supports the idea that Left parties do better in promoting women. For example, Richard Matland (1993) found that it was leftist parties that began sending women to parliament in Norway in the 1980s. Similarly, in a study of 68 political parties across 12 countries, Miki Caul (1999) found that parties on the left sent more women to parliament.

Yet women have also risen to power in Right-leaning parties in recent years. Angela Merkel, who topped *Forbes*' 2012 list of the world's most powerful women, rose to the chancellorship of Germany in 2005 as leader of the Right-leaning Christian Democratic Union. At the same time in some Latin American countries, women's representation in Right-leaning parties began exceeding women's numbers in other parties. Mala Htun (2005:115) suggested that women's party activism played an important role in the transition, arguing that "women's wings [of right-wing parties] reoriented themselves to serve not as support staff but as advocates of female leaders." For example, between 1999 and 2003, the women's wing of Mexico's right-wing National Action Party (PAN) effectively lobbied party leaders to run female candidates—resulting in higher levels of women's representation in the party than in Mexico's two other major parties (Htun 2005).

Not all parties fit easily on a Left–Right spectrum. Some are organized to promote the representation of ethnic or religious minority groups. In an analysis of 260 political parties in 21 countries, Holmsten, Moser, and Slosar (2010) found that 63% of ethnic parties excluded women altogether—more than twice the share of nonethnic parties that did so. But they also found that

Table 6.2   Female Legislators by Political Party, 1975–2005

Country and Party	Percentage of Female Legislators			
	1975	*1985*	*1995*	*2005*
Belgium				
Christian People's (CVP)	12	18	24	33
Socialist (Flemish) (BSP)	3	6	10	35
Liberty (Flemish) (PVV)	0	5	0	36
People's Union (VU)	9	6	20	—
Ecology (Flemish) (AGA)	—	50	0	—
Nationalist (Flemish) (VB)	—	—	9	17
Germany				
Social Democratic (SPD)	5	10	34	36
Christian Democratic/Social Union (CDU/CSU)	6	7	14	20
Free Democratic (FDP)	10	9	19	23
Greens (G)	—	20	59	57
Norway				
Socialist People's (SV)	19	50	31	53
Labour Party (DNA)	19	42	49	48
Center Party (SP)	14	17	44	27
Christian People's (KRF)	5	25	38	45
Liberals (V)	0	—	0	40
Conservatives (H)	17	30	29	22
Progress (FRP)	0	0	10	16
UK				
Labour (LAB)	5	5	14	28
Liberal/Liberal Democrats (LIB/SDL)	0	0	10	16
Conservatives (CON)	3	3	6	8
USA				
Democrats (DEM)	6	5	16	20
Republicans (REP)	2	6	8	10

Sources: Adapted from Caul (1999). Data for 1995 through 2005 collected by the authors.

electoral systems made a difference. In plurality–majority systems, religious ethnic parties were not worse for women, and women actually performed better in ethnic parties than in nonethnic parties. In list-PR systems, alternatively, women's representation in ethnic parties is low, and religious ethnic parties were the worst offenders. Overall, if ethnic minority women are being elected in PR systems, it appears not to be happening within ethnic parties.

Besides party ideology, another important consideration across parties is the composition of their leadership. The attitudes and values of candidate selectors (typically the party elite) matter for who is selected. So, if women are present in the party elite, they may advocate for a greater number of female candidates (Caul 1999; Kunovich and Paxton 2005). As a female legislator from Western Europe stated, "It was the women in the party who encouraged me to get more deeply involved and to register on a list for the elections" (IPU 2000:75). And women may be better able to see what must be done to recruit female candidates in the first place. In Australia, a current female party leader made it possible for a former female party leader to return to politics (and ultimately be elected) by promising to make all the necessary flexible arrangements so that she could juggle the demands of a new baby (Commonwealth Secretariat 1999:20).

It is not only female party elites who make a difference. Miki Caul (1999) found that women in midlevel positions in parties (as delegates to national conferences and women working as local activists) can help create higher levels of female office holders. They do this partly by influencing party rules targeting certain percentages of women as candidates. Women in party leadership positions may also advocate the adoption of quotas for women (Caul 2001). Overall, 78% of women responding to an IPU (2000) survey believed that the presence of women had brought about a change in their party's priorities.

Like entire countries, parties can vary in the extent to which they have clear, consistent, and understandable rules. When candidate selection is transparent and institutionalized, anyone can understand what he or she needs to do to be selected as a candidate. In contrast, if selection rules and processes are unclear, the selection of candidates may seem capricious and based on random criteria. Political outsiders, such as women, should have an easier time breaking in when party rules are clear and transparent (Czudnowski 1975). Indeed, Miki Caul, in her work on 68 parties in 12 democracies, found that parties with clear rules are more likely to elect women to office.

Finally, it is important to note that not all countries have strong party systems. Tens or even hundreds of parties may contest seats in an election, limiting the power and visibility of any single organization. In some countries, disaffection with political parties may even mean that women distance themselves from parties or run as independents. Such has been the case in Afghanistan, for example, where support for political parties is weak. In the last round of elections, female members of parliament (MPs) sometimes ran as independents despite being party members. And in some cases, female MPs were even dishonest about their party alignment, reporting themselves as independents even though they were, in fact, running on party tickets (Lough 2012).

Women's Parties

Some countries have women's parties that run only female candidates. Throughout history, women feeling marginalized by existing political parties have formed their own parties. For example, in the United Kingdom in 1917, when Christabel and Emmeline Pankhurst dissolved the Women's Social and Political Union (WSPU) (see Chapter 2), they formed the Women's Party. The party focused on enlisting women for the war effort, and in the 1918 election, Christabel ran for office but was unsuccessful, and the party dissolved in 1919. Women-only party lists have existed in Israel since 1918, when the Women's Society was elected to the first Representative Assembly (Simmons Levin 1999).

Women's parties have formed in a number of countries since the 1990s, including *Josei-tō*, a feminist party in Japan, and the Hellenic Women's Party in Greece. In 1996, the Northern Ireland Women's Coalition was founded, strongly opposed to violence in the region. Although two women from the party were represented in the Northern Ireland Assembly in 1998 and 2001, both women lost their seats in 2003.

Women's parties have also been formed in many post-Communist countries, including Armenia, Belarus, Bulgaria, Georgia, Kyrgyzstan, Lithuania, Moldova, Russia, and Ukraine. But though these parties may all seek to represent women, they are often quite different, attracting different kinds of supporters. For example, the Women of Russia, founded by elites with links to the past Soviet Bureaucracy, is more traditional in its ideology, whereas the Shamiram Women's Party in Armenia was more successful attracting younger, educated women and received support from feminists (Ishiyama 2003).

Although these parties may have different ideologies, they often share at least one thing—limited electoral success (Moser and Holmsten 2008). Several women's parties have failed to ever win any seats in parliament, including the Democratic Women's Union in Bulgaria, the Women's Party of Georgia, and the Association of Women in Moldova. Moser (2003) argued that the very existence of a women's party can indicate that the women's movement is weak, unable to influence major parties to address women's issues. Further, the presence of women's parties can prevent other parties from believing they can effectively solicit the female vote, leading them not to field female candidates (Moser 2003). So even if a women's party is successful in one election, if it ever fails to win seats in parliament, women's overall representation may decline dramatically. This was the case with the Women of Russia, which obtained 23 seats in 1993 but only 3 seats in 1995 (Ishiyama 2003). Women's overall representation in the legislature simultaneously dropped from 13% to 10%. A similar drop occurred with the Shamiram Women's Party in Armenia, which received 16.9% of the vote in 1995 but failed to claim a single seat in 1999 (Ishiyama 2003). The overall representation of women in parliament in Armenia thus fell from 6% to 3%.

Yet women's parties have had some successes. In Lithuania, the formation of a woman's party encouraged other parties to expand women's participation in the party elite (Krupavičius and Matonytė 2003). In addition, female Prime Minister Kazimiera Prunskiene argued that it was the formation of the women's party and the ensuing pressure that led to the adoption of gender quotas, something that would have been unthinkable just years before. However, Prunskiene is not impartial: She was instrumental in the formation of the party after being pushed out of her own party over her foreign policy stance on dealing with Russia (Krupavičius and Matonytė 2003). And overall, Matland and Montgomery (2003) argued that where women's parties have arisen in the post-Communist world they have been more hurtful to women's representation than helpful.

Although many women's parties have dissolved, for example, in Australia and Iceland, other countries are forming new women's parties. For example, in 2003, women formed the first all-woman party in India, called the Womanist Party of India, or WPI. The party has called for an increase in **reserved seats** for women to 50%, inclusion of women's names in land ownership deeds, and in 2011 unsuccessfully fought to repeal a law that bans women from working after 9:30 p.m. in bars, restaurants, and other establishments unless state exemptions are granted (*The Telegraph* 2004; Thomas 2011). And although Feminist Initiative (F!), a new feminist women's party, has failed to win a single parliamentary seat, in 2010 party members did win four seats on the city council in Simrishamn, home of the F!'s first party spokesperson.

From Candidate to Legislator

Much of the discussion so far has focused on how women move from being aspirants to candidates. But what happens to those female candidates? Are they always elected? No.

Table 6.3 shows that countries send different percentages of their female candidates to political office (Kunovich and Paxton 2005). The table begins by recording the percentage of female candidates in 76 countries, then the percentage of female members of the national legislature, and finally the ratio of the two. Values of one for the ratio indicate a one-to-one relationship between percentage of candidates and percentage of female representatives. Looking at Table 6.3, one can see that the yield of female representatives ranges from values of considerably less than 1 (e.g., 0.3 in Morocco) to values greater than 1 (e.g., 1.22 in the Netherlands). Thus, though the "return" on female candidates is very low in Morocco, 3% female elected officials for every 10% female candidates, the return is greater than expected in the Netherlands. Sheri Kunovich and Pamela Paxton (2005) worked with these numbers and showed that the overall return on female candidates is lower than one-to-one. Across all of the countries, a 1% increase in the number of female candidates results in only a 0.67% increase in female legislators.

Or consider it another way. With the exception of four countries (the Netherlands, Mexico, Grenada, and Seychelles), the percentage of women in the national legislature is never more than 5% higher than the percentage of female candidates. On the other hand, there are numerous examples where the percentage of women in the legislature is substantially lower than the percentage of female candidates. For example, in Iceland, women are 50% of candidates and 25% of representatives.

What determines whether female candidates actually get elected? Obviously, voters are important. Especially in countries with a very negative culture against women in politics, voters may simply not vote for female candidates. But here again political parties play a large role. Political parties are the major source of support for candidates in their bid for public office. Parties in PR systems can support candidates by placing them in favorable list positions whereas parties in plurality–majority systems can improve a candidate's chances of election by running them in winnable districts and by providing additional financial and institutional resources for campaigning. For example, one recent study based in the United Kingdom found that in the 2005 election, women's lower election rates from the Conservative Party compared to the Labour Party could be explained, in part, by the Conservative Party's greater likelihood of running women in unwinnable districts, places where the party received few votes in prior elections (Ryan, Haslam, and Kulich 2010).

Given that female party elites influence how many women appear as candidates, those same elites should also positively affect the ratio of representatives to candidates. Female party elites may try to support female candidates

Table 6.3 Percentage of Female Candidates and Women in National Legislatures

	Percentage of Female:				Percentage of Female:		
	Candidates	Parliament	Ratio		Candidates	Parliament	Ratio
	Western Industrialized				**Asia**		
Australia	27.9	15.5	0.55	Cambodia	4.8	5.8	1.21
Austria	39.3	26.8	0.68	India	4.2	7.2	1.71
Canada	22.1	18.0	0.81	Japan	7.3	4.6	1.59
France	19.2	6.4	0.33	Kiribati	1.5	0.0	0
Germany	29.5	26.2	0.88	North Korea	20.1	20.1	1
Ireland	18.9	13.9	0.74	South Korea	2.2	3.0	1.36
Italy	12.7	11.1	0.87	Laos	10.4	9.4	0.9
Monaco	12.0	5.6	0.47	Mongolia	8.6	7.9	0.92
Netherlands	25.5	31.3	1.22	Nepal	6.0	3.4	0.57
Spain	32.5	24.6	0.76	Philippines	8.5	10.8	1.27
Switzerland	34.8	21.0	0.60	Samoa	4.9	4.1	0.84
United Kingdom	19.4	9.5	0.49	Singapore	3.2	2.5	0.78
				Sri Lanka	2.7	5.3	1.96
				Vietnam	30.3	26.0	0.86

(Continued)

(Continued)

	Percentage of Female:				*Percentage of Female:*		
	Candidates	*Parliament*	*Ratio*		*Candidates*	*Parliament*	*Ratio*
	Scandinavia				**Central and South America**		
Denmark	30.0	33.0	1.1	Argentina	30.0	25.3	0.84
Iceland	50.4	25.4	0.5	Bolivia	16.6	6.9	0.42
Sweden	43.6	40.4	0.92	Brazil	5.7	6.6	1.16
	Eastern Europe and Central Asia			Chile	11.5	7.5	0.65
Armenia	2.5	6.3	2.52	Colombia	8.5	11.7	1.38
Czech Republic	20.2	15.0	0.74	Costa Rica	22.6	15.8	0.7
Georgia	26.8	6.8	0.25	Cuba	22.8	22.8	1
Kazakhstan	11.2	13.4	1.2	Ecuador	10.4	3.7	0.36
Latvia	23.0	9.0	0.39	Grenada	9.8	20.0	2.04
Lithuania	20.6	17.5	0.85	Guyana	16.7	20.0	1.2
Moldova	11.3	4.8	0.42	Jamaica	9.3	11.7	1.26
Poland	13.1	13.0	0.99	Mexico	8.9	14.2	1.6
Romania	11.1	7.0	0.63	Nicaragua	26.4	10.8	0.41
Slovakia	14.6	14.7	1.01				

	Percentage of Female:		
	Candidates	Parliament	Ratio
Slovenia	22.9	7.8	0.34
Tajikistan	5.1	2.8	0.55
Ukraine	9.3	3.8	0.41
Middle East and Northern Africa			
Algeria	2.4	6.6	2.75
Cyprus	9.9	5.4	0.55
Egypt	2.0	2.0	1
Iran	10.0	4.0	0.4
Jordan	0.6	1.3	2.17
Morocco	2.0	0.6	0.3
Tunisia	6.0	6.7	1.12
Yemen	0.8	0.7	0.88

	Percentage of Female:		
	Candidates	Parliament	Ratio
Africa			
Benin	3.3	7.2	2.18
Burkina Faso	3.6	3.7	1.03
Kenya	2.5	3.0	1.2
Malawi	7.2	5.6	0.78
Mali	1.9	2.3	1.21
Namibia	13.8	18.1	1.31
Sao Tome & Principe	9.1	7.3	0.8
Seychelles	21.2	27.3	1.29
South Africa	41.2	25.0	0.61
Zimbabwe	12.6	14.7	1.17

Source: From Kunovich, S., and Paxton, P., "Pathways to power: The role of political parties in women's national political representation," in *The American Journal of Sociology, 111*(2), © 2005. Reprinted with permission of the University of Chicago Press.

in their bids for election by influencing list placement or party contributions to candidate war chests. Consider this West African legislators comment: "Women asked me to stand in the legislative elections and they supported my candidacy in the one-party state system" (IPU 2000:82).

Sheri Kunovich and Pamela Paxton (2005) found that female party elites indeed influence the number of women who run on the party ticket. But the situation is complicated by electoral system. Women's position in party elites translates into gains for women as candidates only under PR systems. In contrast, women's position in party elites increases the likelihood that female candidates will be elected only in plurality–majority systems. This finding makes sense if you consider the difference between PR and plurality–majority systems. Remember that candidate selectors in PR systems feel pressure to balance their party's list between men and women. Thus, it should be relatively easy for female party elites in PR systems to convince the party to field female candidates. But those female elites may be less successful in getting them placed in safe positions on lists. Consider the complaint of a West African legislator: "Women actively participate in the same way as men, but they don't manage to move upwards, always holding subordinated positions in political organizations and on electoral lists" (IPU 2000:60).

Contrast this to the situation of female leaders in plurality–majority systems. Once the battle for who will be a candidate is over, each party has the incentive to fully support its candidate, whether male or female. And female party leaders are in a position to provide additional support to their female candidates in the form of campaign money or better institutional resources for campaigning. In the United States, organizations such as EMILY's List raise money and provide additional training and institutional support for female candidates in their bid for office (see Chapter 10). Female party leaders can tap into these external resources to help women gain a legislative seat once they are nominated as a candidate.

Ultimately, therefore, we see that female elites can help women move from aspirant to candidate in PR systems but not in plurality–majority systems. But female elites can help women move from candidate to legislator in plurality–majority systems and not PR systems.

As for the voters, Kunovich and Paxton (2005) found that once the decisions made by party elites were accounted for, a country's culture did not matter for how many women were elected. This suggests that parties may be overly sensitive to perceived hostility to women as candidates, when in fact women are acceptable as candidates to voters all over the world.

Quotas

I'd give up my seat for you if it wasn't for the fact that I'm sitting in it myself.

—Groucho Marx (quoted in Baldez 2004:231)

On January 4, 2004, the grand council in Afghanistan adopted a new constitution to govern the war-ridden nation. The new constitution included **gender quotas** for both the upper and lower houses of the country's future parliament. Specifically, at least 2 women must be elected to the lower house from each province, guaranteeing a minimum of 65 women. Among the 10 seats set aside for Kuchis, a disadvantaged nomadic people in Afghanistan, 3 are reserved for women, bringing the quota to 27%. For the upper house, the president appoints one third of the members, and 50% of these appointees must be women, assuring women 17 of the 102 seats. But how did Afghanistan, a country formerly governed by one of the most repressive regimes toward women in modern history—the Taliban—adopt provisions that benefit women's parliamentary representation? To answer that question, one must first understand the broader context in which Afghanistan chose to adopt quotas.

Affirmative action strategies to increase women's representation have been around for decades. In the 1950s, Eva Peron lobbied for the use of quotas by the Peronist Party in Argentina, resulting in the election of 15% women to the national Chamber of Deputies in 1952 and 22% in 1955 (Jones 1998). At the time, Argentina had the fourth highest percentage of women in parliament, trailing only the Communist systems of East Germany, the Soviet Union, and Mongolia (Jones 1998). Although Communist countries often do not have explicit quota systems, many researchers note that they operate under informal quota systems, whereby communist party leaders select women to fill seats, guaranteeing their inclusion (Matland and Montgomery 2003; Siemienska 2004). Several Asian countries have a history of quotas. Taiwan, for example, reserved roughly 10% of seats for women beginning in 1953 (Chou and Clark 1994). Upon independence in 1971, Bangladesh reserved 15 of 315 seats in its parliament for women, who were chosen by the 300 parliamentarians elected to the general seats (Chowdhury 2002). And in 1978, a presidential proclamation doubled this number, increasing women's representation to 9.9%. During the 1970s, a small number of political parties in Western industrialized countries also adopted quotas. Reserved seats also appeared in North Africa during the 1970s: in Egypt in 1979, a presidential decree was passed reserving a seat in 30 districts for women, establishing a quota of 8.3% (Abou-Zeid 2003).

Since the 1990s, however, the pace of quota adoption has increased dramatically. National-level quotas spread throughout Latin America after 1990, and after 1995, many African countries followed suit with reserved seats and party-level quotas (Ballington 2004; Tripp 2003). During the 1990s, 22 countries adopted national electoral law quotas that required between 20% and 50% of candidates for legislative office to be women (Baldez 2004). In other countries, scores of political parties voluntarily adopted gender quotas to attract female candidates or voters. In some predominantly Muslim African countries, "the women's quota became part of an effort to contain the growing influence of Islamists" (Tripp 2003:1). Moving into the 21st century, governments and political parties in many additional countries adopted gender quotas, including Australia, Bosnia and Herzegovina, Burkina Faso, Iraq, Niger, and Tanzania, to name a few. In Southeast Asia, the people even started speaking of a sweeping "quota fever" (International Institute for Democracy and Electoral Assistance [IDEA] 2012a). By the end of 2005, more than 100 countries had adopted some form of gender quota. And although a few countries and parties have since backed off quotas, others have adopted them (e.g., Uruguay and Tunisia) or are debating new policies.

At a basic level, gender quotas simply require that women must make up a certain percentage of a candidate list, a parliamentary assembly, a committee, or a government (Dahlerup 2002). As affirmative action policies, gender quotas are designed to help women overcome obstacles to their election such as less political experience, cultural stereotypes, or incumbency. Most governments and political parties adopting quotas are attempting to move beyond token representation to reach at least a critical minority of 20%, 30%, or 40% women in parliament (International IDEA 2012a). And as noted in Chapter 3, many of the largest absolute and relative jumps in the history of women's political representation followed the implementation of gender quotas, allowing countries to move from making slow or incremental gains to running on the "fast track" (Dahlerup 2002; Dahlerup and Freidenvall 2005). Indeed, Aili Mari Tripp and Alice Kang (2008) found that quotas were a very powerful predictor of women's political representation across 149 countries. Quotas are thus pervasive and can also be a game changer for women.

Yet gender quotas exhibit a great deal of variation in how they are developed, implemented, and regulated and in how successfully they increase women's representation. As Mona Krook (2003) accurately stated, "Not all quotas are created equal" (p. 1). Some quotas have proved wholly ineffective in increasing women's representation whereas others have produced substantial gains. In some cases, the same quota legislation has produced completely different outcomes in societies operating under different electoral systems (Krook 2009; Schmidt and Saunders 2004). Furthermore, one has to recognize that quotas raise serious questions about women's representation, and, in some cases, they meet strong resistance.

What Kinds of Quotas Are There and Which Are Better?

Although there are countless ways to classify the vast array of quota regulations, we focus here on three dimensions that are most important for determining how effectively quotas improve the status of women:

1. The threshold required or targeted for representation

2. Whether they are candidate, political party, or reserved seat quotas

3. Which groups are regulated

Threshold for Representation

One clear and simple difference between quotas is the level at which representation is required. Jordan, for example, has a quota of 10%, whereas Spain has set the bar at 40% women in parliament. Many countries choose a number around 30%. One reason for the popularity of this threshold is that the United Nations identified 30% as the level of representation necessary for women to affect the operation and output of parliamentary bodies.

Quota thresholds have increased in some countries over time. For example, the Socialist Party of Chile initially introduced a 20% quota, raising it to 30% for the 1997 and 1998 elections and again changing it in 1999 to a 40% to 60% gender-neutral quota. Some threshold increases are also built into quota legislation. For example, in 1997, a 20% quota was introduced in Ecuador for the Chamber of Deputies, and the percentage increased with each subsequent election until 50% has now been reached.

Although 50% was perhaps an unthinkable mandate just a short time ago, France passed the first such **parity quota** in 2000, and countries like Belgium, Costa Rica, and Tunisia have since followed suit (Baudino 2003; Bird 2003; Murray 2010; Murray, Krook, and Opello 2011; Opello 2004). The increasing popularity of 50% measures has occurred in part because of "50/50" campaigns in which women's organizations and activists have pressed for full gender equality in women's political representation (Bauer 2008; see Chapter 7). But parity laws have often not generated levels of women's representation anywhere close to their stated goals. Until the 2012 elections, women's share of seats in France's National Assembly was even short of the world average. This gap between stated goals and outcomes has been quantified by quota research. For example, Paxton and colleagues (2010) found that for every 1% increase in a quota threshold, women's representation increases by only 0.1%, on average.

The pressure to adopt quotas can also occasionally lead countries to adopt quotas that simply codify levels of representation that were already in place. For example, in China, women's parliamentary representation has remained at a steady 21% to 22% since 1975. When the country adopted a gender quota in 2007, it chose a threshold of 22%, ultimately producing no increase in women's representation. For Chinese women, the new quota did not offer much of a "fast track" to power.

Overall, however, thresholds do matter in the vast majority of cases. Thresholds are particularly important when quotas are implemented in ways to ensure their effectiveness (Schwindt-Bayer 2009). But how quota implementation actually works is also strongly effected on the type of quota countries use. Next, we explore some of these factors as we introduce the three main types of quotas.

Candidate Quotas, Political Party, and Reserved Seat Quotas

The International Institute for Democracy and Electoral Assistance (IDEA) in Stockholm, Sweden, is one of the key sources of data and research on gender quotas. International IDEA classifies quotas into three main types: (1) candidate, (2) reserved seats, and (3) political party (see also Krook 2009). The most common form—**candidate quotas** (also called legal quotas or legislative quotas)—requires all political parties in a country to field a certain percentage of female candidates. In 1990, Argentina became the first country in the world to adopt a candidate quota, called the *Ley de Cupos* or "Law of Quotas" (Bonder and Nari 1995; Gray 2003; Jones 1998). Following the implementation of the Ley de Cupos, the percentage of women in the Chamber of Deputies jumped from 4% to 21%. After this success, the vast majority of Argentina's provinces implemented similar quota regulations for provincial and municipal elections (Jones 1998). Countries throughout Latin America followed the Argentinean example and established candidate quotas, including Bolivia, Brazil, Colombia, Costa Rica, the Dominican Republic, Ecuador, Guyana, Honduras, Mexico, Panama, Paraguay, Peru, and most recently Uruguay (International IDEA 2012b; Schmidt and Saunders 2004; Squires 2004).

Table 6.4 reports all countries that have this type of quota, along with the percentage of women in parliament in the country as of December 2011.

Table 6.4 Legislative Candidate Quotas, 2011

Country	Required Percentage of Women, Lower House or Unicameral	Percentage of Women
Albania	30% of party electoral lists; one of top three spots on list must be of different sex	15.7%
Angola	30% of party electoral lists	38.2%
Argentina	30% of party electoral lists; at least one woman for every two men	37.4%
Armenia	20% of party electoral lists and on at least every 10th position; applies to 69% of seats	8.4%
Belgium	50% of party electoral lists	38.0%
Bolivia	33% of party electoral lists; at least one woman out of every three candidates; applies to 43% of seats	25.4%
Bosnia and Herzegovina	33% of party electoral lists; a woman must be one of top two candidates on list; two among first five candidates; and three among top eight	21.4%
Brazil	30% of party electoral lists	8.6%
Burkina Faso	30% of party electoral lists	15.3%
Colombia	30% of party lists of five or more	12.1%
Costa Rica[1]	40% of electable positions on party lists; 50% and every other position starting in 2014	38.6%
Dominican Republic	33% of seats	20.8%
East Timor	One out of every four candidates on electoral lists	32.3%
Ecuador	50% of party electoral lists and every other position	32.3%

(Continued)

163

(Continued)

Country	Required Percentage of Women, Lower House or Unicameral	Percentage of Women
Egypt	Parties must nominate at least one woman as part of district candidate lists	2.2%
France	50% of candidates; parties and groups cannot present numbers of candidates that differ by any more than 2%	18.9%
Guyana	33% on party electoral lists	31.3%
Haiti[1]	30% in all elected and appointed positions	—
Honduras	30% on party electoral lists	19.5%
Indonesia	At least one in every three candidates on party electoral lists	18.2%
Iraq	No fewer than one out of the first three candidates; no fewer than two of the first six candidates on the list must be a woman and so forth	25.2%
Ireland[1]	30% of female candidates in next elections	15.1%
Kyrgyzstan	30% on party electoral lists	23.3%
Macedonia	One out of every three positions on party electoral lists	30.9%
Mauritania	30% to 50%; where three candidates are to be elected, the lists must include at least one female candidate placed first or second; otherwise, each group of four candidates on the list must include two women	22.1%
Mexico	30% of candidates, excluding 300 districts that use primaries	26.2%
Nepal	At least 33% for entire assembly; 50% on party electoral lists for seats allocated under PR	33.2%
North Korea	20% of candidates	15.6%

Country	Required Percentage of Women, Lower House or Unicameral	Percentage of Women
Panama	30% for party primary elections	8.5%
Paraguay	20% and at least every fifth place on party electoral lists	12.5%
Peru	30% of candidates	21.5%
Poland	35% of party electoral lists	23.7%
Portugal	33% of party electoral lists, except small towns and municipalities	28.7%
Senegal[1]	50% of party electoral lists and every other position, starting in 2012	—
Serbia	30% of party electoral lists	22.0%
Slovenia	35% of party electoral lists	32.2%
South Korea	50% of party electoral lists, 30% of candidates for single-member districts	14.7%
Spain	40% of party electoral lists	36.0%
Tunisia	50% of party electoral lists and every other position	26.7
Uruguay[1]	Every third position for first 15 places or entire list unless only two positions, and then one of two, starting in 2014	—
Uzbekistan	30% of candidates	22.0%
Average Percentage of Women With No Quotas		**13.4%**
Average for Countries With Quotas of This Type		**23.0%**

Note: PR = proportional representation.

1. All or some portion of the quota has not yet been implemented in an election.

Countries with candidate quotas have, on average, 23% women in parliament—more than 10% higher than countries that have no quotas at all (IPU 2012b). (Haiti, Senegal, and Uruguay did not hold elections before 2011 and after quotas were put in place, so the percentage of women in their parliaments is not reported.)

Even a quick look at Table 6.4 shows that requiring women to be candidates offers no guarantee that in the end the women will be elected. One reason is that some parties circumvent or simply ignore quota laws (Ballington 2004:14; Dahlerup 2002). In 1997, Panama instituted a 30% quota requirement for all parties contesting seats in the National Assembly. But in the next national elections, the quota registered gains for women of only a single percentage point. Colombia has quotas at all levels of government, but women comprise only 12% of congressional representatives, 17% of deputies, and 14% of council members (International IDEA 2009).

How can national quota laws be so ineffective? One explanation is differences in quota enforcement (Schwindt-Bayer 2009). The Panamanian law, for example, has weak enforcement. Parties are expected to make a "good faith effort" to find female candidates, but if not enough women register as candidates, parties can ignore the threshold requirements (Jones 2009). On the other end of the spectrum, some quotas are passed along with stiff penalties for parties that do not comply with the laws, called **sanctions for noncompliance**. Even among countries that have sanctions, some are also easier to circumvent or simply accept. According to Dahlerup and Freidenvall (2005), the most effective sanctions require that the electoral commission reject electoral lists that fail to comply with quota regulations. Parties must meet the quota provisions or they cannot run any candidates in the district where they are violating the rules (Schwindt-Bayer 2009). In contrast, monetary sanctions are often less successful at motivating compliance.

The parity quotas in France demonstrate the difference sanctions can make. The quota regulates both municipal and national elections, but sanctions for quota noncompliance are different at the municipal and national levels. At the municipal level, lists are rejected that failed to comply with the quota. Thus, as soon as the quota was applied in 2002, female representation at the local level more than doubled (Ballington 2004). On the other hand, at the national level parties only risked a loss of public funding for failing to following quota provisions, and many parties simply accepted the fines rather than abide by the quota (Freedman 2004). For example, Union for a Popular Movement (UMP), the main right-wing party, nominated only 20% female candidates and was penalized 4 million of its 25 million euros of public funding, but the party won a majority of seats in the assembly (Baudino 2003). And overall, the percentage of women in parliament remained far from parity at 12.2%. Even 10 years later, when women won record numbers of seats in the French National Assembly (27%), parties fell short of full compliance, running only 40% women candidates (IPU 2012a).

Sanctions are only a part of the quota story when quotas are required by the state. The second form of quota, the **political party quota,** is voluntary and occurs when a party chooses to adopt a set of rules or targets that a certain percentage of its candidates be women. Political party quotas are regulated through the internal rules of political parties and are enforced by party leadership. Table 6.5 lists the countries that have political party quotas, the number of parties that have adopted a gender quota, the percentage of parliamentary seats held by those parties, and women's share of parliamentary seats (International IDEA 2012b; IPU 2012b). This list only includes parties that were represented in the national legislature as of December 2011 and also excludes party quotas in countries that go beyond what is required by national candidate quotas (e.g., the National Unity Front in Bolivia, which has a 50% quota, over and above the 33% required nationally). Overall, by 2011, 60 political parties in 33 countries had adopted gender quotas without any national requirement to do so.

By the average numbers, political party quotas appear to be just as successful as legislative quotas. On average, countries with only political party quotas have approximately 23.3% women in their parliaments, again topping countries with no quotas by about 10%. But Table 6.5 also displays a great deal of variation in women's political representation from one country to the next. The success of party quotas is determined, in part, by how successful the parties with quotas are at gaining seats in parliament. For example, Algeria may have a party with a 20% quota for women, but because the party won only 13% of seats in the legislature, the percentage of women remains low at 7.7%. On the other hand, when parties with quotas hold more than 60% of seats, there are usually at least 25% women in parliament, such as in Austria, Germany, Nicaragua, Mozambique, and South Africa.

Still, there are no guarantees, and some party quotas are mainly lip service. For example, Cameroon's grassroots Social Democratic Front promises that at least 25% of its candidates will be women, but in 2007 one woman and 13 men from the party won seats in parliament (Noftsinger 2011). Another such example is in Chile, where there is no national quota, but three major parties have quotas ranging from 20% to 40%. Although these parties hold almost half of the seats in parliament, none of them strongly enforce their quota provision (International IDEA 2012b). Even if parties enforce the quota in one election, parties can lose the will to follow through on their promises over time. Consequently, women's activists around the world often

Table 6.5 Voluntary Political Party Quotas, 2011

Country	Number of Parties	Seats Won	Quota Level	Percentage of Women	Country	Number of Parties	Seats Won	Quota Level	Percentage of Women
Algeria	1	13%	20%	7.7%	Italy	1	34%	50%	21.6%
Australia	1	15%	40%	24.7%	Lithuania	1	9%	33%	19.1%
Austria	3	70%	33%–50%	27.9%	Luxembourg	4	78%	33%–50%	25.0%
Botswana	2	16%	30%	7.9%	Mali	1	78%	30%	10.2%
Cameroon	2	94%	25%–30%	13.9%	Malta	1	54%	20%	8.7%
Canada[1]	2	44%	25%–50%	24.7%	Mozambique	1	76%	30%	39.2%
Chile	3	48%	20%–40%	14.2%	Namibia	1	69%	50%	24.4%
Croatia	1	44%	40%	23.8%	Netherlands	2	27%	?–50%	40.7%
Cyprus	1	9%	30%	10.7%	Nicaragua	2	70%	30%–40%	40.2%
Czech Republic	1	28%	25%	22.0%	Norway	4	57%	40%–50%	39.6%
El Salvador	1	42%	35%	19.1%	South Africa	1	66%	50%	42.3%
Germany	4	78%	33%–50%	32.9%	Sweden	3	45%	50%	44.7%
Greece	1	53%	40%	18.7%	Switzerland	1	23%	40%	28.5%
Guatemala	2	31%	30%–40%	13.3%	Thailand	1	32%	30%	15.8%
Hungary[2]	2	9%	20%	8.8%	United Kingdom	2	48%	20%–50%	22.3%
Iceland	3	68%	40%–50%	39.7%	Zimbabwe	1	93%	33%–50%	15.0%
Israel	3	36%	10%–40%	20.0%					

Total Parties 60

Average Seats Won by Parties With Quotas: 47%

Average Percentage of Women for Countries With No Quotas: **13.4%**

Average Percentage for Countries With Quotas of This Type: **23.3%**

1. Quotas are only targets.

2. One party sets no percentage but requires a maximum of two candidates of the same sex appear in a row on electoral lists.

Sources: Data from International IDEA (2012b) and IPU (2012b).

press for national quotas even in countries where voluntary party quotas are already on the books.

For both kinds of quotas we have talked about so far, one factor that can influence quota success is whether parties place women in winnable positions on party lists or run them in winnable districts. In countries with electoral list systems, parties can run the required number of female candidates but bury women on the bottom of electoral lists. Take Brazil, which has a national quota of 30% for female candidates. However, the law also states that a political party can put forth candidates up to 150% of the number of seats up for grabs in an election (Araújo 2010). So hypothetically, if 100 seats are being contested, a party may put forth 150 candidates. If 30% of the party's candidates are women, there can still be up to 110 male candidates available to fill 100 seats. Therefore, if Brazilian parties and voters want to avoid electing female parliamentarians, they can do so and still be in compliance with the gender quota. It should therefore come as no surprise that Brazil has only 8.6% women in its national legislature.

To deal with this problem, governments and parties have adopted **placement mandates,** rules about the order of male and female candidates on electoral lists (Dahlerup and Nordlund 2004). For example, the Social Democratic Party in Sweden uses what is sometimes called a *zipper system.* The party nomination committee proposes two candidate lists, one for each gender, and these are combined like a zipper, alternating men and women (Dahlerup and Freidenvall 2005). In Africa, these systems have been dubbed *zebra systems,* likening list order requirements to the alternating colors of a zebra's stripes (Ballington 2004). At the national level, combinations of threshold requirements and placement mandates are so powerful that they are sometimes called "double quotas." One country with double quotas is Bosnia and Herzegovina, where not only must women hold 33% of the positions on electoral lists but women also must be one of the top two candidates on the list, two of the first five candidates, and three of the first eight candidates. Some of the other countries with placement mandates at the national level are Costa Rica, Indonesia, Iraq, and Paraguay (International IDEA 2012b; Jones 2004).

But placement mandates only work in countries that have list-based electoral systems. Ensuring quota compliance in countries that use plurality–majority systems is much more complicated (Jones and Navia 1999). Take the United Kingdom, for example, which has used various strategies to implement quotas over the years. One technique introduced by the Labour Party was women-only short lists, requiring all-female lists of party nominees be used in 50% of winnable districts (Squires 2005). The Labour Party has also tried a strategy called twinning, where constituencies are paired according to geography and probability of victory, and one male and one female candidate are selected for each (Squires 2005).

To underscore how quotas and electoral systems interact, we return to the case of France, where the parity quota has largely failed at the national level but had much more successful elsewhere. Taking a second look at the French case, we can see that the failure of the quota to generate change at the national level is not solely a function of differences in sanctions for noncompliance. Indeed, France uses a plurality–majority electoral system at the national level but PR methods at regional and municipal levels of governance (Baudino 2003). Thus, understanding the effects of quotas often means understanding how the quota policies interact with the political systems in which they operate.

But remember that we can make finer distinctions about electoral systems beyond whether or not they use electoral lists. Some list-PR systems use open lists and others use closed lists. Quotas can interact with these rules too. Again, how quotas and such rules interact depends on voter and party support for women, respectively.

What are countries with plurality–majority to do? Some resort to a third way of regulating quotas that avoids making requirements about candidates altogether. Instead, **reserved seats** mandate that a certain percentage of women are elected. Under these systems, certain parliamentary seats may be filled only by women, regardless of the number of female candidates or nominees. Therefore, although women may still compete for unreserved seats, a minimum percentage of women in parliament are guaranteed. Because reserved seats are often criticized as antidemocratic, these quota systems are more commonly found in nondemocratic and semidemocratic countries (Dahlerup and Nordlund 2004). Countries with reserved seat systems include Afghanistan, Jordan, and Rwanda. A full list of countries with reserved seats is presented in Table 6.6, again with the country's percentage of women in parliament.

Like other quota legislation, reserved seat systems vary widely. First, the level of competition for seats differs. In Kenya, for example, between 1997 and 2012, women were appointed by the president to 3% of seats, whereas in Jordan and Rwanda women compete for reserved seats in elections (Dahlerup and Nordlund 2004; International IDEA 2012a). Across countries where women run in elections, some quota systems use an electoral college designed to elect women from each district. In Uganda, for example, a special electorate of men and women in each of the country's 56 districts elects two women to parliament (International IDEA 2012a). Alternatively, some countries use a women-only list in which women compete nationwide for a set of reserved seats regardless of their districts. This type of system is in place in Tanzania, where a quota for women is allocated to parties based

Table 6.6   Reserved Seats, 2011

Country	Required Percentage of Women, Lower House or Unicameral	Percentage of Women
Afghanistan	Electoral law states that women must hold at least twice as many seats as there are provinces; currently 27%, including three women for the 10 seats reserved for the Kuchi minority	27.7%
Bangladesh	13% of seats	19.7%
Burundi	1 in 4 on party electoral lists; co-optation of additional seats to reach 30% representation	30.5%
China	For the 2008 election, Congress declared women's seat share would be no less than 22%	21.3%
Djibouti	10% of seats	13.8%
Eritrea	30% of seats	22.0% (1994)
Jordan	10% of seats	10.8%
Kenya	33% of seats[1]	9.8%
Morocco	9% of seats	17.0%
Niger	10% of seats	13.3%
Pakistan	18% of seats	22.5%
Rwanda	30% of seats	56.3%
Somalia	12% of seats in Transitional Federal Parliament	6.8% (2004)
South Sudan	25% of seats	26.5%
Sudan	25% of seats	24.6%
Tanzania	30% of seats, increasing to 36% starting in 2015	36.0%
Uganda	30% of seats plus 5 out of the 25 representatives of the army, youth, persons with disabilities, and workers	35.0%
Average Percentage in Countries With No Quotas		**13.4%**
Average Percentage in Countries With Quotas of This Type		**24.0%**

1. All or some portion of the quota has not yet been implemented in an election.

on the number of seats won in the election, and parties use women-only lists to fill seats. Still, in other cases such as in Morocco, women compete against each other for reserved seats regardless of district or political affiliation (Tripp 2003).

Many researchers are especially critical of reserved seat systems. For example, Najma Chowdhury (2002) argued that "instead of contributing to women's political agency and autonomy," the reserved seat system in Bangladesh "accentuated their dependence in politics and reinforced their marginality (p. 1). Though the framers of the Bangladesh constitution envisioned that the reserved-seat system would only be necessary for 10 years— a sufficient time to allow women to gain the skills and resources necessary to compete against men on equal footing—this has far from been the case. Instead, the reserved seats served as an extra block of votes for the party in power, the party usually responsible for filling the seats. Though a few women who entered politics through the quota system grew to become active participants in national politics, many more served as placeholders. Often, the party in power elected wives or daughters of deceased members of parliament or women who had close blood or marriage ties to the political leadership (Chowdhury 2002).

Which Groups Are Regulated

Although gender quotas are the most common type of political quota used around the world today, quota policies also target other kinds of groups, including those delineated by race, ethnicity, nationality, religion, caste, language, age, disability, profession, and location of residence (Krook and O'Brien 2010). These types of quotas can sometimes benefit women. Indeed, Hughes (2011) found that quotas targeting racial, ethnic, or religious minority groups improve the representation of minority women in national legislatures.

The vast majority of countries regulate only one identity group at a time. In fact, sometimes quota activists must even promise that gender quotas will not lead to a "slippery slope" to other group-based affirmative action policies (Bird 2003). But some countries have quotas that regulate more than one group, called "tandem" or "mixed" quotas, depending on how various policies are regulated (Hughes 2011). A handful of quotas also promote the representation of more than one marginalized group at once, sometimes dubbed "nested quotas." Afghanistan, for example, reserves 10 seats in the Wolesi Jirga for the Kuchi minority, including at least three seats for women. At the local level in Pakistan, reserved seats for women come out of the seats set aside for Muslims and peasants or workers (Rai 2005). Even without nested quotas, however, Hughes (2011) found that mixing together quotas for women and quotas for minority groups can increase the political representation of minority women.

Gender quotas also regulate different groups. Some quotas explicitly regulate women's seats, whereas others are posed in gender-neutral terms. For instance, in 1988, the Social Democratic Party of Denmark required that 40% of each gender be represented in elections at both the local and regional levels (International IDEA 2012a). Gender-neutral quotas are especially common in Latin America and are framed neutrally to combat arguments that quotas are discriminatory (Ballington 2004). Although gender quotas are almost always adopted to address women's long-standing underrepresentation in politics, gender-neutral quotas do, in some rare circumstances, benefit men (Dahlerup 1988; Freidenvall 2003).

Overall, we have focused on three broad ways of classifying quotas—ways that matter for quota effectiveness. But, the list certainly goes on. And as countries and parties continue to try to increase effectiveness, new strategies may develop. For example, some female legislators have suggested that parties set aside not only a certain share of positions for women but also a specified share of campaign funds and media time (Miguel 2008). Such rules acknowledge that in some countries it takes more to equalize the playing field.

Level of Government

Although so far we have mostly talked about quotas that affect elections to national assemblies, some countries have quotas that operate also or even solely at regional and/or local levels of government. Table 6.7 reports all countries that have quota applied at regional or local levels of government, the type of quota used, along with the percentage of women in affected electoral bodies when available. As of 2011, forty-five countries have subnational quotas in some form.

Just as at the national level, quotas regulating regional and local bodies can have great success at increasing women's representation in local governance. For example, in 1992, Namibia instituted candidate quotas at the local level, requiring that two or three party list candidates were women, depending on the size of local councils. Subsequently that year, women became 37% of local councillors (Ballington 2004). In 1997, the local quota was further strengthened, and the central political parties both called for zebra lists that alternated male and female candidates. Combined, these policies resulted in almost 44% women represented local councils. Namibia is not the only success story. Since Burkina Faso adopted a 30% gender

Table 6.7 Subnational Quotas, 2011

Country	Required Percentage of Women	Type	Percentage of Women
Afghanistan	25% of seats in provincial councils	Reserved seats	
Albania	One in three names on electoral lists for local government organs	Candidate	
Argentina	Provincial regulations vary across the country	Candidate	
Bangladesh	25% of seats in Union Parishads (councils)	Reserved seats	
Belgium	50% of each gender on electoral lists for local elections	Candidate	33% on communal councils; 37% on provincial councils (2006)
Bolivia	30% of party and 50% of citizen group electoral lists for town councils	Candidate	
Bosnia and Herzegovina	33% of party electoral lists; a woman must be one of top two on list; two among first five candidates; and three among top eight; entity, canton, and municipal levels	Candidate	
Brazil	30% of party electoral lists for state and municipal legislative bodies	Candidate	
Burkina Faso	30% of party electoral lists	Candidate	
Colombia	30% of party lists of five or more	Candidate	17% of deputies; 14% of council members (2007)
Costa Rica	40% of electable positions on party lists; 50% and every other position starting in 2014	Candidate	
Dominican Republic	50% of municipal candidates	Candidate	

Country	Required Percentage of Women	Type	Percentage of Women
Ecuador	30% on party electoral lists	Candidate	
Eritrea	30% of seats in regional assemblies	Reserved seats	
France	50% of candidate lists; every other position on candidate lists for regional and municipal councils with more than 3,500 inhabitants	Candidate	48% on regional councils (2004) and 49% on municipal councils (2008)
Greece	50% on candidate lists for local and regional	Candidate	
Honduras	30% on party electoral lists	Candidate	
India	33% in panchayats and municipalities; in 28 states, 50% in only panchayats or also in municipalities	Reserved seats	
Ireland[1]	30% of local council candidates in next elections	Candidate	
Italy	Since 2003, 10 of 20 regions have adopted regional quotas ranging from 20% to 40%; one region requires lists to include women; and one mandates that two preferential votes not both go to men	Candidate	
Lesotho	30% of all local divisions	Reserved Seats	
Macedonia	One out of every three positions on party electoral lists in one municipality	Candidate	
Mauritania	20% of local councils; required electoral list order depends on council size	Candidate	

(Continued)

Country	Required Percentage of Women	Type	Percentage of Women
Mexico	As of 2009, 18 of 32 states had enacted quota laws for state legislative bodies	Candidate	
Namibia	30% candidates for local government	Candidate	43.8% in local government (1998)
Nepal	40% of candidates for Municipal Councils	Candidate	
Pakistan	18% of seats in provincial assemblies and 33% of seats in local government councils	Reserved seats	
Paraguay	On at least every fifth position on party electoral lists	Candidate	
Peru	30% of candidates in regional and local councils	Candidate	
Philippines	A woman must be one of three sectoral representatives that sits in every municipal, city, and provincial legislative council	Reserved seats	
Poland	35% of electoral lists in the bottom two tiers of local administration (gmina and powiat levels)	Candidate	
Portugal	33%, except small towns and municipalities	Candidate	
Rwanda	30% of all district and city councils	Reserved seats	
Senegal[1]	50% of candidates and every other name on lists for regional, municipal, and rural elections, starting in 2012	Candidate	
Serbia	30% of electoral lists for local elections	Candidate	
Sierra Leone	50% of Ward Development Committees, elected at town meetings	Reserved seats	

Country	Required Percentage of Women	Type	Percentage of Women
Slovenia	30% of electoral lists for local elections, increasing to 40% in 2014	Candidate	21.5% of local councillors (2006, when quota was 20%)
South Africa	50% of all electoral lists for local councils	Candidate	38% of all representatives at local level (2011)
South Korea	50% and every other position on electoral lists for city council elections	Candidate	
South Sudan	25% of all state legislatures and executives	Reserved seats	
Spain	40% of regional and local elections, except for villages with fewer than 3,000 people	Candidate	
Tanzania	33% of seats in local governments	Reserved seats	34% of seats in local governments (2011)
Uganda	33% of seats in local councils	Reserved seats	
Uruguay[1]	Every third position for first 15 places or entire list unless only two positions, and then one of two candidates for departmental legislative bodies, starting in 2015	Candidate	
Uzbekistan	30% of candidates for regional, district, and city councils	Candidate	

1. All or some portion of the quota has not yet been implemented in an election.

Note: This table excludes voluntary measures by political parties that operate at the subnational level, for example, in Algeria.

Sources: Ballington (2004) (Namibia); International IDEA (2009) (Colombia); (2012a); Dahlerup and Freidenvall (2008) (Belgium, France, Slovenia); Morna and Nyakujarah (2011) (South Africa).

quota, women's representation on local councils has risen to 35% (National Democratic Institute 2009). And as we discuss in Chapters 8, reservations for women at the local level in India has made a difference beyond numbers.

Quotas also operate for legislative bodies that are supranational, such as regional assemblies. In Africa, for example, quotas are used for the African Union and the Parliamentary Forum of the Southern African Development Community (SADC) (for more on these bodies, see Chapter 15) (Ballington 2004). Some countries in Europe use quotas to decide who represents them in the European Parliament. In the United Kingdom, for example, the Labour Party used a "zipping" mechanism for the European Parliamentary elections in 1999, whereby male and female candidates were placed alternately on the regional lists of candidates, with half of all lists headed by women.

The Adoption of Gender Quotas

How do countries or parties decide to use a quota, and why do they choose a particular type? Research suggests a range of explanations, including (1) internal country structures or characteristics, (2) the influences of women's groups or elites, and (3) extranational forces such as regional **diffusion** and international pressure.

First, researchers have linked quota adoption to a number of internal country characteristics, typically in a similar fashion to women's political representation more generally. For example, PR systems may increase the likelihood that countries adopt quotas in the first place. Indeed, of the 41 countries in Table 6.4 that have candidate quotas, 61% use PR electoral systems, and another 22% use mixed electoral systems. In some countries such as Armenia and South Korea, quotas are only used for seats allocated using PR methods (Jones 2006). And left-wing political parties are often the first parties in political systems to adopt party gender quotas. Other internal factors can affect what kinds of quotas are adopted. For example, long-standing democracies tend to shy away from reserved seats.

Second, research evaluates the roles of key actors in the road to quota adoption. One indispensable pro-quota force in many countries has been the women's movement. In some countries, quota measures are debated extensively, suffer defeats in the legislature, and succeed only after extensive lobbying by women's groups. For example, in Argentina, women "demonstrated notable solidarity and collective action in the struggle for the quota law. . . . Some women also made intense individual efforts to ensure the implementation of the law, often at great personal costs" (Gray 2003).

Yet in other countries, quotas are more top-down and/or are approved without great debate or controversy. In Mexico, for example, grassroots pressure did not play a significant role in quota adoption; it was aggressive activism from second-tier leaders that forced the policy (Bruhn 2003). In Brazil, a national electoral-law quota passed with little fanfare (Araújo 2003). And in Belgium, gender quotas were rather easily accepted as simply one more quota that fit into a normative framework accepted there, the "politics of presence" (Meier 2000).

The role that elites can play in quota adoption is also demonstrated by the effects of regime change. For example, the coming to power of a new king in Morocco was instrumental to the passage of gender quotas (see also Chapter 13). Civil war can have similar effects, opening up space in which women's movements can press for quotas (see also Chapter 15). But on the flip side of the coin, regime change can lead to the dissolution of existing quotas. Indeed, regime change in Egypt has prompted quota cancellation more than once (Abou-Zeid 2003; see also Chapter 13).

Some forces for change originate from outside of a country altogether (Baldez 2004; Bush 2011; Htun and Jones 2002; Jones 2004; Krook 2009). Interestingly, countries within the same region are likely to adopt similar types of quotas, suggesting that countries look to their neighbors as examples. Researchers call this phenomenon diffusion. Even within the same country, one political party may also adopt a quota rule first formulated by another party to avoid losing women's votes, called a **contagion effect** (see Matland and Studlar 1996).

Global forces also influence quota adoption. For example, wars with international dimensions can foster quota adoption (Bush 2011; Krook, O'Brien, and Swip 2010). Bush (2011) found that the presence of international peace-keeping forces, international election monitoring, and dependence on foreign aid all increase the chance that developing countries will adopt quotas. And as discussed further in Chapter 7, international conferences have played key roles in the promotion of women in decision-making roles. Researchers stress the importance of the 1995 Fourth World Conference on Women in Beijing for raising consciousness about women's political underrepresentation, providing transnational activists with the tools necessary to pressure for quotas on a country-by-country basis and increasing the attractiveness of quota proposals to national parliaments (Araújo 2003; Htun and Jones 2002). Further, though Beijing may not have set the process in motion, "international conferences help explain why certain countries moved from party-level to national quota laws" (Baldez 2003:8).

The adoption of quotas often faces opposition on a number of grounds. First, quotas are often criticized as antidemocratic (Gray 2003): Voters should be able to decide who is elected, but quotas mandate that women be elected (Dahlerup 2002). Quotas may also face legal challenges based on gender equality laws. For example, in the United Kingdom in January 1996 the Industrial Tribunal overturned the Labour Party's all-female short lists on the grounds that they violated the Sex Discrimination Act 1975. The British Parliament had to pass an additional law in 2002 —the Sex Discrimination (Elected Candidates) Act—to allow political parties to use affirmative action measures to increase women's share of elected positions.

Quota opponents often argue that there are not enough qualified women to fill the quota (Gray 2003). And including under qualified women may hurt rather than help women's future efforts at representation. For example, as one Lithuanian member of parliament noted, "quotas for women in the Soviet legislature, which existed and which were preserved at any price, spurred a social prejudice that women are incompetent on political matters" (Paliokienė 1999, cited in Krupavičius and Matonytė 2003:94). Further, many women do not want to be elected simply because they are women. For instance, when asked about quotas, one Lithuanian member of parliament made the following response:

> We have enough women working in important positions because of their professional qualities, not because they are women. We don't have women sitting on the working group on NATO enlargement because of a gentlemanly attitude towards including women. It happens because of a pure appreciation of our competence. (cited in Krupavičius and Matonytė 2003:95)

Finally, women's groups argue that quotas may become a ceiling rather than a floor. Because women's presence is guaranteed at a certain level, parties or governments may not pursue strategies to include women in greater numbers. Some opponents argue that quotas are superficial and will not alter the structural and cultural factors that create women's underrepresentation (Squires 1996). Instead, broader political reforms, such as altering the electoral system, are preferable to gender quotas. Quotas alone are no magic fix to women's underrepresentation. Birgitta Dahl, the Swedish speaker of parliament, stated the following:

> One cannot deal with the problem of female representation by a quota system alone. Political parties, the education system, non-governmental organizations (NGOs), trade unions, churches must all take responsibility within their own organizations to systematically promote women's participation from the bottom up. This will take time. It will not happen overnight, or in one year or five years; it will take one or two generations to realize significant change. (quoted in Dahlerup 2002:2)

Therefore, although quotas are one of the most powerful ways of influencing the political demand for women, they may create an artificial demand. They are a way to bypass low party or voter demand for women.

Moving Up the Ladder:
Women in Local Governance

So far in this chapter, we have covered factors that influence women's political candidacy and election in local, regional, and national governments. But it is also important to be aware that political careers at these different levels are not entirely unrelated. Often, politicians begin at lower levels of government—local and state office—and, if successful there, they move up the ladder to the next level, representing a broader constituency (Schreiber and Adams 2008; Stokes 2005). Thus, paying attention to women's representation in the local level is important. If women are less likely to serve in political positions close to home, they are probably less likely to be represented nationally. Further, local government is often responsible for the bulk of local expenditures or local development and investment projects (Vetter 2007).

Research shows that women tend to be better represented in some local and regional political posts than in others. On the one hand, women can be quite successful as local councillors. On the other hand, women mayors tend to be less common (Murray 2010; Verge 2011). One feature of local politics that may facilitate women's participation is the proximity of the town hall to home and the subsequent limited travel requirements, which reduce the burden on family life (Briggs 2000; Neyland and Tucker 1996; but see McDonald and Pini 2004).

Within countries, there can be substantial variation in women's representation in local politics. For example, in Germany, women are only 4.2% of town councillors in the county of Rottweil but 48.3% of town councillors in Gutersloh (Magin 2011). In contrast, women's representation in local government does not vary substantially across the New England states (Ransford and Thomson 2011). In 2009, women were between 25% and 17% of local governing boards in Connecticut, Maine, Rhode Island, Massachusetts, Vermont, and New Hampshire (Ransford and Thomson 2011).

What determines women's representation in local politics? Raphael Magin (2011) asked why women are better represented in some German town councils than in others. As with women's representation in national politics, Magin found that political factors influence women's representation at the local level. Mixed electoral systems with closed lists, high district magnitude, gender quotas, and party competition all significantly increase women's representation at the local level. For social structural factors, the availability of day care increases women's local political representation in the western part of Germany. Magin did not find support for his measure of culture—whether the local area is predominantly Catholic.

Putting It All Together: Democracy, Electoral Systems, and Quotas

In this chapter, we have covered a broad range of political factors that impact women's political representation. But we should not forget that each of these factors does not operate in a vacuum. Democracy, electoral systems, and candidate selection rules ultimately come together to affect women's experiences. Furthermore, these factors are not static. Countries evolve over time, and as they change, so do women's chances for political inclusion.

One case that demonstrates these points well is Bosnia and Herzegovina, which has undergone substantial political changes in just a few decades. Once a Communist country, Bosnia and Herzegovina instituted multiparty democracy, introduced quotas, and changed its electoral rules in stepwise fashion. As shown in Figure 6.1, with each of these changes, women's political representation at the national and in the regional cantons changed too. Bosnia and Herzegovina also reveals how important political factors can be in shaping women's electoral fortunes.

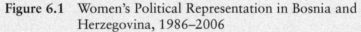

Figure 6.1   Women's Political Representation in Bosnia and Herzegovina, 1986–2006

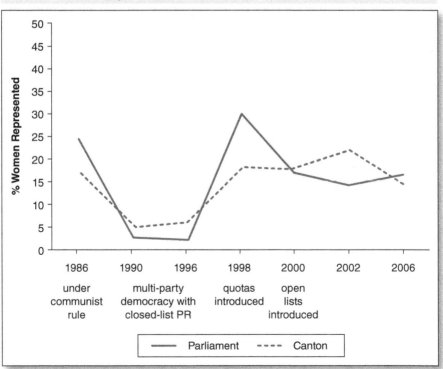

Source: Borić (2005).

7

Explaining the Political Representation of Women— International Factors

I n the previous three chapters, we distinguished two sets of factors that affect women's levels of political representation around the world. Supply factors increase the pool of women with the skills to run for political office, and demand factors make it more or less likely that women will be pulled into office from the supply of willing candidates. In this chapter, we examine international influences on women in politics, explaining how international actors such as the United Nations can increase the supply of women while simultaneously influencing states to increase their demand for women. International influences constitute an overarching explanation that affects both the supply of and demand for women in politics. Returning to the political recruitment process discussed at the beginning of Chapter 4, international factors affect the entire process depicted in Figure 4.1.

To understand the role that international agents such as the international women's movement or the United Nations play in women's political representation, one has to think beyond the level of individual countries. In contrast to explanations within countries, theories of international influence suggest that individual nations do not stand apart from the international arena (Berkovitch 1999; Meyer, Boli, Thomas, and Ramirez 1997; Ramirez, Soysal, and Shanahan 1997). Instead, the connectedness of the world means that nations must pay attention to each other and to the international bodies that write treaties, mediate international disputes, and dispense aid. The connectedness of the world is economic, through trade ties between nations or international economic agreements. Connectedness is also cultural because countries import and export cultural products, such as movies, television shows, and books. Finally, there are political connections between countries because countries exchange diplomats, sign international accords, and create mechanisms for international governance, such as the United Nations.

In this chapter, we demonstrate that this international connectedness can be used by female activists to influence women's political representation (and women's status generally) worldwide. First, we discuss the international women's movement and its goals for women in politics. Then, we discuss how international bodies, especially the United Nations, have adopted this vision for women's political representation. The next section gives examples of how international bodies can affect both the supply of and demand for women in politics. The chapter closes by discussing the Convention on the Elimination of All Forms of Discrimination Against Women (CEDAW), possibly the most important international treaty related to women to date.

The International Women's Movement

The international women's movement grew substantially over time (D'Itri 1999; Rupp and Taylor 1999). From just a few organizations in Western nations in the late 1800s, the international women's movement ultimately grew to encompass more than 40,000 women and men from more than 180 countries, coming together in Beijing for the Fourth Global Conference on Women. As discussed briefly in Chapter 2, unlike women's movements at the national level, which vary in size and strength, the international women's movement has been steadily increasing in size and strength (Berkovitch 1999).

One way to consider the growth of the international women's movement is to chart how many **women's international nongovernmental organizations (WINGOs)** are founded each year. Figure 7.1 shows that WINGOs were founded steadily from 1885 to 1970 except in breaks during wartime periods. Early WINGOs included the World's Woman's Christian Temperance Union (1884), the International Council of Women (1888), and the International Woman Suffrage Alliance (1904). In the 1970s, foundings of WINGOs increased, changing from steady, almost linear growth over time to almost exponential growth.

International women's groups do not all work directly for women's incorporation in politics. But women's political incorporation is often one important goal. Female suffrage was central to the aims of many early

Figure 7.1   Growth in Women's International Nongovernmental Organizations

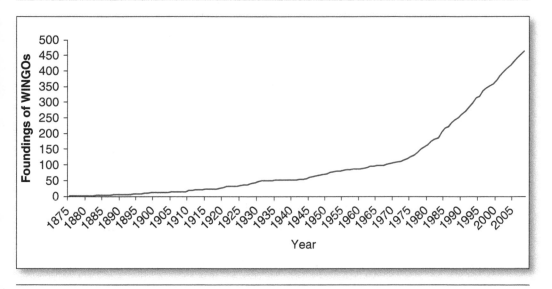

Note: WINGOs = women's international nongovernmental organizations.

Source: Berkovitch (1995, 1875–1985 data).

WINGOs. In fact, many of the first groups were founded with women's suffrage in mind. For example, the International Woman Suffrage Alliance's founding principles state, "Women should be vested with all political rights and privileges of electors" (International Alliance of Women 2005).

The importance of women's political participation to many WINGOs continues today, although the aims of the movement are different. Today, WINGOs are more likely to call for 30%, or even 50%, representation in legislatures. For example, in June 2000, the Women's Environment and Development Organization (WEDO), an international organization that advocates for women's equality in global policy, launched the 50/50 campaign. The campaign's goal is to increase the percentage of women in local and national politics worldwide to 50%, and since its inception, the campaign has been adopted by 154 organizations in 45 countries.

A Brief History of Women's Activism in the United Nations

The international women's movement does not work alone in trying to influence states to increase women's political representation. Instead, women work with the international bodies that connect the world to make sure women's interests are served. Although women and women's movements were active prior to the formation of the United Nations, its creation gave women a place to focus their efforts on influencing large numbers of countries. Therefore, women and women's groups have targeted the United Nations from its inception as a place to work on gender equality. For example, during the United Nations' formation, suffragette Alice Paul and her World Women's Party lobbied for inclusion of the phrase "the equal rights of men and women" in the UN Charter Preamble. Ultimately, the UN General Assembly recommended during its first session in 1946 that all member states fulfill the aims of its charter, "granting to women the same political rights as men" (Resolution 56 (I)). Throughout the rest of the United Nations' history, international feminists worked to keep women— and women's political rights—on the agenda. For example, 18% of all organizations officially allowed to consult with the United Nations during its first decade were women's organizations (Berkovitch 1999:107–108).

The 1970s were especially important for women's global organizing at the United Nations. Motivated by the demands of the Women's International Democratic Federation, the United Nations declared 1975 International Women's Year (Chen 1995). The primary event of the women's year was the first UN World Conference on Women in Mexico City, attended by 133 national delegations. In the same year, the UN General Assembly declared the Decade for Women (1975–1985). The events that followed, including the second and third World Conferences in Copenhagen (1980) and Nairobi (1985), brought worldwide attention to the women's movement.

The international women's movement was an integral part of the planning for these conferences and in participation. In fact, official nongovernmental organization (NGO) forums were held alongside planned conference events to encourage greater participation by a wide range of women's groups. Ultimately, in addition to the thousands of women who participated in these conferences, "tens of thousands were mobilized by the process in countries around the world" (Tinker and Jaquette 1987:419).

During the 1990s and beyond, the international women's movement and women's organizations continued to place women on the international agenda. In addition to participating in the Fourth World Conference on Women in Beijing (1995), international women's organizations successfully drew attention to women's issues at conferences dedicated to a wide range of other issues, including the environment (1992), human rights (1993), population and development (1994), social development (1995), food security, settlements (1996), and food security (1997) (Antrobus 2000; Friedman 2003). Another key success was the incorporation of women's rights into conceptions of human rights (Berkovitch 1999; Joachim 2003; Ruppert 2002).

As we discussed in Chapter 2, early women's movements across the world were dominated by White, upper-class women from Western countries (Chafetz and Dworkin 1986). In the United States, although women of color, such as Sojourner Truth, played significant historical roles in expanding notions of women's rights to include women of all racial, ethnic, and socio-economic backgrounds, not all women felt equally a part of the women's movement. The same divisions have been present in the international arena. Indeed, the first UN global women's conferences were sites of significant conflict between women of the global north and south.

During the first wave of women's organizing, women of the global north sought to incorporate women of color into their suffrage organizations. But the predominance of White Western women in early organizing led national-ists in developing countries to discredit women's movements as bourgeoisie or imperialist. As women's suffrage was attained and the goals of the inter-national women's movement shifted, the rift between women of the global north and south remained. By the second wave of women's organizing, women of the global south were determined to form their own groups that addressed issues of greatest importance to their lives. As women came together in the global conferences, women of the global south accused Western feminists of ignoring their regional concerns, and conflict over the agenda stalled progress. Women also lined up on different sides of the fence on particular issues. For instance, the Second World Conference in Copenhagen was almost torn apart by the Israel–Palestinian conflict, where women of the global north supported Israel, and women from developing countries supported the Arabs or Palestinians (Chen 1995; Moghadam 2005; Zinsser 1990).

Despite these challenges, the 1985 World Conference in Nairobi showed that the world's women could cooperate across all types of boundaries—national, racial, and economic. Researchers note that by the end of the decade for women, there had been a tremendous increase in the number and types of women's organizations across the world as well as networks and alliances to bridge the gaps between. And during the 1990s, groups such as Development Alternatives with Women for a New Era (DAWN), Women Living Under Muslim Law (WLUML), and the Sisterhood Is Global Institute (SIGI) "tran-scended the earlier political and ideological differences" to build a common agenda (Moghadam 2005:9). The integration of global north and global south visions during the 1990s led scholars to argue that women's move-ments had moved from being international to truly being global (Antrobus 2000; Chen 1995; Friedman 2003; Margolis 1993; Moghadam 2005).

Throughout all time periods, WINGOs and the rest of the international women's movement kept the political rights of women on the agenda of the United Nations and its conferences. For example, 1 of 34 resolutions adopted at the First World Conference in Mexico in 1975 called on governments to "pay special attention to political rights of women" (United Nations 2000a). At the outset of the second conference in Copenhagen, conference delegates suggested that one of the obstacles preventing attainment of goals set out in Mexico was that too few women held decision-making positions. At the 1985 NGO forum in Nairobi, the most heavily attended workshop was "If Women Ruled the World," where 18 female parliamentarians from around the world discussed women's contributions as political leaders and the struggle to gain support, even from female voters, for women's political representation (United Nations 2000a). More recently, the 2000 Millennium Goals (MDGs), developed at the United Nations Millennium Summit, target eight specific and measurable development goals including "gender equality and empowering women" (with the subgoal of equality in the "proportion of seats held by women in national parliament"). The international women's movement was also highly involved in the buildup to UN Security Resolution 1325, adopted in 2000, which calls on calling on member states to ensure women's participation in postconflict regimes (Hill, Aboitiz, and Poehlman-Doumbouya 2003).

As the United Nations became a central place for international organizing on women's issues, one issue was whether to pursue women's equality across UN divisions (development, human rights, peace, security, etc.) or to consolidate women's programming. On the one hand, the United Nations itself advocates **gender mainstreaming,** or the idea that a gendered perspective must be independently introduced into all policies and programs of a government. On the other hand, some scholars have argued that consolidation of women's programming under a single entity, a **women's policy machinery,** is crucial for accomplishing coordination and fully representing women's diverse interests (Weldon 2002a). In 2006, Secretary General Kofi Annan appointed a High-Level Panel on Coherence that recommended that gender equality efforts be consolidated and strengthened within the United Nations. Indeed, over time, the resources devoted to women at the United Nations have grown, as indicated in Figure 7.2, which charts the growth in United Nations Development Fund for Women (UNIFEM) resources (in millions of dollars). And in 2011, UN Women, a new unit consolidating the four distinct parts of the UN system focusing on gender equality into a single higher-level entity to be led by an under-secretary-general, was formed. Michele Bachelet is its inaugural executive director.

Figure 7.2   Growth in United Nations Development Fund for Women Resources

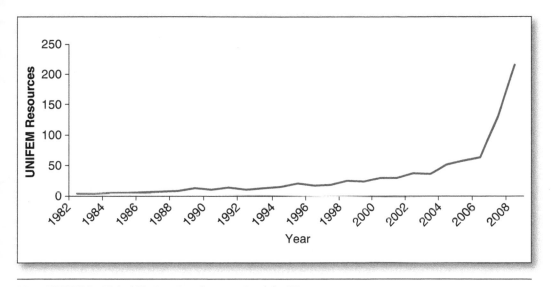

Note: UNIFEM = United Nations Development Fund for Women

To summarize, Figure 7.3 presents a time line of major events related to the international women's movement and the United Nations.

Does It Make a Difference?

To this point, we have discussed women's activity in the international arena, both in international organizations and at the United Nations. Is there any evidence that this activity has made a difference to women in formal politics? Yes. There are a number of pieces of evidence suggesting women's international organizing influenced individual countries. Further, recent research looked at many countries and found an effect of women's international organizing (Paxton, Hughes, and Green 2006; Ramirez et al. 1997).

To begin, international activity can increase the supply of women interested in and able to compete for political office. For example, the international conferences that are so central to women's international organizing inspire and train local women's movements. Participants learn social movement tactics that have been successful in other parts of the world. Women exchange arguments against the enduring cultural beliefs that work against

Figure 7.3   Significant Events for the International Women's Movement and the United Nations

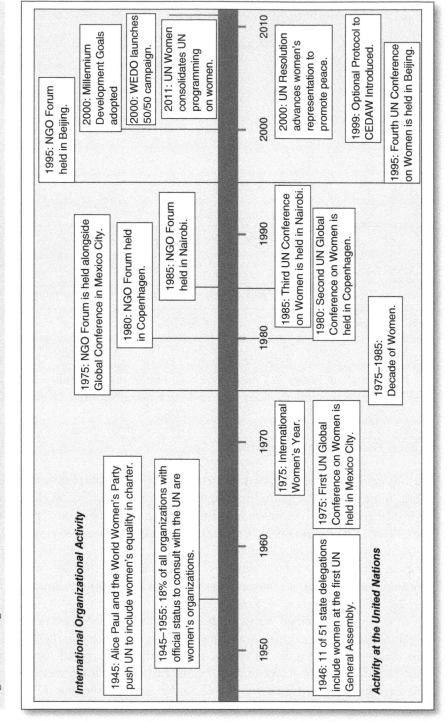

International Organizational Activity

1945: Alice Paul and the World Women's Party push UN to include women's equality in charter.

1945–1955: 18% of all organizations with official status to consult with the UN are women's organizations.

1975: NGO Forum is held alongside Global Conference in Mexico City.

1980: NGO Forum held in Copenhagen.

1985: NGO Forum held in Nairobi.

1995: NGO Forum held in Beijing.

2000: Millennium Development Goals adopted

2000: WEDO launches 50/50 campaign.

2011: UN Women consolidates UN programming on women.

1950   1960   1970   1980   1990   2000   2010

Activity at the United Nations

1946: 11 of 51 state delegations include women at the first UN General Assembly.

1975: International Women's Year.

1975: First UN Global Conference on Women is held in Mexico City.

1975–1985: Decade of Women.

1985: Third UN Conference on Women is held in Nairobi.

1980: Second UN Global Conference on Women is held in Copenhagen.

2000: UN Resolution advances women's representation to promote peace.

1999: Optional Protocol to CEDAW Introduced.

1995: Fourth UN Conference on Women is held in Beijing.

women's participation in politics. Women swap ideas to develop new strategies for action and unite with other women from their home countries to seek common goals. Elizabeth Jane Prichard, an activist from New Zealand, stated the following:

> Attending the Beijing Conference on Women provided for me a much fuller perspective of what can be achieved by any woman who is prepared to participate fully in the work of the conference and then return to address key issues in her own country. (United Nations 2000a)

Similarly, activists from Namibia and Uganda have described how UN conferences on women encouraged domestic women's organizations as they sought to influence their governments to adopt national gender policies (Bauer 2006; Tripp 2006).

International bodies may also work directly to increase the supply of women. For example, the United Nations Development Programme (UNDP) provided training to 144 female candidates in Vietnam. And the UNDP claims that their efforts contributed to a rise in women's representation in Vietnam's national legislature from 18% to 26% (UNDP 2000:97). More indirectly, the United Nations, the International Labor Organization (ILO), the World Bank, and a wide range of international NGOs all provide money, personnel, and training to promote women's empowerment throughout the world. For example, the ILO provides training in employment and skills development. And, in a workshop titled "Rural Women and Land," the UN Food and Agriculture Organization (FAO) brought rural women together from across Senegal to address their access to land and natural resources. Empowering women by helping them get employment training, education, or access to valuable resources such as land can help create the supply of women with the knowledge, skills, and interest to run for political office.

Women's international activity can also increase the demand for female politicians. Most directly, international organizations have pressured states to adopt gender quotas (Childs and Krook 2005; Krook 2004; Towns 2004). For example, in 1997 the male-dominated legislature of Peru approved gender quotas, "without prior pressure from domestic women's organizations and with minimal debate, presumably because then-president Alberto Fujimori had sensed the advantages of such a measure" (Towns 2004:214). What would be the advantage to male political leaders of instituting gender quotas? One advantage could be money. International bodies grant the loans and provide the foreign aid that poor countries so desperately need. When taking money from an international organization, a country may be more willing to listen to suggestions for changes to laws, such as quota laws (Bush

2011). For example, the funding of a $4 million governance program by the UNDP in Bangladesh allegedly led the country not only to extend lapsed quota legislation for women in parliament but also to increase the percentage of women required from 7% to 30% (UNDP 2000:97).

National and local women's organizations may also join with international forces to increase demand for women in politics. Domestic actors search out international allies to bring pressure to bear for their cause. By taking advantage of links to international actors, domestic women's groups can gain leverage, information, money, and other resources that would otherwise be out of reach. Keck and Sikkink (1998) called this process—seeking international support to pressure governments to act—the **boomerang effect.** One active example of this process occurred in Namibia, where women pressing for 50% women in parliament linked to the WEDO's global 50/50 campaign, lending greater resources and legitimacy to their efforts (Bauer 2006).

Whereas domestic actors may sometimes call on international forces for assistance, actors and forces external to nations may also initiate change. International influence is perhaps most apparent in the two recent constitutional transitions in Iraq and Afghanistan. Arguably, neither of these countries had either a strong internal demand or supply of women for political office. But outside agents were central in the formation of their new, postwar constitutions that both include substantial gender quotas. Though Nordlund (2004) found no evidence that the United Nations actively promoted the adoption of a gender quota in Afghanistan, it did strongly advocate increases in women's parliamentary representation. In fact, the United Nations actively worked to get the issue included on the agenda. Further, the international community pressured for women to be represented at the table during constitution building. Women's inclusion during this stage and a lack of other options for increasing women's representation may have been influential in the choice to adopt gender quotas (Dahlerup and Nordlund 2004).

Finally, a recent study statistically tested the impact of women's international organizing on women's acquisition of suffrage and 10%, 20%, and 30% women in parliament. Paxton et al. (2006) looked at data from more than 100 countries from 1893 to 2003. They found that the combination of women's organizing in the form of WINGOs and UN activity had a powerful impact on women's parliamentary representation over time. To give an example of how powerful an effect, at the beginning of the period, a country had a 2.5% chance of attaining suffrage. As international organizing increased, by 1948, the chance of suffrage had increased to 71%. Similarly, another study found that women's international organizing has a profound effect on country adoption of gender quotas as well (Hughes, Krook, and Paxton 2012).

The Convention on the Elimination of All Forms of Discrimination Against Women

The United Nations has many documents that promote equality of men and women's rights, including the UN Charter, the Universal Declaration of Human Rights, and a number of specialized agency resolutions, declarations, and recommendations (Cook 1994). Arguably the most important international treaty for women's rights, however, is CEDAW. CEDAW is also known as the Women's Convention and is sometimes described as the international bill of rights for women. Because it is so important, it is worth discussing CEDAW and its impact in some depth.

CEDAW tries to confront the social causes of women's inequality by addressing "all forms" of discrimination against women, including discrimination in the areas of education, employment, finance, health care, law, marriage and family relations, and politics. Although the United Nations has crafted several international treaties that address women's rights, CEDAW goes further than other treaties in demanding that *states change their laws* to help women. For example, countries that sign the treaty are urged to introduce measures of affirmative action that promote gender equality. Through ratification of CEDAW, countries declare a common goal of gender equality, and they also pledge to pursue policies and practices to reach that goal. Domestic actors may then seek help from the international arena to ensure that states comply with the goals enshrined in the treaty, producing a boomerang effect.

Ratification of CEDAW has increased strikingly over time since the treaty's adoption by the UN General Assembly in 1979. As of March 2005, 180 countries had ratified the treaty, making it one of the most widely accepted treaties in UN history. Although President Jimmy Carter signed CEDAW on behalf of the United States in 1980, the United States has never ratified the treaty and is the only Western country not to do so. Other nonratifying countries are located in the Middle East (Iran, Oman, and Qatar), the Pacific region in Asia (Brunei Darussalam, Marshall Islands, Nauru, Palau, and Tonga), and sub-Saharan Africa (Somalia and Sudan).

Why did the United States never ratify CEDAW? Certainly it had powerful supporters, such as President Bill Clinton:

> I ask you to think about this convention [CEDAW] and its impact. It has a proven record of helping women around the world to combat violence, gain economic opportunity, [and] strike against discriminatory laws. Its provisions are consistent with United States law, which already provides strong protections for women. It offers a means for reviewing and encouraging other

nations' compliance. . . . When you look ahead to this new century and new millennium and you ask yourselves what you would like the story of the next 100 years to be, surely all of us want one big chapter to be about how, finally, in all nations of the world, people of all races and ethnic groups, of many different religious persuasions and cultural practices came together to guarantee that every young girl got a chance to grow up to live up to the fullest of her abilities and to live out her dreams. (U.S. Government Printing Office 2000)

Arguments against the ratification of CEDAW in the United States are made on a number of grounds. Opponents of U.S. ratification stress that, although they support the treaty's goals, they are not sure if CEDAW is the best way to achieve them. Some fear that ratifying the treaty would threaten United States sovereignty, imposing an unnecessary UN bureaucracy to oversee the United States. Many opponents have little belief in the treaty's ability to cause real change, arguing that the pact has no enforcement power. Other opponents maintain that CEDAW could be used by women's groups to impose an objectionable reproductive rights agenda in both the United States and abroad. Along these lines, many Republicans argue that ratification of the treaty would undermine "traditional" moral and social values, including marriage, motherhood, family structure, and even Mother's Day. The treaty's harshest critics attack CEDAW as a "toxic" document that tries to impose "radical feminism" around the world.

CEDAW proponents counter that the treaty takes no position on abortion and that the document is not antifamily. The document calls on ratifying countries to recognize the "common responsibility of men and women in the upbringing and development of their children" and states that "the parents' common responsibility [is] to promote what is in the best interest of the child" (United Nations 1979). Many human rights and women's organizations have placed considerable pressure on the United States to ratify the treaty, arguing that failure to ratify hinders the ability of the United States to exercise political or moral leadership in the human rights field. Furthermore, they contend that by refusing to ratify CEDAW, the United States relinquishes the opportunity to influence further development of women's human rights. They ask how the United States can demand, for example, that India and Pakistan increase efforts to protect women from honor killing when the United States has not even ratified the treaty. Furthermore, by refusing ratification, the United States is barred from appointing a member to the CEDAW committee, leaving the United States unable to influence the body from within (Center for Reproductive Rights 2004).

In 1993, sixty-eight senators signed a letter asking President Clinton to support ratification of CEDAW, and the Senate Foreign Relations Committee has twice voted to send CEDAW to the full Senate for ratification (in 1994 and 2002). However, in neither instance did the measure actually come before the full Senate. Though the measure has failed at the national level, several state and local governments have passed resolutions in support of CEDAW. In April 1998, San Francisco became the first city in the United States to implement the principles of CEDAW locally. A task force now coordinates efforts to identify and combat discrimination against women. The CEDAW framework encourages public policy that explicitly considers the experiences of women, for example, adding streetlights to make neighborhoods safer for women (Hadassah 2004). Other state and local governments that have passed similar measures include Palo Alto and Los Angeles, California; the Connecticut State Senate; Hawaii; the Illinois House of Representatives; Iowa; Maine; Massachusetts; New Hampshire; New York City; North Carolina; and South Dakota.

Has CEDAW made a difference in the status of women across the world? Advocates credit the treaty with encouraging a number of positive developments, including the expansion of women's citizenship rights in Botswana and Japan, inheritance rights in Tanzania, property rights in Georgia, and political participation in Costa Rica (Hadassah 2004). After CEDAW ratification, 22 countries instituted equal employment policies, and a number of countries, such as Guatemala, the Philippines, Poland, and Spain, improved maternity leave and child care for working women (Hadassah 2004). Some researchers also argue that the treaty has been important for securing gains in women's political representation, often through the implementation of gender quotas in various forms.

Despite these favorable arguments by CEDAW's proponents, some research has pointed out that ratification of the treaty is a highly political decision that may have little to do with general attitudes about women (Paxton and Kunovich 2003). Although a nation may succeed in ratifying CEDAW, implementing and fulfilling the provisions of the convention at the domestic level may prove to be a much more difficult task (Holt 1991). Evidence of this difficulty abounds: Though many nations have ratified CEDAW, women still experience oppression around the world and remain strikingly underrepresented in many of the world's parliaments.

Some governments may simply be responding to international pressure and have no real intentions to alter the status quo regarding women's status after ratifying the treaty. A few examples illustrate this point. Kuwait ratified the treaty more than a decade before allowing women to vote, and Saudi Arabia, which only recently allowed women to vote in local elections, ratified CEDAW in 2000. The Taliban government of Afghanistan was one of CEDAW's original signatories; yet clearly the Taliban was not committed to advancing women's political equality. In addition to these notable examples, several empirical studies have investigated the relationship between ratification of CEDAW and the percentage of women in parliament across a large number of countries. Most of this research fails to find that CEDAW has any appreciable effect (e.g., Hughes 2009a; Paxton and Kunovich 2003).

It is important to recognize, however, that one of the main obstacles to CEDAW's success early on was a lack of enforcement mechanisms or ways to hold governments accountable. The **Optional Protocol** was developed to overcome this barrier. In 1999, the United Nations put forth this supplemental treaty to CEDAW. If a country ratifies the Optional Protocol, women are better able to hold governments accountable for their obligations under CEDAW. And the Optional Protocol enables the international CEDAW committee to conduct inquiries into systematic violations of women's rights. As of January 2005, seventy-one countries had already ratified the Optional Protocol (United Nations Population Fund 2005a). But because it has so recently been adopted, researchers do not yet know its effect.

As one way to demonstrate the relationship between CEDAW and women's political status around the world, we use data on women's political equality for 123 countries from 1981 to 2003, available from the Cingranelli-Richards Human Rights Dataset (Cingranelli and Richards 2004b). We separate the 123 countries into two groups: ratifying and nonratifying. Figure 7.4 presents the average political equality scores for these two groups. Because the number of countries that have signed the treaty changes over time, the number of countries in the ratifying group appears in parentheses next to the year on the x-axis. This graph makes it clear that over time countries that ratify CEDAW minimize political inequality between men and women more so than countries that refuse ratification. Although again this does not prove that CEDAW is the cause of women's improving political situation, CEDAW may at least generally indicate a shared commitment to women's political equality.

In sum, women's activity in the international arena can make a difference to women's political representation around the world. This factor influences both the supply of women available for political office and the demand of political actors for women. And finally, it is worth pointing out that, though this chapter focused on the international women's movement and international organizations as an explanation for women's political representation across countries, these same forces for change are also examples of women's political activity.

Figure 7.4   Women's Average Political Equality in 123 Countries, 1981–2003

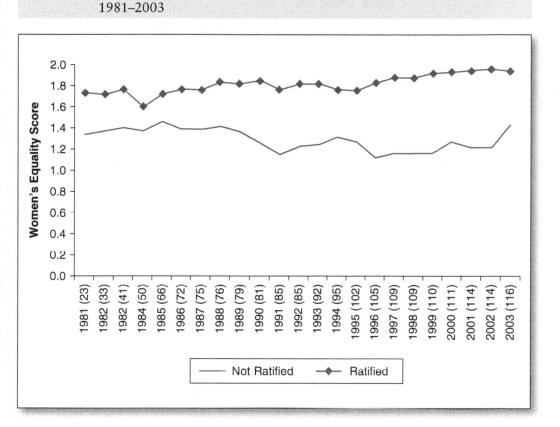

8

Do Women Make a Difference?

In previous chapters, we discussed women's fight for representation and what factors explain women's differential success in gaining power around the world. But a final question remains to be answered—what difference do women make anyway? Put another way, does having women in positions of power change anything? Have women changed the style of politics? Have they influenced public policy? If you viewed the past few chapters as addressing how women gain descriptive representation (see Chapter 1), then this chapter addresses women's substantive representation.

Even if women act and legislate exactly the same way as men, justice arguments imply that, as half the population, women should appear in politics. But arguments for women's representation are even more powerful if women bring to office interests and priorities that are different from those of men (Carroll and Dodson 1991). The difference is whether women are passive representatives, representing women just by being in office, or active representatives, working for women and their interests (Reingold 1992).

Determining whether women make a difference to politics is not easy. To begin, there are any number of questions to be asked and answered:

- Are female politicians, as opposed to male politicians, more likely to see women as a group as important constituents? Do female politicians "see" their female constituents better than male politicians do?
- Do men and women differ in their attitudes and policy priorities? Do women prioritize political issues differently than men do?
- Is there such a thing as a "women's issue" in politics—for example, curbing domestic violence? If we think there are women's issues, how can we define them? Do women's issues vary across countries?

- Do male and female legislators have different voting records? Do female legislators vote more often in favor of "women's issue" bills?
- Are women writing bills on issues of interest to women? Are they taking the initiative to act for women?
- Are women able to get women's issue bills, or any bills, passed once they are initiated? Are women powerful enough to support and shepherd their bills through the legislative process?
- Do women have a different legislative style than men? Do they act through regular and traditional channels of power, or are women changing the rules of the political game?
- Are women better able to sponsor and pass bills related to women—or to support a different legislative style—when there are more of them in office?
- Can women have an effect outside of legislative bodies?

Addressing each of these questions has its own specific problems, and researchers have done a better job answering some than in answering others. Generally, several ongoing limitations in this area of research constrain researchers' ability to make definitive statements about what is "known" about women's impact. First, in the past, most research in the area focused on the United States and a few other Western countries. Only very recently have researchers begun to investigate women's impact in non-Western countries. Second, the way much research discusses women's impact is often Western—defining women's issues as Western feminist issues and assuming democratic channels of power. Again, recent work is beginning to question how to define a "women's issue" and whether issues of interest to women are the same across countries. Third, it is typically very difficult to distinguish women's impact from the surrounding context, including the political party women belong to or the amount of power women hold. These caveats aside, in this chapter, we review the current state of knowledge about women's impact on politics.

Thinking Differently: Women's Views on Women and Their Policy Priorities

We can begin by asking female politicians whether they think they represent women and their concerns. Remember the argument in Chapter 1 that, due to different socialization and life experiences, women may simply be different from men (Phillips 1991; but see Molyneux 1985b). So are female legislators more likely than male legislators to see women as a group of special constituents? Beth Reingold (1992) talked to male and female state legislators from Arizona and California. Thirty-four percent of the women she interviewed spontaneously mentioned women as an important constituency. In contrast, only 6% of male senators mentioned anything about women (i.e., 3 male legislators out of 49). When directly asked whether they thought female legislators were better able to represent women's special concerns, almost 80% of female legislators said yes, whereas only 30% of men said yes. Combining these results suggests that, although male legislators tend to view themselves as capable of representing women's interests, they do not spontaneously mention women as an important constituency. Women seem to do a better job instinctively seeing the special needs or interests of women (see also Carroll 2002; Schwindt-Bayer 2010).

Similarly, Sarah Childs (2002) interviewed female British members of parliament (MPs), nearly half of whom spoke directly about trying to articulate women's concerns. As one female MP explained, "I've become increasingly aware that there are issues that affect women disproportionately and that unless women pursue them nobody else will" (Childs 2002:144). About one third of the women interviewed also said they felt their female constituents were more comfortable talking to them about women's issues. As one MP explained, "Some women actually do say 'Oh I wouldn't have gone to see a man about that; I would never have sat down and told a man that'" (Childs 2002:149). Consider also the female Argentinean legislator who holds weekly office hours to meet with female community leaders from shantytowns to discuss sanitation, health care, and child nutrition (Franceschet and Piscopo forthcoming) or the woman in Rwanda who explains "a woman can easily approach her female friend who is an authority ... [she] understands her well and can help her with her problems" (Burnet 2011:317).

If female legislators see specific issues affecting women, does it affect the kinds of bills they prioritize? Research suggests that female legislators prioritize different political issues than men do. For example, looking at U.S. state representatives, researchers found that, compared to men, women are more likely to prioritize bills related to children, family, and women (Thomas 1991; Thomas and Welch 1991) and health care and social services (Little, Dunn, and Deen 2001). And, in Sweden, female MPs are more likely than men to give high priority to issues such as family policy, elder care, and health care (vs. other priorities, e.g., jobs, the environment, taxes) (Wängnerud 2000, 2006; see also Skjeie 1991, 2002; Solheim 2000).

Similarly, in Latin America, male and female legislators articulate different legislative priorities (Schwindt-Bayer 2006; see also Htun and Power 2006). In a survey of 292 MPs from Argentina, Colombia, and Costa Rica, 65% of female legislators stated "women's equality" is a very high priority, compared with only 25% of male legislators. And 43% of female legislators felt children's and family issues are a very high priority, compared with 28% of men (Schwindt-Bayer 2006). In contrast, male legislators were more likely than female legislators to prioritize agriculture and employment issues.

Much of the work in the United States or Western countries tends to classify policies into those that should be of interest to women and those that would traditionally be of interest to men. This is a top-down approach to determining preferences or priorities. Another, less common, approach is to look from the bottom-up for differences in the preferences or priorities of men and women (Celis, Kantola, and Krook 2008). This is particularly important if we are to consider preferences in an area of policy that is not traditionally associated with either men or women. It is also of critical importance if we are to consider the interests of women outside of the West or the interests of women from marginalized groups.

Apart from different views on so-called women's issues, female legislators may view all issues differently than men do. Lyn Kathlene (1995) looked at legislators in the Colorado House of Representatives and found that women and men saw both the origins of, and solutions to, crime very differently. Female legislators viewed criminals as connected to others and society and as victims of circumstance as well as perpetrators of crimes. Women viewed crime as the result of lifelong issues stemming from early childhood, poor education, and lack of adult opportunities. In contrast, men viewed criminals as independent individuals who are individually responsible for their actions. Men focused more on the crime rather than the fact that it was committed by a person.

Their different views of the people involved led the men and women of the Colorado House to have different policy recommendations. Female legislators were more concerned with prevention (e.g., early childhood education, youth diversion programs, increased job opportunities), whereas men were more reactive in their response (e.g., stricter sentencing, longer prison terms). The women were also more likely to talk about the possibility of rehabilitation than were the men.

What about the interests of women from the global south? How can we understand differences between the policy priorities of men and women in very rural or less developed areas? Raghabendra Chattopadhyay and Esther Duflo (2004) wanted to understand whether men and women in small rural villages in India had different policy preferences. Remembering the "typical day's work" for a woman in Sierra Leone from Chapter 5, it didn't make sense for them to assume that men and women in these villages had preferences like those of men and women in the United States or Britain. Instead, they came up with a clever idea. They looked at the issues men and women brought before the village council as requests or complaints (a time-consuming activity) to look for gender differences in policy preferences. They found that women most frequently brought requests about drinking water and welfare programs to the village council. Men more often raised issues having to do with roads. These differences make sense when you realize that in Indian villages women are in charge of collecting drinking water and are the primary recipients of welfare programs like maternity or widow's pensions. Men, on the other hand, have a need for good roads since they travel frequently out of the village in search of work (Chattopadhyay and Duflo 2004:1430). This example highlights that defining women's interests or issue priorities may require a bottom-up approach, rather than having a western researcher define them from the top down (Celis et al. 2008).

Acting Differently: Women's Voting Patterns and Bill Sponsorship

But do their different views and priorities lead women to act differently than men do? For example, do individual female legislators vote differently simply because they are women? There are two difficulties in trying to demonstrate that female politicians "act differently" or even "act for women" in their voting behavior. The first is that one has to separate women's interests as women from the interest of their party. Women run as candidates and are elected as members of parties—parties that differ widely on public policy. To take a U.S. example, just as male Republicans differ from male Democrats, female Republicans differ from female Democrats (Carroll 1984). The problem is that, because the Democratic Party is generally more politically left than the Republican Party, Democratic candidates and politicians are more likely to espouse and vote for politically left policies that also get defined as "of interest to women." For example, Democrats in general are likely to vote for bills extending family and medical leaves. But family and medical leaves could also be classified as a woman's issue.

The issue of party is even difficult when we consider parliaments with strong norms of party discipline. For example, in Britain, elected MPs, male or female, have little ability to "rebel" on most votes because of the threat of sanction by party whips. British legislators who commonly vote against their party can face severe penalties including the end of their political careers. In such a climate, it is extremely difficult to determine whether women vote differently than men (Lovenduski and Norris 2003). In fact, in Europe individual legislators may have even less freedom because the laws of the European Parliament can supersede the national laws of member states.

Unless male and female legislators have the ability to "rebel" or "defect" from the proposed legislation of their party, we cannot look for gender differences between them.

A similar issue is how to separate a female politician acting for women from her actions in support of her constituents. Nancy Pelosi represents San Francisco in the U.S. House of Representatives. When she votes to support a bill of interest to women (e.g., increasing funding to the U.S. Department of Education), is she voting to represent women or just to represent her largely liberal constituents? Whether San Francisco's politician is male or female, he or she will vote to support funding increases if it is what the voters want. And if liberal constituencies are more likely to elect women, then a critic might argue that female politicians aren't acting for women at all but are only faithfully representing their liberal constituents.

Michele Swers (1998) worked to separate the impact of female politicians in the 103rd Congress (1993 to 1994) from both their party and their constituencies. She looked at how congressmen and congresswomen voted on bills concerning women's issues. The 14 bills she considered women's issue bills included the Family and Medical Leave Act, the Family Planning Amendments Act of 1993, and the Elementary and Secondary Education Act. After accounting for party (Republican or Democrat) and district characteristics (urban vs. rural, constituent income, and percentage of Black constituents), she found that a congressperson's gender made a difference in voting for these bills. Congresswomen were more likely to vote for women's issue bills than their male colleagues were. And this was especially true when she considered the bills most directly related to women, such as reproductive issues or women's health. But party was still important. Democrats, both male and female, tended to vote for these women's issue bills. So it was the defections of Republican women from the way the rest of their party voted that created the gender difference.

A similar pattern of defection occurs in other countries. For example, in New Zealand during early debates on parental leave, conservative women crossed party lines to support parental leave (Grey 2002). And women act for women in Britain as well. Sarah Childs and Julie Withey considered who signed early day motions, which are nonbinding policy statements on a variety of topics that allow MPs to put their views on record. (Although the researchers did not deal with constituency effects, they did deal with party effects by only considering women in the Labour Party.) They found that female MPs were more likely to sign "feminist" early day motions, especially those related to abortion and women's health (Childs and Withey 2004).

An unusual but potent example of women working for women's interests was in the early day motion, initiated by Christine McCafferty and signed by many, that stated female sanitary products should be exempt from the VAT (a European tax) along with other essential items. Childs and Withey (2004) explained that despite constituting only 15% of the Commons, women accounted for 22% of the 249 MPs who signed EDM 89 (99/00):

> That this House believes that sanitary products should be classed in the category of essential to the family budget, just as food, children's clothing and books already are, and that, like such products, they should be classed as VAT-free under EC sixth Directive. (p. 553)

But even if women want to defect from their party or their constituents and act "as women," there are additional constraints that may prevent them from doing so. Female legislators are subject to the same institutional and party constraints that any legislator feels. And a very important factor is whether a female legislator is in a party that is in power or in an opposition party. Women in governing parties have more opportunities to generate legislation but simultaneously have more opportunities to anger party leadership with defection (Swers 2002a:17). Similarly, women in governing parties have more opportunities for leadership positions on committees but are thus concurrently more susceptible to threats of removal upon defection from the party agenda. The importance of institutional context is apparent if one considers what happened to the defections of Republican women from their party in the 104th Congress (1995 to 1996), which followed the 103rd.

At the end of her article on women's impact in the 103rd Congress, Michele Swers (1998) warned that a distinct women's impact might be harder to find in the next, 104th Congress (1995 to 1996). A number of changes in the legislature led to this prediction. Campaigning on the "Contract with America" platform, Republicans had taken over control of the legislature, leading to the most conservative Congress in decades. As part of this change, the newly elected Republican women were also more conservative than their predecessors. Indeed, a number of female Republican freshmen presented Rush Limbaugh (a conservative talk-radio host) with a plaque declaring that none was a "Femi-Nazi" (Hawkesworth, Casey, Jenkins, and Kleeman 2001).

Mary Hawkesworth and colleagues interviewed congresswomen in both the 103rd and 104th Congresses. They concluded that the change in leadership and general conservative turn of Congress had "severe repercussions for bipartisan efforts to develop and promote a women's legislative agenda" (Hawkesworth et al. 2001:17). The new Republican leadership, headed by Newt Gingrich, consolidated power and demanded greater party discipline and adherence to party-line policy stances. Defectors from the party line were threatened with party-endorsed primary opponents if they failed to support the leadership on key votes. Their interviews with congressional staffers suggested that moderate Republican women felt a new caution in focusing on women's issues. "One Congresswoman who had participated in the CAWP research about the 103rd Congress refused an interview after the 104th, with her apologetic staffer explaining that she had to be careful about 'things such as this' (i.e., women) now" (Hawkesworth et al. 2001:17).

The change in power and in climate had an impact. In a later investigation of the 104th Congress, Swers (2002a:117–119) found that Democratic women continued to vote for women's issue bills (on average 13.5 of the 15.0 during the 104th Congress), but Republican women reduced their votes by almost 50% (to only 3.9 of the 15.0 possible). Although Republican women continued to defect from their party at times, it was at a lower rate (Swers 2002a:113–125). Further, although Republican congresswomen had sponsored "feminist" bills during the 103rd Congress, they shifted focus to general social welfare bills in the 104th (Swers 2002b:276). With their party in power and new penalties against defection in place, the moderate Republican legislators who might have defected on women's issues in the past now worried about supporting issues like family planning and child care. They felt it was dangerous to be "perceived as an advocate for Democratic interest groups" (Swers 2002b:277).

Similarly, Sandra Grey (2002) found that party mattered in New Zealand for women's support of parental leave policy. Despite reaching over 29% women in the legislature by 1998, the country's parental leave policy did not substantially change from earlier incarnations. Much of the opposition to broader legislation came from the party to the political Right (the party in power), which was concerned about loss of free-market principles. Thus, "in discussions of the 1998 Paid Parental Leave Bill, four women politicians expressed opposition to the proposed provisions, all from the right of the political spectrum" (Grey 2002:26). Cross-party alliances were also difficult for Chilean women. Waylen (1994) argued that even when women agreed on one issue, such as child support legislation, party divides on other gender issues including divorce and reproductive rights limited amount that women from different parties could connect.

In sum, female politicians work within institutions, institutions that can have a substantial impact on their ability to act for women. Whether or not Republican women wanted to defect in the 104th Congress or women on the right in New Zealand wanted to support Paid Parental Leave, institutional and party forces made it difficult for them to do so.

Besides voting for bills, are women initiating bills related to their policy preferences? That is, on an individual basis, female legislators at times defect from their party or sign particular motions simply because they are women. But do women propose bills that are different from the bills of men? And do they propose bills of special interest to women?

Women do propose bills on women. Bratton and Haynie (1999) found that women in the U.S. Congress are more likely than congressmen to introduce women's interest bills to reduce gender discrimination or to improve the economic status of women (controlling for party and district characteristics) (see also Swers 2002a:32–56). Women are more likely to introduce bills on women's rights in Honduras (Taylor-Robinson and Heath 2003) and initiate 11% more women's issues bills than men do in Argentina, Colombia, and Costa Rica (Schwindt-Bayer 2006).

Women are also more likely to sponsor bills on topics related to women. In Latin America (Argentina, Colombia, and Costa Rica), women are more likely to introduce bills related to children and the family, education, and health (Schwindt-Bayer 2006; see also Franceschet and Piscopo 2008). (But in the Honduran legislature, women are no more likely than men to initiate bills on children or families [Taylor-Robinson and Heath 2003].) In the United States, women are also more likely to sponsor bills related to education, health care, children's issues, and welfare policy (Bratton and Haynie 1999; see also Thomas 1991). Black women, in particular, have been shown to strongly influence state welfare policy outcomes (Reingold and Smith 2012).

The distribution of committee assignments across men and women matters to bill introduction. Legislative committees are expected to produce bills on particular topics. Members of a health and social welfare committee, for example, are expected to produce bills on health and social welfare (Heath, Schwindt-Bayer, and Taylor-Robinson 2005; Schwindt-Bayer 2006). Thus, because women often sit on committees relevant to women's interests, they can use their committee assignments to either propose women's interest legislation or block legislation perceived as harmful to women (Berkman and O'Connor 1993). Committee assignments are one of the processes that could lead to differences across men and women in bill introduction.

Remember that to demonstrate that women make a difference we have to show that a female politician introducing a bill related to women is not merely representing her party or acting to support her constituents. A recent and clever research design by Gerrity, Osborn, and Mendez (2007) addresses this problem by comparing the bill sponsorship of women and men from the same U.S. congressional district. The authors looked at female legislators who replace men in the same district, so they are able to ask whether women and men from the same party and the same district sponsor bills differently. They found that women who replace men introduce more women's issues bills while men who replace women introduce fewer women's issues bills.

When men replace men and women replace women there is no difference in bill introduction (Gerrity et al. 2007:191; see also MacDonald and O'Brien 2011). Overall, Gerrity et al.'s (2007) important research helps demonstrate that women do act differently from men and it is not a function of their party or their constituents.

Returning to the women of the Colorado statehouse, one can ask whether their different views of crime led them to initiate different types of legislation. Lyn Kathlene's (1995) research demonstrates that the attitudinal differences she documented between men and women in their views of crime translated into the kinds of crime and prison bills they proposed. In general, women's solutions were "contextual, multifaceted, and long-term" whereas men rarely "addressed crime from a long-term perspective; rather, they sponsored legislation that responded directly to the crime event" (Kathlene 1995:721).

Table 8.1 reproduces a table from Kathlene's article. Two of the eight bills sponsored by women addressed prevention, compared with none of the bills sponsored by men. (Remember that women were more likely to talk about crime in terms of prevention.) Similarly, only women talked about the victims of crime in their interviews, and the only victim rights bill was sponsored by a woman. In contrast, the bills on crime sponsored by men tended to focus on expanding laws to include new crimes or increasing the penalties of existing laws.

Now let's return to the women and men of rural India studied by Raghabendra Chattopadhyay and Esther Duflo (2004). India has adopted a unique system of gender quotas for leadership of the village councils in its rural villages. In brief, 30% of village chiefs must be female and this leadership is assigned randomly. This quota system allows us to consider whether female village chiefs invest in different public goods than male chiefs (remember that women care about drinking water and men care about roads) in something that approximates an experimental design (the "gold-standard" for quantitative scientific research). And yes, Chattopadhyay and Duflo (2004) found that when a woman is chief there are more public investments in drinking water but not in roads. That is, "women elected as leaders under the reservation policy invest more in the public goods more closely linked to women's concerns" (Chattopadhyay and Duflo 2004:1440).

Acting Successfully: Women's Legislative Effectiveness

But what about legislative effectiveness? Are women effective in actually getting their bills passed? This question has two parts. First, women may be

Table 8.1 Crime Bills Introduced in 1989 Session, Colorado State House, by Sex of Sponsor

Female-Sponsored Bills (n = 8)				Male-Sponsored Bills (n = 12)			
Bill #	Title	Purpose	Outcome	Bill #	Title	Purpose	Outcome
1027	Release of Records Pertaining to Juvenile Offenders	Intervention	Postponed Indefinitely	1091	Concerning Criminal Procedures	Legal procedures	LAW
1072	Crime Prevention Resources Center	Prevention/ Intervention	Postponed Indefinitely	1197	Dismissals of Actions	Legal procedures	LAW
1302	Strengthen Crime Victim Compensation Act	Victim help	LAW	1162	Concerning Crimes	Legal procedures	VETOED
1099	Financing Judicial Facilities	New financing for increased court expenses	Postponed Indefinitely	1231	Discovery in Criminal Proceedings	Legal procedures	LAW
1226	Concerning Court Actions	New financing for police to fight drugs	Postponed Indefinitely	1054	Obstruction of Peace Officer's Animal	Expands law	Postponed Indefinitely

Female-Sponsored Bills (n = 8)				Male-Sponsored Bills (n = 12)			
Bill #	Title	Purpose	Outcome	Bill #	Title	Purpose	Outcome
1205	Criminal Penalities for Animal Owners	Stricter sentencing	Postponed Indefinitely	1245	Safety on Educ. Institution Premises	Expands law	LAW
1111	Driving Privileges of Minors	Stricter sentencing	LAW	1259	Expand Crime of Equity Skimming	Expands law	LAW
1289	Alcohol Related Vehicular Offenses	Expands law, stricter law, stricter sentencing	LAW	1028	Maintenance of Juvenile Records	Stricter sentencing	LAW
				1075	Crime of Sexual Abuse	Stricter sentencing	LAW
				1335	Gang-Related Crimes	Stricter sentencing	LAW
				1166	Driver's License Revocation for Drugs	Stricter sentencing	LAW
				1124	Crimes Involving Acts of Domestic Violence	Rehabilitation	LAW

Source: From Kathlene, L., "Alternative views of crime: Legislative policymaking in gendered terms," in *Journal of Politics, 57*, © 1995. Reprinted with permission of Blackwell Publishing Ltd.

generally less effective in the political process than men are. Because males have controlled legislatures, a male legislating style has dominated throughout most of history. A male-gendered institution may reward "male" qualities, such as competitiveness, rather than "female" qualities, such as collaboration (Eagly and Johnson 1990; Jeydel and Taylor 2003; Rosenthal 1998a). Therefore, women may not be effective legislators because they have the "wrong skills." Of course, to preserve their own power, men may also directly work to undermine the power of female newcomers (Heath et al. 2005).

Second, women may be less effective in getting bills passed that specifically deal with women's issues or that take a woman's perspective. If women have a different outlook on defined social problems, such as crime (Kathlene 1995), or even see new social problems, such as gender discrimination (Bratton and Haynie 1999), then their legislation may be seen as, at best, innovative and, at worst, inappropriate, in ways that make it difficult for women to successfully find support for their proposals.

Despite these gloomy predictions, research suggests that women can be as effective as men in getting their bills turned into law. In U.S. state legislatures, women are more successful than men in getting bills directly related to women, children, and families passed (Thomas 1991). Women in state legislatures are also as good as men at passing bills on topics of broad interest to women (education, health care, etc.) (Bratton and Haynie 1999). And, in the U.S. Congress, women are as successful as men in shepherding all types of bills into law (Jeydel and Taylor 2003). Men are also no more likely than women are to successfully amend other laws, influence domestic spending, or channel money to their home districts. In fact, Anzia and Berry (2011) showed that women are more successful than men in returning federal money to their districts. This research suggests, therefore, that women can be effective legislators, both on issues related to women and, more broadly, on all issues.

But when we look more closely at the bills that get passed by women, the answer to women's effectiveness is more complex. Recent research based in Argentina suggests women can have difficulty passing bills when they deal with women's rights: Between 1999 and 2006, women's rights bills—which women were more likely than men to propose—failed more than twice as often as other bills (Franceschet and Piscopo 2008). Along the same lines, Kathlene (1995) found that female legislators in Colorado were only partially successful in getting their crime-related bills (see Table 8.1) passed. Only the female-sponsored crime bills that addressed crime in "male" terms became law. Women's more innovative bills, addressing crime with a long-term perspective, were not successful. So women were able to pass their bills when they legislated like men.

But it is worth noting a different pattern for female-sponsored prison bills. These had a much higher success rate, and bills with a "female flavor" were passed by the legislature. The difference may have been that prison overcrowding and tight budgets led all lawmakers to consider nontraditional solutions to the problem. In an environment of crisis, the new perspectives brought by female legislators were accepted.

Also, even if women have equal success, it does not mean they enjoy equality in the process. Female politicians are political newcomers with less institutional (and social) power than their male colleagues. This means they have less power in face-to-face interactions, such as in the committee meetings where bills are first discussed and debated. Looking at these committee meetings demonstrates a pattern of male domination:

> Regardless of whether the chair [of the committee] or the sponsor [of the bill] is a man or a woman or the hearing is on a family issue, female committee members engage later, speak significantly fewer words, take significantly fewer turns, and make and receive fewer interruptions than their male counterparts. (Kathlene 1994:569)

Further, women-sponsored bills receive more scrutiny, debate, and hostile testimony than male-sponsored bills do (Kathlene, Clarke, and Fox 1991). And male power is still evident in the treatment of male and female expert witnesses. Consider what Lyn Kathlene (1994) saw in committee hearings in the Colorado state legislature:

> A woman who testified was usually addressed by her first name by male chairs, whether she was an unknown expert, citizen, familiar lobbyist, or bureaucrat; but a witness who was a man received a title in front of his name, both at the time of introduction and at the conclusion of his remarks. Female chairs used titles with both men and women who were unknown to them and reserved first names for witnesses of both sexes with whom they were familiar. The most egregious example of the sexist treatment occurred in a hearing on a health issue, in which several doctors testified. Although the woman witness clearly stated her title and name as "Dr. Elisa Jones," the male chair addressed her repeatedly as "Elisa" and finally thanked "Mrs. Jones" for her testimony. Needless to say, perhaps, none of the male doctors were referred to as anything but "Dr. ___." (p. 572)

The effectiveness of female legislators in getting legislation passed is also highly dependent on context. For example, Swers (2002b) explained that Democratic women were able to influence the legislative agenda when theirs was the party in power during 1993–1994 but were substantially limited in their ability to influence the agenda when their party was out of power in the subsequent congress.

Similarly, nondemocratic systems limit women's ability to influence legislation or otherwise make an impact. Even if women successfully pass legislation in parliament, a powerful president may simply dispose of the parliamentary reforms. Consider women's failed attempts to influence **land tenure** reform in semidemocratic Uganda in the late 1990s. Like many countries in Africa, women in Uganda have limited ownership rights over land. Even where women have the funds to purchase their own land, they often register it in a man's name, giving women limited rights over what the land produces. Thus, in 1997, when the Ugandan government proposed to regularize titling and tenure systems, a coalition of women's groups proposed a clause granting women ownership rights in spousal homestead property. The clause was approved in parliament, where women held 18% of the legislature, but when the Land Act was published a few days later, the clause granting women land rights had been removed. The powerful President Museveni admitted that he had personally intervened to delete the amendment. In the country's semi-democratic system, women had no way to fight back, and women's groups in Uganda continue to fight for land reform (Central Intelligence Agency 2005; Goetz 2003; Goetz and Hassim 2003; Kawamara-Mishambi and Ovonji-Odida 2003; Norris 1993:329; U.S. Department of State 2005; Women of Uganda Network 2005).

Legislating Differently: Women's Legislative Style

What about legislative style? Women may not only change the products of legislatures through different policy priorities and innovative legislation, but they may also change the process of legislating or the procedures of the legislature. Asked as a question, do women change the way business is done in legislatures? Already we explained that women view social problems differently than men do, which leads women to propose different types of legislation. But research suggests that women have a different style of legislating as well—women tend to be more democratic and participatory in their leadership style than men are (Eagly and Johnson 1990). Female legislators also tend to be more collaborative in their leadership styles than men are, answering more positively when asked whether they "try hard to find a fair combination of gains and losses for all sides," "pull people together," and "share power with others" (Rosenthal 1998a:855). For example, Sue Thomas (1994) interviewed state legislators from California,

Georgia, Mississippi, Nebraska, Pennsylvania, and Washington. These female legislators saw women as advocating a different style of politics—one that is more consensus and compromise oriented.

Consider the following account of interviews with state legislators in Ohio:

> One chairwoman emphasized the desire to be more inclusive of as many points of view on an issue as possible, to find a win-win solution, and to use nontraditional decision-making strategies such as facilitator-mediated dispute resolution. By contrast, one of her male colleagues preferred to "develop my own solution to problem, have it drafted, drop in the hopper and watch everyone scream." (Rosenthal 1998a:858–859)

Biographies of women at the highest levels of political leadership suggest that some, such as Corazon Aquino and Violetta de Charmorro, worked for participation and consensus. Others, however, were famously autocratic. Margaret Thatcher was a self-described conviction politician, rather than a consensus politician. She surrounded herself with "yes" men and limited debate and discussion during cabinet meetings. Thatcher would enter a cabinet meeting; tell her cabinet members what she wanted; and then try to bully them through fear, intimidation, control of the agenda, and "sheer force of personality and conviction" (Genovese 1993:199). Indira Gandhi seriously endangered India's 28-year-old democracy by declaring emergency rule when her leadership was challenged. Declaration of emergency rule essentially transformed India into a dictatorship, and Gandhi, as the head of the central government, was able to arrest opposition leaders, censor the press, ban political organizations, and jail more than 100,000 people without trial (Everett 1993).

Differences in legislative style may arise from a different view of power (Kanter 1977:166; Thomas 1994). Feminist theory and studies of female legislators both suggest that women view power as a way to get things done, rather than as a way to control or influence other people. Consider the female legislator interviewed by Cantor, Bernay, and Stoess (1992:40), who explained that "power is basically that sense of strength and understanding about how to pull together resources to get your agendas done." Or consider what Iowa's Lieutenant Governor Jo Ann Zimmerman had to say, "I didn't think about having power myself. There are just things to do, and you get them done" (Cantor et al. 1992:48).

Women may have a different style of doing politics, but does it make a difference to the whole legislature? Has it affected the way business is conducted? A 2001 survey of United States state legislators found that a majority of both men and women say that the increased presence of women has made a difference to the "way legislators conduct themselves on the floor of the legislature" (Center for American Women and Politics [CAWP] 2001:11). These numbers suggest some spillover from female legislators to their colleagues—at least in the United States. Further, women's presence appears to highlight the needs of other traditionally disadvantaged groups. The same survey found that a majority of male and female legislators agreed that women have made a difference in "the extent to which the legislature is sympathetic to the concerns of racial and ethnic minority groups" and "the extent to which the economically disadvantaged have access to the legislature" (CAWP 2001:1). Thus, women may increase awareness not only of "women's issues" but also of issues related to other disadvantaged groups. Consider what Congresswoman Patsy Mink (D-HI) had this to say:

> I think basically that poor women are the ones that have no representation in Congress, other than from congresswomen who feel a sense of commitment to represent their causes. It's the poor women who are left out in much of this debate, certainly the legal immigrant women and legal immigrant children . . . and to some extent elderly women who are also poor and on Medicare, and so forth . . . these are the types of bills that I press on. (quoted in Hawkesworth et al. 2001:10)

Of course, simply asking male and female legislators whether women make a difference to politics cannot directly show whether the legislature objectively changes when women are present. But Bratton and Haynie (1999) found that women are more likely to introduce bills of interest to African Americans (e.g., school integration and funding of sickle cell anemia research). And Black legislators are more likely to introduce bills of interest to women.

And of course, realistically, politics continues to involve zero-sum, win-lose decisions, and women who may naturally have a different legislative style feel pressure to adapt to that environment, at least at times. As explained by state legislator Jean Marie Brough, "I don't like the process, but in order to make a change, you have to get power, and in order to get power you have to play the system" (quoted in Thomas 1994:122). Or consider the views of Maria Rozas, a Chilean parliamentarian: "In order that they do listen to you, women have to shout or swear, but that means adopting masculine behaviour, and it should not be like that" (quoted in Franceschet 2001:215). Generally, the problem is well described by Joni Lovenduski (1993): "A great dilemma for the second wave of feminism has been whether women will change institutions before institutions change women" (p. 6).

In choosing between incremental change and large-scale systematic change, women face serious potential drawbacks to any decision (Thomas 1994:122–127). Do women fight within the system, making small changes but perhaps remaining dissatisfied? Or do women fight to change the entire system, risking marginalization and derision? Consider the dilemma one women's party in Iceland faced. In 1987, the *Kvennalistinn* party (known in English as the Women's Alliance) won six seats in Iceland's election. This was a high enough percentage of seats to make the Kvennalistinn a political player, and the party was asked to join a coalition government. Being a part of the coalition government would increase the party's power and influence substantially. But for the Women's Alliance this was a tough decision because in joining the coalition the party would have to compromise some of its primary goals, such as a minimum wage proposal.

Considering the name of the party, it should come as no surprise that women were central to the objectives of the Kvennalistinn. As stated in the party's platform, it had a goal:

> To make women's perspectives, experience and culture a no less important policy-making force in our society than that of men. The Women's Alliance wants to nurture and develop that which is positive in women's outlook on the world and to harness it for the betterment of society as a whole. (Kvennalistinn 1987)

Thomas (1994:28) explained the following:

> The kinds of political products that members of the Kvennalistinn advocate include women's issues such as childcare, sex education, and fair salaries. Despite a special dedication to these issues, however, members of the alliance insist there is a need for a women's point of view on all domestic and foreign issues. Its platform addresses each issue based on the economic model of a housewife on a limited budget.

Ultimately, the party decided against joining the coalition. As explained by one party member, "We were ready to take part in the government, but only if it would really matter. We didn't want to be flowers to make the government look good to the world" (quoted in Thomas 1994:28). The women of the Kvennalistinn decided it was more important to hold fast to their principles and remain on the outside than to compromise those principles to gain additional power (Koester 1995; Olafsdottir Bjornsson 2001; Thomas 1994).

Did the Kvennalistinn disappear when they wouldn't play politics as usual? No. In fact, in 1988, the Kvennalistinn was the most popular party of

Iceland's six major parties, with support from 31.3% of the population. The party lost ground over time, partly because other parties expanded their numbers of female candidates. But the message of the Women's Alliance continued to resonate over time. It contested and won seats and polled in second place among parties in 1994 (Koester 1995). In 1997, the members of the party split on joining a new coalition, and the party was dissolved.

Do Numbers Matter?
Critical Mass and Women's Impact

An additional question relates to whether the number of women present in a legislature makes a difference for women's impact. That is, are women better able to make a difference when there are a lot of them in office? To understand the question, think about the difference between one or two women struggling for survival in a traditionally male environment and a group of women supporting each other as they bring new ideas to the legislative table. Women may be better able to leave a distinctive imprint on the policy process when there are more of them in place.

Women in politics scholars use the term *critical mass* to suggest that when women reach a certain percentage of a legislature, they will be better able to pursue their policy priorities and legislative styles. The term has its origins in Rosabeth Moss Kanter's (1977) work on women in an American corporation. Although she did not use the term *critical mass,* Kanter made a distinction between four different types of groups:

- Uniform groups have only one type of person (e.g., 100% men, 0% women).
- Skewed groups have mostly one type of person (e.g., 85% men, 15% women).
- Tilted groups are moving toward balance (e.g., 65% men, 35% women).
- Balanced groups have nearly equal numbers (e.g., 50% men, 50% women).

Women in a skewed group are **tokens** and were found by Kanter (1977) to be more visible than men, suffer from stereotyping, and feel compelled to conform to dominant (male) norms. Because token women feel pressure to blend into the male culture, they may find it difficult to form alliances with other token women to further their interests. Although she only studied a skewed group, Kanter suggested that changes in women's behavior and to the culture of a group were possible if a group moved from skewed status to tilted or balanced status.

The theoretical link to women in politics is clear—if the only women in politics are token women, they may not be able to make a difference to policies or legislative style (Dahlerup 1988). But if women reach a critical mass and move out of token status, the increased influence of women and a feminization of the political agenda will be seen.

What exactly constitutes a critical mass? Common use of the term cites 30% women in parliament as the critical cutoff. Indeed, the United Nations used this cutoff when it argued that women need to make up 30% of national elites to exert meaningful influence on politics (United Nations Development Programme [UNDP] 1995). Research has often used 15%, to signify movement out of Kanter's skewed group category.

There is anecdotal evidence for the importance of critical mass. For example, a female politician from southern Europe discussed legislative style as follows: "If . . . the number of women politicians is small as in the case of my country, politics may change women because, in order to survive politically, women may copy the men in their methods and behavior" (Inter-Parliamentary Union [IPU] 2000:23). Especially in highly visible positions, women may also need to be cognizant of sanctions for being seen to act in the interests of women. Relating the experience of Labour MPs in Great Britain, Childs (2002) explained the following:

> The most common perception is that women who seek to act for women act only for women. This results in a tension between a woman MP's parliamentary career and acting for women. If an MP desires promotion, she cannot afford to be regarded as acting for women too often or too forcefully. (p. 151)

When women make up only a small portion of a political party, they are, according to an East African female politician, vulnerable: "The few who are determined to confront the male politicians within the party end up being called all sorts of names—insolent, would-be men, etc.—and they are often ignored and pushed to one side" (IPU 2000:56).

But anecdotal evidence aside, research on critical mass has produced mixed results. In searching for an effect, some research has looked over time at a legislature to see whether something changes when women hit 15% of a legislature (e.g., Grey 2002; Saint-Germain 1989) or has compared U.S. states with different percentages of women to see if they sponsor more women's issue bills (e.g., Bratton 2005; Thomas 1991). This research provides only a little bit of evidence of critical mass effects. For example, in New Zealand, female politicians verbally represent themselves as women more often as they reach 15% of a legislature (Grey 2002). And Michelle Saint-Germain (1989), looking at the Arizona state legislature, found gender differences in the sponsorship of women's interest bills only after women reached 15% of the legislature. But women were not more successful at passing legislation as their numbers rose. In fact, women did better when their numbers were smaller.

In research on critical mass, just like research on women's impact in general, the problem of distinguishing women's impact from the impact of party or district characteristics exists. For example, in 1988, the two states with the lowest percentage of women in their legislature, Mississippi and Pennsylvania, also had the fewest legislators prioritizing bills dealing with women or with children and families (Thomas 1991). But a skeptic might argue that those states might have been more politically conservative than the others, which led to both fewer women appearing in politics and in less legislation related to women and children being sponsored. Kathleen Bratton (2005) looked at the concept of critical mass on women's sponsorship of bills and in their success at passing those bills. She accounted for party and district characteristics in the legislatures of California, Illinois, and Maryland from 1969 to 1999. Women in all three legislatures consistently sponsored more women's interest bills than did men, regardless of the percentage of the legislature they held—suggesting no effect of critical mass. In fact, Bratton found that as the percentage of women in the legislatures of these states rose from around 5% to around 27%, gender differences in bill sponsorship actually diminished. Even more striking, Bratton found that women were better able to pass the legislation they proposed when they were a smaller percentage of the legislature. In discussing her results, Bratton pointed out that, in contrast to women in a corporation, women in politics may never feel that it is a disadvantage to focus on women's issues. Furthermore, when women appear in only small numbers, they may feel an especial need to act for women, resulting in overachievement on sponsoring and passing women's issues.

In contrast, a recent study at the national level that matches male and female representatives from the same U.S. congressional districts finds positive effects of increasing women's numbers (MacDonald and O'Brien 2011). The authors found that, compared to the men that immediately preceded them or followed them in their districts, female congresswomen proposed more "feminist" bills and social welfare bills than men. But importantly, this effect was dependent on the percentage of women in Congress at the time. For example, "female members were significantly more likely to sponsor feminist legislation when at least 5 percent of their House colleagues were women" (MacDonald and O'Brien 2011:478).

As for legislative style, in New Zealand women became more aggressive (making personal attacks and interrupting other MPs) as their numbers rose in the legislature (Grey 2002). Generally, women still made fewer personal attacks than men did. In fact, "male MPs' share of personal attacks was higher than their share of the debates on child care and parental leave in 11 of the 25 years" (Grey 2002:23). But women seem to have adopted more masculine behavior over time, concomitantly with their rise in numbers.

In understanding whether having high numbers of women—a critical mass—makes a difference to women's impact, it is important to recognize that power is not evenly distributed in legislatures. As discussed earlier, being a part of the party in power is important for whether women can influence policy. The party, or parties, in power have a much greater chance than opposition parties of getting their agenda passed. Remember that women in the U.S. Democratic Party had more influence in the 103rd Congress when their party was in power. But Democratic women's ability to pass laws related to women and women's interests declined after Republicans took power in 1994 (Swers 2002a). Similarly, in New Zealand between 1988 and 1990, many discussions of child care and parental leave took place. During this period, women comprised 19.3% of the Labour Party and the Labour Party was in power. But "from late 1990, when women made up only 11.9% of the National group and National was in office, there was a drop in the incidences of debate of the two 'women's issues'" (Grey 2002:22).

Legislators who chair powerful committees or fill cabinet posts also have greater influence on public policy than the regular rank-and-file. Seniority matters in many legislatures, giving long-standing MPs the headships of committees and important cabinet positions. Thus, even if women reach 15% or 30% of a legislature, if they are newcomers, they will still be disadvantaged in positional power. This suggests that though greater numbers may help women develop a voice, it could take more time for women to truly affect policy outcomes (Grey 2002).

It is also important to note theory and evidence that increasing numbers of women can have a *negative* effect on outcomes for women. Kanter's (1977) analysis of proportions is only one way of thinking about how minority groups interact with majority groups. In contrast, sociologist Peter Blau (1977) focused on the social networks possible between minority and majority group members. When minority members are only a small part of a group, they must have more contact with and connections to majority group members (e.g., the only Black student in a high school is likely to have many White friends). The social connections between the minority group member and majority members may increase the support from the dominant group. When numbers of minority members increase, they can have more connections with each other and consequently fewer with majority members. Fewer connections between the majority and minority groups could decrease support from the dominant group and potentially increase discrimination against the minority group.

Further, as women's numbers rise, women become a more threatening minority, and a backlash may result. Janice Yoder's (1991) theory of intrusiveness suggests that when women are a small minority, they can use their token status to draw attention to women's concerns. But when women increase in numbers, they start to threaten the power and privilege of men, leading to competition, hostility, and discrimination. "Numerical surges threaten the majority, who react with heightened levels of discriminatory behaviour in order to limit the power gains of the growing lower-status minority" (Yoder 1991:184).

There is some evidence to support this alternative perspective. In the New Zealand legislature, personal attacks against women rose as women's numbers rose. Just when women reached approximately 15% of the legislature, there was a "rise in hostility toward women politicians" (Grey 2002:25). Female legislators in Colombia are reluctant to address gender because it "threatens men" (Schwindt-Bayer 2006:573). In the United States, Cindy Simon Rosenthal (1998b:88–93) compared men and women's behavior in legislative committee meetings where women held few leadership positions and many leadership positions. She found that women in the committees were more likely to be inclusive, collaborative, and accommodating as the percentage of women in leadership positions increased. But men were less likely to be inclusive, collaborative, or accommodating as the number of women increased in leadership power.

Rosenthal's finding suggests that both Kanter and Yoder may be correct. Women feel more comfortable using a "female" legislative style when there are more of them in power. But men appear to be threatened by female power and subsequently reduce their tendency to compromise or accommodate. Both sides are apparent in a quote from one of Rosenthal's (1998b) chairwomen:

> We're at the point where we have enough women in leadership, a critical mass, that we try to caucus and inform one another about our bills. . . . And I don't see anymore the situation when a woman gets up and blows it, that she's treated as a woman who blew it as opposed to a legislator who blew it. . . . We also have a women's conference committee, it's not for real, we only do it to irritate the men. We just go back in a room by ourselves and talk about something . . . and then they're dying to know what we're doing. (p. 92)

The increase in women has reduced women's token representation of all women (being treated as a woman who blew it rather than a legislator who blew it) in this Texas legislature. But the increase in women is also likely threatening to the men who are "dying to know" what the women are doing.

Ultimately, it may be the **critical acts** of women, as well as their critical mass, that matters for policy influence (Childs and Krook 2005; Dahlerup 1988). Indeed, many female politicians feel that that the quality of female leaders is as important as numbers: "Just one courageous woman can be a vehicle for profound change where 30% may be of little effect" (Pacific politician, cited in IPU 2000:68).

Women's Movements and Women's Policy Machinery as Alternative Sources of Influence

Our discussion of critical mass suggests that even after women achieve a significant number of parliamentary seats, governments may still refuse to address women's concerns. Thus, S. Laurel Weldon (2002a) pointed out that one should also think "beyond bodies" in legislatures. Even in countries and regions where women are woefully underrepresented in political office, women can achieve substantive representation through their participation in women's movements or women's groups. Women's movements "pursue women's gender interests . . . [and] make claims on cultural and political systems on the basis of women's historically ascribed gender roles" (Álvarez 1990:23; see also Beckwith 2005). They are therefore a place outside the government where women can speak for women as everyday citizens and activists (Celis et al. 2008; Waylen 1994:531).

When the voices of female legislators are being pushed to the sidelines, women's movements may push women's interests back into play. For instance, women's groups in Mozambique were critical to getting the New Family Law Act, which allowed women to work without their husband's permission, passed in 2003. Even after elected women held 30% of Mozambique's parliament in 1999, the draft bill was stalled in parliament. Parliamentarians made excuses, did not debate the bill, and generally treated it as a low priority. But in November 2003, more than 1,000 women marched to the National Assembly building and demanded that the New Family Law be debated in parliament. Just 1 month after the march, the bill was passed (Disney 2006:43).

But women's movements need not always be oppositional. When women hold legislative seats, they may provide a sympathetic ear and allow women's groups to help set the agenda. And countries and political parties may also establish structures that help bridge the gap between women's movements and government. An alternative place for women to make a difference is within the **machinery of government**. Governments have various agencies, departments, and ministries that develop and implement policy. Although feminists have traditionally been leery of governments, viewing them as sites of oppression, many now see the benefits to engaging directly with the state to advocate women's rights. Acting within government bureaucracy allows "the development and implementation of gender-sensitive national policy, as well as representation of women's interests within the state" (Friedman 2000:48). And individual women can influence policy in gender-sensitive ways, not just in their position as legislators but also in their position as bureaucrats, or "femocrats" (Sawer 1990).

Today, most national governments have some form of women's policy machinery, or government body devoted to promoting the status of women (Staudt 1998; Stetson 1995; Weldon 2002b). Government-level women's policy machinery can take the form of a national women's agency, a women's commission, or a women's ministry. Having a designated space for women within a government promotes women's interests in a number of ways. First, women's policy machinery can coordinate and consolidate the development and implementation of policy (Stetson 1995; Stetson and Mazur 1995; Weldon 2002a). Without a single site for the creation of gender-sensitive national policy, a government response to gender inequality is likely to be spread across multiple agencies or departments.

> Government response to violence against women . . . requires action in areas as diverse as criminal justice, education, and income assistance policy. But these areas are usually the responsibility of a variety of different agencies, posing considerable coordination problems. (Weldon 2002a:1159)

In contrast, a response to domestic violence can be better designed and more effectively promoted under a single women's agency.

Further, an institutionalized women's policy machinery produces a single, direct route to government cooperation with agents, such as women's movements, who traditionally act outside the state (Friedman 2000; Stetson and Mazur 1995; Weldon 2002a, 2002b). Women's movements may critique or comment on existing agency proposals, assist with policy formation, and help represent the different bases for inequality across women, such as race, ethnicity, or sexuality. Indeed, Weldon (2002a) found that across 36 democratic countries, a strong women's movement acting in conjunction with an effective women's agency predicted the extent of government commitment to domestic violence.

9

Women
From Marginalized Groups

W e have already touched on some of the ways that differences among women can affect their political participation and representation. For example, in Chapter 2, we discussed the exclusion of women of color from mainstream movements for women's suffrage. And in Chapter 6, we addressed the ways that electoral systems and rules can affect majority and minority women differently. Here, we take the opportunity to focus at greater length on the experiences of women who are also members of marginalized groups, including racial, ethnic, and religious minority women and lesbian, bisexual, and **transgender** women. These women may face obstacles in politics because they are women or because they are members of marginalized groups. Yet, as discussed in Chapter 1, one cannot simply add up the disadvantages created by being a woman and the disadvantages created by being a member of a minority group to understand the experiences of minority women. Thus, before we go any further, we first return to the concept of intersectionality, arguably the leading framework for research on women from marginalized groups.

Thinking Intersectionally

In 1989, Kimberlé Crenshaw introduced the term *intersectionality* as a way to better understand the experiences and concerns of Black women in the United States. Crenshaw was critical of the way the forces behind subordination are often viewed in a compartmentalized way. Instead of thinking separately about how sexism affects women and racism affects Black Americans, she argued gender and race should be understood as inter-linked. She further reasoned that the experience of being Black and the experience of being a woman did not sum to the experience of being a Black women. Inequalities intersect in complex and often compounding ways.

Although Crenshaw coined the term *intersectionality,* the idea that women from racial, ethnic, and religious minority groups face multiple bar-riers to power is neither new nor a uniquely American concept. For decades, feminists worldwide have articulated the multiple oppressions faced by women from marginalized groups using terms like "**double barriers**," "dou-ble burden," "double whammy," "double jeopardy," and "double minority" (Black 2000). Over the past two decades, intersectionality research has also grown to encompass a much broader range of intersecting social structures—not just gender and race but also social class, ethnicity, nation, language, and sexuality, to name a few. The concept of multiple oppressions has even been integrated into United Nations resolutions on human rights (Yuval-Davis 2006).

Although meanings of intersectionality have evolved over time and are applied differently, intersectional research involving women typically shares four key elements:

Intersectionality recognizes differences among women. Recognizing and exploring differences among women is at the foundation of intersectionality research (Davis 2008; García Bedolla 2007; Nash 2008). Intersectionality chal-lenges ideas that women are a fixed, monolithic group, and contests essentialism—the assumption that women are defined by a common set of characteristics, attributes, or interests. When faced with assertions about "women," intersec-tionality raises this question: "Which women?" (Smooth 2011).

Intersectionality sees stratifying institutions as inseparable. Systems of stratification like gender and race and forces of oppression like sexism and racism are seen as "interlinked," "interlocking," and "mutually constructed." For example, race is thought to affect the way Black women experience gender, and gender affects the way Black women experience race (Mansbridge and Tate 1992; see also Baca Zinn and Thornton Dill 1996; West and Fenstermaker 1997).

Intersectionality explicitly references power. Differences such as gender, class, race, ethnicity, nationality, religion, and sexuality combine to form intersecting social hierarchies (Glenn 1999; Weber 2001). These intersections are said to create a "matrix of domination," through which individuals may experience both privilege and marginalization, or experience multiple oppressions (Collins 2000).

Intersectionality acknowledges complexity. Understanding life at the intersections is anything but simple. One cannot simply average or add up the experience of being a racial, ethnic, or religious minority and the experience of being a woman to equal being a minority woman. In some cases, the barriers faced by marginalized women may be compounded by the multiplicity of forces of oppression. In other cases, minority women's dual identities can provide strategic advantages or opportunities.

So how does intersectionality play out in politics? In the following sections, we talk about the ways that women from marginalized groups can face multiple barriers to political power. But we also consider the advantages or opportunities that politics at the intersection sometimes provides. We close the chapter by talking about to the political experiences of sexual minorities—lesbians, bisexual, and transgender women.

Double Barriers

Just like women from privileged groups, women from marginalized groups can face barriers to political participation and representation because they are women. Historically, women's suffrage in some countries followed the extension of voting rights to minority men, as occurred in the United States (see Chapter 2). But remember that women's political exclusion is not a thing of the past. As of 2011, seven countries had not a single woman in their national legislature: Belize, Micronesia, Nauru, Palau, Qatar, Saudi Arabia, and Solomon Islands. In these contexts, the multiplicity of women's identities has no effect on their political outcomes. Politics is exclusively a male domain.

In other contexts, women from racial, ethnic, and religious minority groups are excluded from political participation and representation because they are minorities. Historically, some minority groups lacked voting rights long after women received them. Aboriginal peoples in Australia, for instance, did not have full suffrage until over 60 years after women. And in modern times, plenty of marginalized groups continue to lack political representation at the national level. In 2006, some of these groups were the indigenous peoples of Australia, Chile, and Honduras; Turkish groups in Austria, Cyprus, and Switzerland; Roma (also called Romani or gypsies) in Albania, the Czech Republic, and Greece; Afro-descendant peoples in Nicaragua, Panama, Venezuela, and Yemen; and all non-Muslim religious groups in Bahrain and Kuwait. Barriers to political representation were too high for any group member—man or woman—to surmount.

But understanding the double barriers minority women face is more complex than simply acknowledging that either gender *or* minority status may limit them politically. Intersectionality research tells us that we should try to understand the complex ways that gender *and* minority status together influence minority women's experiences. Because of their position in society, their outcomes are often different than the outcomes of majority women and minority men.

Overwhelmingly, minority women's political rights and representation have progressed more slowly than their majority female and minority male counterparts. In the Canadian House of Commons, for example, the first woman was elected in 1920 and the first African Canadian man in 1965, but the first African Canadian woman was not elected until 1972. In New Zealand, the first Maori man was elected in 1868 and the first woman in 1933, but the first Maori woman was not elected until 1949. In the United States, the first Latina was elected to the U.S. House of Representatives in 1989, 41 years after the first woman and 113 years after the first Latino. In some countries, minority women have yet to reach their "firsts." In Greece, for example, the first woman was elected to parliament in 1952 and the first Turkish minority in 1989, but a Turkish woman has yet to serve in the Greek parliament.

In many countries, women are serving in national legislatures, but the representatives of minority groups are all men. Small minority groups—those that win only one or two seats in parliament—are particularly likely to have men representing them. In Macedonia, for example, eight minority Albanian women were sent to parliament in 2008, but elected representatives of the much smaller Turkish, Serbian, and Roma minority groups were all men (Freidenvall 2010). And, looking across more than 400 racial, ethnic, and religious groups in 81 countries circa 2007, Hughes (forthcoming) found that more than three quarters of the groups with only one or two seats in parliament were represented solely by men.

Double barriers also affect women from larger minority delegations. In elections between 1999 and 2005, women were entirely absent among Jews in Russia (5 men), Christians in Jordan (10 men), Arab Muslims in Israel (8 men), Asian Americans in the United States (4 men), Hungarians in Romania (22 men), indigenous peoples of Malaysia (31 men), Arabs in Venezuela (5 men), Shi'a Muslims of Lebanon (27 men), and Ryukyuans in Japan (4 men).

These exclusions of minority women add up. Figure 9.1 displays the composition of the typical population and national legislature by both gender and racial, ethnic, and religious minority status. In the 81 democratic and semidemocratic countries captured by these data, minority women make up approximately 9% of the population but hold less than 2% of national legislative seats (Hughes forthcoming).

Figure 9.1   Composition of the Average Population
               and National Legislature in 81 Countries, 2005–2007

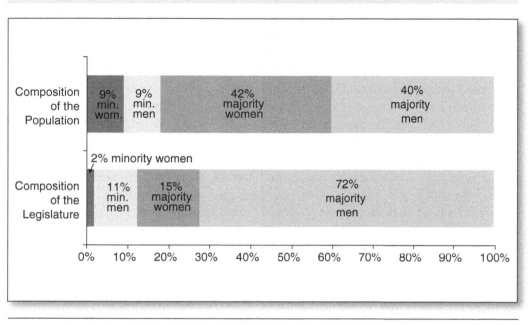

Source: Hughes (forthcoming).

Another way of quantifying the disadvantages faced by racial, ethnic, and religious minority women is to think in terms of the odds that a minority woman is likely to be elected relative to other groups, adjusting for the different sizes of groups in the population. Taking this approach for the same countries and groups in Figure 9.1, we find that majority men are about nine times more likely than minority women to get elected on average. The odds are more even when comparing their chances of election relative to minority men and majority women—about two to one against them—but clearly they still are not good.

The difficulties minority women face go beyond their exclusion in formal politics. Politics at the intersection of gender and minority status also involves conflict over ideals and values. When organizations and movements representing women and minority groups disagree, where do minority women stand? We turn to the answers of these questions in the next section.

When Identities Come in Conflict: Gender Versus Minority Status

As a consequence of the multiplicity of women's identities, women are sometimes pulled in more than one direction. Although intersectionality tells us that race and gender cannot be understood separately, sometimes the two groups of which minority women are a part—minorities and women—explicitly come into conflict. The interests of women's and civil rights or antiracist movements may explicitly collide. As Crenshaw (1994:99) explained, minority women are "situated within at least two subordinated groups that frequently pursue conflicting political agendas."

What happens when women from racial, ethnic, and religious minority groups are faced with the choice between siding with women or with other members of their group? In the United States, at least, research often finds that Black women identify more strongly with race than gender (Gay and Tate 1998). This is not to say that gender is irrelevant to Black women. But when forced, it appears Black women tend to choose race.

As an example, the Clarence Thomas hearings, discussed in Chapter 1, put Black women in America in a difficult position. Anita Hill was a Black woman accusing Clarence Thomas, a Black man, of sexual harassment. What should a Black woman do? Should she support the interests of Blacks? Or should she support the interests of women? It turns out that Black women sided with Black men on this issue and supported Clarence Thomas. Black women were less likely than White women—and even less likely than White and Black men—to believe Anita Hill (Mansbridge and Tate 1992:489).

Jane Mansbridge and Katherine Tate (1992) discussed the Thomas nomination:

> Why did race trump gender for Blacks in the Thomas nomination? Blacks supported Thomas because of their desire to maintain representation on the Supreme Court. In addition, Blacks favored Thomas because of the complicated history of race and gender relations in this country, which led both Black men and Black women to concern at this historical moment with the public image of a Black woman attacking a Black man. The media and organized interest groups also played important roles in shaping public opinion on this matter. The way the media presented the confrontation between Thomas and Hill did not make clear why she had waited 10 years to bring her story forward and why she had not quit or brought charges at the time. For these reasons, Black leaders had difficulty organizing against Thomas.

That paucity of organized opposition greatly benefited his candidacy. (pp. 488–489)

But intersections of gender, race, and ethnicity do not fully explain the nuances of political attitudes. Class differences may also be important. Indeed, Mansbridge and Tate (1992) found that politically active professional Black women appear to have supported Anita Hill more strongly (although too few such women were surveyed for concrete conclusions). And shortly after Clarence Thomas was sworn in on the Supreme Court, more than 1,600 Black university women took out a full-page *New York Times* advertisement expressing support for Professor Hill. Mansbridge and Tate (1992) suggested that working-class women were profoundly suspicious of Hill's decision not to immediately accuse Thomas of sexual harassment when it occurred. In contrast, professional women realized that such accusations could have been profoundly damaging to Hill's career.

Overall, the controversy surrounding Anita Hill and Clarence Thomas is but one example of many in which the multiplicity of minority women's identities can put them in a difficult position. Indeed, tensions between movements to advance women and minorities are not limited to the United States. Historically, feminism has often butted up against anticolonial and nationalist movements (e.g., Cockburn 1998; Moghadam 1994; Yuval-Davis and Werbner 1999). As minority groups press for greater rights within states, for greater autonomy, or even for a state of their own, feminism is often subverted "for the greater good." Furthermore, anticolonial and nationalist movements are frequently gendered in ways that idealize women's roles as mothers. As a result, when these movements win concessions or even control over governance, women from newly empowered groups often continue to face discrimination or marginalization based on their gender.

Recent debates on multiculturalism and feminism in liberal societies highlight similar tensions as religious and cultural minority groups lobby for greater control over personal or **family laws** (Friedman 2003; Kukathas 2001; Kymlicka 1999; Nussbaum 1999; Okin 1999, 2005; Spinner-Halev 2001; Tripp 2002). Because family laws—those involving marriage, divorce, child custody, the division of property and inheritance—often have larger implications for the lives of women in these minority communities, the rights and welfare of minority women are at the center of the debate. Some researchers argue that women's rights are paramount (e.g., Deveaux 2000; Nussbaum 1999; Okin 1999; Tripp 2002), whereas other researchers stress the importance of cultural autonomy, even if it means oppressing women

(Kukathas 2001; Spinner-Halev 2001). Regardless of where one sides on these issues, these debates underscore the importance of allowing minority women the opportunity to speak for themselves through inclusion in decision-making processes (Deveaux 2005; Spinner-Halev 2001; Yeatman 1993). In short, women from marginalized groups need to "have a say" (Spinner-Halev 2001:113).

So far, we have discussed the multiple ways in which minority women face obstacles because of their identities as both women and minorities. But minority women are not always doubly disadvantaged. In the next section, we consider ways in which minority women's political fortunes are not necessarily so dismal.

Strategic Opportunities

Racial, ethnic, and religious minority women are not universally underrepresented in politics. In some cases, the multiplicity of women's identities can sometimes provide them with **strategic opportunities**— advantages that come with being both a woman and a member of another marginalized group (Fraga, Martinez-Ebers, Lopez, and Ramírez 2008; Hughes 2011). Luis Ricardo Fraga and his colleagues (2008) originally used the terminology of strategic opportunities to describe the ability of Latina women legislators in California to leverage their intersectional identities to become particularly effective advocates for working class communities of color. Here, we use the term more broadly, to speak to a range of situations in which women from marginalized groups can be advantaged, or have greater opportunities, than comparison groups.

For example, in several Western industrialized countries, scholars have taken notice of what has been called minority women's **"puzzle of success"**—that women from racial and ethnic minority groups typically occupy a greater share of their group's legislative seats than do women from majority groups (Darcy and Hadley 1988:629). This pattern has been most widely documented in the United States, where women of color have been outperforming majority women in this way at all levels of government since the 1970s (Darcy and Hadley 1988; Darcy, Welch, and Clark 1994; Montoya, Hardy-Fanta, and Garcia 2000; Scola 2006; Takash 1993). For example, at the state legislative level in 2004, women of color held nearly 33% of seats held by their respective groups compared to White women who held 22% of legislative seats held by Whites, a gap that was even wider in the U.S. Congress the same year (Center for American Women and Politics

[CAWP] 2012b; Scola 2006).

Similarly, in Canada in 2006, women's share of seats among visible minority legislators—"persons, other than Aboriginal peoples, who are non-Caucasian in race or non-white in colour"—was more than twice women's share of nonminority seats (41.7% vs. 19.0%) (Bird 2010; Employment Equity Act, S.C. 1995, c. 44). Since 2000, Belgian women of Moroccan and Algerian descent have been elected in numbers higher than their male counterparts, outperforming other Belgian women who have not yet crossed 40% of men's seats (Hughes 2009b).

The puzzle of minority women's success is certainly not universal. Certainly, the representation of women, minorities, and minority women is not static and can change over time. For example, in Brazil in 2006, women who did not identify as being of African descent outperformed Afro-descendant women when measured against the total congressional seats held by their respective groups (11% vs. 7%). But between 2006 and 2010, the numbers of Afro-descendant women elected doubled amidst no growth in women's representation overall; thus, in 2010, women not of African descent held 10% of their group's seats, compared to Afro-descendant who held 16% of all seats held by Afro-descendants) (Paixão and Carvano 2008, cited in Htun 2012).

Research also demonstrates that minority women's success relative to male group members is strongly influenced by the political performance of their group overall (Hughes forthcoming; Scola 2006). Remember from earlier that minority women are often excluded altogether when their group wins only one or two seats in parliament. In absolute terms, then, women tend to do the best when their group has a strong showing. But in relative terms—when measuring women's performance against men's from their group—minority women do better when their group is represented in only moderate numbers. Women can even outpace men from their group, provided that their group does not win more than ten seats in parliament. But as minority groups start looking more like the majority—electing larger numbers of legislators—women no longer outperform men, and the puzzle of minority women's success declines (Hughes forthcoming; Scola 2006).

But beyond these considerations about numbers, what explains minority women's success when it does occur? Scholars have not yet settled on any one reason. But there are plausible cultural, structural, and political explanations why minority women may sometimes perform well relative to men from their groups. When choosing a minority candidate, women may be an attractive option to nonminority parties and populations for cultural reasons (Bird 2010; Hughes 2009b). As Bird (2010) explained, in some contexts ethnic minority women do the following:

[They] tend to carry—or are thought to carry—less of the cumbersome cultural baggage of their ethnic community. They are often viewed as more moderate, with better interpersonal skills, and as better able to negotiate between the mainstream and minority cultures. (pp. 221–222)

But culture may not always help minority women. As shown in Figure 9.2, how minority women perform relative to minority men and majority women varies across the major geographic regions of the world.

Figure 9.2   Majority and Minority Women's Share of Group Seats in 81 Countries, 2005–2007

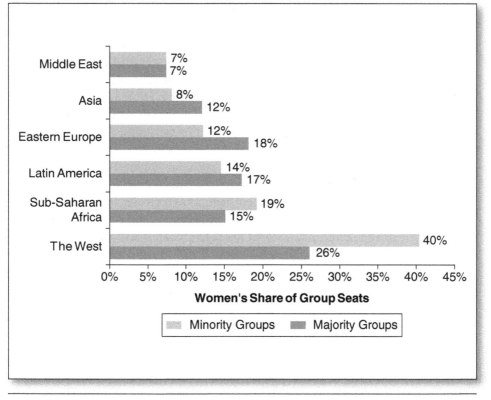

Source: Hughes (forthcoming).

We can also think about the factors that might create a greater demand for minority women in politics. In some countries, policies designed to enhance the representation of women and minority groups may also intersect in ways that benefit minority women (Hughes 2011). Burundi presents one such example.

Burundi

A former Belgian colony, Burundi achieved independence in 1962. Similar to Rwanda, Burundi has three major ethnic groups—Hutu, Tutsi, and Twa—which have been in conflict with one another since independence. As part of the peace process to resolve the long-running civil war, a power-sharing quota system was put in place in the national legislature and the cabinet to ensure that the three ethnic groups each have political representation. The majority Hutus are allotted 60% of seats in the lower house, the minority Tutsi are allocated 40% of the seats, and three seats are reserved for Twa representatives.

But because there is also a national-level quota requiring 30% women, Burundi must balance both the ethnic and gender composition of its national legislature simultaneously. To ensure the proper breakdown by ethnicity and gender, all candidates compete on equal footing for 101 seats, but additional seats are added to produce the right numbers. Following the 2005 election, 18 seats were added to balance the numbers of women and minorities.

Because Tutsi or Twa (minority) women can meet both the ethnic and gender requirement while filling only a single seat, the combination of ethnic and gender quotas has increased their political numbers. In fact, of the female members of Burundi's National Assembly, 57% were minorities (Tutsi or Twa), and of the 18 added positions, more than half are minority women. But the greater participation of Tutsi and Twa women has meant that Hutu women are underrepresented. After the 2005 election, Hutu women made up more than 40% of the population, but they only held 14% of the seats in the assembly.

The case of Burundi is not entirely unique (Hughes 2011). Indeed, how gender and minority intersect with one another can strongly affect the political outcomes of minority women. When national quotas regulate both gender and minority status—what Hughes (2011) called "tandem quotas"—minority women can benefit immensely. If majority group men are attempting to hold on to power, the ability of minority women to improve the statistics for both women's and minority representation simultaneously makes them attractive candidates. But when gender quotas are only voluntarily adopted by political parties, the mix of policies does not create the same incentives to include minority women. Overall, Burundi also demonstrates that at least in some cases, the duality or multiplicity of minority women's identities can be an advantage rather than a detriment.

Acknowledging Differences

Beyond these patterns of double barriers and strategic opportunities, intersectionality research also works to acknowledge differences among women—across groups, over time, and from one state or country to another. In the chapters coming up, we tackle some of this variation, identifying patterns of representation unique to different global regions. As we do this, we will present a series of maps that show variation in women's representation across countries. But, as we have discussed here, women's representation may vary importantly within countries. Therefore, we first show a map showing variation in the legislative representation of women from racial, ethnic and religious minority groups in 81 countries, measured between 2005 and 2007.

Map 9.1 is based on an index that takes the total percentage of minority women in parliament and divides that percentage by their share in the population, adjusted by the sex ratio. Countries with no minority women appear white whereas countries with minority women in the national legislature are shaded in solid gray. Darker shades are associated with higher levels of minority women in the parliament. Countries in which women are at least 50% of the way toward representation proportional to their population are shaded in black. Countries missing from the map are missing from the analysis or are excluded from the analysis based on level of democracy, size, or sovereignty.

Overall, Map 9.1 demonstrates substantial variation in minority women's political power both within and across regions of the world. In Burundi, Ethiopia, and Finland, minority women were overrepresented compared to their share of the population, and in Bosnia and Herzegovina, Costa Rica, Netherlands, and Norway, minority women were represented at levels 50% to 99% of their share of the population. But in 74 countries, minority women are represented in numbers much smaller than their share of the population. On average, around the world minority women are represented at only 17.7% of their population share.

Overall, research on the political representation of racial, ethnic, and religious minority women is new. And although we have described some of the descriptive patterns that exist around the world, it is important to recognize that we know much more about some groups than others. One of the groups of marginalized women we know least about politically is indigenous women. Still, in the next section, we profile some of what we do know, starting with the experience of indigenous women in Latin America and then branching outward.

Map 9.1 Map of Minority Women's Representation in National Legislatures, 81 Countries

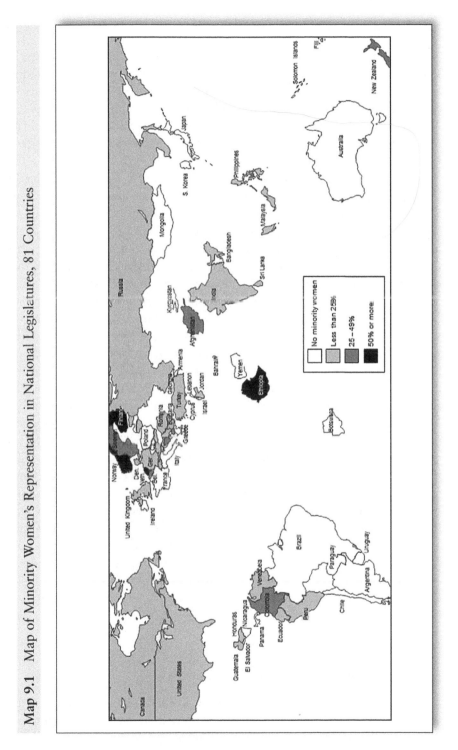

Indigenous Women

Research suggests that indigenous social movements and organizations in Latin America were historically male dominated. But in recent years, indigenous women began to participate in higher numbers, carving out spaces in existing indigenous organizations and forming their own networks. In Mexico, for example, women formed the Coordinadora Nacional de Mujeres Indígenas de México (CNMIM) (Hernández Castillo 2010; Kampwirth 2002, 2004; Sierra 2001, 2007).

During the same time period that women began to play larger roles in indigenous organizations and movements, indigenous movements began to challenge the political exclusion and marginalization they faced for centuries. Often for the first time, indigenous movements took steps to engage actively in local and national electoral politics (Madrid 2005; Van Cott 2005; Van Cott and Birnir 2007; Van Cott and Rice 2006; Yashar 2005). Indigenous women, too, pressed for seats at the table. For example, CNMIM in Mexico demanded women's equal inclusion in all political spaces and institutions.

Politically, indigenous women have enjoyed mixed success. Indigenous women's increasing politicization has not always been met with subsequent gains in formal representation. But in some places, indigenous women have risen to serve as representatives and even political leaders. In Venezuela, two of the three indigenous representatives elected in 2005 were women: Nicia Maldonado and Noelí Pocaterra de Oberto. And in 2006, indigenous Bolivian President Evo Morales chose an indigenous woman, peasant leader Silvia Lazarte, to preside over the Constituent Assembly that drafted the new constitution.

Indigenous women are not universally excluded from political representation elsewhere in the world either. In 2005 in New Zealand, women held nearly 40% of the 21 seats occupied by Maori representatives. Indigenous women held a similar share of seats in Canada. And in Afghanistan and Burundi, women held between 30% and 33% of seats occupied by the Kuchi and Twa indigenous groups in 2005. Overall, indigenous women continue to face political exclusion in some contexts while making headway in others.

So far, we have been talking largely about race, ethnicity, and religion. But women can be marginalized by other identities. In the next section, we focus on women who are also sexual minorities: lesbian, bisexual, and transgender women.

Lesbian, Bisexual, and Transgender Women

Over the past 150 years, legal barriers to the political involvement of minorities have nearly disappeared. But in more than one third of countries, same-sex relationships are illegal. In countries such as Iran, Sudan, and

Yemen, lesbians and bisexual women can be put to death for engaging in same-sex sexual activities. Even where courts do not jail women for their sexuality or gender identity, lesbian, bisexual, and transgender women face violence and discrimination. In 2011, the United Nations issued its first ever report on human rights violations of individuals from the lesbian, gay, bisexual, and transgender (LGBT) community, stating the following:

> In all regions, people experience violence and discrimination because of their sexual orientation or gender identity. In many cases, even the perception of homosexuality or transgender identity puts people at risk. Violations include—but are not limited to—killings, rape and physical attacks, torture, arbitrary detention, the denial of rights to assembly, expression and information, and discrimination in employment, health and education.

Lesbian, bisexual, and transgender women are excluded from politics as well.

But just like women from other marginalized groups, lesbian, bisexual, and transgender women have been elected to public office more often in the last decade than ever before. Perhaps the most visible such event happened in 2009, when Jóhanna Siguðardóttir became prime minister of Iceland, making her the first ever publically lesbian national leader (in addition to becoming the first woman to serve in the post for Iceland). But there are other success stories.

One study of 96 countries identified 105 sexual minority national legislators at the beginning of 2013, up from 35 just 15 years earlier: Most (78) identified as gay men, but 21 identified as lesbians, 5 as bisexual and 1 as transgender (Reynolds forthcoming). As of 2011, more than 90% of LGBT politicians were elected in the West, but there were three in Eastern Europe (including one transgender woman), two in Africa, two in Latin America (including one lesbian), and one each in the Middle East and Asia. Between 1976 and 2012, the United Kingdom elected by far the most LGBT politicians overall, 44, but only 3 of these were women (Reynolds forthcoming). LGBT politicians are also predominantly members of majority ethnic groups; to date, the only known national legislators who are ethnic minorities, sexual minorities, and also women are Georgina Beyer and Louisa Wall, both ethnic Maori New Zealanders. Notably, the vast majority of LGBT national legislators were *out* when they were elected, but Reynolds (forthcoming) identified 40 legislators who came out or were *outed* while in office, 5 of them women.

LGBT individuals have also made gains in the executive. Since 1997, 17 countries have elected or appointed 25 sexual minority cabinet ministers, including 5 women (Reynolds forthcoming). One of these women is lesbian Penny Wong, Australia's first Minister for Climate Change and Water and currently the Minister for Finance and Deregulation. At the regional level, lesbians have also held executive positions. For example, in 2010, Kathleen

Wynne became the first lesbian Minister of Municipal Affairs and Housing and Aboriginal Affairs in the Canadian province of Ontario.

The *T* in LGBT stands for transgender, an umbrella term that does not have an agreed-upon definition but generally is used to describe individuals who do not identify with and/or present as the sex they were assigned at birth. Transgender individuals may eschew binary classifications of gender altogether, embracing a middle area or alternative gender space. Thus, transgender individuals sometimes embrace terms such as *gender queer* or *third gender*. Transgender is a broader term than transsexual, which is typically reserved for a person who lives his or her life as the opposite sex they were assigned at birth and often describes individuals who have taken steps to reassign their sex, for example, by taking hormones or by having surgery.

Aya Kamikawa is a municipal official in Tokyo and the first transsexual individual to seek or win elected office in Japan. In 2003, Kamikawa, then a 35-year-old writer, submitted her application to run for political office, leaving a blank space for "sex." She won a 4-year term as an independent under substantial scrutiny from the media, placing 6th of 72 candidates running for the Setagaya ward assembly, the most populous district in Tokyo. Although the government stated officially that Kamikawa would be considered a male, she stated that she would work as a woman. Kamikawa's platform was to improve rights for women, children, the elderly, the handicapped, and LGBT people. And in April 2007, she was reelected to a second term.

In addition to in Japan, openly transgender politicians have been elected to local or regional office in Cuba (Adela Hernandez), France (Camille Cabral), India (Shabnam Mausi), Spain (Manuela Trasobares), Thailand (Yollada Suanyot), the United Kingdom (Jenny Bailey and Sarah Brown), and the United States (Kim Coco Iwamoto in Hawaii, Althea Garrison in Massachusetts, Jessica Orsini in Missouri, Stacie Laughton in New Hampshire, and Stu Rasmussen in Oregon). All of these transgender individuals were male at birth. To date, there has never been a female-to-male transsexual or female-born transgender politician elected anywhere in the world.

At the national level, three openly transgender women have been elected to national legislatures to date. After New Zealand elected the world's first transgender member of parliament, Georgina Beyer (see Chapter 6), political parties in Italy and most recently Poland have also sent transgender women to parliament—Vladimir Luxuria and Anna Grodzka. Thus, even in majority Catholic countries, sexual minority women have earned their share of the national political spotlight.

Overall, this chapter goes to show that women from marginalized groups can and do participate in politics around the world. These women are a testament to the heterogeneity that exists among women in any city, region or country. In the next six chapters, we turn instead to differences in women's political participation and representation across geographic regions of the world.

10

Regions: The West and the United States

I n the first section of the book, we identified a number of factors and general processes that influence women's political power across the world. But though it is important to understand the big picture, one must also recognize that there is substantial regional variation in both the nature of the obstacles faced by women and the avenues open to women to pursue political inclusion. In parts of the Middle East and the Pacific Islands, women continue to struggle for even the most minimal levels of political representation whereas in Scandinavia women are close to closing the gender gap in political power. Although we cannot delve deeply into the specifics of women's political situations in every country, the next six chapters identify some of the key issues and trends common to particular regions of the world.

The Geography of Women in Politics

To begin, we divide the globe into six regions: (1) Western industrialized countries, (2) Eastern Europe and Central Asia, (3) Latin America and the Caribbean, (4) sub-Saharan Africa, (5) Asia and the Pacific Islands, and (6) the Middle East and North Africa. Countries in each of these categories are fairly geographically concentrated, with the exception of the West, which includes Canada and the United States, Northern and Western Europe, Australia, and New Zealand. Figures 10.1 and 10.2 present an overall picture of the variation in women's political representation and leadership across these six regions.

Figure 10.1 Women's Parliamentary Representation by Region, 2012

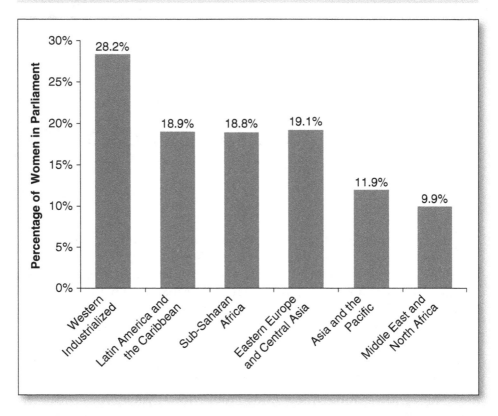

In the following chapters, we examine each region in turn. Overall, we cover a number of topics related to culture, including Scandinavian **political culture,** *marianismo,* Catholicism, **nationalism,** Buddhism, and women in Confucian thought. We also address political and structural matters such as gender quotas at the local level in Southeast Asia and the family law system in the Middle East and North Africa. Building on Chapter 7, where we discussed the myriad ways international factors influence women's political outcomes, we also discuss the complex and contradictory impact of colonialism. These chapters also identify inroads to the political realm that are more commonplace in particular regions, such as women's politicization in democratic movements in Latin America or the family route to political leadership in Asia.

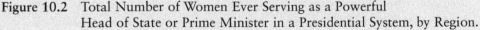

Figure 10.2 Total Number of Women Ever Serving as a Powerful
Head of State or Prime Minister in a Presidential System, by Region.

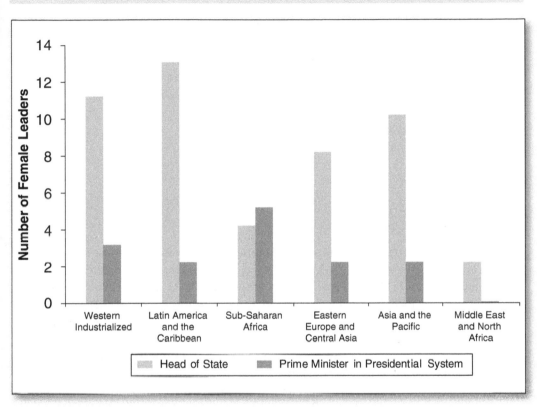

Western Industrialized Countries

*Daddy, on television today they said that a man was prime
minister. Is it possible that a man can be prime minister?*

—Reportedly asked by the child of a news
correspondent after Gro Brundtland,
Norway's former female prime minister,
was ousted from office (Solheim 2000:75)

In no Western industrialized country are women fully excluded from
political representation in national politics. In recent years, no head of state
in the region has appointed an all-male cabinet, and in 2012, only Malta had
less than 10% women in parliament (Inter-Parliamentary Union [IPU]
2012b). However, across the West, substantial differences in women's

political representation and leadership remain. As depicted in Map 10.1, one country, Sweden, has almost 45% women in its parliament, four countries have reached at least 40% women, and many others have more than 20% women. But several countries—France, Greece, Ireland, Malta, San Marino, and the United States—also have less than 20% women in their national legislatures. There is also variation in the histories of female political leadership in the region: Countries such as the United Kingdom elected a truly powerful female head of government, France elected a female prime minister in its presidential system (a position with moderate power), and Ireland elected two women to a largely symbolic national leadership position. Alternatively, countries such as Greece, Italy, San Marino, and the United States have not been led by a woman throughout their entire histories.

Nordic Success

Although women's political representation has increased significantly in a number of Western countries in recent years, since the 1970s, Scandinavia has led the world (see Figure 10.3). Scandinavia is a region of northern Europe that includes Denmark, Finland, Iceland, Norway, and Sweden. With slightly more than 20 million people, Scandinavia comprises small, relatively homogeneous "societies with relatively high standards of living, a fairly common historical tradition and culture, and emphasis on Protestantism, democracy, and social welfare" (Solheim 2000:29). During the 1970s, increasing education, declining birth rates, and a higher cost of living pushed many women into the workforce. But unlike other Western countries, women's political progress in Scandinavia proceeded faster than improvements within the family or the workforce (Solheim 2000).

As of 2012, Nordic countries held 4 of the top 10 positions in the world rankings of women's parliamentary representation. Ranging from a low of 38% in Denmark to a high of 45% in Sweden, the average percentage of women in parliament in Scandinavia is more than 15% higher than the rest of the West (IPU 2012b). This pattern is also evident in the executive branch of government, where by the early 1990s, women cabinet members in Scandinavia totaled 37% whereas the average figure in Western Europe was 9% (Karvonen and Selle 1995). Another impressive political accomplishment of women in Scandinavia is that they have been able to break out of the areas traditionally staffed by women, such as education and family policy, holding cabinet positions in industry, energy, defense, environmental affairs, and justice (Karvonen and Selle 1995). And across the region, only Sweden has yet to elect a truly powerful national female leader.

Map 10.1 Women's Parliamentary Representation in Western Industrialized Countries, 2012

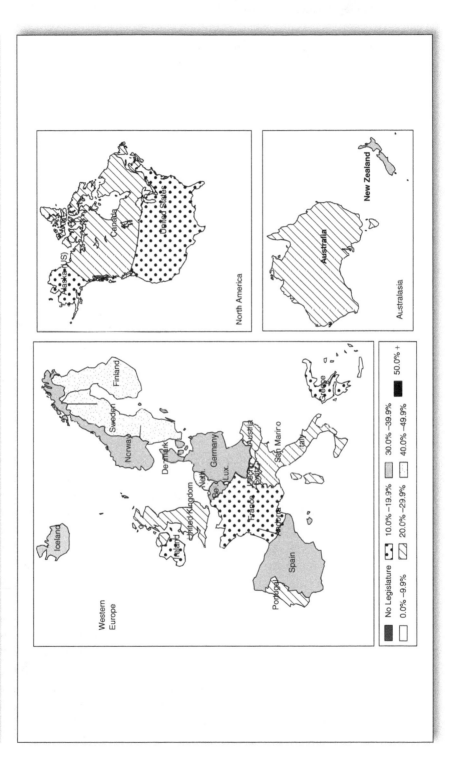

Figure 10.3   Women's Parliamentary Representation
for Scandinavia and the West, 1950–2010

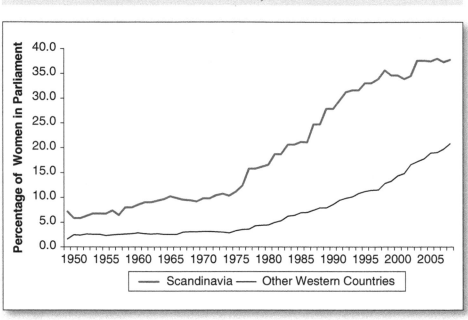

Source: Data from Paxton, Hughes, and Green (2006).

So why are the Nordic countries so different? A number of explanations have been put forth to justify women's exceptional political involvement in Scandinavia, and many of them are discussed in previous chapters: Protestantism, a high level of education and labor force participation for women, the dominance of leftist parties, a proportional representation electoral system, and a well-organized women's movement (Bystydzienski 1995; Haavio-Mannila and Skard 1985; Matland 1993; Norris 1985; Solheim 2000). But scholars also argue that political culture in Scandinavia is different from the political culture in other parts of the world. Scandinavians value equity, consensus, and integration, making politics an arena of accommodation and deference (Solheim 2000). Following **social democratic ideology,** Scandinavians emphasize the collective good, not individual rights or privileges. And since the early 1970s, the new feminist movement in Nordic countries has argued for women's political representation in terms of the collective good (Skjeie 2002). Therefore, the notion of electing women in substantial numbers became integrated with existing ideas about the collective good, democracy, and fair governance.

Not only is the political culture conducive to including women but also the tradition and culture of the region places value on the feminine. For example, anthropologist David Koester (1995) noted that compared with the Hebrew, Greek, and Roman traditions that serve as the foundation for many modern European societies, women are more highly regarded in Icelandic literature. Although women in Icelandic sagas were not equal to men, they were given "relatively authoritative and influential positions" (Koester 1995:574). Furthermore, even in medieval times in Scandinavia, women owned property, ruled households, and had the right to divorce their husbands (Koester 1995).

Although Scandinavian countries currently lead the world in the realm of women in politics, one must be careful not to overglorify women's position in the Nordic countries. Even in Scandinavia, women face obstacles and setbacks. For example, in 1993 elections in Norway, all three major political parties were led by women, but just 4 years later all parties were led by men, and women's parliamentary representation dropped 3%. Further, women still face a number of barriers in other areas of life. Across Scandinavia, women still perform the bulk of unpaid labor, are concentrated in the service sector, and are underrepresented in management in the private sector (Solheim 2000).

France and Parity

Scandinavia may lead the world in women's political representation, but as discussed in Chapter 6, France gets credit for introducing the world's most ambitious quota law in 2000. Known as a parity quota, France was the first country in the world to introduce a 50% gender quota for all parties. What makes the French parity quota even more interesting was its mixed success across parties, elections, and levels of office:

> At its most successful, the law induced near-parity in the composition of local councils, with 47.5 percent women elected in 2001 and 48.5 percent women elected in 2008 where the law applied. However, the law has been less successful at other levels, and its biggest failure has been in the legislative elections, where the proportion of women elected to the National Assembly rose from 10.9 percent in 1997 to just 12.3 percent in 2002, followed by a moderate improvement to 18.5 percent in 2007. (Murray 2010:9)

Overall, the impact of the law has been quite limited, suggesting that its grand claims of equality were not backed up in the corresponding legislation (Baudino 2003; Bird 2003; Fréchette, Maniquet, and Morelli

2008; Freedman 2004; Murray, Krook, and Opello 2011). But the variation in the success of the gender quota law in France highlights the importance of parties to the implementation of quotas (Kittilson 2006; Murray 2010). On the one hand, parties are focused on winning elections and maximizing their votes. If parties see male candidates, particularly incumbents, as electorally more advantageous, then they will resist implementing quota laws such as parity. But Murray (2010) argued that this traditional view of parties does not fully explain why some parties in France did choose to implement parity. Instead, electoral party interests are balanced by the institutional rules under which a party operates and the party's ideological position. Some parties in France were compelled to adopt parity in their candidate lists because they did not have the financial ability to pay the penalty if they did not. Other parties were more willing to implement parity because of their ideological position. For example, the Greens, who both highly valued gender equality and viewed state intervention in elections as appropriate, were willing to incur electoral costs in order to maintain their ideological beliefs (Murray 2010). Party ideology also emerged as an important explanation for differences in quota compliance in 2012, when the Left-leaning Socialist Party came to power, bringing with them record numbers of women. At 27% of seats, women remained far from parity in the French National Assembly, but the Socialist Party elected many more women (37% of party seats) than the previous Right-leaning leading party, the Union for a Popular Movement (UMP) (14% of party seats) (Willsher 2012).

Women in the European Union

No discussion of Western countries, particularly Europe, would be complete without a discussion of the European Union (EU) and its parliamentary institution, the European Parliament. The EU began in 1957 as an economic and political confederation of six countries in Europe and has expanded north, south, west, and finally east to include most Western European countries and some Central and Eastern European countries as well (see also Chapter 11). The EU endorses gender equality as a fundamental value and demands that member states and candidates for membership accept this principle, even if it goes against national preferences (Ellina 2003; Roth 2008). From initial attention solely to equal pay for men and women, over time gender and women's rights have become increasingly important issues on the EU agenda (Ellina 2003; Kantola 2010; Weiner 2009). Although implementation of gender policies has not been perfect (Kantola 2010; Walby 2004), 10 equal opportunity directives have the force of law and have shaped equal pay, social security, pregnancy, parental leave, and sex discrimination in the region (von Wahl 2008; Weiner 2009).

Importantly for women in politics, the EU has explicitly linked democracy to gender equality:

> Democracy is a fundamental value of the European Union, Member States, EEA States and applicant countries. . . . Its full realisation requires the participation of all citizens women and men alike to participate and be represented equally in the economy, in decision-making, and in social, cultural and civil life. (*Community Framework Strategy*, 2001–2005, cited in Weiner 2009)

Further, women's activist organizations and international networks have found the EU to be a fruitful place to push for policies on issues of interest to women. The European Women's Lobby is an umbrella organization of women's nongovernmental organizations (NGOs) in Europe and it has brought many women's issues forward to the EU agenda (Helferrich and Kolb 2001). Still, there is a tension: The EU is a major influence on the national policymaking of its member states while at the same time the national response (implementation or non implementation) is key to the effectiveness of any top-down EU policy (Mazur and Pollack 2009). Thus, the benefit of EU membership for women in a EU member country depends on where the country started. For example, in Ireland and Spain, joining the EU strengthened their national gender equality policies, whereas the Nordic countries "had more to give than to gain from joining the EU" (Roth 2008:4).

The European Parliament is one half of the bicameral legislative branch of the EU and represents over 7% of the world's population. Women make up 35% of the European Parliament overall, but there is significant variation in their representation from the European member countries (see Table 10.1).

The economic integration of the EU has increased the influence of some presidents and prime ministers of Europe. For example, German Chancellor Angela Merkel emerged as an international leader in the eurozone crisis following the United States economic recession that began in 2007. As of 2012, Merkel is the only woman currently leading a G8 country and the second woman to chair the G8. Merkel leads the strongest European economy and the third largest economy in the world, which affords her a prominent leadership position in handling the EU's economic problems (Jalalzai 2011).

Holding a powerful position leads to heightened criticism. Merkel's critics find fault with her policies that promote bailouts and austerity measures for countries struggling with rising sovereign debt. Since Germany has a stronger

Table 10.1 Women's Representation in the European Parliament, by Country

	Seats in the European Parliament	Women	Percent Women
Finland	13	8	61.5
Sweden	18	10	55.6
Estonia	6	3	50.0
Netherlands	25	12	48.0
Bulgaria	17	8	47.1
Denmark	13	6	46.2
France	72	32	44.4
Austria	17	7	41.2
Slovakia	13	5	38.5
Latvia	8	3	37.5
Germany	99	37	37.4
Belgium	22	8	36.4
Hungary	22	8	36.4
Portugal	22	8	36.4
Romania	33	12	36.4
Spain	50	18	36.0
Cyprus	6	2	33.3
Luxembourg	6	2	33.3
United Kingdom	72	24	33.3
Greece	22	7	31.8
Slovenia	7	2	28.6
Ireland	12	3	25.0
Lithuania	12	3	25.0
Italy	72	16	22.2
Poland	50	11	22.0
Czech Republic	22	4	18.2
Malta	5	0	0.0

Source: Data from the IPU (2012b).

economy, many Germans argue it is not their responsibility to fund endless bailouts (Kaden 2012). Other EU members argue against her hard line on austerity measures, which many claim only slow economic growth (Papadimitriou and Wray 2011). Due to her cautious and deliberate leadership approach, foreign pundits criticize her for being unassertive and ambivalent (Ash 2012; Dempsey and Kulish 2011; Henley 2011). This heightened attention to her leadership, however, points to the significant role she plays in economic and foreign policy, realms often associated with masculinity (Jalalzai 2011).

Middle of the Pack: The United States

Because the United States leads the world in a number of ways—the largest economy, the most gold medals in the Olympic games, and the world's largest foreign aid contributor—many people expect that America should lead the world in gender equality as well. But in terms of women in politics, the United States is far from dominant. In fact, with 18% women in Congress, the United States falls in the middle of the pack.

America's mediocrity is evident in Figure 10.4, which displays the distribution of women in parliaments across the world. The figure also includes examples of countries that have reached particular levels of women's incorporation. So, for example, two examples of countries with no women in parliament are Fiji and Saudi Arabia. Most countries in the world fit in the 10% to 14% range, and only Rwanda had over 50% women. The United States falls in the 15% to 19% category along with Indonesia, Zimbabwe, and numerous other countries. The percentage of women in the U.S. Congress is below that of Switzerland, a country where women could not vote until 1971.

In this section, we first discuss women in positions of formal political power—women in the U.S. House of Representatives, and the Senate, women in state legislative bodies, female governors, and women in executive appointed or elected positions, such as members of the president's cabinet. But the vast majority of women in the United States participate in politics more informally. Thus, in the second half of the section, we turn to a discussion of women as citizens, voters, or activists, focusing on the gender gaps that exist between men and women.

Women in the U.S. Senate and House of Representatives: Growing Slowly

One place to start to understand women in U.S. politics is to look at how they have improved their representation in the U.S. House and Senate over

Figure 10.4   Distribution of Women in Parliament With Example Countries

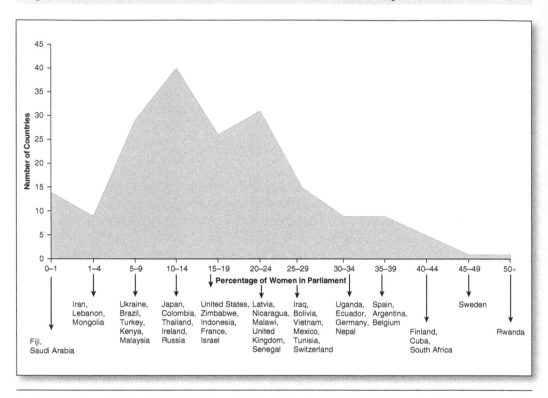

Source: Data from Inter-Parliamentary Union (2010).

time. Make no mistake: Women are still terribly underrepresented—only 17% of the Senate and House today. But Figure 10.5 shows that these percentages are a marked improvement from even 20 years ago.

From the first woman elected to U.S. Congress, Jeannette Rankin in 1917, women slowly increased their numbers in the House until about 1990. By *slowly,* we mean that women did not hold even 5% of the House of Representatives until 1981. After 1981, women continued to slowly increase their numbers until the 103rd Congress (1993–1995), when their numbers increased dramatically, nearly doubling from 6% to 11%.

When women were few in number, it could be rough sailing. In 1972, Pat Schroeder was elected to represent the people of Denver in the House of Representatives. Soon after her arrival, she was appointed to the Armed Services Committee, along with a Black legislator Ron Dellums. Their appointment occurred over the strong opposition (and attempted veto) of

Figure 10.5   Percentage of Women in Congress, 1917–2012

Source: Data from Inter-Parliamentary Union (2010).

the committee's chairman, F. Edward Hebert. Despite their apparent appointment victory, Dellums and Schroeder arrived for their first House Armed Services Committee meeting to find a surprise. Pat Schroeder (1998) recounted the following:

> [Hebert] announced that while he might be unable to control the makeup of his committee, he could damn well control the number of chairs in his hearing room. . . . He said that women and blacks were worth only half of one "regular" member, so he added only one seat to the committee room and made Ron and me share it. Nobody else objected, and nobody offered to scrounge up another chair. (p. 40)

Rather than make a scene, the two sat together "cheek to cheek" and participated in the committee meeting.

Returning to impartial numbers, a similar pattern of slow growth in women's representation appears in the Senate. Between 1917 and 1991, women never held more than 2% of the Senate. Even as late as 1977, women were sometimes not represented in the Senate. But in 1992, women's numbers in the Senate doubled to four women and in 1994 almost doubled again reaching seven. Women's percentage of seats in both the House and Senate continues to rise although they continue to be lower than women's percentage of the general population.

Why the sudden shift after 1992? Most observers explain it with two words—Anita Hill. As discussed in previous chapters, on October 6, 1991, two days before the Senate was scheduled to vote on the nomination of Clarence Thomas to the Supreme Court, a distinguished law professor, Anita Hill, accused Thomas of sexually harassing her in 1981. During the televised Senate judiciary hearings that followed, Americans saw a panel of White men questioning the validity of a Black woman's claims. Angered by the hearings, unprecedented numbers of women were spurred to run for political office. As explained by Barbara Boxer, "America, and in particular, American women, were uncomfortable with the way the whole issue was handled, were uncomfortable with the way the Senate looked—and the Anita Hill incident became a catalyst for change" (Boxer 1994:39–40).

But though women are generally underrepresented, there are differences across states in the percentage of women they send as part of their **congressional delegation.** For example, in the 112th Congress (2011–2013), California sent 19 women, out of 53 delegates (36%), to the House of Representatives, and 2 women were elected to both of California's seats in the Senate. Michigan sent one woman, out of 15 delegates, to the House (7%) and one woman, out of 2 delegates, to the Senate. None of Virginia's 13 delegates (11 to the House and 2 to the Senate) are women.

But Virginia is not alone. Overall, 19 states currently have no women as part of their delegation—Arkansas (5), Georgia (15), Idaho (4), Indiana (11), Kentucky (8), Montana (3), Nebraska (5), New Jersey (15), New Mexico (5), North Dakota (3), Oklahoma (7), Rhode Island (4), South Carolina (8), Utah (5), and Virginia (13)—including four states, Delaware (3), Iowa (7), Mississippi (6), and Vermont (3) that have never sent a woman to the Senate or the House.

The majority of these female national legislators have been White, but some women of color appear in Washington. Early pioneers began to take office in the 1960s. In 1968, Shirley Chisholm (D-NY) was the first Black woman elected to the House of Representatives (see Figure 10.6). And Patsy Mink, elected from Hawaii in 1964, was the first Asian American woman in Congress. Republican Ileana Ros-Lehtinen was the first Hispanic woman in Congress. She was elected in 1988 and continues to serve today. Carol

Moseley Braun, a Democrat from Illinois (1993–1999), was the only woman of color to ever serve in the U.S. Senate.

Figure 10.6   Shirley Chisholm, the First Black Congresswoman

Source: Courtesy of the Library of Congress, Prints and Photographs Division.

In 2012, all Senate women were White. But a quarter of the women in the House of Representatives (24 total) were Black, Asian American, or Hispanic. The distribution of women of color across the two parties is uneven—of these 24 women of color in the House, 92% (22 of 24) are Democrats (Center for American Women and Politics [CAWP] 2012a). Ileana Ros-Lehtinen, mentioned earlier, and Jaime Herrera Beutler are the two Republican women of color in Congress in 2012. See Chapter 9 for a discussion of intersectionality in U.S. politics.

Women in the States

Going by numbers alone, it appears that women have a larger role in state government than at the national level. Compared to the 18% of seats women hold in the U.S. Congress, almost 24% of the state legislators are women. A similar pattern appears in committee leadership. In 2005, no woman chaired a standing committee in the U.S. House of Representatives, and two women chaired committees in the U.S. Senate, but women make up about 19% of committee chairs in state legislatures (Rosenthal 2005). In 2010, women held 16% of state leadership positions (such as senate president or speakers of state houses) (CAWP 2010). In 2012, women made up 17.4% of mayors of U.S. cities over population 30,000 (CAWP 2012d). And though no woman has ever served as the country's commander in chief, Nellie Tayloe Ross became the first female governor in 1925. Since Nellie Ross, 34 other women have served in the position of governor, and a woman has been elected to a statewide executive office in every U.S. state except for Maine (CAWP 2012a). Overall, women's political incorporation has proceeded faster at the state level of government.

Women in the State Legislature

There is considerable variation in women's representation across states. For example, in Colorado, 40% of state legislators are women (CAWP 2012c). Women there have more than four times the share of seats held by women in South Carolina, where women hold only 9.4% of seats. Map 10.2 displays the different levels of women's numbers in state legislatures across the United States (darker shades indicate more women). Women have the highest levels of legislative representation in the West and the Northeast, whereas women are most underrepresented in the South. One surprise in Map 10.2 is Wyoming, which we stated in Chapter 2 is called the Equality State for its status as the first state in which women had the right to vote and hold public office. Wyoming also elected the first female governor, Nellie Ross. Yet women in Wyoming only hold 14.4% of state legislative seats, leaving Wyoming with a rank of 46 out of 50 states.

Women of color have arguably made better inroads into state than national politics. Black women, in particular, perform strongly—holding 13.7% of all seats held by women in state legislatures, outperforming their share of the population, 12.6%, at least among women. On the other side of the spectrum, 66 Latina state legislators comprise just 3.8% of female legislators, a far cry from the 16.3% of the U.S. population that reports Hispanic or Latino origin. When compared to their 4.8% population share, Asian American women fall in between Black women and Latinas with 2.1% of women's seats. Finally, Native Americans and Alaskans make up less than 1% of the U.S. population, but they are represented in the legislatures of several states where they are a significant minority, including New Mexico, Oklahoma, Montana, and Arizona (CAWP 2012b; U.S. Census Bureau 2010).

Map 10.2 Women's Representation in State Legislatures, 2012

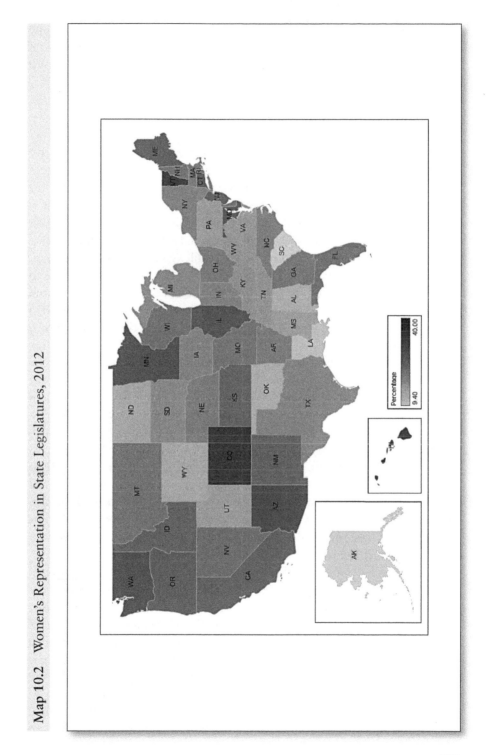

Notably, the distribution of women of color across parties is highly uneven—95% of women of color state legislators are Democrats. Of Republican women of color, most are Asian American or Latinas (CAWP 2012b).

Female Governors

We must also consider women's political representation in the executive branch of state government. Of particular importance is the highest executive position at the state level, the governor's office. Governors are key political players because in many states they are responsible for administering, "large annual budgets and major public programs like welfare" (Weir 1999:248). But even in states where the position does not wield much formal power, as in Texas, governors are highly visible, generating name recognition. And in recent decades, the governor's office has been a main route to the American presidency. Jimmy Carter, Ronald Reagan, Bill Clinton, and George W. Bush all were governors before they became presidents. If a woman is ever to become president, one route may be through the governor's mansion.

Women serving in the governor's office may also be important because they may appoint more women to the executive branch, facilitating the political careers of other women. For example, Christine Todd Whitman, a Republican governor from New Jersey, appointed many women to leadership positions, including attorney general, chief of staff, and the executive director of the New Jersey/New York Port Authority (Weir 1999:253).

Similarly, Ann Richards, the Democratic governor of Texas from 1991 to 1995, promised that state government would no longer be the domain of White men. Of her appointees, 20% were Hispanic, 15% were Black, 2% were Asian, and a full 46% were female (Weir 1999). Two women of color have served as governor: Nikki Haley of South Carolina is Asian American and Susana Martinez of New Mexico is Latina.

So what has been women's share of governorships? In 2012, six states had female governors. North Carolina and Washington elected Democratic female governors; Arizona, New Mexico, Oklahoma, and South Carolina elected Republican female governors. Overall, 34 female governors have served in the United States throughout its history. Arizona deserves special note as the first state to have a female governor succeed another female governor. Indeed, Arizona has now had four women governors (CAWP 2012a). Like the female leaders discussed in Chapter 3 who filled in as political surrogates for their husbands or fathers, the United States has had three female governors who succeeded their husbands to power. Women have also often entered the governor's mansion by moving up from lieutenant governor after a resignation (eight women).

Women and the American Presidency

Scholars sometimes argue that the executive branch is the most masculine branch of government (e.g., Duerst-Lahti 1997). The executive branch is more closely connected to the military than to the other two branches of the government, and the executive branch is more hierarchical in its organization as well. The United States has never had a female president or vice-president. Historically, there has been a general dearth of women in other national-level executive positions but the integration of women in the executive is increasing.

The presidential cabinet administers the branches of the executive and wields substantial power. Examples of cabinet officials include the secretary of state, the attorney general, and the secretary of labor. Including Frances Perkins, who was appointed to be the secretary of labor in 1933 by President Franklin D. Roosevelt, 27 women have received cabinet nominations over nine presidential administrations (Borrelli 2010). Before 1993, women's inclusion in the cabinet was "extremely inconsistent" (Borelli 2010:738). This is evident in Figure 10.7, which shows the percentage of women cabinet secretaries under each president since the Roosevelt administration. Though most presidents since Roosevelt have incorporated women into their cabinets, Presidents Truman, Kennedy, Johnson, and Nixon had male-only cabinets. Since 1993, women's presence in the cabinet has increased markedly. Not only were there greater numbers of women in the cabinets of Presidents Clinton, Bush, and in the initial cabinet of Obama but these women were in diverse cabinet positions including the powerful inner cabinet positions (Borrelli 2010). Over time, the inclusion of women in the president's cabinet has become the norm.

What affects numbers of women in the presidential cabinet? Ultimately, it comes down to the president—members of the cabinet are appointed by, and can be removed by, the president. Consider Richard Nixon, president of the United States from 1969 to 1974, who was captured on tape: "I'm not for women, frankly, in any job. I don't want any of them around. Thank God we don't have any in the Cabinet" (Lithwick 2001). As Nixon explained to his attorney general, "I don't think a woman should be in any government job whatever. I mean, I really don't. The reason why I do is mainly because they are erratic. And emotional" (Lithwick 2001).

Throughout recent American history, women in the U.S. cabinet have often served in positions related to social welfare, health, and education. For

Figure 10.7   Percentage of Women Cabinet Secretaries, by Administration

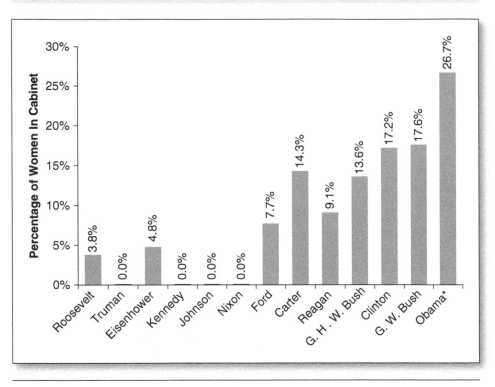

* *Note:* Initial nominations only.

Source: Data from Borrelli (2010).

example, women were the first secretaries of the Health, Education, and Welfare Department (now Health and Human Services) and the Education Department (Borrelli 2002). Some cabinet positions are so often filled with women that they are called the woman's slot (Borrelli 2002; Duerst-Lahti 1997). For example, following in the footsteps of Frances Perkins, seven women have been nominated to the position of labor secretary. But in recent administrations, the appointment of women such as Janet Reno, Madeleine Albright, Condoleezza Rice, and Hillary Clinton to the prominent cabinet posts of attorney general and secretary of state indicates that women are becoming fully integrated into presidential cabinets.

A Woman as Commander in Chief?

In the 1984 presidential election, Geraldine Ferraro was selected by the Democratic Party to run for the position of vice president along with presidential candidate Walter Mondale. The pair challenged the incumbents Ronald Reagan and George H. W. Bush, who were ahead in election polls from the start. Ferraro had served three terms in the U.S. House of Representatives before her nomination, but her credibility and her liberalism, rather than her experience, were the focus of greatest criticism. As a Catholic, Ferraro received criticism from the Church for her support of abortion rights, and then during the campaign she refused to release her husband's tax returns, generating controversy. Ultimately, the majority of voters, both male and female, voted against Mondale and Ferraro. Regardless, Ferraro's nomination was a watershed moment for women in politics in the United States.

In recent presidential races, women have sought their party's nomination for president and have run as a vice-presidential candidate. In 2000, Elizabeth Dole vied for the Republican Party nomination, and in 2004 Carol Moseley Braun, a Black woman, sought the support of the Democratic Party. And in 2008, Hillary Clinton and Sarah Palin electrified the presidential race. Hillary Clinton was the first woman to ever be a serious contender for her party's presidential nomination. For almost a year, she visibly battled Barack Obama for the Democratic Party's nomination and was front-runner for part of that time. At the same time, Sarah Palin became the second woman to be selected as a vice-presidential candidate.

Hillary Clinton and Sarah Palin were very different women with very different political styles. Hillary Clinton was a Yale-educated lawyer, former First Lady, with extensive national-level political experience as a senator from New York. Sarah Palin attended several colleges and community colleges before graduating from the University of Idaho and had political experience as a mayor and briefly as governor of Alaska. Hillary Clinton was criticized for her power pantsuits whereas Palin, who finished third in the 1984 Miss Alaska pageant, was a trendsetter who inspired women to buy rimless eyeglass frames and Naughty Monkey red shoes. Clinton initially played down emotions in her campaign whereas Palin fired up the Republican base with talk of hockey moms. With two such very different but highly visible women in the 2008 presidential field, most women in American could find a role model. In the end, even though neither Clinton nor Palin won the presidency or vice presidency, a generation of young women and men will now grow up having seen women political leaders competing for the very top-level executive positions in the United States.

In fact, the influence of Sarah Palin was seen almost immediately, in 2010, which was called by some pundits "the year of the Republican women." In that year, a record number of Republican women sought federal office—129 in House races and 17 in Senate races. This was a sizable increase over the previous record when, in 1994, 91 Republican women ran for the House and 13 for the Senate. Although GOP women did win eight seats in the House and three new Republican governorships, they generally ran in difficult primaries and races and did not markedly increase their numbers in elected office. Still, the example of Sarah Palin was likely a factor in helping these women decide to step up and run for public office.

The year 2010 was also notable for the amount of money spent by women in their campaigns. For example, Meg Whitman spent $140 million dollars of her own money to attempt to gain California's governor's seat. This set a new record for American politics, beating out the $109 million that Michael Bloomberg spent in New York City. Similarly, Linda McMahon spent $48 million dollars of her own money attempting to take a Connecticut Senate seat (this represents $97 a vote). But this money did not translate into success; both Whitman and McMahon lost their bids for office.

Explanations—Culture

Why are women underrepresented in U.S. politics? And why have women succeeded in gaining political power in some cities or states and not in others? The explanations for women's political power in U.S. politics parallel those found in cross-national research. Cross-nationally, research has shown that what people think about women and a woman's place matters for women's ability to attain political power (Norris and Inglehart 2001; Paxton and Kunovich 2003). Similarly, in the United States, if women are considered too emotional or incompetent, they will not be taken seriously as contenders for power.

Does the United States have a culture that supports women in politics? Lawless and Fox (2010), using data from a variety of polls, compiled attitudes about women in politics in the United States from 1937 to 2007. Figure 10.8 tracks two questions about women: "If your political party nominated a woman for president, would you be willing to vote for her if she were qualified for the job?" and "Tell me if you agree or disagree with this statement: Most men are better suited emotionally for politics than are most women." Figure 10.8 shows that the percentage of Americans willing to vote for a woman for president has risen over time, from a low of 33% in 1937 to over 90% in most of the 1990s. Current support hovers just under 90%.

Figure 10.8   Attitudes Toward a Female President and Women in Politics, 1935–2007

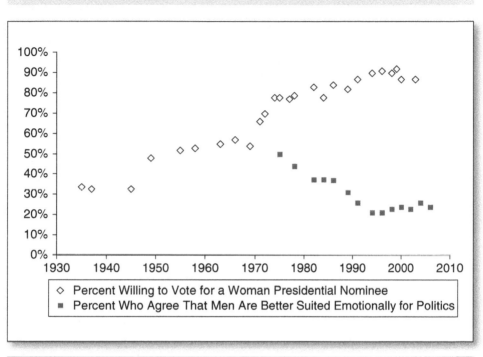

○ Percent Willing to Vote for a Woman Presidential Nominee
■ Percent Who Agree That Men Are Better Suited Emotionally for Politics

Source: Data from Lawless and Fox (2010).

Answers to the other question charted in Figure 10.8, on women's emotional unsuitability for politics, have halved over time, moving from 50% agreement to about 25%. Still, 25% of the population answers in 2007 that men are better suited emotionally to politics. Similarly, in another survey, taken in the late 1990s, 15% of Americans agreed with the statement that "women should take care of running their homes and leave running the country up to men" (Fox and Lawless 2004:270). Thus, though cultural attitudes about women in politics have improved over time, there are still nontrivial numbers of Americans that do not believe women belong in politics. Still, looking at male and female candidates, there is little evidence that voters are biased against female candidates in the present. Though there may be pervasive views about women in politics that prevent women from running or winning, most researchers demonstrate that women receive as many votes as men do (e.g., Darcy, Welch, and Clark 1994). In fact, gender does not appear to matter to men, but female voters seem to prefer women as candidates (Dolan 1998; Seltzer, Newman, and Leighton 1997; Smith and Fox 2001).

Can culture explain differences across U.S. states in the percentage of women in their state legislatures? Kevin Arceneaux ranked states on their citizens' positive views of women in politics using two of the questions discussed earlier: Do you agree that "women should take care of running their homes and leave running the country up to men" and that "most men are better suited emotionally for politics than are women" (Arceneaux 2001:148)?

Map 10.3 presents a map of attitudes toward women in politics, using Arceneaux's (2001:157) state rankings. Darker colors indicate more accepting views of women in politics. The darkest states have attitudes about women that are at least 1 **standard deviation** above the average for all states. The second darkest have attitudes between 0.5 and 1 standard deviation above the average. The lightest states have attitudes at least 1 standard deviation below the average of all states. (Georgia and South Carolina were the only two states with attitudes between 0.5 and 1 standard deviation below the average, so they are combined with the other "average" states.)

Map 10.3 suggests that region makes a difference to women in politics. Southern states generally have less approving attitudes about women in politics than other regions. The Northwest and Northeast tend toward more lenient attitudes. But even within regions with different political cultures and across conservative and liberal states, specific attitudes about women in politics make a difference to women's numbers. Arceneaux (2001) found that region, a conservative ideology, and a direct measure of gender-role attitudes are all independently important in explaining the percentage of women in state houses.

Explanations—Structure (Eligibility)

Social eligibility is the U.S. counterpart to the social structural explanations discussed in Chapter 5. Recall that social structural arguments focus on men's greater money, time, and access to education and certain professions. In the United States, most legislators are more educated than the general public and come disproportionately from a few occupations. The most common occupation for a U.S. state legislator or congressperson is law—approximately 45% of the members of the U.S. House of Representatives are lawyers. Thus, getting women into elected office requires a pool of educated women and women's participation in political pipeline occupations, such as law.

Though today women outnumber men in law schools around the country, this is only a recent development. In the 1960s, women made up only 4% of

Map 10.3 Positive Attitudes About Women in Politics Across 38 U.S. States

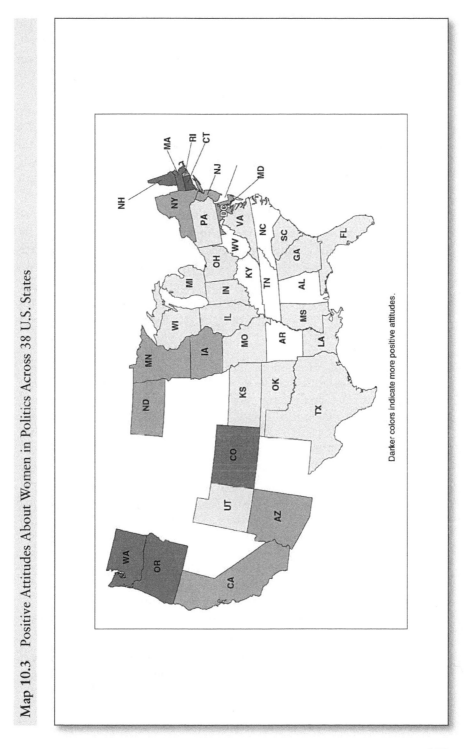

Darker colors indicate more positive attitudes.

law school students; in 1972, they made up 9%; and in 1978 the figure had risen to 29%. In 1960, women obtained only 35% of all bachelor's degrees, and almost 40% of those degrees were in education (National Center for Education Statistics 2006). Harvard Law School first admitted women in 1953. And Yale University first admitted female undergraduates in 1969.

A pipeline analogy is apt—one has to remember that the pool of women available for office was likely educated 20 or more years prior to running for office. Thus, the extremely small numbers of women in law school in the 1960s were the women in the pipeline for office in the late 1970s and 1980s. The women available to run for office around 2000 were part of the only 29% of women in law school in the late 1970s.

Though many women were likely socialized against pursuing high levels of education or professional careers, the low percentages of women in the law profession were not simply a matter of choice. Women were overtly discriminated against in education and employment until the 1970s when a variety of anti-gender–discrimination laws were passed. And the first pioneering women in law experienced active discrimination. Consider the following story related by Pat Schroeder (1998), U.S. congresswoman from 1973 to 1997:

> The best preparation for infiltrating the boys' club of Congress was the boys' club of Harvard Law School. In 1961 there were fifteen women in my first-year class, and the five hundred men acted as if we constituted estrogen contamination. I was stunned when several of them insisted on changing their assigned seats in the lecture halls, as if mere proximity to women could be hazardous. . . . Maybe *none* of them thought women belonged there!
>
> The dean certainly didn't. Erwin Griswold was . . . a member of the United States Civil Rights Commission, but the idea of gender equity had not penetrated his comprehension. The first week of school, he invited the freshman women to his home and informed us that he was opposed to women attending law school but that the board had outvoted him. He said that the admissions committee counted the number of women in the class and then admitted that many additional men, certain that the women would never use the degrees and the world might otherwise be deprived of enough Harvard lawyers. Then he . . . ordered each of us to state why we were there, occupying . . . no, wasting such sacred space.
>
> In stark terror, sitting uncomfortably on our chairs placed in a circle, each of us tried to sound profound and controlled in our answers. I said something trite and predictable like, "Oh, I am here to bolster my love of the law." But one of the women blithely said, "I'm here because I couldn't get into Yale." (pp. 93–95)

Imagine trying to get an education under such hostility and pressure. These were the women in the pipeline for political office in the 1970s and 1980s.

Research across states shows that the pool of available women makes a difference to the number of women elected to state legislatures. Having more women in pipeline occupations such as law leads to more female state legislators (Arceneaux 2001; Norrander and Wilcox 2005) and state executives (Oxley and Fox 2004).

Now, certainly not all office holders are lawyers, or even highly educated. And women both in and out of the workforce participate in churches, school boards, and political parties, giving them valuable political experience (Burns, Schlozman, and Verba 2001). Women have successfully run for public office as homemakers. But attaining political office even among homemakers requires that the women have name recognition in the community. Thus, there must be women who have "held local office, who have been active in community affairs, and who have name recognition in the community, ties to important established political groups, or other resources that help win elected office" (Norrander and Wilcox 2005:182).

To combat low numbers of female candidates, a number of organizations have grown to support women's bids for public office. As mentioned in Chapter 4, one of the most successful women's political finance organizations in the United States is EMILY's List, a political action committee (PAC) that supports pro-choice, Democratic women. EMILY is an acronym standing for "Early Money Is Like Yeast" because it helps the dough rise. The premise is that during campaigns, early financial support suggests to other potential donors that a candidate is viable, so more money is likely to follow, and early money also discourages potential challengers from entering the race. Thus, by providing money to female candidates early in their campaigns, EMILY's List seeks to improve women's political chances. Founded in 1985, EMILY's List was instrumental in the election of the female senator Barbara Mikulski in 1986. And since then, it has helped to elect 87 congresswomen, 16 senators, 9 governors, and hundreds of women to state and local office (EMILY's List 2012).

A Republican counterpart to EMILY's List, called The WISH List, was founded in 1992. The organization attracted 1,500 members and raised $250,000 in the first year of its operation, and in 1994, The WISH List distributed $370,000 to women candidates (Burrell 1998; Thomas 1998). In total, The WISH List distributed 3.5 million dollars to Republican women before merging under the Republican Majority for Choice (The WISH List 2012). Like EMILY's List, The WISH List supported pro-choice candidates. To fill this gap, the Republican PAC Susan B. Anthony List was founded in

1994 to support prolife Republican women running for political office. And today, the Susan B. Anthony List has over 80,000 members (Susan B. Anthony List 2006).

Explanations—Politics

Just as different countries have different levels of political demand for women, U.S. states can have differential demand for women. It is easy to understand that nations vary in their political systems, but the U.S. states are also actually 50 different institutions (Sanbonmatsu 2002b). States vary in their electoral systems, how many **open seats** are available, whether legislating is considered a full-time job, and how expensive it is to win political office. In explaining women's access to political power in the United States, researchers have therefore also turned to these political explanations. Some are unique to the United States, whereas others are similar to those we discussed in Chapter 6.

Political scientists have turned to incumbency as one important explanation for women's lack of representation in politics in the United States. In the United States, incumbent reelection rates are typically more than 90%. Candidates who currently hold public office are more likely to have higher name recognition, an effective campaign organization, and more money. High incumbency reelection rates are also due to political **gerrymandering** by both parties that ensures incumbents well over 60% of the vote. For example, 99% of incumbents were reelected in 2004 (Abramowitz, Alexander, and Gunning 2005). Any challenger, male or female, contesting a seat against an incumbent, faces serious opposition. For women, therefore, the logic is straightforward:

- Incumbents seek reelection 75% of the time.
- Incumbents typically win reelection (99% of them did in 2004).
- Most incumbents are male.

In the 2004 elections, only one woman who won a seat in the House of Representatives defeated an incumbent. The other seven women to win seats in the House did so in open seats or seats where the incumbent did not run for reelection (Ruthven 2005). Similarly, among candidates for governor, since 1970 women have won only about 32% of the races in which they have participated (CAWP 2006). But 35% of the time they ran as challengers to male incumbents and only 12% of the time as incumbents.

When researchers focus on individual legislators, incumbency stands out as very important, especially at the national level. Mathematical analyses demonstrate that incumbency creates glacial pace of change in women's numbers over time (Darcy and Choike 1986; Darcy et al. 1994). Researchers also show that in special elections (with no incumbent) women do as well as men (Gaddie and Bullock 1997).

But trying to show the effects of incumbency across states has been more difficult. States vary in ways that make it harder or easier for incumbents to keep their seats. For example, some states have **term limits** that force long-term incumbents out of office. To try to measure the effect of incumbency at the state level, researchers have modeled turnover, or the number of seats that are contested in a given year. Based on what we know about incumbency, states with higher turnover rates should have higher numbers of female legislators. But turnover rates do not predict women's share of state legislatures (Arceneaux 2001; Norrander and Wilcox 2005) or only weakly predict it (Nechemias 1987). The lack of an effect of turnover across large numbers of legislators may be partly due to less-than-optimal numbers of women in the pipeline to run.

And what about term limits? Term limits cut off how long incumbents can stay in office and should increase turnover. Theoretically, fewer incumbents should benefit women because they can contest in open seats. But evidence for the benefits of term limits to women is not generally positive (e.g., Carey, Niemi, and Powell 1998; Carroll and Jenkins 2001). One study demonstrated that term limits increase numbers of women in upper houses but decrease them in lower houses. Norrander and Wilcox (2005:192) explained that of the 11 states that instituted term limits between 1994 and 2002, seven had more women in the state senate but experienced a leveling-off or drop in women in the lower house.

Another political explanation in the United States is the professionalism of the legislature. Professional legislatures meet more often, pay more, and generally have larger staffs. Because professional legislatures are more prestigious and have more perks, getting elected to them is generally more desirable than getting elected to a less professional legislature (Diamond 1977). In less desirable races, women face less opposition from men and should gain seats in greater numbers. State legislatures vary in their degree of professionalism.

There is some evidence that the attractiveness of the office partly explains women's representation. Research studies show that states where legislative salaries are higher have fewer women in state legislatures (Arceneaux 2001; Hill 1981) or that when the power of a state executive office (e.g., governor) is higher, fewer women hold it (Oxley and Fox 2004). Generally, states with weak executives or legislatures had a higher percentage of women holding office.

But the explanation of the professional legislature is not only about the attractiveness or desirability in terms of power and pay of the office to men. It could also reflect the attractiveness of the office to women. There is wide variation in how often state legislatures meet. Nine states have full-time legislatures, the legislatures of six states meet once every other year, and the remaining meet annually for a limited time (Norrander and Wilcox 2005:183). Women traditionally make up a larger percentage of part-time legislatures (Norrander and Wilcox 2005). It may be that women are happy to have the flexibility afforded by part-time legislatures to pursue an occupation or to devote time to their family if they have spousal monetary support. Further, it could also be that greater weight is given to the education or profession of candidates in races for professional legislatures, and some women who run for office run as homemakers or have largely civic experience.

Finally, it may surprise you to find out that U.S. states differ in their electoral system and that some states have multimember districts where multiple people represent the voters of a particular electoral district (see Chapter 6). Thirteen states have at least some multimember districts (Norrander and Wilcox 2005). And just like in countries with multimember districts, party leaders feel some pressure to balance their ticket to appeal to important groups of voters, such as women.

Multimember districts benefit women in the United States. Women do better in states with multimember districts compared to states with only single-member districts (Arceneaux 2001; Sanbonmatsu 2002b). And within states that use both systems, women get elected at higher rates in the multi-member races (Darcy et al. 1994:160–166; Matland and Brown 1992). Finally, in states that changed their electoral system and dropped multimember districts in the past 30 years, a drop in the number of female legislators has occurred (Darcy et al. 1994; King 2002).

Gender Gaps in American Politics

Although women's formal roles in politics have historically been limited, women in the United States have participated widely in the public realm since before the American Revolution. During revolutionary times, women organized public demonstrations, boycotted English tea, formed organizations, signed public petitions, raised money in the name of the revolution, and published their ideas (Burrell 2004). Thus, women have long participated in causes for the general good of the society in which they lived. This practice has continued into the modern era, when women have voted, petitioned, lobbied, demonstrated, and protested to affect public policies from gun control to nuclear proliferation (Burrell 2004).

Thus, women act politically not only as legislators or governors but as average citizens, voters, and activists. But women do not always act the same way as men. If female voters or citizens hold different political positions on issues or participate in different numbers than their male counterparts, there is said to be a gender gap in political orientation or in political participation (Conover 1988; Manza and Brooks 1998; Shapiro and Mahajan 1986). For example, there were significant gender differences in the Super Tuesday races of February 5, 2008, with a higher percentage of women voting for Hillary Clinton than Barack Obama in all but 2 of the 16 states that voted that day (CAWP 2008). Here, we consider the differences between men and women in their party affiliations, vote choices, and types of participation.

Party Affiliation

Historically, the Republican Party has been more supportive of women's rights than the Democratic Party (Freeman 1987). As the first major party to favor women's suffrage, the Republican Party played a leading role in securing women the right to vote. In fact, 26 of 36 state legislatures that voted to ratify the 19th Amendment granting women suffrage were under Republican control. Republicans were also the first major party to place the **Equal Rights Amendment (ERA)** on their party's platform in 1940. And prior to the 1960s, women were more often Republicans (Inglehart and Norris 2000).

But beginning in the 1960s, and especially since the 1980s, women's attitudes and beliefs have more often aligned with the Democratic Party. Women are more likely to identify as Democrats, and women are also more likely to approve of the job performance of Democratic legislators. For example, women have been more likely than men to disapprove of the job performance of the past four Republican presidents (CAWP 2005a). Alternatively, Bill Clinton's approval ratings as president were higher among women (CAWP 2005a). And there has been a consistent gender gap of about 6 percentage points in approval of Barack Obama's job performance since 2009, with women more approving than men (Crabtree 2012).

Of course, women's attitudes toward the political parties also translate into differences in voting behavior. For example, in the 2008 presidential election, women favored Barack Obama by 7 percentage points over men. This was about equal to the gender gap in 2004 where 48% of women voted for George W. Bush whereas 55% of men did so (CAWP 2004). This difference also held across all key segments of the population—Blacks, Whites, Hispanics, and Asians; those in the highest income and educational brackets and those in the lowest; and all age groups (CAWP 2004, 2005b). Looking over time, there has been a significant gender gap in presidential elections since 1980 (see Figure 10.9).

Figure 10.9 Percentage of Men and Women Voting Democrat and Republican in U.S. Presidential Elections, 1980–2008

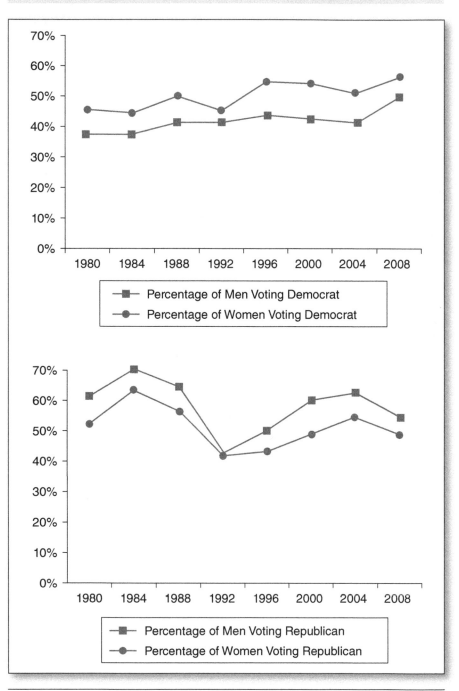

These differences are not only evident in presidential elections but carry to other races as well. In 2010, there was a 7 percentage point gap in races for the House of Representatives. Forty-nine percent of women voted for the Democratic congressional candidate in their district compared to 42% of men (CAWP 2010). Gender gaps also appeared in 17 of 18 gubernatorial races, of up to 19 percentage points. Likewise, in 25 of 26 Senate races, gender gaps of up to 17 percentage points appeared. The gender gap is about party, not the gender of the candidate. Women voters in 2010 were less likely than men to support Republican women running for office. For example, in South Carolina, Nikki Haley, the Republican candidate for governor won 49% of women's votes but 55% of men's votes. Similarly, Meg Whitman won 39% of women's votes but 45% of men's votes in her race for the governorship of California (CAWP 2010).

Voter Turnout

But how women affect an election is not just a function of their political attitudes but also their numbers. From when women gained the vote in 1920 throughout the 1970s, women cast their ballots less often than men did. But during the 1980s, women began to outnumber men at the polls, and in the 2008 presidential election nearly 10 million more women voted than men (CAWP 2011b). As depicted in Figure 10.10, the key transition year was 1980, when President Ronald Reagan was elected. The same pattern holds in off years, when there is not a presidential race; women began turning out in greater numbers in 1986 and have since voted more often than men (CAWP 2011a). And predictably, women also outnumber men as registered voters since the 1980s (CAWP 2011a).

Of course, looking closely at Figure 10.10, it does not tell a story of women substantially increasing their percentage turnout. Instead, men are decreasing their turnout at a faster rate than women, and that has led to the transition.

When Does the Gender Gap Matter?

In recent years, women have more often voted for Democrats and voted in higher numbers, so why aren't Democrats dominating the political arena? It is important to understand that the gender gap will not necessarily affect the outcome of an election. For instance, if 60% of men favor the Republican candidate and 60% of women favor the Democratic candidate, their different preferences cancel each other out, but the Democratic candidate would win because more women vote. But even if women turn out in higher

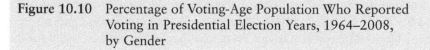

Figure 10.10   Percentage of Voting-Age Population Who Reported
Voting in Presidential Election Years, 1964–2008,
by Gender

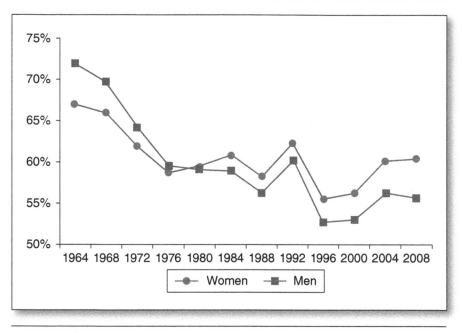

Source: Data from CAWP (2011a, 2011b).

numbers, if males have stronger preferences than women, it is men's votes
that will determine the outcome. This is what happened in 2004, when 51%
of women favored John Kerry, but 55% of men favored George W. Bush.
Even though 8 million more women voted, men's stronger Republican leanings outweighed women's more marginal Democratic preference. And in
2010, women split their votes almost evenly between Republican and
Democratic congressional candidates of the two parties with only a slight
advantage for Democrats, while men strongly preferred Republican candidates. This resulted in an overall advantage for Republican candidates
(CAWP 2010).

Campaign Activities

Voting is far from the only form of political activity. There are many other
ways to influence an election. Surveys conducted by National Election Studies
(NES) have asked Americans about their participation in five such activities

since the 1950s: talking to others to try to influence their vote, attending rallies and other political meetings, displaying support for a candidate through buttons or bumper stickers, volunteering for a campaign, and contributing money. Overall, the most popular form of political participation is engaging in a discussion to try to influence someone's vote. Significantly fewer Americans attend a political meeting or volunteer for a campaign, and less than 5% of Americans report making a campaign donation.

How does women's participation in these activities compare to men's? In short, women's greater participation in voting does not appear to carry over to these other political activities. Burrell (2004) reported the following:

> Women have consistently reported lower levels of involvement, and the gap has not diminished over the course of the contemporary era. . . . With respect to the 2000 election, for instance, 48 percent of men and 39 percent of women reported having participated in at least one of these activities. (p. 101)

In general, over time, men have been consistently more likely to try to influence votes through debate. Differences across the genders for other political activities are much smaller. For instance, during the 2004 election, 51% of men and 45% of women reported talking to others to try to influence their vote—a 6-point gender gap—whereas 22% of men and 19% of women wore a campaign button or displayed a bumper sticker—only a 3-point gender gap. There were no gender gaps for some activities: During the 2004 election, men and women volunteered, attended a political meeting or rally, and donated money at the same rates.

The rarest, but perhaps most influential, form of political participation is the campaign donation. Using data from the Federal Election Commission for the 2000 election, Burrell (2004) found that just 0.5% of men donated $200 or more to candidates for national office, and 0.2% of men donated $1,000 or more. Though this is quite a small fraction of the population, the percentage of women making contributions was less than half that of men, 0.2% at the $200 level and 0.09% donating $1,000 or more.

11

Eastern Europe and Central Asia

Ideologies favorable to women's political participation are a significant part of the history of the former Communist world. Social equality for women was a central tenet of Communist ideology. In 1920, Vladimir Lenin stated the following:

> In law there is naturally complete equality of rights for men and women. And everywhere there is evidence of a sincere wish to put this equality into practice. We are bringing the women into the social economy, into legislation and government. All educational institutions are open to them, so that they can increase their professional and social capacities.... In short, we are seriously carrying out the demand in our programme for the transference of the economic and educational functions of the separate household to society. That will mean freedom for the woman from the old household drudgery and dependence on man. That enables her to exercise to the full her talents and her inclinations. (Zetkin 1920)

Thus, across all domains, including the political, women were to be treated as equals to men. Communist regimes called for the dissolution of public and private spheres, instituted higher levels of education for women, and enforced female participation in the labor force and in politics.

Influenced by this ideology of gender inclusiveness, many public policies and practices during Communist times were beneficial to women. Scholars generally agree that Marxist–Leninist governments actively attempted to erase gender differences (Gal and Kligman 2000:5; Matland and Montgomery 2003). For example, East Germany (or German Democratic Republic [GDR]) passed a decree on equal pay for equal work in 1946, which was some of the earliest legislation targeted to benefit women in world history

(Einhorn 1991). And several countries in Eastern Europe provided abortions for free within the first trimester.

Across the Eastern bloc, women's numbers in politics were also boosted by gender quotas that set mandatory levels for women's participation. Gender quotas ensured that, compared to women in the West, women in most Communist countries experienced relatively high levels of political representation. In the former Soviet Union, for example, women held 17% of seats in the national legislature in 1946, the highest level of female representation at the national level in the world at the time. In 1967, East Germany became the first country to reach 30% women in parliament, followed by the former Soviet Union in 1970 and Romania in 1980. Alternatively, a democratic country did not achieve this feat until 1985, when Sweden elected 31.5% women to parliament. In some countries, such as Poland, women held an even larger share of political offices at the regional and local levels (Shaul 1982).

However, in reality, women living under Communism were still marginalized by the patriarchal system (Fodor 2002). For example, although extensive welfare programs allowed women to participate in the labor force, women were concentrated in lower prestige positions that earned lower wages, and women were still expected to perform the bulk of household and child rearing duties (Gal and Kligman 2000). Thus, although Communist systems use the language of feminist emancipation, power is not shared equally between men and women. Women appear in such high numbers in Communist systems because their political participation is considered mandatory, and states reserve a certain share of parliamentary seats for women.

The Fall of the Soviet Union: Women Fall Too

Transitions to democracy in Eastern Europe in the early 1990s raised fundamental questions about the resilience of women's political power. In short, would women's past roles in government allow them to compete against men for positions in newly democratic countries? The simple answer to this question is no. During the 1990s, women's political representation in former Communist countries plummeted, often dropping from levels around 30% to less than 10%—and sometimes less than 5% (Matland and Montgomery 2003; Saxonberg 2000). Now, two decades later, the average level of representation in Eastern Europe and Central Asia falls right around the rest of the world at 19%, but still a full 6% lower than the 1988 average (Inter-Parliamentary Union [IPU] 2012b; Paxton, Green, and Hughes 2008).

Map 11.1 Women's Parliamentary Representation in Eastern Europe and Central Asia, 2011

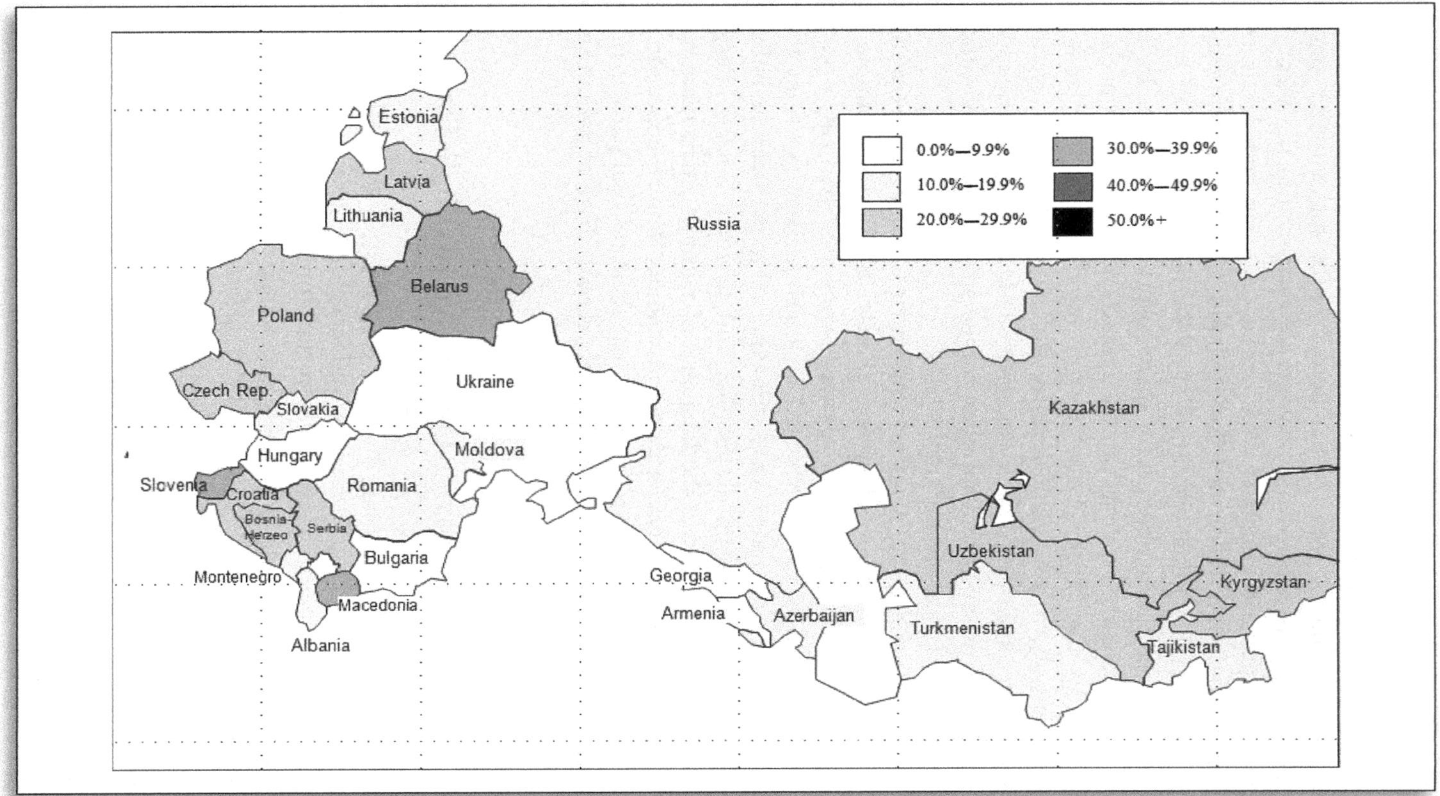

Legend:
- 0.0%–9.9%
- 10.0%–19.9%
- 20.0%–29.9%
- 30.0%–39.9%
- 40.0%–49.9%
- 50.0%+

See Map 11.1 for variation in women's representation across the countries of Eastern Europe and Central Asia.

Looking back, it is now clear that "women were ill prepared to influence the State and the newly active political parties during the very rapid collapse of the old order" (Waylen 1994:347). First, the women chosen to serve in Communist parliaments were not likely to pursue politics once countries transitioned to democracy. Describing the Communist situation in Bulgaria, Kostova (1998) stated the following:

> Many of the women . . . were weavers, seamstresses, heroes of socialist labor, and women with low-status jobs. The fact that these women did not have experience to be taken seriously in important decision-making was exactly the reason they were chosen. (p. 211)

But this pattern was not unique to Bulgaria. Across the Communist world, women's representation was acknowledged as token, and women were known as "milkmaid" politicians (Waylen 1994).

Furthermore, women's representation in the legislatures of Communist countries did not mean they had genuine power. Under Communism, the real power is held in the central committee or **politburo**—the executive body that governs the Communist Party—whereas legislatures serve only as "rubber stamps" (Matland and Montgomery 2003:6). And though Lenin argued that a "woman communist is a member of the Party just as a man communist, with equal rights and duties" (Zetkin 1920), men held the positions of power in the politburos (Einhorn 1991; Montgomery 2003). For example, in East Germany, not a single woman entered the politburo during its history (Einhorn 1992, cited in Waylen 1994). Women's party participation and share of leadership positions were greatest during the period before and immediately after the Communist revolution but declined as Communism was consolidated (Wolchik 1981, 1994).

Women were further marginalized during the politics of transition. As elites negotiated the forms that new social, political, and economic institutions would take, women were swept aside. As Einhorn (1991) described, "In all those cases where past dissidents formed or were important in the first democratically elected governments—in pre-unification East Germany, in Slovenia, in Czechoslovakia, in Poland—it is men . . . who became government ministers" (p. 17). For example, during the transition period in Czechoslovakia, of the 21 positions of ministerial rank in the interim government, there was only one woman (Wolchik 1994). Women "were present at the big demonstrations, on the happy streets, but disappeared from the negotiating tables" (Kiss 1991:51).

One explanation for women's exclusion is that during the process of transition there was little to no activity by women's movements. In part, this is a legacy of Communist policy. Lenin argued that the Communist women's movement should be a part of the greater revolution against capitalism, so women should not form special organizations (Zetkin 1920). "No independent women's organizations were tolerated, and those women's organizations that did exist were essentially part of the Communist Party apparatus" (Waylen 1994:345). Although these restrictions on organizing were lifted once Communist dominance ended, it is not so easy to create a vibrant civil society with active citizen participation (Putnam 1994). Instead of motivating them to action, women's loss of position in their new democratic system created a sense of shock that perpetuated women's inactivity (Einhorn 1991). Overall, with no underlying structure of activism to push for women's incorporation, women's individual demands could simply be ignored.

But there are also reasons why women retreated from the public realm. Regional experts often note that though Communism espoused an ideal of gender equality, the revolution was incomplete. Women living under Communism were still marginalized by the patriarchal system (Fodor 2002; Gal and Kligman 2000). The policies establishing women's equality were part of a "revolution from above" that left the everyday structures of life and the relations between men and women at the most basic levels relatively unchanged. In addition to their workplace roles, women continued to shoulder the overwhelming majority of domestic work and child care. This double burden of work and family roles was further extended into a **triple burden**—participation in politics. Therefore, once the requirements on women's work and political participation were removed, it was not difficult to push women back into traditional patterns (Einhorn 1991; Kiss 1991).

Variation in Recovery

Since the transition to democracy and market economics, women in some former Communist countries have been more politically successful than others. For example, women now hold less than 10% of seats in countries like Armenia and the Ukraine, whereas Bulgaria has even surpassed its high point of women's legislative representation under communism, electing 26.2% women in 2001. Variation across the region is so great that the patterns we introduced in Chapter 3—Flat, Increasing, Big Jump, Low Increasing, and Plateau—all appear in the trajectories of women's representation in post-Communist since 1990. Figures 11.1 and 11.2 display countries that follow each of these five trajectories from 1991 to 2011.

Figure 11.1   Trajectories Since 1991—Georgia, Macedonia, Slovenia

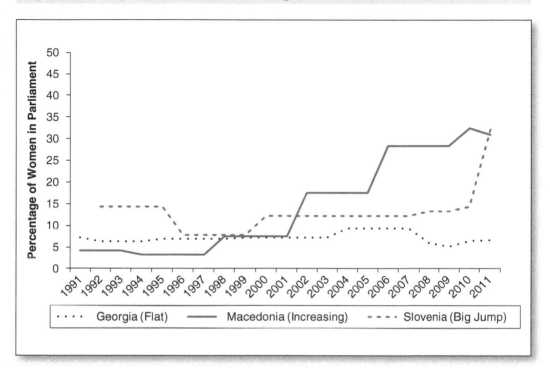

Several countries in the region have flat trajectories, exhibiting little real change over the past two decades. Georgia shows this pattern in Figure 11.1, but countries like Armenia, Georgia, and the Ukraine are no different. In contrast, other post-Communist countries have demonstrated substantial improvement in women's political representation over time. Some, like Macedonia, experienced steady gains, following an increasing pattern. As shown in the figure, Macedonia's growth occurred primarily after 1997, although other countries like Lithuania experienced earlier successes. The third country depicted in Figure 11.1 is Slovenia, marked by a gray dashed line. Slovenia experienced little change until 2011, when women's descriptive representation more than doubled.

Figure 11.2 displays countries that fit the low increasing and plateau trajectories. Albania, shown with a black line, shows no change in women's legislative inclusion until recent years, when minimal gains finally began to appear. Other countries showing recent promise include Albania, Azerbaijan, and Tajikistan.

Turkmenistan arguably mirrors the pre-1990 pattern for the region—the plateau. Although women dropped from the parliament for a few years

Figure 11.2   Trajectories Since 1991—Albania and Turkmenistan

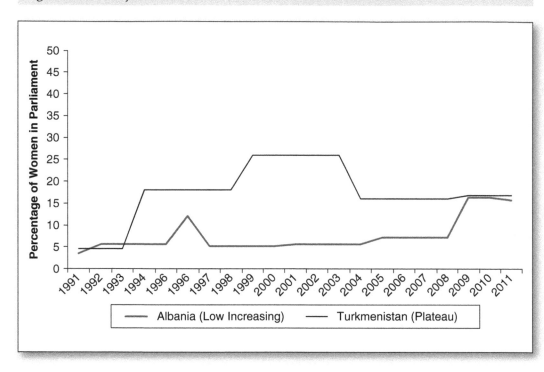

during the 1990s, Turkmenistan recovered more quickly than other countries in the region, crossing 25% women in parliament during the late 1990s. Women's legislative representation suffered a drop-off in 2004 but has remained at a steady 16% to 17% since.

Explaining Women's Political Power Since 1990

What explains these trajectories? Why were some countries able to rebound but others were not? What are the barriers to women's political incorporation today? To answer these questions, one must consider the cultural, economic, and political circumstances faced by women throughout Eastern Europe and Central Asia since the fall of the Soviet Union.

Like in other parts of the world, women seeking political office across Eastern Europe and Central Asia must now contend with traditional beliefs about women's proper roles as well as negative stereotypes about women in politics. Across the region, there has been "an explicit rebirth of the ideology of women's primary role as wife and mother, tender of the domestic hearth"

(Einhorn 1991:18). And because women held token positions under communism, male politicians often do not take female politicians seriously. For example, Ekaterina Lakhova, former head of the Presidential Commission on Women, Families, and Demography in Russia, stated, "Men see us as women, but not as deputies. You're explaining something to him about infant mortality, and he says that it doesn't become you to talk about such serious things; that you have to be a woman" (cited in Sperling 1998:159).

One significant problem for women seeking to organize for change is the prevalence of antifeminist attitudes. Across the region, feminism carries negative associations because of both its connections to the West and its association with the Communist period. In fact, "'gender equality' is a term that most politicians, male and female alike, hesitate to use" (Rueschemeyer 1994:233). The discrediting of feminism limits both the abilities of women to successfully organize and the ability of female politicians to represent women's interests (Goven 1993; Jaquette and Wolchik 1998; Matland and Montgomery 2003; Rueschemeyer 1994). A female candidate speaking about equal wages risks accusations that she is a Communist. Therefore, female politicians may be more likely to toe the party line to acquire or hold on to power. Birch (2003) stated, "Female politicians in Ukraine are clearly using the institution of the political party to their advantage; the question remains as to whether they are using it to the advantage of Ukrainian women" (p. 149).

But although traditional beliefs about women's gender roles and antifeminism are quite common across the region, there is also significant variation in cultural support for women in politics both across and within Eastern European countries. According to data from the World Values Survey, support for women as political leaders is lowest in Georgia and Armenia and highest in Slovenia and Macedonia (Wilcox, Stark, and Thomas 2003). And across the region, older, less educated, politically conservative, and Muslim citizens were less supportive of women in politics than their younger, more educated, more liberal, and Christian counterparts (Wilcox et al. 2003).

Some stereotypes about women have even served them well politically. For example, across Eastern Europe, women have been marketed as especially good candidates for fighting corruption. "With an image as an outsider, women can be seen with brooms sweeping out the corruption that still exists in the halls of power" (Matland 2003:329). One particularly interesting example of the relationship between gender and corruption is Yulia Tymoshenko, former prime minister of Ukraine. During Ukraine's transition to democracy, Tymoshenko was accused of selling abroad enormous quantities of stolen Russian gas, earning her the nickname "gas princess" (Zarakhovich 2005). But Yulia later cast herself as an economic reformer in the political realm. She said, "I want to say to people, 'Forget about paying bribes. Pay taxes'" (Tymoshenko 2005).

Women have also had trouble translating their high levels of education and employment, encouraged during the Communist period, into political gains in the post-Communist period. Under Communism, approximately 92% of working-age women in the Soviet Union either participated in the labor force or were furthering their education (Wejnert 1996). But since democratization, women make up the majority of the unemployed. In Ukraine, for example, women make up 70% of the unemployed population, even though two thirds of these women have higher education (Birch 2003). Women's exit from the workforce matters for the usual structural reasons. But to combat negative stereotypes about female politicians' lack of qualifications holding over from the Communist era, women today may even need to be overqualified. In Poland, for example, female parliamentarians hold more university-level degrees than their male counterparts and often have longer records of party and trade union service (Siemienska 2003).

In terms of political factors, many of the patterns established in research on the West hold for Eastern Europe: Proportional representation (PR) systems tend to favor women, leftist parties also more consistently field a larger number of female candidates, and high party magnitudes can ensure that women, who are often placed lower on party lists, will gain seats (Kunovich 2003; Matland and Montgomery 2003). Of course, there are exceptions. In Russia's mixed system, for example, women have fared better competing in the plurality half of the system than in the party-list system (Moser 2003). And in Lithuania, the conservative Homeland Union Party included just as many women as other parties with more leftist ideologies (Krupavičius and Matonytė 2003; Matland 2003).

Level of democracy is another political factor that continues to affect countries across the region. It is a lack of democracy that explains the post-1990 trajectory of Turkmenistan. Unlike many other countries that ousted their Communist leaders, First Secretary of the Turkmen Communist Party Saparmurat Niyazov led Turkmenistan from the fall of the Soviet Union until his death in 2006. Niyazov's rule was far from democratic, and he gained a reputation for his strange decrees. For example, he banned lip synching at public concerts and female news anchors from wearing makeup on television. Under Niyazov's regime, candidates were hand-selected by the government and were all members of Niyazov's Democratic Party. Thus, like other authoritarian regimes, Niyazov placed women into power. After Niyazov's death, the country was taken over by President Gurbanguly Berdymukhamedov, who began dismantling many of Niyazov's policies. In 2008, a new constitution was adopted, and in 2012, Berdymukhamedov called for multiparty elections. Only time will tell if the transition will hasten a new drop in political representation for Turkmen women.

In a few cases, post-Communist countries have also experienced armed conflicts that have fueled changes in women's representation. For example, after Tajikistan's 1992 to 1997 civil war, women's parliamentary representation increased 10%. After the war, women moved in greater numbers into the nongovernmental sector and began to organize conferences and meetings. These activities resulted in the passage of the 1998 National Plan of Action on Improvement of Women's Status, which included provisions for women's political incorporation. But the Tajik civil war was unlike African conflicts in other ways that matter for women's empowerment: Tajik women did not comprise a significant percentage of combatants, the war did not produce regime change, and traditional attitudes toward women's status and roles were unshaken (Hughes 2009a). Ultimately, therefore, Tajikistan has not seen increases in women's political representation as dramatic as seen in Africa (see Chapter 15).

Another country that has recently experienced both political turmoil and changes for women is Kyrgyzstan. During the Soviet period, women made up 33% of the legislature (Hunt 2007), but after democratization, their participation in politics dropped dramatically. In 2005, women held not a single seat in parliament. And only one member of the cabinet of ministers was a woman (Bedelbaeva and Kuvatova 2010). But in recent years, women in Kyrgyzstan politics have been more of a success story. In 2007, women were elected to 25% of the national legislature, and between 2010 and 2011, Roza Otunbayeva served briefly as president. There are two major explanations for this remarkable change in such a short period of time. First, the United Nations and other international agents have been very active in promoting women's political representation by fostering ties between nongovernmental organizations (NGOs) and female candidates and by training women as activists and leaders. Second, in 2007, Kyrgyzstan introduced a 30% quota with placement mandates and sanctions for noncompliance. One new female parliamentarian, Gulnora Derbisheva, attributes her election to the quota. "There were so many obstacles on my path to politics," she said (Najibullah 2010).

Yet, gender quotas have not always had a warm reception in post-Communist countries. The requirements for women's inclusion in politics during the Communist era largely delegitimized quotas as a strategy for enhancing women's representation (Matland and Montgomery 2003). Thus, during the 1990s, post-Communist governments resisted national-level quotas (Dahlerup and Freidenvall 2005; Tripp and Kang 2008). After 2000, a few post-Communist countries came around. In 2001, Bosnia and Herzegovina became the first country in the region to adopt a national quota above 10%, followed by Serbia and Uzbekistan in 2004, Slovenia in 2006, Armenia and Kyrgyzstan in 2007, Albania in 2008, and Poland in 2011.

Today, gender quotas still have their critics, even among women. But others see the opposition to gender quotas as missing the ways that men are privileged in politics. As one Kyrgyz activist stated, "When we are talking about men, nobody cares about the fact that they're using whatever resources, whatever tools, corrupt or not corrupt. When it comes to women, immediately there's a double standard" (Najibullah 2010).

Eastern and Central Europe and the European Union

Like countries in Western Europe, the countries in Central and Eastern Europe have been influenced by the European Union (EU)—specifically the desire of many countries to become members of the union and the reforms to their economic and political institutions that membership entailed. In 2004, the first Eastern European countries joined the EU—Hungary, Estonia, the Czech Republic, Poland, Latvia, Lithuania, Slovakia, and Slovenia. In 2007, Bulgaria and Romania followed. Croatia is scheduled to become a member in 2013, and Macedonia, Montenegro, and Serbia are all acknowledged candidates for membership.

The countries in Central and Eastern Europe wishing to become members of the EU (called candidate countries) had to undertake political, economic, and social policy reforms. Candidate countries have to adjust their laws and institutions to strengthen neoliberal market economies and democratic practices. Among the changes required are those that relate to gender equality including equal pay for men and women, parental leave, work–family balance, sexual harassment and the institution of gender mainstreaming. Although attention to gender policies in candidate countries by the EU during the accession process was not perfect (Bretherton 2001), the accession process did provide the EU and local activists with a tool to put pressure on candidate state governments to improve their gender equality legislation (Haskova and Krizkova 2008; Roth 2007).

As explained by Angelika von Wahl (2008:19–20), the post-Communist states entering the EU found themselves at a crossroads of four paths: "their own socialist legacy, the transition to capitalist economy, the states' desire to reinvent and invigorate their own national heritage, and the EU." The EU accession process forces these states down a particular path—to a market-driven economy with social concerns heavily influenced by external (EU) regulations.

And the Eastern European countries wishing to join the EU had to address gender equality: "It constitutes the dense policy framework that national and local political actors must deal with in some form or other, whether that is to implement, reframe, call upon, contend, compromise with, support, get around or evade" (von Wahl 2008:20). In short, no matter how they ultimately responded, the countries of Central and Eastern Europe that joined the EU were forced to address gender equality. As a result, gender equality legislation has been adopted and women's policy machineries and gender mainstreaming introduced in a wide range of Eastern European countries (Roth 2008)—for example the Czech Republic (Anderson 2006).

So what has EU accession meant for women's political representation in the region? It is hard to say. On the one hand, we can point to success stories among new member states, places like Slovenia. Between 1990 and 2005, Slovene women maxed out at three ministers in the government, 6% of mayors, 12% of local councillors, and 14% of members of parliament (MPs) (European Forum 2008). But in 2001, women formed the Coalition for Parity and took advantage of the Slovenian accession period (2001–2004) to lobby for change. The first breakthrough was a new 40% gender quota for the European Parliament. After the quota proved successful, women pushed for other changes. Slovenia enacted a 20% quota for local elections and women's share of councillors rose from 12% to 21% (European Forum 2008). Finally, in 2006, the parliament passed a quota for national legislative seats, designed to start at 25% in 2008 and subsequently increase to 35%. Although these numbers fell short of the 40% threshold lobbied for by the Coalition for Parity, women's representation in parliament climbed to 32.2% in 2011, catapulting Slovenia to the spot of regional leader in women's political representation.

But Slovenia may be the exception rather than the rule. Most Central and Eastern European countries that have joined the EU have experienced stability or incremental gains in women's political representation in recent years. And although EU member states and candidates generally outperform non-EU countries in the region, these differences were present in the early 2000s. If anything, gaps between EU and non-EU countries in Central and Eastern Europe have closed over time because of countries like Albania and Belarus (nonmember states), which doubled or tripled their levels of women's representation in the decade after 2000.

In conclusion, we should not romanticize the high number of women in Communist governments. The drop in women's legislative representation associated with the transition to democracy may be striking, but there are also increasing opportunities for women to gain true political power in the new democracies of this region. As Lithuanian scholars Krupavičius and Matonytė (2003) described, "While the number of women in formal positions of power has dropped precipitously from the Soviet period, the women who are active in politics have been able to carve out more authentic places for themselves, with meaningful power" (p. 103). Competing in elections may present new obstacles for women and change may be slow, but the benefits are real.

12

Latin America
and the Caribbean

Who would have said, 10, 15 years ago, that a woman would be elected president?

—Michelle Bachelet, president of Chile, 2006

In April 2012, women held approximately 19% of the seats in the national legislatures of Latin America and the Caribbean. Although 19% is still far from equality, women have clearly made gains in the region in recent years. Only five countries have less than 10% women in their lower house of parliament—Brazil, Panama, Belize, Saint Kitts and Nevis, and Haiti—while six countries have more than 30%—Argentina, Ecuador, Guyana, Costa Rica, Nicaragua, and Cuba (see Table 12.1). At the subnational level, women appear in legislative office at approximately the same rate as at the national level—21% in 2010 (Htun and Piscopo 2010:14)—although they have yet to be elected to subnational executive positions such as governor or mayor in any great numbers (see Hinojosa and Franceschet forthcoming).

One example of women's success in the region was the election of Michelle Bachelet, who won a runoff election in 2006 to become the first female president of Chile. As a separated mother of three and a self-described agnostic, Michelle Bachelet does not conform to conventional ideas about womanhood in her conservative and Catholic homeland. Yet, as we discuss later, like

Table 12.1   Women in Parliament, Women Ministerial Appointments, and Female National Leaders in Latin America and the Caribbean, 2012

Country	Percentage of Women in Parliament	Percentage of Women Ministers	Current or Former Female Chief Executive
South America			
Argentina	37.4%	17.6%	Isabel Peron, Christina Fernández de Kirchner
Ecuador	32.3%	40.0%	
Guyana	31.3%	29.4%	Janet Jagan
Bolivia	25.4%	45.5%	Lydia Gueiler Tejada[1]
Peru	21.5%	16.7%	
Venezuela	17.0%	37.8%	
Chile	14.2%	18.2%	Michelle Bachelet
Paraguay	12.5%	7.1%	
Colombia	12.1%	33.3%	
Uruguay	12.1%	7.1%	
Suriname	11.8%	11.1%	
Brazil	8.6%	27.0%	Dilma Rousseff
Average	19.7%	24.2%	
Central America			
Costa Rica	38.6%	29.2%	Laura Chinchilla
Nicaragua	40.2%	46.2%	Violeta Chamorro
Mexico	26.2%	21.1%	
El Salvador	26.2%	11.1%	
Honduras	19.5%	17.6%	
Guatemala	13.3%	0.0%	
Panama	8.5%	29.4%	Mireya Moscoso de Arias

(Continued)

(Continued)

Country	Percentage of Women in Parliament	Percentage of Women Ministers	Current or Former Female Chief Executive
Belize	3.1%	0.0%	
Average	22.0%	19.3%	
Caribbean			
Cuba	45.2%	22.6%	
Trinidad and Tobago	28.6%	18.4%	Kamla Persad-Bissessar
Dominican Republic	20.8%	13.0%	
Saint Vincent and the Grenadines	17.4%	18.2%	
Saint Lucia	16.7%	15.4%	
Grenada	13.3%	21.4%	
Jamaica	12.7%	20.0%	Portia Simpson-Miller
Dominica	12.5%	13.3%	Eugenia Charles
Bahamas	12.2%	0.0%	
Antigua and Barbuda	10.5%	11.1%	
Barbados	10.0%	11.8%	
Haiti	4.2%	16.7%	Ertha Pascal-Trouillot[1]
Saint Kitts and Nevis	6.7%	11.1%	Claudette Werleigh[2]
Average	16.2%	14.9%	

1. Interim or acting leader.

2. Prime minister in mixed system.

Note: Ministers include ministers and deputy prime ministers.

Source: Data from Inter-Parliamentary Union (IPU) (2012b).

many women across Latin America, she was politicized by the struggle for democracy and liberation from brutal military rule. During her tenure, Bachelet was a vocal supporter of women's rights and instituted gender parity in her cabinet by appointing 10 women and 10 men to cabinet positions (Hunt 2007). In 2010, Bachelet became head of the United Nation's new entity, UN Women, which consolidated UN efforts to address women's empowerment and gender equality. Other important leaders in the region are Cristina Fernández de Kirchner of Argentina, Laura Chinchilla of Costa Rica, and Dilma Rousseff of Brazil. In fact, Latin America leads the world in the number of countries that have elected female presidents or prime ministers.

Another example of marked improvement in recent years is in Costa Rica (see Figure 12.1). Costa Rica is exceptional in the region of Latin America for its governmental stability, suffering only two brief periods of war in its long democratic history (Central Intelligence Agency 2006). Prior to the 1990s, women's political representation increased only slowly and inconsistently (Quesada 2003). But in 1996, the adoption of a 40% quota for women on party lists accelerated women's involvement, increasing representation at the national level from 15.8% to 19.3%. Once placement mandates were added to the law in 2002, women's parliamentary representation jumped even further. Female parliamentarians have also had significant legislative success. Studies have shown that laws submitted by female deputies have been approved 81% of the time whereas for men the statistic is only 48% (de Figueres 2002 but see Sagot 2010).

Women's political advancement in Chile and Costa Rica highlights two forces that are important for women's political progress across Latin America. First, women's participation in revolutionary struggles has changed ideas about women's proper roles. Political transitions have fostered women's integration into newly ruling parties, furthered public policy that benefits women, and catapulted women like Michelle Bachelet into political leadership. Second, the wave of national quota legislation that has washed over the region since the 1990s has also fostered real improvements in women's political situations in some countries (Bonder and Nari 1995; Htun and Jones 2002; Jones 1998, 2004, 2009; Quesada 2003; Sacchet 2008; Schmidt and Saunders 2004; Zetterberg 2008). For example, Argentina, the first country in the world to adopt a national quota law, is now among the leaders of the region with 37.4% women in its lower house.

Before discussing these two forces for women's advancement, however, we review the historical and cultural obstacles to women's political empowerment, including the Catholic Church, **machismo** and *marianismo,* and

Figure 12.1   Women's Political Milestones and Representation
                   at the National and Municipal Levels in Costa Rica, 1982–2010

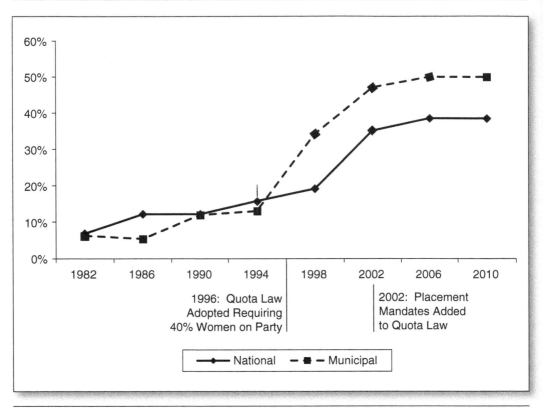

Sources: Data from de Figueres (2002); Jones (2004); Sagot (2010).

repressive exclusionary governments. These forces help us understand why women's participation in democratic movements does not always guarantee gains in women's formal political roles after a regime has been toppled, for example, in El Salvador. And where women have entered formal politics, they continue to be hindered by restrictive gender cultures.

Cultural Barriers to Women in Politics in Latin America

As in countries across the world, gender roles in Latin America have traditionally been constructed to exclude women from the public realm. The ideal woman does not work outside the home but focuses on her responsibilities as mother and housewife. Mothering and nurturing are considered women's natural roles. Even in recent times, while women are increasingly participating in paid labor, women still view motherhood as their primary identity (Craske 1999). Traditional gender roles and the ideal of motherhood are reinforced by the Catholic Church, which has remained a powerful force across the region. As Mair (1991) stated, "Catholic patriarchal dogmas have been the major element in glorifying women as mothers, and thereby confining them to domesticity" (p. 159). Central to Catholicism is the symbol of the Virgin Mary, which reinforces a female ideal of selfless motherhood (Craske 1999).

Cultural attitudes about appropriate behavior for men and women are summarized in the extremes of machismo and **marianismo.** The male ideal, machismo, not only calls for arrogance and sexual aggression in the relations between men and women but also cultural standards such as having a large family and women staying home are linked to male virility (Craske 1999). In politics, this refers to "an extremely aggressive or competitive style of speech and a condescending or patronizing attitude towards women" (Franceschet 2001:215). The female counterpart, marianismo, depicts the female ideal as the selfless mother—morally superior and spiritually strong but submissive to men and therefore dependent, timid, and conformist (Craske 1999). Women are expected to derive their identities from the males in their lives, fathers, husbands, sons, and are expected to derive fulfillment as the counterparts to these males, as daughters, wives, and mothers (Saint-Germain and Metoyer 2008). Consider the statement by Argentinean businesswoman Carmen Olaechea:

> Even though my family is a matriarchy where intelligence is valued, I was educated in the first place to be a mother and wife and to support my man. From an early age, I received messages like the following: "If you are more intelligent than the man, don't let him notice." . . . Looking back, I believe that the strongest manifestation of the family mandate consisted in the fact that up until I was 30 years old, I didn't even have a vision for myself apart from my role as a mother, wife, and daughter. Simply, it never occurred to me. (quoted in Cosgrove 2010:97)

Many people across Latin America believe that to a greater or lesser extent these ideals reflect the biological nature of man and woman (Seitz 1991).

Gender roles and the feminine ideal have structured both women's political exclusion and the forms of their participation. Women who conform to the ideals of docility, morality, and spirituality receive social approval. But women who deviate from these ideals experience disapproval and contempt. Because politics is viewed as a corrupt arena, women should not participate unless to influence social issues. Women may be encouraged to enter politics at times of crises, when their feminine characteristics (honesty, humanity) are needed, but "when crises pass and politics-as-usual returns, women are expected to return to their social roles as mothers and community caretakers" (Franceschet 2005:2).

When women enter the halls of power, cultural attitudes are not left at the door. For example, in her 1960s study of women in politics in Chile and Peru, Elsa Chaney (1973) found that female politicians often see themselves as *supermadres*, or supermothers, who must manage a particularly large family in the large "house" that is their municipality or country. Chaney (1973) also demonstrated that women were segregated into women's wings within political parties and marshaled into areas that dealt with "appropriate" issues for women, such as education, health, and the general social welfare. More than 40 years later, women have expanded their view of their political role (Furlong and Riggs 1996; Schwindt-Bayer 2006), but the practice of assigning women to committees dealing with social issues continues (de Figueres 2002; Heath, Schwindt-Bayer, Taylor-Robinson 2005).

Democratization and Women's Political Empowerment

Most citizens across Latin America live under democratic or semidemocratic administrations (Freedom House 2012). But for much of the region's history, this was not the case. In countries where democracy existed, it was often interrupted by military interventions and rule by brutal authoritarian regimes. Because such regimes place significant limitations on political activism of all types, women seeking political recognition of any type faced substantial barriers (Craske 1999). As Nikki Craske aptly stated, "Women's growing participation has to be understood in the context of a generalized exclusion which has characterized the region's political systems and the long-term struggle for democracy" (p. 3).

Across Latin America, transitions from **military authoritarianism** to democracy did not proceed smoothly but were fueled by popular protest, guerrilla warfare, and revolution. And in each of these forms of struggle, women played key roles.

Women's Participation in Guerrilla Warfare and Revolutionary Movements

Women were an active part of the guerrilla warfare and political uprisings that swept Latin America in the 1970s and 1980s. By the late 1970s, across the region, "women of all social classes defied their historical exclusion from things political and joined the opposition in unprecedented numbers" (Sternbach, Navarro-Aranguren, Chuchryk, and Álvarez 1992). For example, following the 1973 military takeover of Chile and the murder of as many as 30,000 people within the first few months, women were the first to mobilize against the repression (Baldez 2002; Chuchryk 1991; Noonan 1995). During the 1992 demobilization in El Salvador, 30% of the demobilized war participants were women, and at the high point of the Nicaraguan insurrection, women were reported to be a quarter of combatants (Luciak 2001).

Consider the experience of women in the overthrow of Nicaragua's brutal Somoza regime. The Somoza family dynasty ruled Nicaragua from 1936 to 1979, controlling as much as 40% of the economy and impoverishing the people. Nicaragua's poor economic situation had severe implications for poor and working-class women. Faced with the inability to support their families, many fathers and husbands abandoned their families. Responsible for the survival of themselves and their children, mothers entered the labor force in large numbers. Nicaraguan women made up a large proportion of the country's agricultural field workers, making them the first to be affected by unemployment, inflation, and shortages.

When the Marxist Sandinista National Liberation Front (FSLN) organized in the 1960s and began its first campaign against the Somoza regime in 1974, women were motivated to joining the revolution. Women were involved in every facet of the opposition movement (Luciak 2001). They demonstrated on the streets, participated in strikes, fought on the front lines, participated in support tasks, worked undercover in government offices, and helped to hide undercover soldiers and weaponry. By the final offensive in 1979, women made up 30% of the revolutionary army and held important leadership oppositions, commanding everything from small units to full battalions. As revolutionary Amada Pineda recounted, women were also repressed and victimized by Somoza's regime:

> They took us away—seven men and me. I was the only woman. They locked us all together in the same room, in a house they had nearby. . . . They used different kinds of approaches. Sometimes they used torture—they would beat me. Sometimes it was soft talk. When they came to rape me, after a while it was just . . . unbearable. [They] raped me seventeen times. . . . Toward the end, they said they were going to take me up in a helicopter and drop me from the sky. . . . But they didn't. Instead, they took the other prisoners and tortured them in front of me. They beat them. They burned them. They half-buried them in ant hills. After six or seven days of that, they let me go. . . . It was terribly traumatic. I felt like I smelled bad, and I couldn't get rid of the smell. . . . There

are many women in Nicaragua who can tell of the barbarities they've suffered. And many others who didn't live through the nightmares. (quoted in Randall 1981:86–90)

Women experienced significant hardships under Latin America's dictatorships and during their subsequent revolutionary struggles. But participation in these revolutionary struggles also provided women with experiences and skills that "bended gender" (Kampwirth 2002:76; Viterna forthcoming). Women participated in actual combat, in leadership roles, and in logistics and infrastructure. For example, "Roxana" participated in the El Salvadorian guerrilla war and received formal training as a war medic. She worked with a special forces unit, carried a gun, and used it. "Lupe" spent 4 years in the guerrilla camps, also worked as a medic, and experienced the heat of battle. Both women had children during their time in the struggle (Viterna forthcoming:6).

Participation in warfare can increase women's self-confidence and help them to see themselves as competent activists (Viterna forthcoming). For example, Roxana, described in the previous paragraph, is involved in a feminist organization, has served multiple times on her village council, and was elected to the governing regional council of her political party. As recounted in Viterna (forthcoming:7) she attributes her political participation and leadership abilities to her wartime experiences: "We women did so much in the war. How would it be possible that after the peace accords, in a more tranquil climate, that we wouldn't be capable of doing more?" Women were active participants in the new parties that grew out of former guerrilla movements (Luciak 2001). Both Michelle Bachelet, former president of Chile, and Dilma Rousseff, current president of Brazil, were actively involved in their country's democratization movements and, indeed, were both arrested and tortured during the struggle.

In addition to the politicization of individual women, women in many Latin American countries launched "vibrant autonomous feminist movements" in the aftermath of these revolutionary struggles (Kampwirth 2004:165, 2010:112; Luciak 2001). Women noticed that their roles in opposition movements or parties were constrained by gender roles that helped them develop a feminist consciousness. Women could take their experiences and translate them into service in new feminist movements. Consider the experience of Mary Bolt, who had a history as a guerrilla with the Sandinistas, then became a party activist in the new democracy, and finally became an activist in the feminist movement when the Sandinistas lost political power:

After, with the new election, an emptiness opened up and I think this happened to a lot of Nicaraguan men and women. It was a political emptiness. . . . for us it was very strong; it was a cause for grieving. . . . So for me this emptiness was filled by the feminist movement. (interview cited in Kampwirth 2010:115)

Women's Participation in Protest Movements

Besides outright participation in war or guerrilla insurgencies, women were active participants in organized resistance to the human rights violations of authoritarian governments. Perhaps the most famous example of women fighting for democratization is the Mothers of the Plaza de Mayo (see Figure 12.2), a group of mothers who protested the "disappearance" of their children by the Argentinean military. Beginning in 1977, mothers gathered on Thursdays on the Plaza de Mayo, wore distinctive white headscarves, and processed in front of the presidential palace carrying pictures of their kidnapped children. The Mothers also published demands in newspapers requesting information on the whereabouts of their children and worked with international agents to expose human rights abuses. Over time, the number of women participating in the weekly demonstration grew and drew international attention to human rights abuses in Argentina. Other women's groups fighting against authoritarian regimes across Latin America followed the lead of the Mothers and framed their protests as mothers, daughters, sisters, and grandmothers rather than individuals (Jaquette and Wolchik 1998).

The example of the Mothers of the Plaza de Mayo illustrates two important points about women's activism in democratization movements in the region. First, because women were traditionally excluded from mainstream political activities such as political parties or unions, women had the unique opportunity to mobilize precisely when mainstream activities were being repressed (Noonan 1995). Women's and other social movements are an important source of political activism when political parties, for example, are banned (Jaquette and Wolchick 1998). The opportunity for women presents itself because, in contrast to men, women's sources of power are often informal and nontraditional (Jaquette 1994). If women are invisible in the public sphere, then they can be political actors during times when political action is dangerous (Chuchryk 1991). For example, when the government of Chile cracked down on street demonstrations by unions, women's human rights groups continued to protest (Noonan 1995:102). In places where public meetings were banned, women could meet in groups because their interaction was perceived as "harmless gossiping" (Craske 1999:119).

The second unique feature of women's activism exemplified by the Mothers of the Plaza de Mayo is the use of gender in the fight for democratic principles. The Mothers felt that they had the right to protest, as mothers,

Figure 12.2   Mothers of the Plaza de Mayo

Source: Eduardo Di Baia, AP.

about their concern for their children and how their families were profoundly impacted by a disappearance (Fisher 1989). Similarly, housewife
organizations in Latin America demonstrated and held purchasing strikes
against the high cost of living, arguing that their children were going hungry
because of economic crises and the regime's economic policies. These housewives organizations were responsible for helping organize larger urban
protests against deteriorating living standards (del Carmen Feijoo and
Gogna 1990). As an identity that crosses ethnicity and class, the ideal
of motherhood allowed women to unite against oppression (Craske 1999).
To describe this pattern, Álvarez (1990, 1994) coined the term *militant
motherhood.*

Using gendered frames can be a particularly effective strategy against
regimes that use gendered imagery to consolidate power. The military had

difficulty dealing with the Mothers in Argentina and in other countries such as Chile because it had claimed moral authority to defend family values (Noonan 1995). Across Latin America, regimes reinforced traditional views of a woman's place, co-opted traditional symbols of feminine morality, spirituality, and motherhood, and made "Family, God, and Liberty" the cornerstone of the militaristic authoritarian regime (Álvarez 1990:5–8). When women in turn used this same imagery to protest, regimes had little recourse. As explained by Jo Fisher (1989:60), the presence of "silent, accusing" mothers on the Plaza de Mayo exemplified the very things the regime claimed to protect. In short, women can strategically challenge state power by seeming to act within traditional gender roles.

Furthermore, the Catholic Church, which has served to restrict women to traditional gender roles, legitimized their participation in social and political struggles (Mair 1991). Throughout Latin America during the 1960s and 1970s, sectors of the Church aligned against the military regimes and supported women's organizing (Jaquette 1994). Women's participation was in line with a Christian ideal of womanhood, which called for a focus on improving family welfare or defending life. And as Craske (1999:126) noted, "It was difficult for partners, parents and the authorities to criticize women for participating in something endorsed by the Church."

Women may also be safer than other groups when they use their gender against an authoritarian regime. It is difficult for a regime to retaliate against women who are only fulfilling their duties as "good" mothers. Women themselves stated that they felt safer than other family members when protesting. In the words of a Mother of the Plaza de Mayo, "a mother always seems more untouchable" (quoted in del Carmen Feijoo and Gogna 1990:90). By using a maternal frame for their activities, women's activism meshed with state discourse and was therefore safer than a more oppositional frame (Noonan 1995). But safer does not equal safe; the first president of the Argentinean Mothers was one of many women disappeared during the authoritarian period.

Women's activism for democracy was often linked to more general feminist activism. Rising concerns over women's secondary status in other movements, such as worker's unions, and in political parties led to the formation of many autonomous women's groups—both before and after the region's democratic transition (Ray and Korteweg 1999; Richards 2004). As women gained political experience, they attempted to influence the state for a variety of causes that would help mothers and women. Consider the famous slogan of the Chilean women's movement: "We want democracy in the nation and in the home" (quoted in Noonan 1995:81).

Women's Current Activism

Today, women's mass movements have been replaced by a more grass-roots and sometimes fragmented approach. Jane Jaquette (2009) argued that "women's movements today are not seen as significant actors in Latin American politics" (p. 6). Instead, feminist activism occurs within a subset of feminist or grass-roots groups through elected women and through women in government bureaucracies. While feminist efforts at national legal reforms continue, there is not sufficient coordination or consensus among groups to be called a movement (Jaquette 2009:6). Instead more effort is dedicated to local service provision (Maier and Lebon 2010). Women's groups have worked at the local level to rebuild their communities after war and to provide the community services that were scaled back during economic reforms in the region.

Critical to women's activism in the region after democratization were the neoliberal economic policies adopted by many countries during the 1980s and 1990s. Faced with severe debt crises in that period, many countries in the region adopted the economic policies prescribed by the World Bank and International Monetary Fund (IMF), which included market deregulation, debt control and repayment, trade liberalization, and privatization of both industry and government-supplied social services (Metoyer 2000). These policies—which often meant the reduction or elimination of free education and health care—created severe hardships for many women, whose participation in the informal economy combined with continued responsibilities at home led to double and triple workdays (Maier and Lebon 2010). In some countries, such as Argentina, women mobilized in large numbers to protest the implementation of these policies (Borland and Sutton 2007). Describing the protests in Buenos Aires in 2001, Borland and Sutton (2007) wrote the following:

> Women shaped the city's landscape as they marched with baby strollers, played drums and chanted protest songs outside the cathedral, put their bodies on the line in roadblocks, rallied demonstrators with megaphones, and distributed bread and roses to pedestrians as a symbolic act. (p. 709)

Unable to afford the costs of many services and lacking institutional remedy, women frequently turned to local grassroots feminist organizations and international nongovernmental organizations (NGOs), which sprang up to fill the gaps (Álvarez 1999; Ewig 1999). This transition from large-scale movement politics to civil society organizations, which Sonia Álvarez (1999) famously dubbed the "NGOization" of the women's movement, continues to influence women's social and political participation throughout the region (Jaquette 2009; Silber 2011).

Women's organizations created communal kitchens, opened health clinics, and offered critical services for women experiencing domestic violence—among others (Barrig 1996; Rosseau 2009). Although operating primarily at a local level, these women's NGOs also organized into issue networks or coalitions to change laws, influence policy, and acquire additional rights, particularly in the areas of domestic violence and reproductive and sexual health (Kampwirth 2004). In Nicaragua, for example, the Women's Network against Violence, formed in the early 1990s, successfully advocated for the implementation of women's police stations that provide comprehensive services for victims of domestic violence throughout the country (Kampwirth 2003). Successful movements to address various aspects of violence against women have also occurred in Brazil, Peru, Costa Rica, and Mexico (Maier and Lebon 2010). In Venezuela, intense mobilization by women during the drafting of the 1999 Constitution led to the inclusion of gender-sensitive language, numerous references to women's equality and citizenship, as well as concrete rights for mothers, such as social security benefits for housework (Rakowski 2003).

A long-standing division also persists between feminist *politicas* (those who work within political parties) and *autonomas* or *feministas* (those who struggle for women's rights via independent groups). Some women argue for autonomous women's groups that can prioritize their own agendas and not fear being subsumed under the agendas of a union or a political party. Other women argue that autonomous groups lack elite connections and allies and cannot address large-scale issue of discrimination. Women who continue to be involved in politics through political parties or other organizations argue for a "double militancy" approach, or the pursuit of gender justice alongside party politics (Franceschet 2005; Richards 2004).

Participation to Representation?

What were the ultimate consequences of women's political activism? Not only were women politicized in the democratic transitions in Latin America but once regimes toppled and democratic institutions began to form, women were potentially positioned to press for their own inclusion. But although women were part of the insurrectionist elites, they were often excluded from the formal peacemaking process. As Saint-Germain and Metoyer (2008) explained the following:

> Women active in peace negotiations from guerrilla or opposition groups constituted only a small part of the entire leadership, and generally did not (or

could not) introduce women's interests or women's demands with sufficient strength into the negotiations. This is reflected in the fact that all of the Esquipulas documents detailing the plans for the pacification and development of Central America used male pronouns and made little or no reference to women's contributions, women's rights, or women's conditions. (p. 226)

Women's participation in democratization movements didn't necessarily mean that women achieved formal political representation in the newly democratic regime. Jocelyn Viterna and Kathleen Fallon (2008) compared women in the aftermath of democratization in Argentina and El Salvador. In both countries, women were active participants in the democracy movement and actively engaged the new state. In Argentina, feminists argued that if democratic reforms were necessary to make Argentina a "modern state" then so too were gender policies to allow women better access to democratic decision making (Towns 2010; Viterna and Fallon 2008:677). Although women were not a large part of the initial government, the 1991 quota law did increase women's representation in the legislature.

Women were likewise important participants in the El Salvadorian democratic transition. The women's groups that formed under the Farabundo Marti National Liberation Front (FMLN) became feminist NGOs. This new women's movement argued that women had been active and effective members of the revolutionary movement and therefore deserved an "equal role in the democracy they had helped to create" (Viterna and Fallon 2008:680). But women were not well incorporated in the first parliament after the peace accords (11%) and this number remained the same 10 years later in the 2003 elections.

So although women were highly mobilized in both cases, only in Argentina did women gain representation in the newly democratic regime. Viterna and Fallon (2008) argued that the difference between the Argentine and El Salvadorian cases is that there was a foundational change in the state structure in Argentina that allowed women the opportunity to interact with and help shape new state institutions (like quotas). In contrast, El Salvadorian feminists did not have a formal opportunity to change the state apparatus. As seen in earlier chapters, women's representation can be profoundly influenced by political factors including political parties, electoral system, quotas, and so on. Latin America highlights that during moments of transition, institutional factors, specifically the openness of newly forming institutional rule to changes promoted by women, can be extremely important for women. In short, to understand whether women will be successful in translating activism in a movement for democracy into representation in the new democratic government requires understanding the institutional context of the transition.

As for today's movements, the success of women's activism has depended on both the receptivity of established political actors and the strategic approach of women's demand-making. A comparison of Brazil and Peru reveals, for example, that while political parties in Brazil actively courted feminist organizations (who ultimately received institutional representation), in Peru livelihood struggles remained separate from feminist efforts, and little political gains were made (Ray and Korteweg 1999). However, Peru was also the first country to pass a law criminalizing domestic violence against women (Boesten 2006).

Gender Quotas

Gender quotas are an extremely important piece of women's political advancement in the Latin American region. As discussed in Chapter 6, Argentina was the first country in the world to adopt an electoral law quota (Jones 1998). Remember that electoral law quotas apply to all political parties in a country rather than just select political parties. Countries throughout Latin America followed the Argentinean example and established electoral law quotas, including Bolivia, Brazil, Colombia, Costa Rica, the Dominican Republic, Ecuador, Honduras, Mexico, Panama, Paraguay, Peru, and Venezuela (International Institute for Democracy and Electoral Assistance [IDEA] 2012a). Threshold percentages vary from 50% in Bolivia; to 40% in Costa Rica, Argentina, and Mexico; to 33% or lower in Brazil, the Dominican Republic, Guyana, Honduras, Ecuador, Panama, Paraguay, and Peru (Htun and Piscopo 2010).

Although electoral law quotas can be found around the world, they are most concentrated in Latin America. Maps 12.1 and 12.2 illustrate how—especially in South and Central America—the overwhelming majority of countries have a statutory gender quota.

In Latin America, the influence of quotas outweighs every other factor in producing women's formal political representation (Htun and Piscopo 2010). Latin American countries with gender quotas elect more women than countries without them. Of course, "Though the effects of quotas are strong, they are not a panacea" (Htun and Piscopo 2010:7). Since quotas are written in vastly different ways across the region, some have been successful in ensuring women's representation but others have not. Some quotas have placement mandates; some do not. Others have strong enforcement mechanisms while others have weak enforcement mechanisms. Leslie Schwindt-Bayer (2010:54) created an index of quota strength for countries in Latin America based on the threshold of the quota, whether it has a placement

Map 12.1 Quotas in Central America

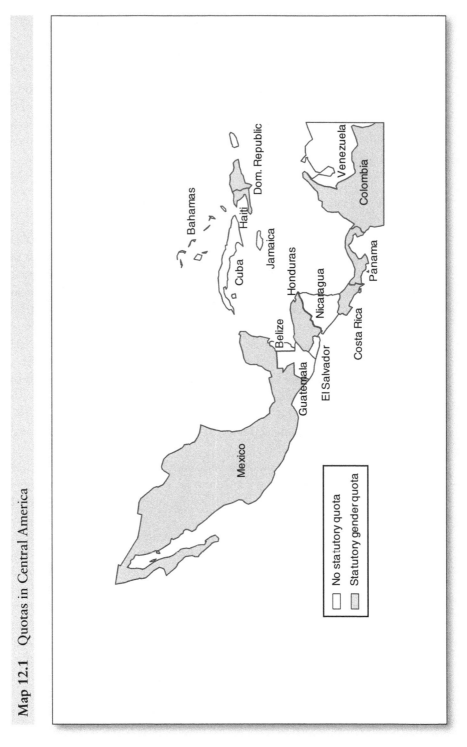

Map 12.2   Quotas in South America

mandate, and whether it has strong enforcement mechanisms. Her index shows significant differences among the quotas in Latin America—from a value of 30 for Honduras to 270 for Ecuador. Costa Rica's revised quota law (post-2002) has the second highest index value among the countries in Latin America, and as illustrated in Figure 12.1, markedly increased women's representation.

Regardless of the strength of quotas or other electoral rules, informal norms and rules can make it difficult for women to increase their numbers and to advance to powerful leadership positions (Franceschet and Piscopo forthcoming; Hinojosa and Franceschet forthcoming). And unlike some countries, like Rwanda, which are electing more women than mandated by their quota, countries in Latin America are electing exactly the numbers of women legislated by the quotas, making the quotas a ceiling rather than a floor. Regardless, Latin America stands out as a region where quotas have been successfully implemented, and the face of politics is changing.

13

Middle East and North Africa

The Arab Spring gave women a golden opportunity, but time is limited and if they don't benefit from it, it will become an Arab Winter for them.

—Sultana Al-Jeham, Executive Director
and Chairwoman of Woman's Affairs,
Civic Democratic Initiatives
Support Foundation, Yemen

Across the Middle East and North Africa, women are still struggling for the most basic of rights. In Saudi Arabia, women cannot drive, and in Lebanon, proof of education is required for a woman to vote. Women's political situation in the region is also rather grim. As of 2011, women held only 9.9% of parliamentary seats, less than 7% of ministerial positions, and only one woman has led her country as the head of government: Golda Meir of Israel (Inter-Parliamentary Union [IPU] 2012b). Viewed pictorially and especially in contrast to Western Europe (Map 10.1), the low levels of women's parliamentary representation in the Middle East and North Africa are striking (see Map 13.1).

Women's political representation across the region has historically been the lowest in the world. Women, on occasion, appeared in prominent political positions. Iraq was the first Arab country to appoint a female minister in 1959 (Pinto 2011). And throughout the 1960s, 1970s, and 1980s, women occasionally led social affairs and cultural ministries in Egypt, Syria, Jordan, and Algeria. Generally, however, the region saw few changes to women's

Map 13.1 Women's Parliamentary Representation in the Middle East and North Africa, 2011

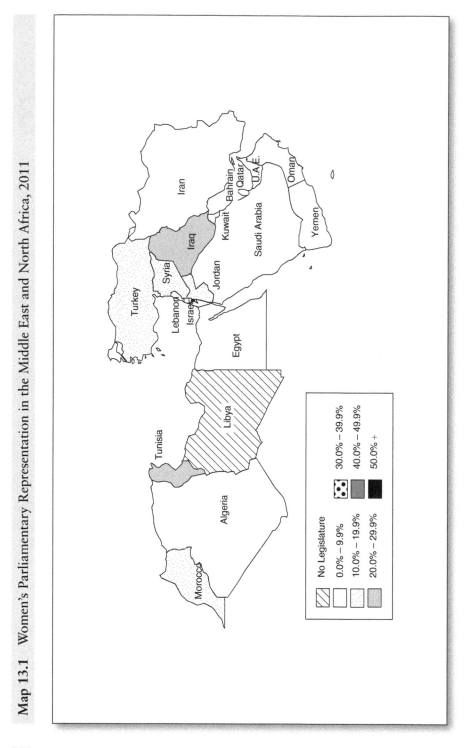

status or empowerment until after 2000. As women began making strides in political representation in Latin America and sub-Saharan Africa, women remained on the fringes of formal politics across the Middle East and North Africa.

One explanation for the stagnation of women's political representation in the Middle East and North Africa is that there were few political changes in the region whatsoever. Unlike in other parts of the world, where wars and revolutionary movements created spaces for women to enter politics, the leadership of most countries in the Middle East and North Africa remained stable. Leaders and political parties came to power and then stayed in power for decades at a time.

Since 2000, however, remarkable political and institutional changes have come to the region. Starting in 2002, women's suffrage spread across the Arab Peninsula. In 2003, the United States led a war in Iraq that ended the 24-year reign of Saddam Hussein, and international influences helped to establish a 25% gender quota in the Council of Representatives (Krook, O'Brien, and Swip 2010; Nordlund 2004). And the region was further shaken in 2011 and 2012, when a wave of pro-democracy protests and revolutionary movements spread from one country to the next, ending the 23-year rule of the Tunisia's Constitutional Democratic Rally (RCD) party, the 30-year reign of Egypt's Hosni Mubarak, the 42-year leadership of Libya's Muammar Gaddafi, and the 22-year presidency of Yemen's Ali Abdullah Saleh.

In the following sections, we will examine these winds of change that have come to the Middle East and North Africa. But first we will provide a brief background of the diversity of the region, discuss the ways women have participated politically, and introduce some of the historical barriers to the empowerment of women who live there.

An Overview and Brief History of the Region

In the minds of many people in the West, Arab culture and Islamic fundamentalism dominate the Middle East and North Africa. And both are conceived as oppressive to women. Karam (1999) effectively put it this way:

> In much of western popular imagination, the Arab world is frequently associated with veiled women, men with long beards, religious fundamentalism (inevitably Islamic), terrorism, war, and hostage-taking. . . . All together, both the region and its women remain interesting objects of (mis)information. (pp. 5–6)

But one should resist overgeneralizing about the region and its women. There are several populations that live in Middle East and North Africa who are not Arab either by ethnic or linguistic definition. Examples include the Berbers of North Africa and the Kurds of Iraq, Syria, and Turkey. There are also three countries in the region that are not predominantly Arab: Israel, Iran, and Turkey. Islam, too, is not a singular cultural force. There are two major schools of thought in Islam, Sunni and Shi'a, and there are more than 150 distinct sects. Major divisions include the Wahhabis or Salafis (mostly in Saudi Arabia), the Ibadhi (mostly in Oman), and the *ijtihadists,* or liberals. There are also religions linked to Islam, such as the Druze and the Alawites (mostly in Syria). Furthermore, a number of other religious beliefs persist in the region, most notably Judaism and Christianity. As discussed in Chapter 4, these other religions are not necessarily helpful to women's quest to attain political power. Indeed, in Israel, from the early 1980s until recently, there were no women Knesset members representing religious parties.

Scholars of the Middle East and North Africa also work to dispel the idea that women in the region are not political actors. They remind us that the "politics of the personal"—that all interactions, inside or outside the home, involve power and authority, and thus politics as well (Karam 2000). Women sometimes wield substantial political power in certain parts of family life. Judith Tucker (1993) noted, "The political importance of marriage alliances, for example, given that marriage arrangements are often controlled by women, has accorded women considerable power in the sphere of informal politics" (p. xiii).

Middle Eastern and North African women also participate in critical ways in civil society. Experts estimate that there are thousands of organizations across the Arab world that deal with women's issues. "Assessments of their role in promoting women's political participation differ, but there is overall consensus that . . . they are filling in a vacuum and performing a useful function in mobilizing public opinion and making visible women's issues" (Karam 1999:14).

In recent years, some women's organizations in the region have been successful pressing for greater political rights or representation of women. In Turkey, for example, the Association for the Support of Women Candidates (KA-DER) has been working to raise awareness about the underrepresentation of women in politics (Bigili 2011). Before the 2007 elections, KA-DER publicized photographs of women artists, businesswomen, and other well-known women with mustaches and ties drawn on the pictures along with this question: "Is it mandatory to be male to enter parliament?" (Bigili 2011:114). KA-DER also lobbied the major political parties, asking them to field at least 30% female candidates. KA-DER's efforts ultimately enjoyed success, doubling women's representation from 2002 levels to 9.1%. Building on their achievements in 2007, KA-DER pursued a similar strategy in the run-up to the 2011 elections. This time, the organization used pictures of male political party leaders pictured as women performing domestic tasks along with the question, "What if you were a woman?" (Bigili 2011:115; see Figure 13.1). KA-DER hoped to point out that if these political leaders were women, they might spend their time cooking, knitting, and tending to children rather than running the country. Using humor worked, and women's representation in Turkey's parliament increased again, now to 14.2%.

Figure 13.1   Media Campaign by the Association for the Support of Women Candidates (KA-DER) Superimposing Pictures of Male Turkish Political Party Leaders on Women's Bodies, 2011

Source: Ya Kadın Olsaydın Tayyip Bey? KADER' in Kampanyası Çok Konuşulacak, 28 March, 2011, in Bigili (2011).

Yet as the case of Turkey well illustrates, for women in the Middle East and North Africa, success in politics is best found when comparing to the past or to one's neighbors. When using the rest of the world as a yardstick, women's participation in formal politics in the Middle East and North Africa is still abysmally low. Out of 19 countries in the region, more than half had less than 5% women in their national legislature and/or cabinet ministry. It was not until 2012 that any country in the region surpassed the barrier of 30% women in parliament. And no country in the region has even come close to that threshold in executive government.

Explaining Women's Underrepresentation

Why is women's political representation in the Middle East and North Africa so low? One reason is that politically active women historically did not prioritize women's rights (Karam 1999). As in other regions, women's struggle for political incorporation was set aside in favor of other goals—freedom from colonial rule, the implementation of socialism and Arab nationalism, or democratization and human rights. Summarized in the words of a Palestinian legislator, "How are we going to argue for women's rights above all else, when our human right to exist and truly govern ourselves as a people, is denied us?" (Karam 1999:10).

Women throughout the region also face numerous structural challenges. One obstacle to women's political advancement in many Arab countries is their limited freedom of movement, which can prevent women from voting and from obtaining support for their political candidacies (Sabbagh 2007; Tiltnes 2000). As discussed in Chapter 5, Ross (2008) also argued that women's lack of power derives from women's low levels of labor force participation, a consequence of oil wealth. Women's labor force participation in the Middle East and North Africa is indeed the lowest in the world. In Turkey, women have even been working less over time. In 1955, 72% of Turkish women participated in the labor force, whereas in 2008 the number fell to 22% (Bigili 2011).

Unlike in other parts of the world, where international influences have often helped foster positive changes for women in politics, in the Arab world external forces and pressures have had some unfavorable outcomes for women. As Karam (2000:70) explained, "what are considered to be authentic values are restated and redesigned in the face of threats of cultural 'absorption.'" Patriarchal attitudes about women's roles are embraced as part of a society's culture and tradition, creating distance from what is seen as cultural imperialism from the West.

Another reason for women's lack of formal power across the region has been that women's subordination is institutionalized in personal status, or family laws, that are often based on shari'a, or Islamic law (Moghadam 2003; Molyneux 1985a; Shehadeh 1998). Family law regulates marriage, divorce, child custody, inheritance, and division of marital assets. Typically, family law in the Middle East and North Africa is linked to religious law and places women in a subordinate position to men. Below are a few examples of shari'a laws that continue to impact laws in Muslim-majority countries today:

- Instant and Final Divorce by men is allowed for husbands even under torture, compulsion, influence of alcohol, narcotics and as a matter of jokes. (Shafi'I Law # n.3.5)
- The only way for a wife to get divorce is to convince the shari'a court and also to pay money to her husband. (Shafi'I Law # n.5.0)
- Custody goes to the mother for boys 9 years old, and girls 7 years old, provided the mother prays and does not marry a stranger during this time. After 9 and 7 years, boys and girls go to the father. (Shafi'I Law # m.13.0)
- Husbands are not obliged to provide to their wife's doctor's fees, medicines and cosmetics. They must provide only for food, clothes and a house. Rebellious wife doesn't get anything. (Shafi'I Law # m.11.4)

Valentine Moghadam (2003) explained that "religiously-based family laws reinforce the distinction between the public sphere of markets and governance—which are cast as the province of men—and the private sphere of the family, with which women are identified" (p. 70). Or alternatively, as human rights activist Asma Khadar (quoted in Charrad 2001) succinctly stated, "Family law is the key to the gate of freedom and human rights for women" (p. 5).

Although the family laws of the Middle East and North Africa are typically detrimental to women, laws vary across countries in their level of repressiveness. Mounira Charrad (2001) discussed family law and women's status in three countries in North Africa: Algeria, Morocco, and Tunisia. As these countries achieved independence, the relationship between the ascending political elite and tribal kin groupings affected the family laws that were ultimately put in place. Whereas Algeria and Morocco adopted legal systems that limited women's rights, the political elites of Tunisia, to undermine the power of traditional kin elites, established a family legal structure that expanded women's rights. Tunisia's liberal family laws created a climate where women could make political gains more easily.

In recent years, however, these historical patterns have shifted as a consequence of regime change. In 1999, the death of Morocco's King Hassan II ended 42 years of repressive rule. The new king, Mohammed VI, promised at his accession that he would work to improve human rights in the country, and he has proved to be much more open than his father on issues of women's rights. He issued a royal decree that the Committee on the Elimination of All Forms of Discrimination Against Women (CEDAW) be given legal force, he created a new women's ministry to advance gender equality, he consulted with women's rights activists, and he appointed a commission to revise the *Moudawana,* Morocco's family code (Tavaana 2010). In 2004, the parliament passed a landmark reform to the family code that accorded women the right to marry without guardian approval, placed limitations on polygamy, raised legal marriage age for women from 15 to 18, gave women equal access to divorce, and made sexual harassment illegal (Welborne 2010). These changes in Morocco coincided with political victories for women as well—victories we return to next.

Few in the Middle East and North Africa have seen changes as broad as those in Morocco. In some parts of the region, women are just beginning to take their first steps into local politics. This is certainly true of women living in the Arab Gulf, to where we now turn.

Changes Come to Women of the Arab Gulf

Although women's political representation has been almost universally low across the Middle East and North Africa, the six countries on the Arab Peninsula that border the Persian Gulf—Bahrain, Kuwait, Oman, Qatar, Saudi Arabia, and the United Arab Emirates—maintained the most extreme levels of women's political exclusion for the longest. As of 2001, none of these Arab Gulf countries had universal suffrage or had ever appointed a woman to a single position in executive government (Pinto 2011).

But during the first decade of the 21st century, women's political rights in Arab Gulf countries finally began to change. For the first time, women began to win battles to extend their rights.

The Blue Revolution:
Women's Struggle for Suffrage in Kuwait

The passage of women's suffrage in Kuwait on May 16, 2005, marked the culmination of decades of struggle by women's rights activists and their allies. Compared to other countries in the Middle East, women in Kuwait have a good deal of freedom (see Figure 13.2). Unlike Saudi Arabia, for example, Kuwaiti women drive and are allowed to travel without a male escort. Contraception is available without a prescription, women are a majority of university graduates, and the country has one of the highest female labor force participation rates in the Gulf region.

The passage of women's suffrage in 2005 followed several failed attempts, the first of which came during the early 1980s, when the prime minister promised women would soon get the vote. Although a bill granting women's suffrage was proposed in the legislature, legislators proclaimed that "the time is not

Figure 13.2   A Woman Voting in Kuwait, 2009

Source: Gustavo Ferrari/AP.

opportune for receiving the idea in the light of well-established traditions" (Morgan 1984:409). A week later, 10,000 women demonstrated for suffrage, sent messages to the assembly, and organized delegations to confront members who voted against the bill. But their efforts to sway the National Assembly were unsuccessful, and the bill was defeated by a vote of 27 to 7.

A second almost-win for women unfolded during the 1990s. In August 1990, Kuwait was invaded by neighboring Iraq. Kuwaiti women reacted immediately. Two days after the occupation began, women organized their first demonstration against the occupation. Throughout the war, Kuwaiti women participated in the underground struggle against Iraq just as their male counterparts did. Those captured faced prison, torture, rape, and death. As Dr. Alqudsi-Ghobra (2002), a professor at the University of Kuwait, stated, "The high percentage of Kuwaiti women among those executed or imprisoned during the occupation is a matter of shocking record." When the Iraqi occupation ended, Kuwait's emir, Sheik Jaber Al-Ahmed Al-Sabah, returned from exile with praise for his country's women and promises of equality. But in 1999, when he decreed women could vote and run for parliament, a powerful coalition of tribal interests and Islamists in the legislature opposed him, and suffrage failed by the closest vote in Kuwait's 37-year parliamentary history (Equality Now 2001).

Despite continual failures to convince the parliament to extend rights to women, protests and other social agitation for women's suffrage continued. On February 1, 2000, for example, hundreds of women marched to voter registration centers and demanded to be registered as voters. Protest activity continued to ramp up in the years that followed such that, by 2005, the issue had both captured the public's attention and fuelled staunch Islamists to form a new anti-suffrage campaign. In March 2005, approximately 1,000 demonstrators peacefully gathered outside of the Kuwaiti parliament to again demand voting rights for women. Many of the female demonstrators wore pale blue, leading some eventually dub the struggle for rights Kuwait's "Blue Revolution." After exerting considerable pressure on the members of the legislature, the emir forced a vote on May 16. This time, however, the outcome was different. By a vote of 35 to 23 with one abstention, a bill for women's suffrage finally passed in the National Assembly.

After the vote, women danced and sang in the streets. Sheikha Suad al-Sabah, a well-known Kuwaiti poet from the al-Sabah ruling family, told reporters, "I have been struggling for this moment for more than 20 years through my writings, the media, conferences, and through all sorts of activities." Rola Al-Dashti, Kuwaiti activist, remarked, "We made it. This is history" ("Quote of the Day" 2005). And in 2006, Kuwaiti women also made history when they cast ballots for the first time in a municipal by-election.

Gender Quotas

Countries located elsewhere in the Middle East and North Africa have not limited women's formal roles in politics to the degree seen in the Arab Gulf. But across much of the region, ruling leaders and parties have shared a resistance to gender quotas. When national quotas were adopted, they were often a low level—around 5% to 9%. For example, from 1979 to 1986, a quota reserving 30 of the 360 parliamentary seats was implemented in Egypt; however, women were excluded from competing for the other seats, effectively creating a 92% quota for men. When the quota was revoked, one justification was that, while in office, the women did not affect Egyptian law or women's status. From 1984 to 1987, women only raised five political issues, and none submitted a single draft law (Abou-Zeid 2003).

Recently, however, some countries in the Middle East and North Africa have adopted more ambitious targets for women's inclusion. For example, Moroccan political parties came to a "gentlemen's agreement" that 30 national seats were reserved for women in the 2002 elections. Although the quota was not guaranteed by law, the measure increased the percentage of women in the national legislature from 0.7% to 10.8%. After the elections, the legislature refused to institutionalize the quota in law on the grounds that it would violate the constitution. But the quota system—along with reform to family law discussed earlier—led to other milestones for women in the years that followed (Liddell 2009). Women were appointed in greater numbers to senior positions in both the judiciary and the executive. In 2002, King Mohammed took a female royal advisor for the first time, and in 2007, he appointed a record number of women ministers (Liddell 2009). Morocco made further progress in the quota arena in 2009, when the country reserved 12% of local council seats for women. Unlike in 2002, when only 127 women were elected to local councils, the new local quota resulted in the election of more than 3,400 women to local public office, the most in any Arab country (Monjib 2009; Tahri 2003).

Quotas have also moved forward as a consequence of the Arab Spring. Algeria instituted a gender quota in 2012, requiring between 20% and 40% women on party lists depending on the number of seats in each electoral district. In the subsequent 2012 election, women were elected to 31% of seats in the National People's Assembly, making Algeria the new regional leader in women's political representation.

Yet not everyone hails the quotas in Morocco and Algeria as all-out victories for women. Some say that gender quotas are just a smoke screen put up by Arab rulers to stave off pressure for greater women's rights. Gender quotas are an "easy fix," especially in countries like Morocco and Algeria that have limited civil liberties. It is useful, then, to also consider the pro-democracy protests that swept the region in 2011 and 2012. Based on what we already know about women's informal political participation, it should perhaps not come as a surprise that women were a force to be reckoned with when people took to the streets. In the next section, we discuss women's roles during the Arab Spring.

Women and the Arab Spring

On December 17, 2010, Tunisian street produce vendor Mohamed Bouazizi had reached his limit. That day, police in the town of Sidi Bouzid had confiscated Bouazizi's scales, allegedly just one of many acts of harassment and humiliation Bouazizi regularly experienced at the hands of police and municipal officials. Within a half hour of the incident, Bouazizi stood outside the governor's office in the middle of traffic and shouted, "How do you expect me to make a living?" He then doused himself in gasoline and set himself on fire. Angered by Bouazizi's self-immolation, protests began in Sidi Bouzid within hours.

In the weeks that followed, a wave of pro-democracy protests and demonstrations spread across the Middle East and North Africa in what became known as the Arab Spring. Regimes in Tunisia, Egypt, Libya, and Yemen came toppling down. In other countries, civil uprisings and major protest movements failed to unseat ruling leaders and parties but still fueled social or political change. The Arab uprisings have thus altered the lives of millions of women and men across the Middle East and North Africa.

Although the Arab Spring may have been first sparked by the desperate act of one Arab man, women played influential and visible roles in the Arab uprisings from the beginning. In Yemen, for example, democratic protests were triggered by the arrest of Tawakul Karman, head of Women Journalists Without Chains, who later won a Nobel Peace Prize for her efforts. And in Libya, attorney Salwa Bugaighis led a protest in Benghazi that, after drawing fire from security forces, escalated into the rebellion that ended the 42-year rule of Muammar Gaddafi.

Regardless of women's status in a given country at the time of the uprisings, women across the Arab world took to the streets in massive numbers (Radsch 2012). In Yemen, which has by some measures the world's worst record on women's empowerment, thousands of women took to the streets, sometimes burning their veils in protest. Yemeni women resisted requests by the president that they stay at home to "protect their honor" and even demands by government officials that men assert control over their female relatives to stop their activism. Even in Tunisia, which occupies the other end of the women's rights spectrum in the region, it was still unusual to see women flooding the streets and leading protests. Women participated in sit-ins, strikes, and demonstrations; they wrote articles. As activist Lina Ben Mhenni put it, "Women were everywhere" (Radsch 2012:21). But unlike the older mothers who famously protested for peace and democracy in Latin America (see Chapter 12), it was young, sometimes single, women who played visible protest roles in the Middle East and North Africa.

Young women, in particular, played key roles as cyberactivists—organizing demonstrations and communicating with journalists through blogs and social media sites. Esraa Abdel Fattah, dubbed "Facebook girl" after her 2008 arrest for Facebook group she started to support a textile workers' strike, reemerged in 2011 to report on her experiences in Tahrir Square, ground zero of the Arab uprising in Cairo (Robbins 2011). And women such as Egypt's Mona Eltahawy, Libya's Danya Bashir, and Bahrain's Zeinab al-Khawaja became known as the "Twitterrati" for their coverage of protests on Twitter (Radsch 2012). These women inspired others to take action, coordinated efforts on the ground, and brought international media attention to the events unfolding in their respective countries.

Even in countries where massive protests did not take place, the Arab Spring still made a mark. In Saudi Arabia, for example, in the spring of 2011, activist Manal al-Sharif was filmed driving a car, violating the national ban on women driving. After the video was posted on YouTube and Facebook, al-Sharif was arrested and detained by the Saudi government. In the month following al-Sharif's detention, an estimated 70 cases of women driving were publically documented. Some credit the protests as helping to influence King Abdullah's September 2011 announcement that women would be able to vote in the 2015 municipal elections and stand in the Consultative Assembly (for more on the battle for suffrage in Saudi Arabia, see Chapter 2).

Across the region, many hoped women's revolutionary efforts during the Arab Spring would be rewarded with greater inclusion in formal politics. As discussed in Chapter 12 and 15, women's roles in democratic movements and armed conflicts can sometimes change views about women's roles and create political openings for their entry into political leadership. Yet as numerous examples demonstrate, democratic movements and regime change do not guarantee women's subsequent political empowerment. Once governments start returning to business as usual, women can be pushed aside or advised to return to their traditional roles.

One particularly concerning sequence of events unfolded in Egypt, where women helped put an end to the 30-year reign of Hosni Mubarak. Women protested shoulder-to-shoulder with men in Cairo's Tahrir Square. But after Mubarak was removed from power by the military in February 2011, the new regime's record on women worsened. Female protesters were harassed, beaten, detained, and subjected to forced "virginity checks." In December 2011, one female protester was savagely beaten by Egyptian military forces, her abaya (a black Islamic cloak) torn from her body, revealing jeans and a blue bra. Photographs snapped of the woman during the brutal attack spread rapidly on the Web, and one image of one of the military officers poised to stomp the woman's bare stomach with his boot was published in newspapers across the world (see Figure 13.3). Thousands of women and men marched in protest of the brutal attack, holding up copies of newspapers and posters bearing the image of the woman wearing the blue bra (see Figure 13.4). By some accounts, the demonstration was the largest public women's demonstration in Egypt in decades (Coleman 2011).

Figure 13.3   "The Girl in the Blue Bra" Attacked After Clashing With
Egyptian Security Forces at a Protest in Tahrir Square,
Cairo, Egypt, 2011

Source: Reuters/Stringer/Files

Despite women's visible roles in the revolution before and after Mubarak's removal, events in Egypt continued to unfold in ways that would limit women's power. The military appointed no women to the constitutional committee and replaced the 12% of seats reserved for women in the national legislature with a weak candidate quota. As a result, in January 2012, there were 498 men and only 10 women who were elected to Egypt's People's Assembly, a 10% drop in women's representation from the 2010 election. Shortly after taking office, the parliament began considering changing the personal status law to strip women of the right to initiate divorce and reduce women's child custody rights. Yet legislators had only a few months to govern before the Supreme Court ruled the parliament unconstitutional, and the body was dissolved, spurring more protests.

Why did the situation in Egypt deteriorate for women so rapidly? Some reason that the dominant force in post–Mubarak Egypt has been the military, an institution that rarely promotes women's interests anywhere in the

Figure 13.4 Woman Holds Up a Photograph
of Woman in the Blue Bra at Egyptian Protest, 2011

Source: Amir Nabil, Associated Press, In-Depth Africa 2011.

world. Others suggest the events in Egypt follow the traditional pattern in the region, where women's rights are set aside in favor of other goals. Still another explanation involves the empowerment of moderate and radical Islamists, who won the first and second-largest shares of parliamentary seats in the 2012 election. The more moderate Muslim Brotherhood, one of the world's largest and influential Islamist movements, was the dominant political force in Egypt's new parliament. The Muslim Brotherhood takes the position that women cannot and should not lead countries. Further, women's representatives from the party have counseled Egyptian women against protesting, stating that it is more "dignified" to let their husbands and brothers demonstrate for them.

Women's future is also uncertain in Tunisia, where state policies have long ranked among the most progressive toward women in the Arab world. During the 23-year reign of Ben Ali, the women's movement enjoyed both ideological and financial backing from the government (Goulding 2010). But it was precisely those close ties that left women's future uncertain after the

Arab Spring, since those associated with the prior regime were excluded from participating in the transitional government. Still, regime change also offered great promise, as Tunisia adopted a parity gender quota for the National Constituent Assembly, the body tasked with writing a new Tunisian Constitution. Even though the parity quota included placement mandates requiring alternating men and women on party lists, a large number of political parties contested seats, and many parties sent only a single representative to the Assembly. Since women only headed 7% of the candidate lists, women ultimately only won 27% of seats, a far cry from 50%.

Although women's representation in Tunisia's Constituent Assembly far exceed those of Egypt's new People's Assembly, the two countries share at least one common denominator—both sets of elections have brought Islamists to power. And Tunisia and Egypt were not alone. In many countries in the region, the Arab Spring was followed by an Islamist Summer. Exactly how democracy and Islamism will combine to impact women's rights in the Middle East and North Africa is yet unproven. And only time will tell what the next Arab season will bring.

Overall, across the Middle East and North Africa, there are examples where women are making gains in the formal political arena. However, compared with other regions of the world, these gains have been much smaller, slower, and more prone to reversals. Still, recent trends toward democratization in the region foster hope. Although we know that women's increased political representation under democratic institutions is far from guaranteed, such developments may allow women's organizations to turn their focus from the broader goal of democracy to the plight of women.

14

Asia and the Pacific

If women will be empowered the society will be empowered. Women will not sit around playing cards.

—Male focus group in Jorausi,
India (Redlund 2004)

Addressing women's political experiences in Asia and the Pacific is an important task if only because of sheer numbers. As of 2010, more than half the world's population—4.2 billion people—occupied the region (United Nations 2011). China and Japan also have the second- and third-largest economies in the world today, and three of the five fastest-growing economies in the world are in Asia: Singapore (2nd), India (3rd), and China (4th) (International Monetary Fund [IMF] 2012).

Politically, Asia also stands out as having a particularly large number of women serving in national leadership as their country's president or prime minister, eclipsed only by Latin America. As we noted in Chapter 3, Sri Lanka was the first country to elect a female head of government in 1960. Since then, Bangladesh, India, Pakistan, and Thailand have elected female prime ministers, and Indonesia, the Philippines, and Sri Lanka have elected female presidents. Three of these countries have even been led by more than one female leader. Women in Burma, Malaysia, and Papua New Guinea have also served as **opposition leaders**.

Remember, however, that many female leaders act as a surrogate for their politically powerful husband or father. Although this phenomenon is not unique to Asia, the importance of family connections for women's political empowerment is particularly prevalent. Of the region's 10 powerful heads of government to date, 3 were wives, 6 were daughters, and 1 was a sister of politically powerful men. For example, Gloria Macapagal-Arroyo, president of the Philippines from 2001 to 2010, is the daughter of former Philippine president Diosdado Macapagal. She has stated that her role model is her father, and her living role model is Corazon Aquino, former president of the Philippines, who was the wife of assassinated opposition leader Benigno Aquino Jr.

Research on women leaders in Asia emphasize that it is not just ties to powerful men that fuel women's rise to power but, in particular, their ties to martyrs. Women's suffering is the ticket to political acceptance in the largely patriarchal societies they come to rule. They initially appear "weak, vulnerable and manipulable," only entering politics to carry on the will of the fallen (Hellman-Rajanayagam 2008:224). But the women leaders that have risen to power as "vicarious martyrs" do not stay weak for long. Once they are at the top, they are active, determined, and begin to shape the polities they lead. They integrate themselves into conventional politics and often become career politicians (Fleschenberg 2008).

We might expect that women's presence in positions of national leadership might "trickle down" such that national legislatures and executive cabinets would enjoy increases in women's representation. But Asia shows that women's national leadership and electoral performance more generally do not go hand in hand. In fact, countries in Asia and the Pacific have, on average, one of the worst records for women's representation in cabinets and parliaments in the world. As of 2011, women held an average of only 9.9% of executive cabinet positions and 12.5% of seats in national legislatures. Women's total exclusion from political bodies, today a rarity in much of the world, is not entirely uncommon in the region. In 2011, Bhutan, Papua New Guinea, Singapore, and Vanuatu had no women cabinet ministers; Palau and Micronesia lacked even one female parliamentarian; and in Nauru and the Solomon Islands, women were excluded from both the cabinet and parliament. In countries without local gender quotas, women often do no better than at the national level (Inter-Parliamentary Union [IPU] 2012b). For example, following 2006 elections in Sri Lanka, women were only 3% of municipal councils, 3.4% of urban councils, and 1.6% of Pradeshiya Sabha (Centre for Women's Research 2009).

Women have made limited political gains in recent years. For example, in 1997, women's share of seats in the National Assembly of Laos rose from 9.4% to 22.4% (Paxton, Green, and Hughes 2008). Perhaps the most obvious change has been in Afghanistan, where, prior to 2005, women peaked at 3.7% of parliamentary seats but now hold the highest percentage of seats in the region—27.7%. As of 2011, sixteen countries in Asia and the Pacific exceeded the world average in parliamentary representation, and both Nepal and East Timor had crossed the barrier of 30% women in their national legislatures (see Map 14.1). Maldives and the Federated States of Micronesia have 21% and 22% women in their cabinets, respectively.

Overall, however, women seeking to ascend the political ladder in Asia face numerous barriers. Similar to other regions of the world, women's exclusion from the public realm is justified by a number of ideas about culture, tradition, and "natural" gender roles. For example, Quirina Tablo, a 65-year-old mother of nine from the Philippines, "has seldom missed voting in an election. But her candidates of preference have always been men because she believes that 'politics is not for women'" (Mission 1998). Women also face a range of structural barriers that contribute to their disadvantaged status and marginalization:

- In Afghanistan, violations of women's human rights remain widespread. Women face forced marriage, domestic abuse, abduction and rape, honor killings, and "daily discrimination from all segments of society as well as by state officials" (Amnesty International 2005).
- Women in Fiji and Samoa have the highest suicide rate in the world. Suicide, usually by ethnic-Indian women, has become Fiji's biggest killer (United Nations Development Fund for Women [UNIFEM] 2005). Forty-one percent of the suicides reported in 1992 were related to domestic violence (Dutton 1992).
- Although women in Japan comprise about 34% of nonmanagerial positions in the workforce, they hold only 3% of director positions and 5% of section manager positions (Japanese Ministry of Health, Labour, and Welfare 2005).
- In Bangladesh, the average age at first marriage for women is 14 years (Haub and Cornelius 2000).
- In Vietnam, the practice of *Doi moi* means that women's spare time must be dedicated to income generation, not involvement in public life. Women's political participation is therefore effectively hampered not by any specific government policy prohibiting their involvement, but by their lack of time (Yarr 1996).
- In Papua New Guinea, intimate partner violence is endemic; two thirds of women report having been beaten by their husbands or partners, a figure that closes in on 100% in some parts of the country (Kidu 2012).

With these obstacles to women's equality, it is not surprising that women across the region struggle to obtain positions of political power.

Although we speak of Asia and the Pacific as a single region, the 36 countries we discuss are quite different, incorporating both religious and secular

Map 14.1   Women's Parliamentary Representation in Asia and the Pacific, 2011

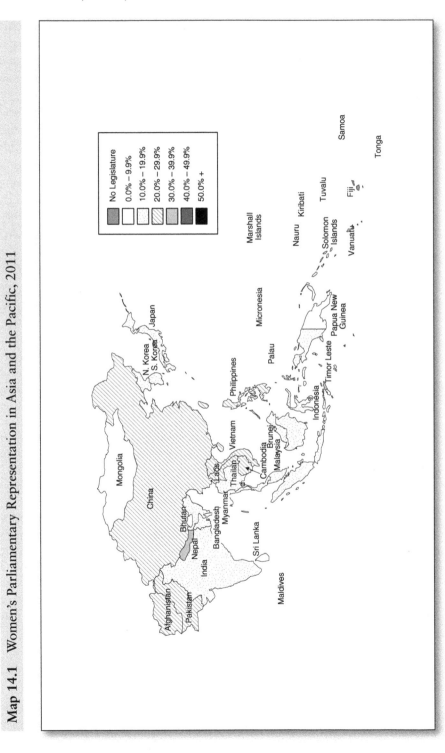

societies, highly industrialized states and poor agricultural nations, a diverse array of political systems, and multiple distinct civilizations. Thus, we do not present a unified theme explaining women's political representation across Asia and the Pacific. We do, however, focus on some of the distinct features of the region that do not appear in force elsewhere, for example, its philosophies and religions (Confucianism, Buddhism, and Hinduism). We orient our discussion around the four subregions of East Asia, Southeast Asia, South Asia, and Oceania.

East Asia

We begin East Asia, the smallest subregion with only five countries: China, Japan, Mongolia, South Korea, and North Korea. But there is not much else that is small about East Asia. First, there is China, the world's most populous country. For our purposes, China demonstrates that ascension to national leadership but lack of substantial political representation does not hold for all countries in the Asia-Pacific region. Indeed, in China, 40% of Chinese government officials are women, and 22% of seats in the National People's Congress are held by women, but few women hold positions of senior leadership (Mong 2011). In six decades of Communist rule, there have been only six female politburo members (Howell 2008; International Tibet Network 2012). Currently, the highest-ranking woman in Chinese politics is Liu Yangdong, the sole female member of the politburo and the only female state councillor (comparable to a cabinet minister position). Overall, the pattern of women in politics in China more closely resembles Eastern Europe prior to the 1990s than most Asian countries today.

But unlike in Eastern Europe, women in China and other Asian countries are affected by the philosophy of Confucianism. Although sometimes thought of as a religion, Confucianism is an ethical and philosophical system developed from the Chinese sage Confucius. The Confucian tradition has had tremendous influence on the history of the Chinese civilization and therefore a number of countries in Asia, including all of the East Asian countries.

Under Confucianism, women at every level are to occupy a position lower than men. The following statements are popular sayings (see Women in World History 2006), quotes from Confucian philosophers, and remarks attributed to Confucius himself:

- A woman ruler is like a hen crowing.
- Women are to be led and to follow others.

- The woman with no talent is the one who has merit.
- Disorder is not sent down by Heaven; it is produced by women.
- Man is honored for strength; a woman is beautiful on account of her gentleness.
- Women's nature is passive.
- A woman should look on her husband as if he were Heaven itself, and never weary of thinking how she may yield to him.
- Lay the (girl) baby (at birth) below the bed to plainly indicate that she is lowly and weak, and should regard it as her primary duty to humble herself before others.

The Confucian *Book of Rites* presents an ideal model that women were supposed to follow in traditional China: "The woman follows (and obeys) the man: in her youth, she follows her father and elder brother; when married, she follows her husband; when her husband is dead, she follows her son" ("The Single Victim at the Border Sacrifices" 1885).

As we discussed in Chapter 4, when a culture dictates that women are subordinate to men and should follow the opinions of their husbands and fathers, they are less likely to be politically active. Simultaneously, in culturally hostile environments, the few women who are politically active are not taken seriously by political leaders or regular citizens. Therefore, Confucian ideals can suppress women's political participation and representation.

Another feature of a number of Asian countries is their rapid and recent **modernization.** As discussed briefly in Chapter 5, theorists have long asserted that the forces of economic modernization would inevitably liberate women. As societies transition from "traditional" to "modern," standards of living rise, giving women more free time, and individuals move to the cities, undermining traditional extended kinship systems that oppress women. Further, increased access to education and labor force participation provide women with more individual resources and autonomy.

Yet Asia helps one understand that economic modernization and industrialization are not sufficient for women's political power. Across a range of newly industrializing countries, such as those in Asia, as women entered the labor force they were often relegated to low status and unskilled positions, and new agricultural techniques were dominated by men, marginalizing women in agricultural production as well (Boserup 1970; Horton 1995; Ward 1984). Thus, we must make a distinction between jobs that provide skills and resources to women and jobs that exploit women for the low cost of their labor. Can women translate their labor force participation into political capital? Are women simply working too many hours to find the time to participate politically? Women's factory labor across Asia may boost women's labor force participation rates, but such work roles are unlikely to supply women experience or skills that will benefit them politically (Kunovich and Paxton 2005; but see Ross 2008).

As the most economically developed country in the region, Japan demonstrates that national wealth and economic power do not necessarily foster women's political participation. Japan has one of the lowest levels of women in parliament, arguably the worst in the developed world (IPU 2012b). At the local level, female governors and mayors are also a relative rarity in Japan (Iwanaga 2008b).

So in this truly industrialized and modernized country, what explains women's poor political performance? Some assert that the highly patriarchal culture of Japan prevents women from competing successfully against men. Although Japanese women are among the most educated in the world, Japanese culture often privileges women's traditional roles as wives and mothers. In 2003, former prime minister Yoshiro Mori even stated that childless women should not receive government pensions:

> The government takes care of women who have given birth to a lot of children as a way to thank them for their hard work. . . . It is wrong for women who haven't had a single child to ask for taxpayer money when they get old, after having enjoyed their freedom and had fun. (quoted in Doi 2003, p. 78)

In response, many men in the crowd nodded in approval.

To explain women's political underrepresentation, some research also highlights a unique combination of characteristics of the political system in Japan—namely, strict campaign regulations and strong personal support networks. In Japan, door-to-door campaigning is prohibited, media advertising is strictly limited, fund-raising activities and campaign spending are highly regulated, and even the number of posters and pamphlets that may be distributed is controlled. But organizations provide a loophole through which candidates can interact with the electorate:

> A candidate or election worker may not canvas door-to-door in Japan, but the same worker may go door-to-door visiting members of an organization. The number of campaign mailings is strictly limited, but an organization may provide information on its endorsements to all of its members without state oversight or regulation. (Christensen 2000:31)

Because of this loophole, political candidates invest their time and energy developing personal support organizations, called *kōenkai*. A combination of existing organizations and a candidate's personal contacts, kōenkai are the core of political campaigns.

Kōenkai is difficult to develop, but there are a number of ways that an aspiring politician can gain a kōenkai, such as inheritance through a politician in the family. But most ways of gaining kōenkai exclude women. For example, male politicians often only pass down their kōenkai to their sons or sons-in-law, not their daughters or daughters-in-law. Further, it is easier to build a kōenkai as a member of a cohesive minority group. Yet in Japan, women as a group are not unified or cohesive. They are divided by other identities, such as social class, religion, and ethnicity. These ideas suggest that women's underrepresentation in politics is a function of both the political environment, which makes personal support networks so important, and the larger cultural context, which makes it difficult for women to build or inherit them.

Overall, the specific institutional and cultural barriers to women's political representation are unique in each East Asian country. But across the region, unfavorable attitudes toward women in politics means that women often obtain lower levels of support than men when they run for office. In 2003, there were 44% of Japanese men who ran successfully for office, whereas the share of successful women was only 23% (Iwinaga 2008b). The pattern is the same in South Korea, where women are much more likely than men to run as "sacrificial lambs" in districts that are strongholds of rival political parties (Jones 2006). It may "take a candidate" for women to get elected, but if East Asian countries are to see more women in politics, it will also take more supportive political parties and more voters willing to cast ballots on their behalf.

Before moving on, it is also noteworthy that not all women politicians in Asia rise to power through their blood relations to male politicians. In this regard South Korea stands apart—not just from other Asian countries but from countries like the United States as well (Shin 2004). Looking historically, Kim (1975) showed that 34 of 86 U.S. congresswomen who served between 1917 and 1974 were widows of male politicians, whereas between 1948 and 1973, not a single woman legislator in the Korean National Assembly succeeded her father or husband.

Southeast Asia

Although tied together by geography, the ethnic, religious, and cultural makeup of this subregion varies widely. The region includes two countries that are overwhelmingly Catholic (East Timor and Philippines) and three that are majority Muslim (Brunei, Indonesia, and Malaysia). But the most common majority religion in the region is Buddhism (in Cambodia, Laos,

Myanmar, Singapore, Thailand, and Vietnam). Like other major world religions, Buddhism has many incarnations, but there are two main branches: Theravada (The Teachings of the Elders) and Mahayana (The Great Vehicle). In countries where Buddhism is the majority religion, Theravada is more common in all but Vietnam.

Scholarship focusing on Buddhist-majority countries often traces women's marginal roles in many of these countries to Buddhism, which provides "a moral framework for men's hierarchical precedence over women" (Lindberg Falk 2002:104). Furthermore, under Buddhism, women are seen as "polluters" (Iwanaga 2008a). In Thailand, for example, women are forbidden from physical contact with, much less from becoming, Buddhist monks. Within the faith, there also exists the fear that women will contaminate or otherwise lessen sacred images, so women are typically refused entry to places where sacred relics are kept. And there is a common fear that, in the public sphere, women can sap the strength from men (Iwanaga 2008a).

In many parts of Southeast Asia, the cultural dominance of Buddhism often trumps women's rights. This story is well illustrated through the story of Senator Rabiaprat Pongpanit, a Thai politician and women's activist (Hamburg 2008). In July 2004, Senator Pongpanit visited Wat Doi Suthep, regarded as one of the most important temples in Northern Thai culture. When she was refused entry to a part of the temple that contains important relics because she is a woman, she protested the rule on human rights grounds and set off a widespread controversy. The senator was subjected to hate speech and mail, was accused of "not being a good Buddhist," and protesters even burned her in effigy (Hamburg 2008:98). The senator representing the district where the temple was located also admonished her, arguing there was "a limit to women's rights" (Hamburg 2008:98). Ultimately, Senator Pongpanit apologized and retracted her request.

In Cambodia, Buddhism has historically been a central part of national identity. Proper behavior is codified for different groups in Buddhist-inspired *chbap* (rules). One such set of rules, the *chbap srey,* explains ideal behavior for traditional Cambodian women. Chbap srey establishes men's dominance and women's subordinate position in society through verses such as the following: "When you reach the world of human beings, you are to remember that you are the only personal servant of your husband and you should always highly obey your husband" (Lilja 2008). The Committee on the Elimination of Discrimination Against Women (CEDAW) Committee criticized the rules, arguing they were a root cause of persisting gender inequalities in Cambodia. In response, Ms. Ing Kantha Phavi, the minister of women's affairs, defended the chbap srey as part of school curriculums in Cambodia on the grounds that the rules were part of national identity (Lilja 2008).

Despite these barriers, Cambodian, or Khmer, women have won limited victories in recent years. When Cambodia's first multiparty elections at the local level took place in 2002, the women's movement rallied to place women candidates on 30% of party lists, and nearly 13,000 women stood for election to more than 1,600 commune councils. Ultimately, 954 women were elected to the commune councils, 8.5% of seats across the country (McGrew, Frieson, and Chan 2004). Although these numbers may seem small, the election was perceived as a significant victory for Khmer women and helped changed attitudes towards women's political participation and representation. For example, between 2001 and 2003, national surveys reported a 12% increase in the share of people who thought women should make their own choice for voting, rather than allowing men to advise her (Kraynanski 2007). Then, following elections in 2007, women's representation on commune councils increased to 14.6%.

In Cambodia's northeast provinces, increases in the political representation of women have also extended to indigenous women. Yet interviews with the councillors demonstrate the importance of looking beyond just numbers. For example, one female councillor from Khavet reported the following:

> I have been the second deputy since 2007. I was selected by the authorities, who came to the village and said that they needed a woman on the list. Villagers selected me, then they asked me and I agreed. But my role in the commune council is not relevant: I prepare tea, boil water, and welcome guests during meetings. The chief of the commune and the commune clerk make all the decisions. The clerk manages the commune budget, I don't know about money, planning or anything else. We only follow the chief's and the clerk's decisions. I don't really know what the programs are, everything is managed by the clerk; he receives and manages the money of the commune. I have never seen money for women's and children's affairs, or even discussed a project. (Maffii 2010:22)

Nonetheless, the same study found that many indigenous women were willing to engage more fully in local politics and believed that women could make important contributions to their communities through public service, particularly in environmental arenas because of women's ties to the land and its resources (Maffii 2010).

Buddhist-majority or not, many of the patterns of representation in this subregion fall in line with the broader story for the region—women's political success often happens at least in part due to family ties. The most prominent example of this pattern of late is the rise of Yingluck Shinawatra, prime minister of Thailand since 2011. She is unlike other national leaders in Asia in that she followed her elder brother (instead of a father or husband) into power. Shinawatra's brother Thaksin was ousted from the prime minister position by a coup d'état 5 years before her rise to power. Remember, however, that the importance of family reaches all the way down to the local level. Whether a woman is competing for a position in a local council or for a headship position, "the larger, more supportive, and more extensive the kinship network a woman has, the more success is anticipated" (Vichit-Vadakan 2008:144).

South Asia

South Asia, our third subregion, includes Afghanistan, Bangladesh, Bhutan, India, Maldives, Nepal, Pakistan, and Sri Lanka. Although much of past research about women in politics in South Asia has focused on female leaders or grassroots movements, recent developments have increased attention to local-level governance in the region as well. Whereas women have rarely made inroads into legislatures at the national level, gender quotas have provided women access to political positions at the local level— for example, in city and village councils (Raman 2002; United Nations 2000b). In South Asia, gender quotas at the local level have been implemented in Afghanistan, Bangladesh, India, Nepal, and Pakistan. But perhaps the most well-known and well-researched local gender quota system is for the village government system in India, or *Panchayat Raj*.

Local Gender Quotas in India: Women in the Panchayat Raj

Like many societies across the world, Indian culture and tradition dictate that politics is a man's world. Men often tell their wives how to vote, and although a small number of elite women from political families have ascended to political leadership, women's political representation at the national level (at 10% of cabinet positions and 11% of parliamentary seats in 2011) is far below the global average. Of those few women who have successfully won seats at the national level, most are women from privileged backgrounds, leaving poorer women from lower castes without representation (Rai 2002).

This picture is dramatically different at the local level, however. In 1992, India amended its constitution to revitalize its village government system, the Panchayat Raj. The changes included new requirements that marginalized castes and tribes be represented in proportion to their population and that one third of seats be reserved for women. The 30% gender quota applied to seats for both dominant and marginalized groups, to all three tiers of the new local government structure—the village cluster, block, and district—and to both member and leader positions (Raman 2002). In the first elections after the new legislation came into effect, nearly 1 million women of all backgrounds entered local political institutions, shattering the myth that Indian women are fundamentally disinterested in the political process (Hust 2004; Raman 2002; Singla 2007).

Research suggests that women's *panchayat* membership and leadership have allowed them to challenge men and alter the political agenda (Raman 2002; Singla 2007). Remember from Chapter 8 the research of Chattopadhyay and Duflo (2004) who find that when a woman is chief of a panchayat it results in more public investments in drinking water (what women care about) but not in roads (what men care about). Women's priorities have also included issues such as alcohol abuse, domestic violence, education, health, and water. The panchayat system is also credited with affecting women and society in positive ways beyond the policymaking arena, including improvements in women's self-esteem and small but significant changes in gender roles (e.g., Hust 2004). Women's incorporation into local government has also empowered women from different sectors of Indian society. Although chairperson positions continue to be occupied by women from more well-to-do sectors of society, substantial numbers of women in panchayats are from marginalized communities or groups.

Despite these advances, we should not gloss over the continued barriers faced by women seeking political power in India. Men have refused to work with female panchayat members, and when women oppose men, they may be subject to physical violence. Female members of lower castes may also face opposition by upper caste women. And even when women perform well as leaders, they may not receive the credit they deserve. For example, one study of 2,304 villages found the people may not give women credit for their successes (Duflo and Topalova 2004). Researchers visited all of the villages and evaluated the drinking water infrastructure—using measures such as the number of public taps and hand pumps. In villages with women leaders, infrastructure was at least as good, if not better, than in villages without reserved leadership for women. But, the villagers did not necessarily see it that way. Whereas in men-led villages, better infrastructure meant villagers were happier with the water system, in women-headed villages the people were unhappy with the water system regardless of its actual quality (Duflo and Topalova 2004).

But research also shows that negative assessments of women's leadership change over time. Using survey data, Lori Beaman and her colleagues (2009) showed that when leadership positions were initially reserved for women, Indian voters typically evaluated them more harshly than men, but these opinions changed if women continued to lead for a second term. Furthermore, in districts that reserved the leadership position for women for two consecutive terms, more than twice as many women stood for, and won, positions in panchayats compared to councils led by men for one or two of the prior terms (Beaman et al. 2009).

Since its initial implementation, the quota has expanded. In 2009, the government approved an increase in the reservation to 30% women to 50%. Although not yet formalized, 12 of 29 states increased their reservations from 33% to 50% by the end of 2011 (Andhra Pradesh, Bihar, Chhatisgarh, Himachal Pradesh, Jharkhand, Kerala, Madhya Pradesh, Maharashtra, Orissa, Rajasthan, Tripura, and Uttarakhand).

Even in states that have not yet instituted parity, some villages have elected women in numbers beyond what is required by law. For example, in the western state Gujarat, Chief Minister Narendra Modi offered financial incentives to villages that elected their panchayats through consensus rather than traditional electoral methods—bodies dubbed *samras gram* (harmonius village) panchayats. Of these consensus bodies, more than 240 elected in 2011 were all women, about 2% of all village panchayats in Gujarat (Das 2012). One village, Siswa, is now on its third all-women panchayat, although this time Siswa elected a 12 member panchayat comprised entirely of single, educated, college-aged women, an atypical profile for panchayat women (Hust 2004). As one former village head explained, "Women are convincing. Villagers tend to listen to them better. This time, we decided to go a step further and appoint young, educated girls who are brimming with fresh ideas" (Das 2012).

Women have not had such success pressing to extend a gender quota to the national legislature (Sumbul 2004). An amendment to establish a 33% quota at the national level was put forth in 1995, but in successive legislative meetings, the measure has failed to pass. One often-lodged criticism of the amendment, which is called the Women's Reservation Bill, is that it does not guarantee representation to marginalized minority groups or castes (see Figure 14.1). Thus, critics assert that power would remain in the hands of elites, and female members of parliament (MPs) would simply be relatives of those already in power. Still, the bill has almost unanimous support from national women's organizations, which continue to exert pressure on male legislators.

Figure 14.1   Women Protest for Passage
of Women's Reservation Bill in India, 2005

Source: From the Press Trust of India Photo Library. © 2005 by the Press Trust of India.
Reprinted by permission of the publisher.

India is not the only South Asian country to have local quotas. In 1997, Bangladesh set aside three reserved seats for each Union Parishad, part of the local government. Although the quotas enhanced women's political access and offered women a voice on "women's issues"—such as disputes related to dowry, divorce, and polygamy—women elected through the quota are often ignored or even subjected to sexual harassment by their male counterparts (Ahmed 2008; Pathways of Women's Empowerment 2011).

Another South Asian country that has garnered a great deal of scholarly attention of late is Afghanistan, where the downfall of the Taliban and the adoption of gender quotas created new political space for women (see also Chapter 6). But as we will discuss, women's fight for rights and representation in Afghanistan is far from over.

Women in Afghanistan

They will kill me but they will not kill my voice, because it will be the voice of all Afghan women. You can cut the flower, but you cannot stop the coming of spring.

—Malalai Joya, former member of parliament

Although the downfall of the Taliban in 2001 improved many women's lives and opened space for modest gains in women's rights and status, today Afghan women confront discrimination and violence at levels that many of us cannot comprehend. Women's lack of power derives, in part, from limited access to resources. Although educating girls is becoming more common, the gender gap in secondary education in Afghanistan remains among the worst in the world. And in 2008, women accounted for only 8% of Afghanistan's entire paid labor force (Afghanistan National Risk and Vulnerability Assessment). But to really understand women's current position in Afghanistan, one first has to acknowledge the country's history, which has not been kind to women.

For more than a century, women's place in Afghan society has been characterized by "an ideological tug of war" between modernizing and conservative forces (Kabeer, Khan, and Adlparvar 2011:6). The Soviet occupation of the 1980s was much like Afghanistan today—who was winning the "tug of war" depended on where in the country you looked (Lough 2012). Women in government-controlled Kabul experienced opportunities for participation in public life: Women were part of the central committing of the ruling political party, they served as delegates in the traditional council (Loya Jirga), and they were present in parliament in token numbers (Moghadam 1999). But in areas controlled by the Afghan *mujahedeen,* women were victims of a conservative backlash.

When the Soviet-backed government collapsed, the mujahedeen assumed power, and women's lives became difficult no matter where they lived. The new government issued an edict that required women to veil in public and banned women from offices and radio and television stations. All women's schools, dubbed "the hub of debauchery and adulterous practices," were closed down (Lough 2012:6). Yet who would rule the country was not immediately settled, and different factions of the mujahedeen vied for power in a 4-year civil war. Women everywhere were caught in the cross fire. As one women's rights activist recounted, "Under the mujahedeen, the weapon of one community against another was to attack, to jail, to rape, to hit in public the female members of the other community" (Povey 2003:269).

When the Taliban rose to power in 1996, the new regime was quick strengthen limitations on women's rights. Immediately, women could not leave their homes without wearing a burka and the escort of a close male relative, or *mahram*. Women's medical treatment was limited to female doctors, effectively barring them from many surgical procedures that only men were trained to perform. All ground and first floor residential windows were painted or screened to prevent the visibility of women on the street, and women were forbidden access to residential balconies. Women that refused to obey were publically mutilated or executed. Even public places that included the word *women* were renamed. Women all but vanished from public and political life.

Even during Taliban rule, in the face of possible imprisonment, torture, and death, Afghan women resisted (Povey 2003). For example, in secret, the Women's Association of Afghanistan funded and managed sewing, knitting, and handicraft courses for women. Many former teachers opened clandestine schools in their homes, risking their lives to teach basic numeracy and literacy to hundreds of women and girls (Povey 2003). Although tragic, these secret organizations empowered many women. The small sums of money women earned kept some women from having to beg or resort to sex work, and the organizations generated networks of trust and reciprocity that facilitated women's organizing after the Taliban fell.

In 2001, when the U.S. military attack on Afghanistan brought an end to Taliban rule, life for many women, especially those living in Kabul, changed immediately. Women could appear in public unveiled and unescorted. Representatives of the anti-Taliban forces, along with other Afghan groups signed the Bonn Agreement, which would serve as a guide as the country transitioned to new leadership. Under the agreement, the transitional administration was tasked with ensuring women's equal access to health care, education, politics, and with safeguarding "their full participation in all spheres of Afghan life" (Afghanistan Government 2001). But outside of Kabul, many women's lives remained unchanged or even worsened as women became vulnerable to indiscriminate sexual abuse, rape, and acid attacks (Roshan 2004).

In line with the Bonn Agreement, women were included in the interim government from the beginning (Bauer 2002; Dahlerup and Nordlund 2004). Women served as government ministers, including in the new Afghan Ministry of Women's Affairs. Women were also 20% of the delegates to the Constitutional Loya Jirga and served on all committees tasked with drafting and reviewing the constitution (Grenfell 2004; Office of International Women's Issues 2003). But looking beyond women's numbers, the picture was less rosy: During the transition, women representatives were sometimes not allowed to speak, had their microphones silenced, and were threatened and harassed (Krook, O'Brien, and Swip 2010). But at least one woman would not be silenced. Malalai Joya, a 25-year-old social worker from rural Afghanistan and a delegate to the Constitutional Loya Jirga, gained international attention for speaking out publically against corruption in the interim government and the empowerment of Taliban-era warlords. Despite the obstacles to women's full participation during the transition, their mere presence on constitutional bodies still set a standard for future political inclusion (Krook et al. 2010).

Ultimately, the 2004 constitution included a reserved seat quota system, ensuring that women's political presence would continue. And in the 2005 election, women candidates stood for office in record numbers. Women also came out to vote, making up almost half of all voters in 2005 (Reynolds 2006), and survey research suggests even more women would have voted if they had not been prevented from doing so (Asia Foundation 2006). Ultimately, 68 women were elected to the new parliament in 2005, including Malalai Joya and 18 other women who received enough votes to be elected even without the reserved seats (Reynolds 2006). Afghanistan now had the highest level of women's political representation in its region. And surveys showed broad support among Afghan people for women's equal participation in voting and political leadership (Asia Foundation 2006).

In the years that followed, women activists and politicians continued to fight, pushing forward for change and against forces that would return women to their pre-2001 status. But not all women parliamentarians saw eye-to-eye on women's rights. And as the first decade of post-Taliban rule drew to a close, some suggested Afghan officials were "selling out" women to hold onto their own power. Take, for example, the Shi'a Family Law, signed into law by President Karzai in 2009. Many women parliamentarians voted for the law despite provisions stripping rights from Shi'a women, a minority religious community in Sunni-majority Afghanistan. Under the new law, a Shi'a woman cannot refuse intercourse with her husband, cannot work or go to school without her husband's permission, and must dress in public according to her husband's wishes. Men can also legally sanction Shi'a women who do not comply with the law by refusing to feed them.

The tenuous political position of Afghan women is also well illustrated by the intimidation of female candidates in the run-up to the 2010 parliamentary elections. Women faced threats from the Taliban in the south but also from warlords in the north (Boone 2010). Many women candidates did not feel safe campaigning in rural areas at all, where women working outside the home were receiving death threats, and local religious councils were issuing edicts forbidding women to leave their homes without a male relative (Baker 2010). And in the cities, campaign posters displaying faces of women candidates were ripped down or defaced. Figure 14.2 shows one such campaign poster for parliamentary candidate Tahere Sajjadi, as seen on a wall in the city of Herat. In at least one province, women were the targets of roughly 90% of candidate-specific threats (Boone 2010). As a government minister summarized, "As women get stronger and they find a voice among the public, there are many people who lose power. There are many traditional people who lose so they try to create problems and trouble" (Boone 2010).

Figure 14.2   Defaced Campaign Poster of Parliamentary Candidate Tahere Sajjadi on a Public Wall in Herat, Afghanistan, 2010

Source: Raheb Homavandi, Reuters.

It is important to understand that in 2010 women candidates were not facing idle threats. In 2006, Ministry of Women's Affairs director Safia Ahmed-jan was assassinated. Malalai Kakar, the only female police commander in the country, was murdered in similar fashion in 2008. In 2009, women's activist and regional parliamentarian Sitara Achakzai was gunned down by the Taliban. And during the 2010 campaign season, five male volunteers of Fauzia Gilani's campaign were kidnapped and murdered (Boone 2010).

But Afghan women would not be deterred. Between 2005 and 2010, the number of women parliamentary candidates more than doubled. And ultimately, one district even elected a woman outside of the reserved seat system, bringing the number of women in the new parliament to 69.

What does the future hold for Afghan women? As the United States moves toward withdrawal from Afghanistan, women are left in a precarious position. In March 2012, President Karzai endorsed an edict from the country's highest Islamic authority stating, "Men are fundamental and women are secondary" and counseling women against "mingling with strange men in various social activities such as education, in bazaars, in offices and other aspects of life." The economy minister told a gathering of women leaders that they will have to "sacrifice their interests" for the sake of peace in the country. If reconciliation with the Taliban succeeds and so-called Talib moderates are welcomed into government, there is no telling how extreme a sacrifice Afghan women may have to make. Although Afghanistan's constitution protects women's rights and their seats in parliament, countries do change their constitutions. The economy minister, for one, would love to see an end to the gender quota. He claims, the quota for women "makes them lazy" (Baker 2010). But if Aghanistan's history proves anything, it is that Afghan women will not go down without a fight.

Oceania

More than 20,000 islands scatter the Pacific Ocean. Sometimes called Oceania as a collective, these tropical islands include both dependent territories and independent countries. In this section, we focus on 12 sovereign countries located in the Pacific region: Federated States of Micronesia, Fiji, Kiribati, Marshall Islands, Nauru, Palau, Papua New Guinea, Samoa, Solomon Islands, Tonga, Tuvalu, and Vanuatu. Although New Zealand and Australia could be considered part of this group geographically, we treat them as part of the West and thus discuss them in Chapter 10.

As a subregion, these countries in Oceania have the fewest women in politics of any part of the world, averaging only 2.6% women in their national legislatures. As of December 2011, Kiribati (pronounced *kir-i-bas*) led the group with four women (8.7%), Papua New Guinea included just one woman out of 109 seats, and four countries—Micronesia, Nauru, Palau, and the Solomon Islands—had parliaments comprised entirely of men. This level of exclusion is not a new phenomenon. Vanuatu and Tonga both elected fewer than five women MPs throughout their entire histories and never more than one in a single year (Bowman, Cutura, Ellis, and Manuel 2009; Guttenbeil-Likiliki 2006). And between 1968 and 2004, women were

38% of parliamentary candidates in Nauru, but only one woman was ever elected (Lauti and Fraenkel 2006).

Why is women's political representation in Oceania so low? Traditional customs and other cultural factors are typically offered as a main explanation. Across Oceania, gender roles are typically seen as complementary, where men's and women's labor are viewed as separate and distinct, and women's power is limited to the domestic realm. For example, in Vanuatu, men often say, "Women do have a voice—but from the kitchen" (Office of the Prime Minister and Department of Women's Affairs 2004). In some Oceanic countries, traditional social structures offer women high status and prestige but negligible access to political leadership. For example, in the low-lying islands of Tonga, the traditional system of *fahu* confers a high value on female children and high status for women in Tongan society, but the complementary system of *'Ulumotu'a* means that women are afforded little decision-making authority and tend to vote in line with elder men in their households (Guttenbeil-Likiliki 2006). Similarly in the matrilineal societies of Micronesia and Tuvalu, identity, titles, land rights, and property traditionally was passed down through women, giving them considerable influence over domestic affairs, but politics was considered the domain of men.

For cultural reasons, women pursuing political careers also typically lack broad political support from women voters (Guttenbeil-Likiliki 2006). In 2008, when a record number of women ran in the Tongan parliamentary elections and not a single woman was elected, several of the female candidates attributed their loss to women not voting for them. As one female candidate summarized, "The reason why a woman did not get elected was the women themselves" (Heleta 2008). Some men also see the problem as one resting with women, reporting that "it's a woman's thing and they need to deal with it themselves first before they can go any further" (Guttenbeil-Likiliki 2006:146). Thus, Tonga demonstrates well that when culture serves as an obstacle to women's political representation, it can operate through the attitudes of both men and women (see Chapter 4).

The lack of support for women politicians—whether real or perceived—means that women can have a hard time gaining the backing of political parties and the men who lead them. Vanuatu's male political leaders have voiced strong opinions that women should stay out of politics. For instance, in 2002, the Council of Chief president, who presides over the island chain's 2,000 chiefs, publicly stated his belief that women had "no place in politics or the judiciary," and in 2004, the chair of the Port Vila Council of Chiefs told the media categorically that women should not serve as presidents or prime ministers (Donald, Strachan, and Taleo 2002:50; Office of the Prime Minister and Department of Women's Affairs 2004). Women faced even more difficult political conditions in 1995 and 1998, when none of the political parties in

Vanuatu fielded a single female candidate, leaving all women to stand for office as independents. Women's nongovernmental organizations (NGOs) in Vanuatu tried to fill the gap by offering support and training to female candidates (Donald et al. 2002). But in a country where almost all elected officials are affiliated with political parties, women's battle for political power was an uphill one. Not all Oceanic countries have strong party systems, however, and women still struggle politically. Nauru, for example, has no political parties and women similarly fail to win legislative seats (Lauti and Fraenkel 2006).

Although numerically rare, women politicians in Oceania have still played visible and important political roles. Nauru's first and only female MP to date, Ruby Dediya, at different times served as the minister of health, speaker of parliament, minister of finance, and acting president. Dame Carol Kidu, Papua New Guinea's sole female legislator in 2011, served in the parliament for 15 years and as minister for community development for 9 years. In addition to standing out because she is a woman, Kidu stood out as a White Australian-born immigrant in a country populated by hundreds of different indigenous ethnic groups. In 2012, Kidu became the first woman opposition leader when all other members of her party protested Prime Minister Peter O'Neill rise to power by refusing to take seats in parliament. Although Kidu fought for a wide range of causes over the years, she began fighting for gender quotas in 2005 in the form of the Equality and Participation Bill, which would create 22 new women-only seats in parliament. In November 2011, the bill came up one vote shy of the supermajority needed to be enacted, but women's groups have vowed to continue to push for the measure (Sauer 2012). Quotas have suffered similar fates in the Federated States of Micronesia, Kiribati, Samoa, and the Solomon Islands, where reserved seats have been discussed or even formally proposed but not enacted (International Institute for Democracy and Electoral Assistance [IDEA] 2012b; Lee 2009; Radio New Zealand International 2011).

Before moving on, it is worth acknowledging that the Oceanic country in which women historically had the greatest political success was in Fiji, where women were elected to 11.3% of seats in parliament in 2006 before a coup d'état established military rule. Although Fiji still lacks a democratically elected parliament, the interim government has expressed that it sees including women in the new government as key to the country's future development. The existing leadership backed up this rhetoric in 2012, when the commission formed to draft a new Fijian constitution became the country's first female-majority representative body. Still, only time will tell if Fiji will again assume its position as regional leader in women's political representation.

To learn more about women in politics in the Pacific Islands, see www.pacwip.org, which provides a range of information and news about women in politics in the region.

15

Sub-Saharan Africa

My administration shall empower Liberian women in all areas of our national life. We will support and increase the write of laws that restore their dignity and deal drastically with the crimes that dehumanize them.

—Ellen Johnson Sirleaf, Africa's first elected
woman president, in her inauguration speech,
January 16, 2006, Liberia

In 2008, Rwanda, a country roughly the size of Maryland located in the center of sub-Saharan Africa, made world history by becoming the first country to elect a national legislature with more women than men. Although Rwanda is no longer the only country to have elected a female-majority legislature, Rwanda still leads the world in women's representation at 56%.

Just a few decades ago, Rwandan women's political success would have been unthinkable. Researchers' depiction of women's political situation in Africa was grim. Naomi Chazan (1989) summarized the following:

The female experience in African politics during the past century is . . . one of exclusion, inequality, neglect, and subsequent female consolidation and reaction. Women have neither played a significant part in the creation of the modern state system on the continent, nor have they been able to establish regular channels of access to decisionmakers. (p. 186)

When women did enter politics, their participation was judged to be "little more than an extension of their submissive domestic role" (Geisler 1995:547).

Women who attained seats in national parliaments often did so through the women's wings of political parties, which left women marginalized and alienated from the policy formation process. Furthermore, the conservative culture of women's wings often meant that women were expected to reinforce the very traditions that subjugated them. For example, during the 1970s and 1980s, female leaders of the Women's League of the United Independence Party (UNIP) in Zambia worked to assure men that women's participation in the political realm was, in fact, not a challenge to male authority and that they still sought to serve their husbands. This pattern meant that young professional women seeking empowerment often rejected formal political membership and instead joined or formed civic associations (Geisler 1995).

Since the early 1990s, however, women's standing in African politics has changed dramatically. Since 1960, no region has experienced a rate of increase in women's political representation higher than in sub-Saharan Africa, which jumped from 1% in 1960 to 18% in 2010 with a major boost between 1990 and 2010 when rates tripled (Tripp 2003). In addition to Rwanda, 6 other countries in the region are among the top 20 in women's parliamentary representation (Inter-Parliamentary Union [IPU] 2012b). And in 2011, women in Africa held, on average, 18.8% of the legislative seats (in the single or lower house)—just shy of the world average. Map 15.1 displays women's legislative representation across the countries of sub-Saharan Africa.

African women's political success is not limited to seats in national legislatures. Until the 1990s, it was virtually unheard of for an African woman to run for president. But, between 2000 and 2009, women ran in about one third of all African presidential elections, and in 2005, Liberia's Ellen Johnson Sirleaf became Africa's first elected woman president. Across the continent, women have also been assuming positions as prime minister, speaker of the house, and vice president. For example, Specioza Kazibwe was Uganda's vice president from 1994 to 2003. In 2012, women averaged 20% of cabinet positions overall and claimed powerful ministerial positions in many countries. And at the local level, women have topped one third of government seats in countries like Namibia, Uganda, Mozambique, and even as high as 60% of the local seats in Seychelles and Lesotho.

Although the impact of this transformation on the substantive representation of women has varied across time and across the region, researchers generally find that climate surrounding women's rights and gender equality is fundamentally different than a few decades ago. Burnet (2008) explained the following in the Rwandan case:

> While there are still those Rwandans . . . who label independent or outspoken women as "loud" or "loose," these voices are no longer met with social silence

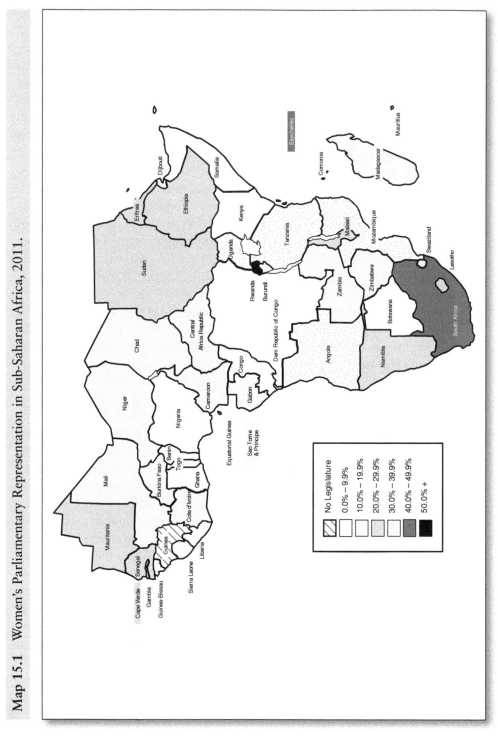

Map 15.1 Women's Parliamentary Representation in Sub-Saharan Africa, 2011.

No Legislature

0.0% – 9.9%

10.0% – 19.9%

20.0% – 29.9%

30.0% – 39.9%

40.0% – 49.9%

50.0% +

or tacit approval. Instead, they are pointed out as "un-evolved" points-of-view, which hearken back to the "Old Rwanda." (p. 382)

What explains the transformation in women's political representation in Africa? Although not all countries enjoying legislative gains for women have gender quotas (Yoon and Bunwaree 2008), the spread of gender quotas across Africa is certainly part of the story (Tripp 2005; Tripp, Morna, and Konaté 2006; Yoon 2004; see also Chapter 6). Nearly half of sub-Saharan African countries used gender quotas in their most recent election, typically through reserved seats (International Institute for Democracy and Electoral Assistance [IDEA] 2012b). A handful of ruling political parties have also voluntarily adopted quotas. Examples include the African National Congress (ANC) in South Africa, Front for the Liberation of Mozambique (FRELIMO) in Mozambique, and South West Africa People's Organization (SWAPO) in Namibia. Overall, in 2011, sub-Saharan African countries with candidate quotas, reserved seats or voluntary party quotas had, on average, 10% more women in parliament than African countries without gender quotas.

Yet on their own, quotas cannot fully explain African women's political success in the last few decades. Quotas may be the way, but they do not answer the why. Why did so many African countries adopt quotas? One explanation for the rapid growth of women's representation in Africa has been the role of major armed conflicts (Ballington 2004; Bauer and Britton 2006; Hughes 2009a; Tripp, Casimiro, Kwesiga, and Mengwa 2009; Zuckerman and Greenberg 2004). Rwanda, for one, was ravaged by political and economic upheaval, civil war, and a horrific ethnic genocide before women successfully ascended to political leadership. Women also claim large numbers of parliamentary seats in other post-conflict countries like South Africa (42%), Mozambique (39%), Angola (38%), Uganda (35%), and Burundi (31%). As of 2010, women held 25% of the parliamentary seats, on average, in African post-conflict countries, compared with the remaining countries, where women held only 14% of seats (Hughes and Tripp n.d.).

Other research points to the effects of international and regional forces (see also Chapter 7). The 1985 UN Conference on Women in Nairobi, in particular, served as a catalyst for women's mobilization throughout the continent. Tripp (2000) has shown how Ugandan women activists returned from Nairobi with a new sense of urgency to begin revitalizing and creating autonomous women's associations. The Ugandan participants, who were coming out of 15 years of armed conflict, gained a sense of how far women in other countries had come. Similarly, scholars point to the 1995 UN Conference on Women in Beijing as a watershed moment for women's movements everywhere, including in Africa. Particularly after 1995, women's movement began pressing political parties and leaders to adopt gender quotas.

Regional organizations such as the Southern African Development Community (SADC) and the African Union have also played key roles in the region. Women's movements placed pressure on these organizations that, in turn, pressured countries to increase women's political representation. In November 1997, SADC heads of government adopted a "Declaration on Gender and Development" in which they committed themselves to achieving 30% representation of women in politics and decision making by the year 2005, and targets have subsequently increased to 50% (Hughes and Tripp n.d.). Similarly, the African Union, an association of all African states except Morocco, has called for 50% women's representation at all levels of political decision making by 2015.

It is also important to remember that gains in sub-Saharan Africa did not develop in the absence of barriers to women's political inclusion. Indeed, sub-Saharan African countries have helped to show that Islam does not always inhibit women's legislative representation. In the Middle East and North Africa, the dominance of Islam is often offered as an explanation for women's continued struggle for a political voice (see Chapter 13). And in Asia, despite women's rise to national leadership in Muslim-majority countries like Indonesia and Pakistan, women's legislative representation remains low (see Chapter 14). In sub-Saharan Africa, however, numerous countries with majority or substantial Muslim populations have adopted gender quotas (Eritrea, Mali, Mauritania, Niger, Senegal, South Sudan, Sudan, and Tanzania) (Hughes and Tripp n.d.). These countries are motivated by many of the same factors as elsewhere in the region: urging from women's movements and female elites, the desire to win women's votes, and the pressure to accommodate changing international norms among others. Countries with sizeable Muslim populations may also seek to dissociate themselves from Islamist political influences (Hughes and Tripp n.d.).

Overall, there are many possible explanations for women's political gains in Africa. As women's political representation in countries in sub-Saharan Africa has soared, researchers have tested theories developed for Western Europe in the African context and explored new topics or paths to political power. In addition to exploring effects of gender quotas, armed conflict, international organizations, and religion, recent research on gender and politics in Africa has focused on civic participation and activism, colonial history, democracy and democratization, development, electoral systems, ethnicity and nationalism, foreign aid, and women's impact on government policy. Although we do not explore all of these topics in detail—we limit our discussion to the lasting effects of colonialism, issues of ethnicity and nationalism, and the transformative power of armed conflict—it is clear that research on women in politics in Africa is burgeoning.

Colonialism

No discussion of the political situation in Africa today can occur without first acknowledging the enormous effects of European intervention in the region through colonialism. By the late 1800s, the "scramble for Africa" was under way as European powers, such as England, France, Spain, and Portugal, sought to conquer and rule indigenous societies across the African continent. European governments imposed foreign political and legal structures, drew arbitrary territorial boundaries, extracted valuable resources, spread disease, and enslaved, slaughtered, evangelized, and attempted to "civilize" indigenous populations. But colonialism was far from uniform across Africa. European powers brought their own distinct ideas about how indigenous cultures should be governed or assimilated, colonies were populated and governed differently, and colonial governments faced varying levels and types of indigenous resistance over time and place. It makes sense, therefore, that colonialism's impact has been both complex and contradictory.

Colonialism undermined women's power and status in Africa relative to their position in precolonial times. In many traditional societies, men and women were not equal, but gender relations were characterized by interdependence—men and women had different but complementary roles (Waylen 1996:50). For example, among the Baule in what is now the Ivory Coast, or Cote d'Ivoire, subsistence was traditionally based on the production of yams and cloth. Although men and women both took part in the production of these items, men initiated the production of yams and controlled their distribution, while women initiated the production of cloth and therefore took responsibility for it (Etienne 1980; Waylen 1996).

But when colonial governments came to power, they fostered **export-oriented economies** that interfered with the economic interdependence of men and women (Waylen 1996). Not only did European powers limit the extension of important resources such as credit and training in new technologies to men only but women's workloads also increased as men withdrew from subsistence agriculture to focus on cash crops. Because men became the sole wage earners, women became dependent on men to pay the tax demanded by colonial governments.

Colonialism also brought important legal changes that affected women's power, such as changes in land tenure. Property rights were individualized, and women lost their rights to customary land, transforming women from economic partners to the status of laborers in men's fields (Etienne 1980; Waylen 1996). Colonial governments also codified male power over women through separate "customary" legal systems. Men sought to maximize power by exaggerating their authority in traditional arrangements to male colonial administrators, who were willing to assist African men with controlling their women (Barnes 1992:602). Thus, as many scholars have strongly emphasized, the customary laws put in place during colonialism are not based on African practices surviving from precolonial times but instead are a product of the colonial imposition (Channock 1982; Oyewumi 1997).

Women's political roles in traditional societies also often disappeared with the advent of colonialism. For example, in precolonial Ghana, there was a female counterpart to the male "king" called the *omanhemaa,* or queen mother. Not only was the conduct and welfare of the girls and women in the state her direct responsibility but "as the authority on kinship relations, she determined the legitimacy of an aspirant to the royal stool-ship, or throne, and had the prerogative of nominating the *omanhene* (king), subject to the ratification by a council of elders" (Okonjo 1994:288). Furthermore, if the king had to leave his throne to lead his soldiers into battle, the queen mother ruled the state until his return. When the British took control of the region, however, authorities instituted political structures that defined governance as a male domain. Formal contact between the indigenous states and the Europeans was between Black and White males, isolating women from the state establishment (Okonjo 1994).

African women did not accept their changing circumstances passively. The colonial state was a site of gender struggle, and "some women attempted to use the limited spaces which had opened up to their advantage" (Waylen 1996:68). For example, in the early colonial period, young Swazi women used the colonial courts to bring charges of assault and rape against men (Booth 1992). And in some areas, women benefited somewhat politically. For example, women in colonial Sierra Leone were elected as paramount chiefs in areas where women had never served in positions of formal executive authority (Day 1994). But Day (1994) also argued that this transition to formal chiefship was grounded in women's authority as lineage heads, founders of towns, and secret society officials prior to colonial times, which left them well situated to move into chief positions. For example, in Baoma, the town founder, war champion, and head of the village's prominent people was Madam Nenge. Recognized as chief by the British, her descendants have claimed the right to rule, and her daughter as well as two of her granddaughters held office after her death (Day 1994:489). But overall, this research indicates that women's political position was undermined by the colonial project.

Colonialism may continue to have effects on women's empowerment today through structures established during colonial times. For example, in Zimbabwe, the current school curriculum is modeled on the colonial British education system, which educated girls for domesticity (Gordon 1998). Although the formal curriculum appears gender neutral, girls are expected to focus their education on religion, fashion, fabric, and nutrition, while boys are taught science, geography, history, and mechanical skills. Textbooks are rife with traditional gender stereotypes. In a study of textbooks by Brickhill, Hoppers, and Pehrsson (1996), women were represented as "housewives who cook and clean and nag their children and husbands" whereas "the father is the provider and makes important decisions" (quoted from Gordon 1998:55). Thus, decades after reaching independence, the socialization of children is still influenced by colonial history.

Indeed, recent research supports that cultural links between colonies and European powers continue to affect women's political representation to this day. Specifically, Hughes (2005) found that former colonies tend to mirror their former colonial rulers in their current levels of women's parliamentary representation. For example, among the European imperial powers, France has the lowest rate of female parliamentary representation at the national level. Former French colonies tend to mirror these low levels—for example, Benin (8.4%), Djibouti (13.8%), and the Ivory Coast (8.4%)—and have lower percentages of women in parliament on average than former Spanish or Belgian colonies (IPU 2012b).

One reason why former colonies may share similar levels of representation with their former colonizers is that links may shape patterns of quota adoption. For example, research suggests continuing links between Argentina and Spain may have fostered quota adoption in one or both of the countries (Krook 2009). If colonial ties do facilitate quota adoption, France may ultimately help lead its former colonies out of the doldrums of women's representation if they follow France's lead of parity quota laws, as happened in the former French colonies of Senegal and Tunisia. Indeed, though the era of colonialism has now passed, its impact may continue to extend far past its historical decline.

Women, Ethnicity, and Nationalism

Although countries in Africa share many features, women in the region are far from a monolithic group. Christianity and Islam coexist alongside a diverse array of indigenous beliefs. And, across the continent, hundreds of ethnic groups speak distinct languages. Each of these groups has its own relationship to state power, influenced by group resources (including ties to other groups in the region), precolonial and colonial relations, the road to independence, and strategies used by government actors to balance or usurp power. Thus, a woman's religion or ethnicity may exclude her from power even more so than her gender. And the resources and political access of peasant women are clearly different from the resources and access of the privileged women of the urban bourgeoisie. For these reasons, countries in Africa serve as particularly important cases for the study of how gender intersects with ethnicity and nationality.

It is impossible to discuss ethnic and race relations in Africa without returning to colonialism. European powers often negotiated their borders, drawing country boundaries without regard to the homelands of distinct populations. This meant that single tribal groups were often divided among two or more countries or that traditional enemies were forced to live alongside each other with no buffer between them. Furthermore, European powers often sought to dominate indigenous populations by privileging one group or class over another—often empowering groups that were not in the numerical majority. Different ethnic groups received different levels of education, training, and employment, and they were often allotted different political roles. This practice fostered hatred and mistrust between ethnic groups that was not present prior to colonization. But after colonialism came to an end, ethnic tensions often boiled over into massive civil conflicts. Perhaps the most devastating example of this practice occurred in Burundi and Rwanda, where ethnic tensions between Tutsis and Hutus nourished under German and Belgian colonialism eventually gave rise to the ethnic genocide of 1994.

As the women and men in colonial societies fought for independence, group identities were formed that continue to influence racial and ethnic relations in Africa today. Specifically, the struggle of a people to define themselves and fight for self-rule generates nationalism. Nationalism is a political belief that groups bound by common ethnicity, language, or values have the right to self-govern within an independent territory. The relationship between women and nationalism is quite controversial (Jayawardena 1986; Moghadam 1994). On the one hand, Bystydzienski (1992:209) argued that nationalism has "empowered millions of women . . . created pride in indigenous cultures, a demystification of innate superiority of foreign oppressors, and a recognition of community." Yet, on the other hand, in nationalist struggle women are often constructed as the symbolic form of the nation whereas men are represented as the nation's chief agents (Pettman 1996). This means that when statehood is achieved, men emerge as the major beneficiaries (Wilford 1998). There is no acknowledgment of women's greater economic and political roles prior to the colonial imposition nor of their role in the independence struggle. Women face an uphill battle to be recognized as political actors, and "male politicians who had consciously mobilized women in the struggle, push them back into their 'accustomed place'" (Jayawardena 1986:259; Pankhurst 2002).

On the other hand, when ethnic conflict becomes armed conflict and topples governments, women's political representation may subsequently increase. Women are often perceived as consensus builders and capable of crossing ethnic divides. More cynically, some scholars argue that focusing on women allows ruling governments to divert attention away from persisting ethnic inequalities. Although evidence for such allegations is difficult to come by, research does show that in African national legislatures, ethnic inequality and gender inequality are inversely related. Countries with lower ethnic inequality—places like Djibouti, Ghana, Liberia, Malawi, Mauritius, Sierra Leone, and Zambia—have relatively high levels of gender inequality in representation (Shella 2011). In contrast, countries like South Africa and Burundi are found to have more balanced parliaments by gender but higher levels of inequality by ethnicity (Shella 2011). Overall, African governments may tend to focus on one dimension of inequality—gender or ethnicity—at a time.

Where does this leave ethnic minority women? Although the paucity of research on minority women in places like Africa means it is hard to guess, research does suggest that minority women can benefit from mechanisms designed to promote the representation of either women or minority groups. But they can benefit the most from a combination of the two. As discussed in Chapter 6, one case that illustrates this point is Burundi, which uses both gender and minority-based quotas and where 57% of women representatives are from the minority Tutsi or Twa groups (Hughes 2011). But these policies did not appear from nowhere. Like many other African countries, Burundi recently emerged from a brutal civil war. In the next section, we more directly explore the mechanisms through which such conflicts can increase women's political representation.

Armed Conflict: Devastation Yet Hope?

Armed conflict between or within countries is a horrible and disastrous occurrence. Therefore, although war may be a force for change, we must first acknowledge the tremendous suffering that is involved—particularly for women. Whereas men more often die on the battlefield, women disproportionately suffer crimes such as mass rape, forced prostitution, torture, and other atrocities. Rape in particular is employed systematically by armed forces to undermine social stability or even as a form of ethnic cleansing (Meznaric 1994; Sideris 2001). For example, in the ongoing conflict in the Democratic Republic of the Congo, rape of women has become systemic—with forces on both sides of the conflict acting as perpetrators. Women in post-conflict situations are also more often displaced, as widows struggle to hold onto property in societies that do not recognize their rights.

But even out of the most devastating of circumstances, hope for change may rise. In the history of any nation, wars serve as defining moments, turning points, and catalysts for change. Armed conflict often alters the very fabric of society, shifting the ideas, beliefs, and social positions of its members. Although such events are devastating to the makeup of society and often leave thousands or even millions of individuals scarred by loss, these crises may also create opportunities for women to gain political representation (Goetz 1995; Hughes 2009a; Lipman-Blumen 1973; Putnam 1976).

Although wars happen everywhere, understanding the role of openings at the end of armed conflicts in Africa is particularly important because after 1985 many long-standing conflicts across the continent came to an end, and new civil conflicts became rarer events. Wars of national liberation ended in Namibia and South Africa after 1990. Civil conflicts came to an end in countries like Mozambique (1992), Rwanda (1994), Chad, (2002), Angola (2002), Sierra Leone (2002), Liberia (2003), Burundi (2004), southern Sudan (2005), and northern Uganda (2007).

So, why exactly does war benefit women? Revolutionary movements or armed conflict may increase women's subsequent political representation for a number of reasons: increased supply of female candidates, influence of cultural beliefs about women's participation in ways favorable to their election, or alteration of the political opportunity structure to facilitate women's entry into the halls of power. In the next sections, we talk about each of these mechanisms for change in turn.

Increasing the Supply of Female Candidates

War has historically allowed women to operate outside of the constraints of traditional gender norms and to gain access to roles that were previously closed to them (Geisler 1995; Meintjes 2002; Waylen 1994). As men are pulled into combat and away from their jobs, women enter the labor force to fill the vacancies. One familiar example of this phenomenon is the influx of women into the labor force during and after World War II. Although women's participation may have been taboo prior to the war, women are able to gain a foothold in the public realm. And once conflict has subsided, it may be difficult to reinstitute sharp boundaries between public and private spheres. As discussed in Chapter 5, participation in the workforce may provide women experience that allows them to run for public office.

Yet during wars women's participation is not limited to serving as place-holders for men. Women play supportive roles, such as nursing the dying or wounded, and they also serve as armed combatants. Although the image of a soldier is usually male, women have fought in battles throughout history and around the world (Enloe 1980; Goldman 1982). For example, during the 18th and 19th centuries in the Dahomey Kingdom in West Africa, an all-female combat unit numbering in the thousands fought for the king (Goldstein 2001). More recently, during the Ethiopian civil war of the 1980s, roughly one third of the rebel fighters were women (Bloomfield, Barnes, and Huyse 2003). Wartime heroism is one important channel through which women can rise to positions of power (Denich 1981). Serving in combat may make female candidates better able to compete with men by providing them experience with matters of state defense or security.

In addition to providing women with access to the labor force and the military, conflict situations may also cause women to enter the public realm through participation in social movements. (See Chapter 12 for a discussion of women's social movement participation in Latin America.) In conflict situations, women create campaigns and demonstrations, institute human rights reporting, lobby for cease-fires, and build networks to care for refugees and support victims of war (Rehn and Sirleaf 2002). At national, regional, and international levels, women organize to end the use of land mines, enforce treaties, end sexual violence, and recognize specific acts of violence against women (Bop 2001). And national peace movements are often led by women, who "are committed to finding alternatives to violence" (Kelly 2000:51). Although women's efforts to promote peace are not always politically popular (remember our discussion of Jeannette Rankin in Chapter 3), women can gain experience in such movements that proves useful in the pursuit of formal political careers once conflict ends.

The expansion of women's roles can also happen after conflict has subsided. The killing, imprisonment, or exile of men may force many women into positions as heads of their households. For example, in Rwanda, women took over everyday tasks that were previously taboo such as milking cows and putting roofs on houses but also new societal roles such as entrepreneur or government administrator (Burnet 2008, 2011). Rwandan women seized opportunities to change their lives by going back to school, starting businesses, and entering politics (Burnett 2011).

Increased organizational activity during periods of reconstruction may also provide women with a route to political influence. Faced with the aftermath of violence, women have learned to unite and organize. For instance, after the war and genocide subsided in Rwanda, "women's organizations, both new and old, took a leading role in efforts to help women reconstruct their lives" (Longman 2006:138). And many women moved through these organizations into political office. In sum, through their experiences serving as armed combatants, activists, organizational members, and movement leaders during and after conflicts, women may gain the skills necessary to compete with men for political power.

Changing Culture

In addition to affecting the pool of qualified female candidates, wars and revolutions provide important moments for reshaping beliefs and ideas about gender and women's proper role. As Sambanis (2002) suggested, civil war is "a disruption of social norms that is unparalleled in domestic politics" (p. 217). And case studies have demonstrated that under conditions of change that undermine tradition, women in developing countries may rise to political leadership positions (Chaney 1973). For example, in Rwanda, parliamentarian Berthe Mukamusoni explained the following:

> Men and women both took part in the fight against the genocide, even at the front. When the men saw how tough the women were, healing the sick and cooking the food, as well as their presence at the front, they saw what women were capable of and the value of collaborating with them. (Women for Women International 2004:12)

Sometimes cultural changes that come with war are a direct consequence of new visions of society advanced by groups struggling for independence or to overthrow regimes. Certainly, not all wars and revolutions advance ideas favorable to women. Indeed, international feminist scholars point out that state military organizations have historically and cross-culturally depended on maleness (Enloe 1987). And during struggles for liberation, movement leaders may draw on ideas of the nation as a family, casting women as symbols of the nation and voicing support for women's "traditional" roles (Yuval-Davis 1997). Acknowledging variation in the ideas put forth by different movements, Moghadam (1997) categorized two types of revolutions: patriarchal and modernizing. **Patriarchal revolutions** connect national liberation to discourse about women in traditional familial roles. Women are cast as mothers of the revolution rather than actual revolutionaries. **Modernizing**

revolutions, on the other hand, advance models that serve to emancipate women.

Even for modernizing revolutions, the postwar context often leaves revolutionary promises about gender unfulfilled. Some researchers argue that to date no revolution has ever successfully maintained "an emancipating atmosphere for women" after the war subsided and the honeymoon period ended (Hale 2001:123). But although the promises of change may remain unfulfilled, the ideas developed and spread by modernizing revolutions may still inspire feminist consciousness (Moghadam 1997; Shayne 2004). One former woman fighter in Eritrea described this tension:

> [Our families] were happy at first that we came back alive. But after a year it changed. We have very different ideas from the rest of society. Women must stay at home and take care of their children, not go out and talk with men. We do not accept these traditional ideas of our parents, but it is difficult to change them. It is very hard for us because we were used to equality in the field. (Hale 2001:127)

Thus, though the entire society may not welcome women into politics following a war or revolution, armed conflict may still alter the beliefs and attitudes of individual women.

Changing Politics

It is also important to consider how armed conflict may produce openings in the political opportunity structure. Even if the pool of female candidates and ideology toward women remain stable, wars and revolutions may create windows of opportunity where it is easier for women to succeed in elections. One reason is that the male candidate pool may be significantly depleted due to the death or imprisonment of large numbers of men. Following the Rwandan genocide, for example, women and girls significantly outnumbered in the country's population, and an estimated 90,000 men were imprisoned (Powley 2003; Remmert 2003). Women may therefore be encouraged to fill the gap in candidates simply out of necessity.

The new roles women assume may also help them generate pressure for change. Notably, Africa's first elected female president Ellen Johnson Sirleaf links her own political success to women's efforts during and after the conflict. In her inauguration speech in 2006, she explained the following:

> Until a few decades ago, Liberian women endured the injustice of being treated as second-class citizens. During the years of our civil war, they bore the brunt of inhumanity and terror. They were conscripted into war, gang

raped at will, forced into domestic slavery. Yet, it is the women who laboured and advocated for peace throughout our region. It is therefore not surprising that during the period of our elections, Liberian women were galvanized—and demonstrated unmatched passion, enthusiasm, and support for my candidacy. They stood with me; they defended me; they worked with me; they prayed for me. The same can be said for the women throughout Africa. I want to here and now, gratefully acknowledge the powerful voice of women of all walks of life. (Sirleaf 2006)

Another political opportunity explanation for women's rise in post-conflict situations is that the former regime is often replaced. Research indicates that incumbency effects often hinder the access of women and minority groups (Darcy and Choike 1986; Putnam 1976). Therefore, when governments are toppled and incumbent politicians are pushed out of office, space is created for new candidates. Such situations may create favorable conditions for women to run and win (Hughes 2007). Surveys based in Africa show that women are often perceived as less corrupt and as caring more about basic needs of the community than men (British Council 2002). Women can serve also as powerful symbols of healing and rebirth. Such perceptions may help women win elections as societies struggle to stitch themselves back together after wars.

In addition to case study evidence, statistical research on developing countries suggests that the regime changes created by wars may be an important part of the story. Specifically, Hughes (2009a) found only civil wars that challenged the central government led to increases in female parliamentary representation in subsequent years. On the other hand, wars fought over territory that failed to displace the regime did not increase women's political presence. Table 15.1 shows how the distinction between civil wars fought against the central government and civil wars fought over territory produce different political gains for women. Even 15 to 20 years after conflict subsided, women are better represented in the legislatures of countries that experienced government-centered civil wars.

One of the ways regime change matters for women is that such moments create opportunities for new political structures. Indeed, after wars, new constitutions are often written and electoral systems are altered. Although historically women did not fare well during peace processes and constitution writing (Pankhurst 2003), post-conflict governments in recent years have had contend with pressure from domestic and international women's movements. In Burundi, Liberia, Mozambique, Namibia, South Africa, Rwanda, and Uganda, women's organizations vigorously took advantage of political openings to press for increased representation (Hughes and Tripp n.d.). They demanded

Table 15.1   Civil Wars and Women's Political Gains

Challenging the Government		Women in Parliament			
Country	Years	Prewar	2000	Change	2010
Angola	1990–1994	14.5	15.5	1.0	38.6
Ethiopia	1976–1991	1.6	7.7	6.1	27.8
Mozambique	1981–1992	12.4	30.0	17.6	39.2
Rwanda	1991–1992	17.1	25.7	8.6	56.3
Uganda	1981–1989, 1991	0.8	17.8	17.0	31.3
Average		9.3	19.3	10.1	38.6

Territorial Civil Wars		Women in Parliament			
Country	Years	Prewar	2000	Change	2010
Ethiopia	1974–1991	1.6	7.7	6.1	27.8
Sudan	1983–1992	8.5	9.7	1.2	25.6
Average		5.1	8.7	3.7	26.7

Source: Adapted from Hughes (2009a).

a seat at the peace talks, on constitutional commissions that drafted new constitutions, and in interim and newly formed governments. Often, backed by international pressures and norms, they explicitly demanded gender quotas (see also Chapter 6).

In summary, conflict situations may alter the supply of women, attitudes about women's roles, and the political opportunity structure in combinations of ways that subsequently increase female representation. Certainly, not all war situations lead to women's inclusion in politics after peace is negotiated. But beginning in the 1990s in sub-Saharan Africa, women were able to emerge from conflict situations with greater political representation. Perhaps the most notable example of post-conflict gains occurred in Rwanda, but researchers have stressed the importance of armed conflict in many other cases across the African continent (Bauer 2004; Boyd 1989; Byanyima 1992; Goetz 1995; Pankhurst 2002; Tripp 1994; Urdang 1989; Wakoko and Labao 1996). Overall, post-conflict environments in Africa have offered new beginnings for women who were ready to embrace change and take the lead.

Continuing Challenges

So far, we have described Africa largely as a success story—a place where exclusion and unthinkable violence have given way to women's increasing empowerment. But as we discussed in Chapter 8, the representation of women does not end with their presence alone. Even in countries that have made substantial progress toward gender equality, "discriminatory statutory, customary, and religious laws still pose significant obstacles to women" (Yoon 2001:170). And the region faces a host of other problems—escalating debt, government repression, HIV/AIDS, infant mortality, poverty, and starvation to name just a few.

One important limitation to women's power across Africa is that gains are sometimes concentrated in one part of government—in the executive or the legislative, at the national, or at the local level. This can be especially problematic if the issues of upmost importance to women are largely dealt with in a part of government in which women have less presence or influence. According to Jo Beall (2005), this is exactly the scenario in South Africa. Although women have made remarkable inroads into politics at the national level, the influence of traditional authorities in local governments have erected substantial barriers to the land rights of rural women (Beall 2005).

Another continuing struggle facing many women in African politics is how to successfully have influence on policy in undemocratic regimes (Abbas 2010; Burnet 2008; Longman 2006; Yoon 2011a). For example, in authoritarian countries like Rwanda, policy is often developed from the top down, limiting women's ability to influence policy outcomes. Jennie Burnet (2008) argued that as women's legislative representation has increased, their policy influenced has decreased. Prominent women's movement leaders left to take positions in the government, and once there, they had to toe the party line or risk being forced out of government. At the same time, the young women who took over leadership of the women's movement did not have the knowhow to "negotiate the levers of power" in a nondemocratic government (Burnet 2008:379). Some of the harshest critiques of women's high levels of representation in nondemocratic Africa have suggested that women's presence is being manipulated by authoritarian regimes ways to maintain power and improve their international reputation (e.g., Reyntjens 2010).

Because reserved seats often helped women achieve greater levels of representation in Africa, scholars have also cautioned that separate systems for women's election could pose challenges to women's ability to influence policy or to make gains beyond the seats that are set aside for them (Devlin and Elgie 2008; Disney 2006; Tripp 2006; Yoon 2011b). By using separate mechanisms to fill women's seats, women elected through these rules risk being dubbed "quota women," a label that could presumably limit their effectiveness as politicians (Goetz and Hassim 2003). And even if voters and other legislators do not stigmatize women who rise to power through quotas, this fear may lead female legislators to distance themselves from what are seen as women's issues—to show they are *real* politicians.

Regardless of how women rose to power in African governments and despite the numerous challenges they will face as executives and legislators, the expansion of women's political representation in Africa is nothing shy of remarkable. Women's political gains across the region have been hard fought. And women's lives have been transformed by the process. Although women face many battles on the horizon, things are looking up for African women.

16

Where Do We Go From Here?
And How Do We Get There?

W e do not have a crystal ball that will allow us to gaze into the future of women in politics. But in this chapter, we review where women have been with an eye to where women may be going. In doing so, we introduce a new measure of women's political representation that accounts for the distribution of the world's population, called the **Women Power Index.** We also summarize the lessons learned in previous chapters and present several ways for countries and citizens to influence women's incorporation into formal politics in the future.

Where Are We Now?

During the past 100 years, women around the world have made inroads into every area of political decision making. From the scattered and sporadic power of queens and tribal leaders, women are today presidents, prime ministers, parliamentarians, and mayors. In fact, women are not only political leaders but also grassroots activists, revolutionaries, and everyday voters. Truly, the increase in women's political representation over the past century is one of the success stories of the modern world.

But women have not yet achieved political equality with men. As one way to measure women's political power, we created the Women Power Index. Table 16.1 presents the Women Power Index for 2011. This index focuses on one measure of women's political power, their representation in national legislatures. But unlike a simple world average, the Women Power Index accounts for differences in population across countries. Thus, the index acknowledges that more people (1.2 billion) live under India's 11% women than the people (4.9 million) who live under Norway's 40% women. The Women Power Index therefore depicts the level of female representation experienced by the typical person in the world. To calculate the index, take each country's percentage of women in parliament and multiply it by the proportion of the world's population that lives in that country. Then add all countries to give a measure of the percentage of women governing the population of the world.

Table 16.1 The Women Power Index, 2011

World	Free	Partly Free	Not Free
17.6%	16.1%	18.6%	18.8%

Sources: Freedom House (2012); Inter-Parliamentary Union (IPU) (2012b); United Nations Statistics Division (2012).

Overall, the world's population is governed by national legislatures that are 17.6% women. In Table 16.1, we also account for broad differences in governance by creating separate measures for countries that are **free, partly free,** and **not free** (Freedom House 2012). (Territories that are not independent countries are excluded from our calculations, as are countries such as Brunei that had no legislature at the time.) Looking at Table 16.1, one can see that there are notable differences in the Women Power Index across different types of societies. In 2011, citizens of free countries were governed by legislatures that were 16.1% female, whereas partly free and not free societies were less male dominated, living under 18.6% and 18.8% women. These differences provide further evidence of a pattern for women's power that we have seen throughout this book: Women hold a greater share of political positions that are less powerful.

But looking across time, one can see increases in women's political power. Figure 16.1 displays values of the Women Power Index from 1975 to 2005 for free and partly free countries.

Overall, Figure 16.1 shows that women have been gaining power over time but at a generally slow rate. Women move from a power index value of about 4% in both free and partly free countries in 1975 to 13.6% for free

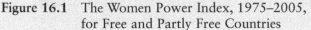

Figure 16.1 The Women Power Index, 1975–2005,
              for Free and Partly Free Countries

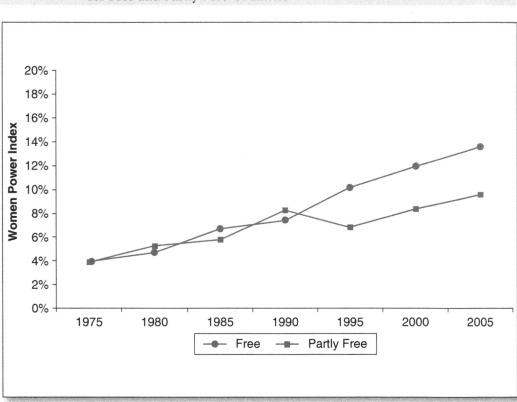

countries and only 9.6% in partly free countries in 2005. Also, whereas free
and partly free countries were similar in their index scores until the 1990s,
free countries pulled ahead during the 1990s and elected more women to
power. Yet, after 2005, partly free countries closed the gap and even pulled
ahead of free countries by 2011 (see Table 16.1).

We can also consider women's political progress across time in other
ways. Table 16.2 presents a snapshot of the number of countries that have
reached certain thresholds of women's representation—10%, 20%, 30%,
40%, and 50%—by the end of 2011.

Although there are some notable successes, it is clear from this table that
women still have far to go. Two countries, Rwanda and Andorra, have
achieved gender parity, 50% women in parliament, and seven other countries have come close, crossing the threshold of 40% women in parliament.

Table 16.2   Thresholds of Women's Parliamentary Representation
for 193 Countries, December 2011

Threshold	None	10%	20%	30%	40%	50%	Total
Number of Countries	46	67	46	21	7	2	193
Percentage of Total	24.3%	35.5%	24.3%	11.1%	3.7%	1.1%	100.0%

Source: IPU (2012b).

Twenty-one countries have at least 30% women in their parliaments, representing all regions of the world, and more than twice that number have passed the threshold of 20%. It is sobering to see, however, that almost 60% of countries have less than 20% women in parliament, and nearly one quarter of countries have not even reached 10% women.

Where Are We Going?

Will women reach 50% of more national legislatures in the next 10 years? Will the United States have a female president in 20 years? Will women in Afghanistan ever vote at levels similar to those of men? Obviously, we can only speculate about the answers to these questions. But some research offers guidance in thinking about the future of women in politics.

To begin, gender quotas offer a powerful prescriptive for women's future access to positions of political authority. As we discussed in Chapter 6, the implementation of quotas has in some countries allowed women to make large jumps in political representation in a relatively short period of time. In fact, the "typical picture" of women's acquisition of political power may be changing from slow and steady progress to fast-tracked power (Dahlerup and Freidenvall 2005). As Drude Dahlerup (2003) explained, "The Scandinavian experience cannot be considered a model for the 21st century because it took 80 years to get that far. Today, the women of the world are not willing to wait that long" (p. 4).

Not only are more countries adopting quotas but quotas are also becoming more effective. Higher quota levels, placement mandates, and sanctions for noncompliance are creating quotas that better guarantee women a seat at the table. It is probably safe to say that quotas will continue to increase levels of women in politics where they are effectively adopted and appropriately enforced. What is less clear is whether some countries will ever feel comfortable enough with levels of female participation to remove quotas. We hope that the question of whether to dismantle quotas because they are no longer needed will be debated sooner rather than later.

Another important trend is the election of female heads of state. Women are getting elected as presidents and prime ministers at an increasing rate. It took 20 years for the first five women to be elected as president and prime minister. The next five were elected in 10 years. Fourteen women came to power in the 1990s. As of June 1, 2012, approximately 7% of the world's governments were headed by women. It is probably safe to say that this number will grow over time but is likely to remain a small percentage of all leaders for some time.

Understanding where various countries of the world are going requires looking at where they have been. In Chapter 3, we introduced five basic historical paths to power: (1) Flat, (2) Increasing, (3) Big Jump, (4) Low Increasing, and (5) Plateau. Extrapolating forward from these trends suggests certain groups of countries, such as those in the increasing category, where one is likely to see even larger gains in the future. Low increasing countries should also be watched because their small increases may turn into long-term increases in women's representation. Another point to remember from our discussion in early chapters is that countries making significant gains in women's representation over the next 10 years are just as likely to be from the global south as the global north.

The female leaders of tomorrow are the girls of today. And girls growing up today in most countries are the first generation to see women participating at the highest levels of politics in even moderately large numbers. Apart from a few pioneer countries in Scandinavia and Eastern Europe, women's major gains in politics in most countries of the world occurred in just the past two decades. As Figure 16.1 shows, most women of the free world were living under less than 10% women as recently as 1993. And the average citizen of the partly free world has never lived under more than 10% women in power.

So what will happen when a generation of girls who see women in political life as normal and appropriate grows up? Will they participate at even higher levels, helping push the percentage of women in politics to 50% and beyond? As discussed in Chapter 4, we have some help in answering this question in the research of Christina Wolbrecht and David Campbell (2007). Looking across 27 countries, Wolbrecht and Campbell found a pure role model effect of women in politics. In countries with greater numbers of women in parliaments, adolescent girls envisioned themselves participating in politics more often (see also Atkeson 2003; Campbell and Wolbrecht 2006; Koch 1997).

Indeed, Lisa Murkowski, Republican senator from Alaska, experienced some hero worship from young girls:

> I am encouraged by the young girls that I see, those still in high school. They are really excited. They are almost giggly, movie-star excited—"Wow! You are a woman in the United States Senate!" You feel kind of silly, but you have to stop and think: This is something that they can look to and say, "I could be there." That is so incredibly important. They can visualize themselves here. (quoted in Victor 2005)

How Do We Get There?

Can one take away any lessons from this book? In this section, we draw on the lessons learned in previous chapters to present ways that countries and citizens can influence women in politics.

Furthering Women's Position in the Social Structure

We discussed that for women to succeed in politics they must have the knowledge, skills, and resources to compete against men. Therefore, organizations, political parties, and governments seeking to empower women politically should work to increase educational and training opportunities for both women and girls. And one must also remember that structural change takes time. Indeed, years will pass before the law student of today becomes the politician of tomorrow. So in the fight for women's representation, the time to arm women with the tools to succeed is now.

A more short-term strategy to improve women's political circumstances is to bolster their financial resources. Running for political office certainly requires money. But countries can level the playing field through public financing of campaigns. Political action organizations, such as EMILY's List, that finance women's campaigns are also key to increasing women's political representation. And individuals seeking to make a difference can contribute to such organizations or to individual female candidates.

Resources such as education and money matter everywhere. But it is also important to remember that the proper solution to the problem of political gender inequality varies depending on the context. And in different countries, women must overcome unique barriers. For instance, across parts of the Islamic world, family laws prevent women from effectively participating in the public realm. There, it is the reform of such laws that is the place to start in affecting women's representation.

Influencing Culture

We also explained that changing cultural beliefs may facilitate women's political participation and representation. Although cultural beliefs may seem slow to change (and probably are), change can be enacted when individuals challenge stereotypes and biases when they see them. Beliefs grounded in religion are no exception. When thinking about religion, remember that millions of adherents belonging to all major world religions accept women in politics while maintaining their religious beliefs. Work on political ambition suggests that socialization and early family experiences can shape women's later beliefs about politics. So parents should talk to their male and female children about politics and stress their competence in this arena.

One must also acknowledge that in some parts of the world, cultural beliefs seem to present almost an insurmountable obstacle to women's political equality. In these contexts, we detailed how the growing interconnectedness of countries across the globe may help to facilitate change. Because countries are part of a global community with global norms and standards, activists and media sources can mobilize information strategically to generate pressure on countries and parties to incorporate women. Further, the international women's movement and the United Nations continue to redefine global norms and standards and to exert pressure on countries. Finally, post-conflict reconstruction efforts (such as in Afghanistan and Iraq) may also be places where people can concentrate efforts to benefit women.

Disrupting Politics as Usual

When considering lessons learned about political influences, it is clear that some factors are more amenable to change than others. Although a number of countries have experimented with a variety of constitutional forms, realistically most countries are wedded to their particular electoral system. Still, we encourage citizens to become informed about the variety of electoral systems that exist around the world. Some electoral systems promote not only the representation of women (and other minority groups) but also the representation of a variety of political views.

But even if electoral systems are unchanged, electoral rules may be altered to hasten women's gains in politics. In recent years, quota policies have been adopted in a wide range of countries. But we have learned that the construction of quota laws matters greatly for their efficacy. Therefore, citizen-activists pushing for change should remember that placement mandates and sanctions for noncompliance are critical components of successful gender quota legislation.

In this text, we also argued that political parties serve important functions as gatekeepers to public office. But because political parties operate in a competitive environment, they must be responsive to citizens. Thus, individuals can help women gain political power by expressing their preferences for female candidates to party leaders. And using the power of the vote, citizens can interrupt politics as usual.

Citizens can also look to successful countries for ways to make parliaments and national legislatures more women friendly. For example, in South Africa (with 42% women), the parliamentary calendar was reorganized to match the school calendar. That is, when children are out of school, parliament is out of session. To further recognize that many parliamentarians have family responsibilities, debates end early in the evening and day care is provided (Britton 2006:70). And as we showed, pushing for the formation of women's policy machinery can provide women outside traditional political circles access to government.

Finally, knowing that women are less likely to aspire to or run for public office, we encourage all women to consider running for office at the local, state/regional, or national level. Remember, Fox and Lawless (2004) suggested that women are more qualified than they think. And to men who aspire to public office, Tremblay and Pelletier (2000) remind readers that men can also act as feminists, producing positive action on behalf of women. In the following list are Web resources that can help both men and women further understand women's descriptive and substantive representation:

International IDEA (Institute for Democracy and Electoral Assistance) Women in Politics, www.idea.int/gender/

IPU PARLINE Database, www.ipu.org/parline-e/parlinesearch.asp

UN Women, www.unwomen.org/

Development Alternatives With Women for a New Era (DAWN), www.dawnnet .org/

Center for American Women and Politics (CAWP), www.cawp.rutgers.edu/

In Conclusion:
What Would a 50/50 World Look Like?

In closing, we should stop and consider for a moment what a 50/50 world would look like. What would legislative meetings look like and sound like if 50% of the members were women? What would nuclear arms nonproliferation talks look like and sound like if the leaders negotiating were female? What would the U.S. cabinet and U.S. Supreme Court look like under a string of female presidents?

Anne Phillips (1991) provided one vision of a future:

> People are no longer defined through their nature as women or men. In this future scenario, . . . men and women . . . would vary as individuals rather than sexes in their priorities or experience, and would be equally attracted to (or repulsed by!) a political life. In such a context, the notion of the citizen could begin to assume its full meaning, and people could participate as equals in deciding their common goals. (p. 7)

But this 50/50 world is not reality. And we will not know what one looks like until women achieve such levels of power across many countries. And, ultimately, the women of the world need to be educated about their levels of representation in politics. Kira Sanbonmatsu (2003) found that one area in which women know less about politics than men is in estimating the percentage of women in office. Women are more likely than men to overestimate women's political presence. Sanbonmatsu (2003) suggested that "women would be even more supportive of electing women to office if they were as knowledgeable as men about the extent of women's underrepresentation" (p. 367). We hope that this book contributes to this process.

References

Abbas, Sara. 2010. "The Sudanese Women's Movement and the Mobilisation for the 2008 Legislative Quota and its Aftermath." *IDS Bulletin* 41(5):100–108.

Abou-Zeid, Gihan. 1998. "In Search of Political Power—Women in Parliament in Egypt, Jordan and Lebanon." *Women in Politics: Beyond Numbers*. Available online at www.vintob.com/elections/docs_6_g_6_6a_3.pdf.

Abou-Zeid, Gihan. 2003. "Introducing Quotas in Africa: Discourse in Egypt." Paper presented at the meeting of the International Institute for Democracy and Electoral Assistance, November 11–12, Pretoria, South Africa.

Abramowitz, Alan I., Brad Alexander, and Matthew Gunning. 2005. "Incumbency, Redistricting, and the Decline of Competition in U.S. House Elections." Prepared for the annual meeting of the Southern Political Science Association, January 6–8, New Orleans, LA.

Acker, Joan. 1992. "From Sex Roles to Gendered Institutions." *Contemporary Sociology* 21:565–569.

Adams, Melinda and John A. Scherpereel. 2010. "Variation in Women's Ministerial Representation Across Space and Time: Towards Explanations." Paper presented at the annual meeting of the American Political Science Association, September 2–5, Washington, DC.

Afghani, Jamila. 2005. "The Current State of Affairs for Afghan Women." Paper presented at the Afghan Women Leaders Speak Conference, November 16–19, Columbus, OH.

Afghanistan Government. 2001. "Afghan Bonn Agreement." Retrieved June 4, 2012 (http://www.afghangovernment.com/AfghanAgreementBonn.htm)

Ahmed, Kamal Uddin. 2008. "Women and Politics in Bangladesh." Pp. 276–296 in *Women's Political Participation and Representation in Asia*, edited by Kazuki Iwanaga. Copenhagen: Nordic Institute of Asian Studies.

Ahmed, Leila. 1992. *Women and Gender in Islam*. New Haven, CT: Yale University Press.

Alexander, Herbert E. 2001. "Approaches to Campaign and Party Finance Issues." P. 198 in *Foundations for Democracy: Approaches to Comparative Political Finance*, edited by K. Nassmacher. Baden-Baden: Nomos.

Almond, Gabriel Abraham, R. Scott Appleby, and Emmanuel Sivan. 2003. *Strong Religion: The Rise of Fundamentalisms Around the World*. Chicago: University of Chicago Press.

Alqudsi-Ghobra, Taghreed. 2002. "Women in Kuwait: Educated, Modern and Middle Eastern." Available online at http://www.wrmea.org/wrmea-archives/132-washington-report-archives-1988-1993/july-1991/2095-as-a-middle-eastern-woman-what-i-would-change-in-my-countrythree-views-v15-2095.html.

Álvarez, Sonia E. 1990. *Engendering Democracy in Brazil: Women's Movements in Transition Politics*. Princeton, NJ: Princeton University Press.

Álvarez, Sonia. 1994. "The (Trans)formation of Feminism(s) and Gender Politics in Democratizing Brazil." Pp. 13–63 in *The Women's Movement in Latin America*, edited by J. S. Jaquette. Boulder, CO: Westview Press.

Álvarez, Sonia E. 1999. "Advocating feminism: The Latin American Feminist NGO 'Boom.'" *International Feminist Journal of Politics* 1(2):181–209.

Amin, Sajeda, Ian Diamond, Ruchira T. Naved, and Margaret Newby. 1998. "Transition to Adulthood of Female Garment-Factory Workers in Bangladesh." *Studies in Family Planning* 29(2):185–200.

Amnesty International. 2004. "Saudi Arabia: Women's Exclusion From Elections Undermines Progress." Available online at http://www.amnesty.org/en/library/asset/MDE23/015/2004/en/3ae0ee3c-d55c-11dd-bb24-1fb85fe8fa05/mde230152004en.pdf.

Amnesty International. 2005. *Afghanistan: Women Still Under Attack—A Systematic Failure to Protect*. Available online at http://www.rawa.org/ai-wom05.htm.

Anderson, Leah Seppaneri. 2006. "European Union Gender Regulation in the East: The Czech and Polish Accession Process." *East European Politics and Societies* 20:101–125.

Anderson, Nancy Fix. 1993. "Benazir Bhutto and Dynastic Politics: Her Father's Daughter, Her People's Sister." Pp. 41–69 in *Women as National Leaders*, edited by M. A. Genovese. Newbury Park, CA: Sage.

Antrobus, Peggy. 2000. "Transforming Leadership: Advancing the Agenda for Gender Justice." *Gender and Development* 8(3):50–56.

Anzia, Sarah F. and Christopher R. Berry. 2011. "The Jackie (and Jill) Robinson Effect: Why Do Congresswomen Outperform Congressmen?" *American Journal of Political Science* 55(3):478–493.

Araújo, Clara. 2003. "Quotas for Women in the Brazilian Legislative System." Paper presented at the workshop of the International Institute for Democracy and Electoral Assistance, February 23–24, Lima, Peru.

Araújo, Clara. 2010. "The Limits of Women's Quotas in Brazil." *IDS Bulletin* 41(5):17–24.

Arceneaux, Kevin. 2001. "The 'Gender Gap' in State Legislative Representation: New Data to Tackle an Old Question." *Political Research Quarterly* 54: 143–160.

Ash, Timothy Garton. 2012. "Angela Merkel Needs All the Help She Can Get: Few Had Anticipated the Leadership Dilemmas of a European Germany in a German

Europe," *The Guardian,* February 8. Available online at http://www.guardian
.co.uk/commentisfree/2012/feb/08/angela-merkel-all-help-can-get.

Asia Foundation. 2006. "Afghanistan in 2006: A Survey of the Afghan People."
Retrieved May 14, 2012 (asiafoundation.org/pdf/AG-survey06.pdf).

Associated Press. 2004. "Nobel Laureate Speaks Out for Women." Available online at
http://www.apnewsarchive.com/2004/Nobel-Laureate-Speaks-Out-for-Women/
id-451f754fad32dcf2c01550098a74b33e.

Atkeson, Lonna Rae. 2003. "Not All Cues Are Created Equal: The Conditional
Impact of Female Candidates on Political Engagement." *Journal of Politics*
65:1040–1061.

Avicenna. [~1000] 1963. "Healing: Metaphysics X." Pp. 98–111 in *Medieval Political
Philosophy,* edited by R. Lerner and M. Mahdi, translated by Michael
E. Marmura. New York: The Free Press.

Azize-Vargas, Yamila. 2002. "The Emergence of Feminism in Puerto Rico, 1870–
1930." Pp. 175–183 in *Latino/a Thought: Culture, Politics, Society,* edited by
F. H. Vazquez and R. D. Torres. Lanham, MD: Rowman and Littlefield.

Baca Zinn, Maxine and Bonnie Thornton Dill. 1996. "Theorizing Difference From
Multiracial Feminism." *Feminist Studies* 22:321–331.

Baker, Aryn. 2010. "Afghan Women and the Return of the Taliban." *Time Magazine.*
August 9.

Baker, Paula. 1994. "The Domestication of Politics: Women and American Political
Society, 1780–1920." Pp. 85–110 in *Unequal Sisters: A Multicultural Reader in
U.S. Women's History,* 2nd ed., edited by V. L. Ruiz and E. C. DuBois. New York:
Routledge.

Baldez, Lisa. 2002. *Why Women Protest: Women's Movements in Chile.* Cambridge,
UK: Cambridge University Press.

Baldez, Lisa. 2003. "Elected Bodies: The Gender Quota Law for Legislative Candidates
in Mexico." Paper presented at the meeting of the American Political Science
Association, August 28–31, Philadelphia.

Baldez, Lisa. 2004. "Elected Bodies: The Gender Quota Law for Legislative Candidates
in Mexico." *Legislative Studies Quarterly* 29:231–258.

Ballington, Julie, ed. 2004. *The Implementation of Quotas: Africa Experiences.*
Stockholm, Sweden: IDEA.

Barber, E. Susan. 1997. *One Hundred Years Toward Suffrage: An Overview.* Available
online at http://memory.loc.gov/ammem/naw/nawstime.html.

Barnes, Teresa A. 1992. "The Fight for Control of African Women's Mobility in
Colonial Zimbabwe, 1900–1939." *Signs: Journal of Women in Culture and
Society* 17:586–608.

Barrig, M. 1996. "Women, Collective Kitchens and the Crisis of the State in Peru." in
Emergences: Women's Struggles for Livelihood in Latin America, edited by John
Friedmann, Rebecca Abers, and Lilian Autler. Berkeley: University of California
Press.

Baudino, Claudie. 2003. "Parity Reform in France: Promises and Pitfalls." *Review of
Policy Research* 20: 385–400.

Bauer, Antje. 2002. *Afghan Women and the Democratic Reconstruction of Afghanistan: Findings and Interviews From a Journalist's Field Trip*. Berlin: Berghof Research Center for Constructive Conflict Management.

Bauer, Gretchen. 2004. "'The Hand That Stirs the Pot Can Also Run the Country': Electing Women to Parliament in Namibia." *Journal of Modern African Studies* 42:479–509.

Bauer, Gretchen. 2006. "Namibia: Losing Ground Without Mandatory Quotas." Pp. 85–110 in *Women in African Parliaments*, edited by G. Bauer and H. Britton. London: Lynne Rienner.

Bauer, Gretchen. 2008. "50/50 by 2020: Electoral Gender Quotas for Parliament in East and Southern Africa." *International Feminist Journal of Politics* 10(3): 348–368.

Bauer, Gretchen and Hannah Evelyn Britton, eds. 2006. *Women in African Parliaments*. Boulder, CO: Lynne Rienner.

Bauer, Gretchen and Manon Tremblay, eds. 2011. *Women in Executive Power: A Global Overview*. New York: Routledge.

BBC News. 2001. "Candidate Selection." Available online at http://news.bbc.co.uk.

BBC News. 2005a. "Profile: Liberia's 'Iron Lady.'" *BBC News*, November 23.

BBC News. 2005b. "UK Women Earn 27% Less Than Men." *BBC News*, August 30.

Beall, Jo. 2005. "Decentralizing Government and Decentering Gender: Lessons From Local Government Reform in South Africa." *Politics Society* 33:253–276.

Beaman, Lori, Raghabendra Chattopadhyay, Esther Duflo, Rohini Pande, and Petia Topalova. 2009. "Powerful Women: Does Exposure Reduce Bias?" *The Quarterly Journal of Economics* 124(4):1497–1540.

Beckwith, Karen. 2005. "The Comparative Politics of Women's Movements." *Perspectives on Politics* 3:583–596.

Bedelbaeva, Aidai and Jyldyz Kuvatova. 2010. "Widening Women's Political Representation in Kyrgyzstan." *United Nations Development Programme Newsroom*, August 11. Retrieved January 17, 2013 (http://content.undp.org/go/newsroom/2010/july/20100716-women-kyrgyzstan.en).

Berkman, Michael B. and Robert E. O'Connor. 1993. "Do Women Legislators Matter? Female Legislators and State Abortion Policy." *American Politics Quarterly* 21:102–124.

Berkovitch, Nitza. 1995. "From Motherhood to Citizenship: The Worldwide Incorporation of Women Into the Public Sphere in the Twentieth Century." PhD dissertation, Stanford University, Stanford, CA.

Berkovitch, Nitza. 1999. *From Motherhood to Citizenship: Women's Rights and International Organizations*. Baltimore: Johns Hopkins University Press.

Beyer, Georgina. 2005. "Biography." Available online at http://www.ps.parliament .govt.nz/mp137.htm.

Bielby, William T. and James N. Baron. 1986. "Men and Women at Work: Sex Segregation and Statistical Discrimination." *American Journal of Sociology* 91:759–799.

Bigili, Nazlı Çağın. 2011. "Bridging the Gender Gap in Turkish Politics: The Actors Promoting Female Representation. *European Perspectives* 3(2):105–129.

Birch, Sarah. 2003. "Women and Political Representation in Contemporary Ukraine." Pp. 130–152 in *Women's Access to Political Power in Post-Communist Europe,* edited by R. E. Matland and K. A. Montgomery. Oxford, UK: Oxford University Press.

Bird, Karen. 2003. "Who Are the Women? Where Are the Women? And What Difference Can They Make? Effects of Gender Parity in French Municipal Elections." *French Politics* 1:5–38.

Bird, Karen. 2010. "Patterns of Substantive Representation Among Visible Minority MPs: Evidence From Canada's House of Commons." Pp. 207–229 in *The Political Representation of Immigrants and Minorities: Voters, Parties and Parliaments in Liberal Democracies,* edited by Karen Bird, Thomas Saalfeld, and Andreas W. Wüst. New York: Routledge.

Bjarnegard, Elin. 2009. *Men in Politics: Revisiting Patterns of Gendered Parliamentary Representation in Thailand and Beyond.* Doctoral thesis. Uppsala University.

Black, Jerome H. 2000. "Entering the Political Elite in Canada: The Case of Minority Women as Parliamentary Candidates and MPs." *Canadian Review of Sociology and Anthropology* 37(2):143–166.

Black, Jerome H. and Lynda Erickson. 2000. "Similarity, Compensation, or Difference? A Comparison of Female and Male Office-Holders." *Women and Politics* 21:1–38.

Blatch, Harriot Stanton and Alma Lutz. 1940. *Challenging Years: The Memoirs of Harriot Stanton Blatch.* New York: G. P. Putnam's Sons.

Blau, Peter M. 1977. "A Macrosociological Theory of Social Structure." *American Journal of Sociology* 83:26–54.

Blondel, Jean. 1980. *World Leaders: Heads of Government in the Postwar Period.* Beverly Hills, CA: Sage.

Blondel, Jean. 1988. "Introduction: Western European Cabinets in Comparative Perspective." Pp. 1–16 in *Cabinets in Western Europe,* edited by J. Blondel and F. Muller-Rommel. London: Macmillan.

Blondel, Jean. 1991. "Introduction." Pp. 1–4 in *The Profession of Government Minister in Western Europe,* edited by J. Blondel and J. Thiebault. London: Macmillan.

Bloomfield, David, Teresa Barnes, and Luc Huyse, eds. 2003. *Reconciliation after Violent Conflict: A Handbook.* Halmstad, Sweden: International Institute for Democracy and Electoral Assistance.

Blumberg, Rae L. 1984. "A General Theory of Gender Stratification." *Sociological Theory* 2:23–101.

Boesten, J. 2006. "Pushing the Boundaries: Social Policy, Domestic Violence, and Women's Organisations in Peru." *Journal of Latin American Studies* 38(2): 355–378.

Bonder, Gloria and Marcela Nari. 1995. "The 30 Percent Quota Law: A Turning Point for Women's Political Participation in Argentina." Pp. 183–193 in *Rising Public Voice: Women in Politics Worldwide,* edited by A. Brill. New York: Feminist Press.

Bonevac, D. W. B., William Boon, and S. Phillips. 1992. *Beyond the Western Tradition: Readings in Moral and Political Philosophy.* Mountain View, CA: Mayfield.

Boone, Jon. 2010. "Afghanistan Election: Five Campaigners for Female Candidate Shot Dead," *The Guardian,* August 29. Retrieved June 3, 2012 (www.guardian .co.uk/world/2010/aug/29/afghanistan-election-campaigners-shot-dead).

Booth, Alan R. 1992. "European Courts Protect Women and Witches: Colonial Law Courts as Redistributors of Power in Swaziland 1920–1950." *Journal of Southern African Studies* 18:253–275.

Bop, Codou. 2001. "Women in Conflicts, Their Gains and Their Losses." Pp. 19–34 in *The Aftermath: Women in Post-Conflict Transformation,* edited by Sheila Meintjes, Anu Pillay, and Meredeth Turshen. London: Zed Books.

Borić, Besima. 2005. "Application of Quotas: Legal Reforms and Implementation in Bosnia and Herzegovina." Pp. 38-42 in *The Implementation of Quotas: European Experiences Quota Report Series,* edited by Julie Ballington and Francesca Binda. Stockholm, Sweden: International Institute for Democracy and Electoral Assistance.

Borland, Elizabeth and Barbara Sutton. 2007. "Quotidian Disruption and Women's Activism in Times of Crisis, Argentina 2002–2003." *Gender and Society* 21(5):700–722.

Borrelli, MaryAnne. 2002. *The President's Cabinet: Gender, Power, and Representation.* Boulder, CO: Lynne Rienner.

Borrelli, MaryAnne. 2010. "The Contemporary Presidency: Gender Desegregation and Gender Integration in the President's Cabinet, 1933–2010." *Presidential Studies Quarterly* 40:734–749.

Boserup, E. 1970. *Women's Role in Economic Development.* London: Allen and Unwin.

Boudreaux, R. 1991. "The Great Conciliator," *Los Angeles Times Magazine,* January 6, pp. 9–13.

Bowman, Chakriya, Jozefina Cutura, Amanda Ellis, and Clare Manuel. 2009. *Women in Vanuatu: Analyzing Challenges to Economic Participation.* Washington, DC: World Bank.

Boxer, Barbara. 1994. *Strangers in the Senate: Politics and the New Revolution of Women in America.* Washington, DC: National Press Books.

Boyd, Rosalind E. 1989. "Empowerment of Women in Uganda: Real or Symbolic." *Review of African Political Economy* 45/46:106–117.

Bratton, Kathleen A. 2005. "Critical Mass Theory Revisited: The Behavior and Success of Token Women in State Legislatures." *Gender and Politics* 1:97–195.

Bratton, Kathleen A. and Kerry L. Haynie. 1999. "Agenda Setting and Legislative Success in State Legislatures: The Effects of Gender and Race." *Journal of Politics* 61:658–679.

Braun, Carol Moseley. 2003. "Giving Life to Declaration of Intent: A Call to Citizenship." Paper presented at Roosevelt University, February 26, Chicago, IL.

Bretherton, Charlotte. 2001. "Gender Mainstreaming and EU Enlargement: Swimming Against the Tide?" *Journal of European Public Policy* 8:60–81.

Brickhill, P., C. O. Hoppers, and K. Pehrsson. 1996. *Textbooks as an Agent of Change.* Stockholm, Sweden: SIDA.

Briggs, Jacqui. 2000. "What's in It for Women? The Motivations, Expectations and Experiences of Female Local Councillors in Montreal, Canada and Hull, England." *Local Government Studies* 26:71–84.

British Council. 2002. *Effective Leaders, View From Central and East Africa.* London: Mimeo.

Britton, Hannah E. 2005. *Women in the South African Parliament: From Resistance to Governance.* Urbana: University of Illinois Press.

Britton, Hannah E. 2006. "South Africa: Mainstreaming Gender in a New Democracy." Pp. 59–84 in *Women in African Parliaments,* edited by G. Bauer and H. E. Britton. London: Lynne Rienner.

Bruhn, Kathleen. 2003. "Whores and Lesbians: Political Activism, Party Strategies, and Gender Quotas in Mexico." *Electoral Studies* 22:101–119.

Burn, Shawn Meghan. 2005. *Women Across Cultures: A Global Perspective.* 2nd ed. New York: McGraw-Hill.

Burnet, Jennie E. 2008. "Gender Balance and the Meanings of Women in Governance in Post-Genocide Rwanda." *African Affairs* 107(428):361–386.

Burnet, Jennie E. 2011. "Women Have Found Respect: Gender Quota, Symbolic Representation, and Female Empowerment in Rwanda." *Politics & Gender* 7(3):303–334.

Burns, Nancy, Kay Lehman Schlozman, and Sidney Verba. 2001. *The Private Roots of Public Action: Gender, Equality, and Political Participation.* Cambridge, MA: Harvard University Press.

Burrell, Barbara C. 1994. *A Woman's Place Is in the House: Campaigning for Congress in the Feminist Era.* Ann Arbor: University of Michigan Press.

Burrell, Barbara C. 1998. "Campaign Finance: Women's Experience in the Modern Era." Pp. 26–37 in *Women and Elective Office: Past, Present, and Future.* Oxford, UK: Oxford University Press.

Burrell, Barbara C. 2004. *Women and Political Participation: A Reference Handbook.* Santa Barbara, CA: ABC-CLIO.

Burrill, Emily, Richard Roberts, and Elizabeth Thornberry, eds. 2010. *Domestic Violence and the Law in Colonial and Postcolonial Africa.* Athens: Ohio University Press.

Bush, Sarah Sunn. 2011. "International Politics and the Spread of Quotas for Women in Legislatures." *International Organization* 65:103–137.

Bussey, Jane. 2000. "Campaign Finance Goes Global." *Foreign Policy* 118(Spring):74–84.

Byanyima, Karagwa W. 1992. Women in political struggle in Uganda. Pp. 129–142 in *Women Transforming Politics: Worldwide Strategy for Empowerment,* edited by J. M. Bystylzienski. Bloomington: Indiana University Press.

Bystrom, Dianne G., Mary Christine Banwart, Lynda Lee Kaid, and Terry A. Robertson. 2004. *Gender and Candidate Communication: VideoStyle, WebStyle, NewsStyle.* New York: Routledge.

Bystydzienski, Jill M., ed. 1992. *Women Transforming Politics: Worldwide Strategies for Empowerment.* Bloomington: Indiana University Press.

Bystydzienski, Jill M., ed. 1995. *Women in Electoral Politics: Lessons From Norway.* Westport, CT: Praeger.

Cahill, Spencer E. 1986. "Childhood Socialization as Recruitment Process: Some Lessons From the Study of Gender Development." Pp. 163–186 in *Sociological Studies of Child Development,* edited by P. Adler and P. Adler. Greenwich, CT: JAI Press.

Calasanti, Toni M. and Carol A. Bailey. 1991. "Gender Inequality and the Division of Household Labor in the United States and Sweden: A Socialist-Feminist Approach." *Social Problems* 38:34–53.

Caldwell, John C. 1986. "Routes to Low Mortality in Poor Countries." *Population and Development Review* 12:171–220.

Camp, Roderic A. 1998. "Women and Men, Men and Women: Gender Patterns in Mexican Politics." Pp. 167–178 in *Women's Participation in Mexican Political Life,* edited by Victoria E. Rodriguez. Boulder, CO: Westview Press.

Campbell, David and Christina Wolbrecht. 2006. "See Jane Run: Women Politicians as Role Models for Adolescents." *Journal of Politics* 68:233–247.

Cantor, Dorothy W., Toni Bernay, and Jean Stoess. 1992. *Women in Power: The Secrets of Leadership.* Boston: Houghton Mifflin.

Carey, J. M., R. G. Niemi, and L. W. Powell. 1998. "The Effects of Term Limits on State Legislatures." *Legislative Studies Quarterly* 23:271–300.

Carroll, Susan J. 1984. "Women Candidates and Support for Feminist Concerns: The Closet Feminist Syndrome." *Western Political Quarterly* 37:307–323.

Carroll, Susan J. 2002. "Representing Women: Congresswomen's Perceptions of Their Representational Roles." Pp. 50–68 in *Women Transforming Congress,* edited by Cindy Simon Rosenthal. Norman: University of Oklahoma Press.

Carroll, Susan J. and Debra L. Dodson. 1991. "Introduction." Pp. 1–11 in *Gender and Policymaking: Studies of Women in Office,* edited by D. L. Dodson. New Brunswick, NJ: Center for the American Woman and Politics.

Carroll, Susan J. and Krista Jenkins. 2001. "Do Term Limits Help Women Get Elected?" *Social Science Quarterly* 82:197–202.

Casas-Zamora, Kevin. 2005. "Political Finance Regulation in Guatemala: A Comparative Survey." IFES White Paper II. Available online at http://www.money andpolitics.net/researchpubs/pdf/Political_Finance_Guatemala.pdf.

Catt, Carrie C. 1918. "Do You Know? Voting Facts About Women." Washington, DC: Library of Congress, Rare Book and Special Collections Division, National American Woman Suffrage Association Collection.

Caul, Miki. 1999. "Women's Representation in Parliament: The Role of Political Parties." *Party Politics* 5(1):79–98.

Caul, Miki. 2001. "Political Parties and the Adoption of Candidate Gender Quotas: A Cross-National Analysis." *Journal of Politics* 63(4):1214–1229.

Celis, K. Sarah Childs, Johanna Kantola, and Mona Lena Krook. 2008. "Rethinking Women's Substantive Representation." *Representation* 44(2):113–124.

Center for American Women and Politics. 1997. *The Gender Gap: Attitudes on Public Policy Issues.* New Brunswick, NJ: Center for American Women and Politics.

Center for American Women and Politics (CAWP) is an outstanding reference for students of American women in politics. We drew from the data on their website and from many of their fact sheets in writing Chapter 10. We suggest that anyone interested in women in American politics bookmark CAWP's site (www.cawp .rutgers.edu) as an essential resource.

Center for American Women and Politics. 2001. *Women State Legislators: Past, Present, and Future.* New Brunswick, NJ: Center for American Women and Politics.

Center for American Women and Politics. 2004. *Gender Gap Persists in the 2004 Election.* New Brunswick, NJ: Center for American Women and Politics.

Center for American Women and Politics. 2005a. *The Gender Gap: Party Identification and Presidential Performance Ratings.* New Brunswick, NJ: Center for American Women and Politics.

Center for American Women and Politics. 2005b. *Sex Differences in Voter Turnout.* New Brunswick, NJ: Center for American Women and Politics.

Center for American Women and Politics. 2006. *Women Candidates for Governor 1970–2004: Major Party Nominees.* New Brunswick, NJ: Center for American Women and Politics.

Center for American Women and Politics. 2008. *Presidential Watch: Proportions of Women and Men Who Voted for Hillary Clinton in the Super Tuesday Races of February 5, 2008.* New Brunswick, NJ: Center for American Women and Politics.

Center for American Women and Politics. 2010. *Fact Sheet: Women in State Legislative Leadership Positions 2010.* New Brunswick, NJ: Center for American Women and Politics.

Center for American Women and Politics. 2011a. *Gender Differences in Voter Turnout.* Retrieved June 7, 2012 (http://www.cawp.rutgers.edu/fast_facts/voters/ documents/genderdiff.pdf).

Center for American Women and Politics. 2011b. *Sex Differences in Voter Turnout.* New Brunswick, NJ: Center for American Women and Politics.

Center for American Women and Politics. 2012a. *Fact Sheet: Statewide Elective Executive Women 2012.* New Brunswick, NJ: Center for American Women in Politics.

Center for American Women and Politics. 2012b. *Fact Sheet: Women of Color in Elective Office 2012: Congress, Statewide, State Legislature.* New Brunswick, NJ: Center for American Women and Politics.

Center for American Women and Politics. 2012c. *Fact Sheet: Women in State Legislatures 2012.* New Brunswick, NJ: Center for American Women and Politics.

Center for American Women and Politics. 2012d. *Women Mayors in U.S. Cities, 2012.* New Brunswick, NJ: Center for American Women and Politics.

Center for Reproductive Rights. 2004. "CEDAW: The Importance of U.S. Ratification." Item F021. Available online at http://www.reproductiverights.org/pub_fac_ cedaw.html.

Central Intelligence Agency. 2005. *The World Factbook.* Available online at http:// www.cia.gov/cia/publications/factbook/.

Central Intelligence Agency. 2006. "Chile." *CIA Factbook*. Available online at http://www.cia.gov/cia/publications/factbook/geos/ci.html.

Centre for Women's Research. 2009. "Status of Women." Retrieved May 31, 2012 (http://www.cenwor.lk/status_of_women.html).

Chafetz, Janet S. 1984. *Sex and Advantage: A Comparative Macro Structural Theory of Sex Stratification*. Totowa, NJ: Rowman and Allanheld.

Chafetz, Janet S. 1990. *Gender Equity: An Integrated Theory of Stability and Change*. Newbury Park, CA: Sage.

Chafetz, Janet S. and Anthony Gary Dworkin. 1986. *Female Revolt: Women's Movements in World and Historical Perspective*. Totowa, NJ: Rowman and Allanheld.

Chaney, Elsa. 1973. "Women in Latin American Politics: The Case of Peru and Chile." Pp. 104–139 in *Male and Female in Latin America*, edited by A. Pescatello. Pittsburgh, PA: University of Pittsburgh Press.

Channock, Martin. 1982. "Making Customary Law: Men, Women and Courts in Colonial Northern Rhodesia." Pp. 53–67 in *African Women and the Law: Historical Perspectives*, edited by M. J. Hay and M. Wright. Boston: Boston University.

Chari, A.V. 2011. *Gender, Social Norms and Voting: Female Turnout in Indian State Elections*. RAND Labor and Population Working Paper Series. Retrieved May 21, 2012 (http://www.rand.org/content/dam/rand/pubs/working_papers/2011/RAND_WR900.pdf).

Charrad, Mounira M. 2001. *States and Women's Rights: The Making of Postcolonial Tunisia, Algeria and Morocco*. Berkeley: University of California Press.

Charrad, Mounira M. 2009. "Kinship, Islam, or Oil: Culprits of Gender Inequality?" *Politics & Gender* 5(4):546–553.

Chattopadhyay, Raghabendra and Esther Duflo. 2004. "Women as Policy Makers: Evidence From a Randomized Policy Experiment in India." *Econometrica* 72:1409–1443.

Chazan, Naomi. 1989. "Gender Perspectives on African States." Pp. 185–201 in *Women and the State in Africa*, edited by J. L. Parpart and K. A. Staudt. Boulder, CO: Lynne Rienner.

Chen, Martha A. 1995. "Engendering World Conferences: The International Women's Movement and the United Nations." *Third World Quarterly* 16(3):477–495.

Childs, Sarah. 2002. "Hitting the Target: Are Labour Women MPs 'Acting for' Women?" *Parliamentary Affairs* 55:143–153.

Childs, Sarah and Mona Krook. 2005. "The Substantive Representation: Rethinking the 'Critical Mass' Debate." Paper presented at the American Political Science Association, September 1–4, Washington, DC.

Childs, Sarah and Julie Withey. 2004. "Women Representatives Acting for Women: Sex and the Signing of Early Day Motions in the 1997 British Parliament." *Political Studies* 52:552–564.

Chou, B. E. and J. Clark. 1994. "Electoral Systems and Women's Representation in Taiwan: The Impact of the Reserved-Seat System." Pp. 161–170 in *Electoral*

Systems in Comparative Perspective: Their Impact on Women and Minorities, edited by Wilma Rule and J. F. Zimmerman. Westport, CT: Greenwood.

Chowdhury, Najma. 2002. "The Implementation of Quotas: Bangladesh Experience— Dependence and Marginality in Politics." Paper presented at the regional workshop of the International Institute for Democracy and Electoral Assistance, November 11–12, Jakarta, Indonesia.

Christensen, Ray. 2000. "The Impact of Electoral Rules in Japan." Pp. 25–46 in *Democracy and the Status of Women in East Asia,* edited by R. J. Lee and C. Clark. Boulder, CO: Lynne Rienner.

Chubb, Catherine, Simone Melis, Louisa Potter, and Raymond Storry. 2008. *The Global Gender Pay Gap.* International Trade Union Confederation, February. Available online at http://www.ituc-csi.org/IMG/pdf/gap-1.pdf.

Chuchryk, Patricia. 1991. "Feminist Anti-Authoritarian Politics: The Role of Women's Organizations in the Chilean Transition to Democracy." Pp. 149–184 in *The Women's Movement in Latin America: Feminism and the Transition to Democracy,* edited by Jane S. Jaquette. Boulder, CO: Westview Press.

Cillizza, Chris. 2005. "Emily's List Celebrates Clout as It Turns 20: Pro-Abortion-Rights Candidates Championed." *The Washington Post,* October 18, p. A13.

Cingranelli, David L. and David L. Richards. 2004a. *The Cingranelli-Richards (CIRI) Human Rights Database Coder Manual.* Manual Version 8.01.04. Available online at http://ciri.binghamton.edu/documentation/web_version_7_31_04_ciri_coding_guide.pdf#search=%22The%20Cingranelli-Richards%20coder%20manual%22.

Cingranelli, David L. and David L. Richards. 2004b. *The Cingranelli-Richards (CIRI) Human Rights Dataset.* Available online at www.humanrightsdata.org.

Clift, Eleanor. 2003. *Founding Sisters and the Nineteenth Amendment.* Hoboken, NJ: Wiley & Sons.

Coalition on Revival. 1999. *The Christian Worldview of the Family.* Available online at www.reformation.net/cor/cordocs/family.pdf.

Cockburn, Cynthia. 1998. *The Space Between Us: Negotiating Gender and National Identities in Conflict.* New York: Zed Books.

Cole, Judith K. 1990. "A Wide Field for Usefulness: Women's Civil Status and the Evolution of Women's Suffrage on the Montana Frontier, 1864–1914." *American Journal of Legal History* 34:262–294.

Coleman, Isobel. 2011. "Is the Arab Spring Bad for Women?" Overthrowing Male Dominance Could Be Harder Than Overthrowing a Dictator." *Foreign Policy,* December 20. Retrieved May 30, 2012 (http://www.foreignpolicy.com/articles/2011/12/20/arab_spring_women?page=full).

Collins, Patricia H. 2000. *Black Feminist Thought: Knowledge, Consciousness and the Politics of Empowerment.* New York: HarperCollins.

Commonwealth Secretariat. 1999. *Women in Politics: Voices From the Commonwealth.* London: Commonwealth Secretariat.

Connell, R. W. 1987. *Gender and Power: Society, the Person, and Sexual Politics.* Cambridge, MA: Polity.

Conover, Pamela Johnston. 1988. "Feminists and the Gender Gap." *Journal of Politics* 50:985–1010.

Conover, Pamela Johnston and Virginia Gray. 1983. *Feminism and the New Right: Conflict Over the American Family.* New York: Praeger.

Cook, Rebecca J. 1994. "State Accountability Under the Convention on the Elimination of All Forms of Discrimination Against Women." Pp. 228–256 in *Human Rights of Women: National and International Perspectives,* edited by R. J. Cook. Philadelphia: University of Pennsylvania Press.

Coole, Diana H. 1988. *Women in Political Theory: From Ancient Misogyny to Contemporary Feminism.* Sussex, UK: Wheatsheaf Books.

Corder, Kevin and Christina Wolbrecht. 2006. "Political Context and the Turnout of New Women Voters after Suffrage." *Journal of Politics* 68(1):34–49.

Cornwall, Marie, Eric C. Dahlin, and Brayden G. King. 2005. "Mobilization, Strategies, and Elite Support: An Institutionalist Analysis of State-Level Woman Suffrage Movement Outcomes." Unpublished manuscript.

Cosgrove, Serena. 2010. *Leadership From the Margins: Women and Civil Society Organizations in Argentina, Chile, and El Salvador.* New Brunswick, NJ: Rutgers University Press.

Costa, Paul T., Jr., Antonio Terracciano, and Robert R. McCrae. 2001. "Gender Differences in Personality Traits Across Cultures: Robust and Surprising Findings." *Journal of Personality and Social Psychology* 81:322–331.

Crabtree, Steve. 2012. "Gender Gap in Obama Approval Constant Since Term Began." *Gallup,* May 9. Available online at http://www.gallup.com/poll/154562/gender-gap-obama-approval-constant-term-began.aspx.

Craske, Nikki. 1999. *Women and Politics in Latin America.* New Brunswick, NJ: Rutgers University Press.

Crenshaw, Kimberlé W. 1989. "Demarginalizing the Intersection of Race and Sex: A Black Feminist Critique of Antidiscrimination Doctrine, Feminist Theory and Antiracist Politics." *University of Chicago Legal Forum* 139–167.

Crenshaw, Kimberlé W. 1991. "Mapping the Margins: Intersectionality, Identity, Politics and Violence Against Women of Color." *Stanford Law Review* 43: 1241–1299.

Crenshaw, Kimberlé W. 1994. "Mapping the Margins: Intersectionality, Identity Politics, and Violence Against Women of Color." Pp. 93–118 in *The Public Nature of Private Violence,* edited by M. A. Fineman and R. Mykitiuk. New York: Routledge.

Czudnowski, Moshe M. 1975. "Political Recruitment." Pp. 155–242 in *Handbook of Political Science: Micropolitical Theory,* vol. 2, edited by F. I. Greenstein and N. W. Polsby. Reading, MA: Addison Wesley.

D'Amico, Francine. 1995. "Women National Leaders." Pp. 15–30 in *Women in World Politics: An Introduction,* edited by Francine D'Amico and Peter R. Beckman. London: Bergin and Garvey.

D'Amico, Francine and Peter R. Beckman, eds. 1995. *Women in World Politics: An Introduction.* London: Bergin and Garvey.

D'Itri, Patricia Ward. 1999. *Cross Currents in the International Women's Movement, 1848–1948.* Bowling Green, OH: Bowling Green University Popular Press.

Dahlerup, Drude. 1988. "From a Small to a Large Minority: Women in Scandinavian Politics. *Scandinavian Political Studies* 11:275–298.

Dahlerup, Drude. 2002. "Using Quotas to Increase Women's Political Representation." Pp. 91–106 in *Women in Parliament: Beyond Numbers,* edited by A. Karam. Stockholm, Sweden: IDEA.

Dahlerup, Drude. 2003. "Quotas Are Changing the History of Women." Paper presented at an International Institute for Democracy and Electoral Assistance conference, November 11–13, Pretoria, South Africa.

Dahlerup, Drude and Lenita Freidenvall. 2005. "Quotas as a 'Fast Track' to Equal Representation for Women." *International Feminist Journal of Politics* 7:26–48.

Dahlerup, Drude and Lenita Freidenvall with the Assistance of Eleonora Stolt, Katarina Bivald and Lene Persson-Weiss. 2008. "Electoral Gender Quota Systems and Their Implementation in Europe." Directorate General Internal Policies of the Union. PE 408.309. Brussels: European Parliament.

Dahlerup, Drude and Anja Taarup Nordlund. 2004. "Gender Quotas: A Key to Equality? A Case Study of Iraq and Afghanistan." *European Political Science* 3:91–98.

Darcy, R. and James R. Choike. 1986. "A Formal Analysis of Legislative Turnover: Women Candidates and Legislative Representation." *American Journal of Political Science* 30:237–255.

Darcy, R. and Charles D. Hadley. 1988. "Black Women in Politics: The Puzzle of Success." *Social Science Quarterly* 69:629–645.

Darcy, R., Susan Welch, and Janet Clark. 1994. *Women, Elections, and Representation.* Lincoln, NE: University of Nebraska Press.

Das, Soumitra. 2012. "Siswa Grampanchayat's Powerpuff Girls." *The Times of India,* January 8. Retrieved June 3, 2012 (http://articles.timesofindia.indiatimes .com/2012-01-08/people/30604104_1_samras-panchayat-meeting-woman-sar-panch).

Davis, Kathy. 2008. "Intersectionality as Buzzword: A Sociology of Science Perspective on What Makes a Feminist Theory Successful. *Feminist Theory* 9(1):67–85.

Davis, Rebecca. 1997. *Women and Power in Parliamentary Democracies: Cabinet Appointments in Western Europe, 1968–1992.* Lincoln: University of Nebraska Press.

Day, Lynda R. 1994. "The Evolution of Female Chiefship During the Late Nineteenth-Century Wars of the Mende." *The International Journal of African Historical Studies* 27:481–503.

de Figueres, Karen Olsen. 2002. "A People Marching-Women in Parliament in Costa Rica." Available online at http://archive.idea.int/women/parl/studies3a.htm.

del Carmen Feijoo, M. and M. Gogna. 1990. "Women in the Transition to Democracy." Pp. 79–114 in *Women and Social Change in Latin America,* edited by E. Jelin. London: Zed Books.

Dempsey, Judy and Nicholas Kulish. 2011. "With Strong Leadership Demanded, Merkel Waits and Sees," *The New York Times,* August 15. Available online at

http://www.nytimes.com/2011/08/16/world/europe/16iht-merke116.html?
    pagewanted=all.

Denich, Bogdan. 1981. "Women and Political Power in a Revolutionary Society: The
    Yugoslav Case." Pp. 115–123 in *Access to Power: Cross-National Studies of
    Women and Elites,* edited by C. F. Epstein and R. L. Coser. London: George Allen
    & Unwin.

Deveaux, Monique. 2000. "Conflicting Inequalities? Cultural Groups and Sex
    Equalities." *Political Studies* 48(3):522–538.

Deveaux, Monique. 2005. "A Deliberative Approach to Conflicts of Culture." In
    Minorities Within Minorities: Equality, Rights and Diversity, edited by Avigail
    Eisenberg and Jeff Spinner-Halev. Cambridge, UK: Cambridge University Press.

Devlin, Claire, and Roger Elgie. 2008. "The Effect of Increased Women's Representation
    in Parliament: The Case of Rwanda." *Parliamentary Affairs* 61(2):237–254.

Diamond, Irene. 1977. *Sex Roles in the Statehouse.* New Haven, CT: Yale University Press.

Disney, Jennifer Leigh. 2006. "Mozambique: Empowering Women Through Family
    Law." Pp. 31–57 in *Women in African Parliaments,* edited by G. Bauer and H.
    Britton. London: Lynne Rienner.

Dodson, Debra L. 1997. "Change and Continuity in the Relationship Between Private
    Responsibilities and Public Officeholding: The More Things Change, the More
    They Stay the Same." *Policy Studies Journal* 25(4):569–584.

Doi, Ayako. 2003. "Japan's Hybrid Women." *Foreign Policy,* November 1. Retrieved
    June 1, 2012 (http://www.foreignpolicy.com/articles/2003/11/01/japans_hybrid_
    women?page=full).

Dolan, Kathleen. 1997. "Support for Women's Interests in the 103rd Congress: The
    Distinct Impact of Congressional Women." *Women and Politics* 18:81–94.

Dolan, Kathleen. 1998. "Voting for Women in the 'Year of the Woman.'" *American
    Journal of Political Science* 42:272–293.

Donahoe, Debra Anne. 1999. "Measuring Work in Developing Countries." *Population
    and Development Review* 25:543–576.

Donald, Isabelle, Jane Strachan, and Hilda Taleo. 2002. "Slo Slo: Increasing Women's
    Representation in Parliament in Vanuatu." *Development Bulletin* 59:54–57.

Dowd, Maureen. 1991. "7 Congresswomen March to Senate to Demand Delay in
    Thomas Vote," *The New York Times,* October 9, p. A1.

Dubeck, Paula J. 1976. "Women and Access to Political Office: A Comparison of
    Female and Male State Legislators." *Sociological Quarterly* 17(1):42–52.

DuBois, Ellen C. 1998. *Women's Suffrage and Women's Rights.* New York: New York
    University Press.

Duerst-Lahti, Georgia. 1997. "Reconceiving Theories of Power: Consequences of
    Masculinism in the Executive Branch." Pp. 11–32 in *The Other Elites: Women,
    Politics, and Power in the Executive Branch,* edited by M. A. Borrelli and J. M.
    Martin. Boulder, CO: Lynne Rienner.

Duflo, Esther and Petia Topalova. 2004. "Unappreciated Service: Performance,
    Perceptions, and Women Leaders in India." Working Paper. Retrieved May 14,
    2012 (poverty-action.org/sites/default/files/unappreciated.pdf).

Dutton, M. A. 1992. *Empowering and Healing the Battered Woman*. New York: Springer.

Duverger, Maurice. 1955. *The Political Role of Women*. Paris: UNESCO.

Eagly, Alice H. and Mary C. Johannesen-Schmidt. 2001. "The Leadership Styles of Women and Men." *Journal of Social Issues* 57:781–797.

Eagly, Alice H. and B. T. Johnson. 1990. "Gender and Leadership Style: A Meta-Analysis." *Psychological Bulletin* 108:233–256.

Eagly, Alice H. and S. J. Karau. 2002. "Role Congruity Theory of Prejudice Toward Female Leaders." *Psychological Review* 109:573–598.

Eagly, Alice H., M. G. Makhijani, and B. G. Klonsky. 1992. "Gender and the Evaluation of Leaders: A Meta-Analysis." *Psychological Bulletin* 111:3–22.

The Economist. 2002. "Rape Laws: Crime and Clarity." Retrieved September 2, 2012. Available online at www.economist.com/node/21561883.

Ehrick, Christine. 1998. "Madrinas and Missionaries: Uruguay and the Pan-American Women's Movement." *Gender and History* 10:406–424.

Einhorn, Barbara. 1991. "Where Have All the Women Gone? Women and the Women's Movement in East Central Europe." *Feminist Review* 39(Autumn):16–36.

Einhorn, Barbara. 1992. "German Democratic Republic: Emancipated Women or Hardworking Mothers?" Pp. 125–54 in *Superwoman and the Double Burden,* edited by C. Corrin. London: Scarlet Press.

Ellina, Chrystalla A. 2003. *Promoting Women's Rights: The Politics of Gender in the European Union*. New York: Routledge.

EMILY's List. 2012. "Emily's List." Available online at http://www.emilyslist.org.

EMILY's List Australia. 2005. "Welcome to EMILY's List Australia." Available online at http://www.emilyslist.org.au/.

Employment Equity Act, S.C. 1995, c. 44. (Canada).

England, Paula, Marilyn Chassie, and Linda McCormack. 1982. "Skill Demands and Earnings in Female and Male Occupations." *Sociology and Social Research* 66:147–168.

Enloe, Cynthia. 1980. "Women as the Reserve Army of Labor." *Review of Radical Political Economics* 12(Summer):42–52.

Enloe, Cynthia. 1987. "Feminist Thinking about War, Militarism, and Peace." Pp. 526–547 in *Analyzing Gender: A Handbook of Social Science Research,* edited by Beth B. Hess and Myra Marx Ferree. Newbury Park, CA: Sage.

Equality Now. 2001. "Kuwait: The Struggle for Women's Suffrage." January 1. Available online at www.equalitynow.org/node/230.

Escobar-Lemmon, Maria and Michelle M. Taylor-Robinson. 2005. "Women Ministers in Latin American Government: When, Where, and Why?" *American Journal of Political Science* 49(4):829–844.

Escobar-Lemmon, Maria and Michelle M. Taylor-Robinson. 2008. "How Do Candidate Recruitment and Selection Processes Affect Representation of Women?" Pp. 343–368 *Pathways to Power: Political Recruitment and Candidate Selection in Latin America,* edited by Peter M. Siavelis and Scott Morgenstern. University Park, PA: Penn State University Press.

Escobar-Lemmon, Maria and Michelle M. Taylor-Robinson. 2009. "Getting to the Top Career Paths of Women in Latin American Cabinets." *Political Research Quarterly* 62(4):685–699.

Etienne, Mona. 1980. "Women and Men, Cloth and Colonization: The Transformation of Production-Distribution Relations among the Baule (Ivory Coast)." Pp. 518–535 in *Women and Colonization: Anthropological Perspectives,* edited by M. Etienne and E. Leacock. New York: Praeger.

European Forum. 2008. "Short Analysis of the Slovenia General Elections From the Gender Point of View." Retrieved June 8, 2012 (http://www.europeanforum.net/news/497/short_analysis_of_the_slovenia_general_elections_from_the_gender_point_of_view).

Everett, Jana. 1993. "Indira Gandhi and the Exercise of Power." Pp. 103–134 in *Women as National Leaders,* edited by M. A. Genovese. Newbury Park, CA: Sage.

Ewig, C. 1999. "The Strengths and Limits of the NGO Women's Movement Model: Shaping Nicaragua's Democratic Institutions." *Latin American Research Review* 34(3):75–102.

Fallon, Kathleen M. 2008. *Democracy and the Rise of Women's Movements in Sub-Saharan Africa.* Baltimore: Johns Hopkins University Press.

Fallon, Kathleen M., Liam Swiss, and Jocelyn Viterna. 2012. "Resolving the Democracy Paradox: Democratization and Women's Legislative Representation in Developing Nations, 1975 to 2009." *American Sociological Review* 77(3): 380–408.

"Finnish Women." 1911. *Dawson Daily News,* March 22. Available online at http://www.explorenorth.com/library/vignettes/bl-FinnWomen1911.htm.

Firebaugh, Glenn and Kevin Chen. 1995. "Vote Turnout of Nineteenth Amendment Women: The Enduring Effect of Disenfranchisement." *American Journal of Sociology* 100(4):972–996.

Fischer, Audrey. 1994. "Winning the Vote for Women." *Library of Congress Information Bulletin,* April 15. Available online at http://www.loc.gov/loc/lcib/9607/suffrage.html.

Fisher, J. 1989. *Mothers of the Disappeared.* London: Zed Books.

Fleschenberg, Andrea. 2008. "Asia's Women Politicians at the Top: Roaring Tigresses or Tame Kittens?" Pp. 23–54 in *Women's Political Participation and Representation in Asia,* edited by Kazuki Iwanaga. Copenhagen: Nordic Institute of Asian Studies.

Flexner, Eleanor. 1975. *Century of Struggle: The Woman's Rights Movement in the United States.* Cambridge, MA: Belknap Press.

Fodor, Eva. 2002. "Smiling Women and Fighting Men: The Gender of the Communist Subject in State Socialist Hungary." *Gender and Society* 16(2): 240–263.

Food and Agriculture Organization. 2003. *One Woman's Day in Sierra Leone.* Available online at http://www.fao.org/NEWS/FACTFILE/FF9719-E.HTM.

Fox, Richard L. and Jennifer L. Lawless. 2004. "Entering the Arena? Gender and the Decision to Run for Office." *American Journal of Political Science* 48:264–280.

Fox, Richard L. and Jennifer L. Lawless. 2010. "If Only They'd Ask: Gender, Recruitment, and Political Ambition." *Journal of Politics* 72(2):310–326.

Fox, Richard L. and Jennifer L. Lawless. 2011. "Gendered Perceptions and Political Candidacies: A Central Barrier to Women's Equality in Electoral Politics." *American Journal of Political Science* 55(1):59–73.

Fraga, Luis Ricardo, Valerie Martinez-Ebers, Linda Lopez, and Ricardo Ramírez. 2008. "Representing Gender and Ethnicity: Strategic Intersectionality." Pp. 157–174 in *Legislative Women: Getting Elected, Getting Ahead,* edited by Beth Reingold. Boulder, CO: Lynne Rienner.

Franceschet, Susan. 2001. "Women in Politics in Post-Transitional Democracies: The Chilean Case." *International Feminist Journal of Politics* 3:207–236.

Franceschet, Susan. 2005. *Women and Politics in Chile.* Boulder, CO: Lynne Rienner.

Franceschet, Susan, and Jennifer M. Piscopo. 2008. "Gender Quotas and Women's Substantive Representation: Lessons from Argentina." *Politics & Gender* 4(3): 393–425.

Franceschet, Susan and Jennifer M. Piscopo. Forthcoming. "Sustaining Gendered Practices? Power, Parties, and Elite Political Networks in Argentina." *Comparative Political Studies.*

Franklin, Mark, Patrick Lyons, and Michael Marsh. 2004. "Generational Basis of Turnout Decline in Established Democracies." *Acta Politica* 39(2):115–151.

Fréchette, Guillaume R., Francois Maniquet, and Massimo Morelli. 2008. "Incumbents' Interests and Gender Quota." *American Journal of Political Science* 52(4):891–907.

Freedman, Jane. 2004. "Secularism as a Barrier to Integration: The French Dilemma." *International Migration* 42(3):5–27.

Freedom House. 2012. *Freedom in the World 2012: The Arab Uprisings and Their Global Repercussions.* Washington, DC: Freedom House.

Freeman, Jo. 1987. "Feminist Influence in the Democratic and Republican Parties." Pp. 215–244 in *The Women's Movements of the United States and Western Europe: Feminist Consciousness, Political Opportunity and Public Policy,* edited by M. C. M. Katzenstein. Philadelphia, PA: Temple University Press.

Freidenvall, Lenita. 2003. "Women's Political Representation and Gender Quotas— The Swedish Case." *Stockholm Working Paper Series* 2. Stockholm, Sweden: Stockholm University.

Freidenvall, Lenita. 2010. "Intersectionalising Representation: Ethnicity, Gender and Political Representation in Multicultural Europe." Working Paper No. 1. Femcit. Retrieved June 8, 2012 (http://www.femcit.org/files/WP1_WorkingpaperN01 .pdf.).

French, Marilyn. 1992. *The War Against Women.* New York: Summit Books.

Friedman, Elisabeth J. 1998. "Paradoxes of Gendered Political Opportunity in the Venezuelan Transition to Democracy." *Latin American Research Review* 33:87–135.

Friedman, Elisabeth J. 2000. "State-Based Advocacy for Gender Equality in the Developing World: Assessing the Venezuelan National Women's Agency." *Women and Politics* 21:47–80.

Friedman, Elisabeth J. 2003. "Gendering the Agenda: The Impact of the Transnational Women's Rights Movement at the UN Conferences of the 1990s." *Women's Studies International Forum* 26(4):313–331.

Furlong, Marlea and Kimberly Riggs. 1996. "Women's Participation in National-Level Politics and Government: The Case of Costa Rica." *Women's Studies International Forum* 19:633–643.

Furnham, Adrian, and Richard Rawles. 1995. "Sex Differences in the Estimation of Intelligence." *Journal of Social Behavior and Personality* 10:741–748.

Gaddie, Ronald Keith and Charles S. Bullock III. 1997. "Structural and Elite Features in Open Seat and Special U.S. House Elections: Is There a Sexual Bias?" *Political Research Quarterly* 50:459–468.

Gal, Susan and Gail Kligman. 2000. *The Politics of Gender after Socialism: A Comparative Historical Essay*. Princeton, NJ: Princeton University Press.

Gallagher, Michael and Michael Marsh, eds. 1988. *Candidate Selection in Comparative Perspective: The Secret Garden of Politics*. Beverly Hills, CA: Sage.

Gamson, William A. 1990. *The Strategy of Social Protest*. Belmont, CA: Wadsworth.

García Bedolla, Lisa. 2007. "Intersections of Inequality: Understanding Marginalization and Privilege in the Post-Civil Rights Era." *Politics & Gender* 3(2):232–248.

Gardner, Catherine Villanueva. 2006. *Historical Dictionary of Feminist Philosophy*. London: Scarecrow Press.

Gay, Claudine and Katherine Tate. 1998. "Doubly Bound: The Impact of Gender and Race on the Politics of Black Women." *Political Psychology* 19:169–184.

Geisler, Gisela. 1995. "Troubled Sisterhood: Women and Politics in Southern Africa: Case Studies From Zambia, Zimbabwe, and Botswana." *African Affairs* 94: 545–578.

General Accounting Office. 2003. "Women's Earnings: Word Patterns Partially Explain Differences Between Men's and Women's Earnings." Washington, DC: General Accounting Office.

Genovese, Michael A., ed. 1993. *Women as National Leaders*. Newbury Park, CA: Sage.

Gerami, Shahin. 1996. *Women and Fundamentalism: Islam and Christianity*. New York: Garland.

Gerami, Shahin and Melodye Lehnerer. 2001. "Women's Agency and Household Diplomacy: Negotiating Fundamentalism." *Gender and Society* 15:556–573.

Gerrity, Jessica C., Tracy Osborn, and Jeanette Morehouse Mendez. 2007. "Women and Representation: A Different View of the District?" *Politics & Gender* 3: 179–200.

Geschichte-Schweiz. 2004. "Switzerland's Long Way to Women's Right to Vote." Retrieved June 12, 2007 (http://history-switzerland.geschichte-schweiz.ch/chronology -womens-right-vote-switzerland.html).

Giddings, Paula. 1996. *When and Where I Enter: The Impact of Black Women on Race and Sex in America*. New York: Quill William Morrow.

Gidengil, Elisabeth and Joanna Everitt. 2003. "Tough Talk: How Television News Covers Male and Female Leaders of Canadian Political Parties." in *Women and*

Electoral Politics in Canada, edited by Manon Tremblay and Linda Trimble. Toronto: Oxford University Press.

Giele, J. Z. and A. C. Smock, eds. 1977. *Women, Roles, and Status in Eight Countries.* New York: Wiley and Sons.

Glaser, Kurt and Stefan T. Possony. 1979. *Victims of Politics: The State of Human Rights.* New York: Columbia University Press.

Glenn, Evelyn N. 1999. "The Social Construction of Institutionalization of Gender and Race: An Integrative Framework." Pp. 3–43 in *Revisioning Gender,* edited by M. M. Ferree, J. Lorber, and B. B. Hess.

Goetz, Anne Marie. 1995. "The Politics of Integrating Gender to State Development Processes: Trends, Opportunities and Constraints in Bangladesh, Chile, Jamaica, Mali, Morocco, and Uganda." Occasional Paper #2, Fourth World Conference on Women. Geneva, Switzerland: United Nations Research Institute for Social Development.

Goetz, Anne Marie. 2003. "Women's Political Effectiveness: A Conceptual Framework." Pp. 29–80 in *No Shortcuts to Power: African Women in Politics and Policy-Making,* edited by A. M. Goetz and S. Hassim. London: Zed Books.

Goetz, Anne Marie and Shireen Hassim, eds. 2003. *No Shortcuts to Power: African Women in Politics and Policy Making.* London: Zed Books.

Goldman, Nancy, ed. 1982. *Female Soldiers—Combatants or Noncombatants? Historical and Contemporary Perspectives.* Westport, CT: Greenwood.

Goldstein, Joshua S. 2001. *War and Gender: How Gender Shapes the War System and Vice Versa.* Cambridge, UK: Cambridge University Press.

Goot, Murray and Elizabeth Reid. 1975. *Women and Voting Studies: Mindless Matrons or Sexist Scientism.* Beverly Hills, CA: Sage.

Gordon, Rosemary. 1998. "'Girls Cannot Think as Boys Do': Socialising Children Through the Zimbabwe School System." *Gender and Development* 6:53–58.

Goulding, Kristine. 2010. "The Quandary of Gender Quotas in Tunisia: Representations and Perceptions at the Local Level." Retrieved May 29, 2012 (http://www.womenpoliticalparticipation.org/upload/file/the%20Quandary%20of%20Gender%20Quotas%20in%20Tunisia_web%20site.pdf).

Goven, Joanna. 1993. "Gender Politics in Hungary: Autonomy and Anti-Feminism." Pp. 224–240 in *Gender Politics and Post-Communism: Reflections From Eastern Europe and the Soviet Union,* edited by N. Funk and M. Mueller. New York: Routledge.

Gray, Tricia J. 2003. "Electoral Gender Quotas: Lessons From Argentina and Chile." *Bulletin of Latin American Research* 22:52–78.

Grenfell, Laura A. 2004. "Paths to Transitional Justice for Afghan Women." *Nordic Journal of International Law* 73(4):505–534.

Grey, Sandra. 2002. "Does Size Matter? Critical Mass and New Zealand's Women MPs." *Parliamentary Affairs* 55:19–29.

Gronlund, Paula. 2003. "Women Members of Finland's Parliament." Available online at http://www.eduskunta.fi/efakta/opas/tiedotus/naisede.htm.

Guttenbeil-Likiliki, Ofa. 2006. "Report 4: Advancing Women's Representation in Tonga." Pp. 143–208 in *A Woman's Place is in the House*. Suva, Fiji: Pacific Islands Forum Secretariat.

Haavio-Mannila, Elina and Torild Skard, eds. 1985. *Unfinished Democracy: Women in Nordic Politics*. Oxford, UK: Pergamon Press.

Hadassah. 2004. "Focus On: Women's Rights Worldwide." Available online at http://www.hadassah.org/news/content/per_american/archive/2004/04summer/focus.html.

Hale, Sondra. 2001. *Liberated, But Not Free: Women in Post-War Eritrea*. London: Zed Books.

Halsall, Paul. 1997. "Modern History Sourcebook: Sojourner Truth: 'Ain't I a Woman?' December 1851." Fordham University. Available online at http://www.fordham.edu/halsall/mod/sojtruth-woman.asp.

Hamburg, Cambria G. 2008. "Prohibited Spaces: Barriers and Strategies in Women's NGO Work in Isaan, Northeastern Thailand." Pp. 95–124 in Women and Politics in Thailand: Continuity and Change, edited by Kazuki Iwanaga. Copenhagen: Nordic Institute of Asian Studies.

Hancock, Ange-Marie. 2005. "When Multiplication Doesn't Equal Quick Addition: Examining Intersectionality as a Research Paradigm." Paper presented at the annual meeting of the American Political Science Association, September 1–4, Washington, DC.

Hannagan, Rebecca J., Jamie P. Pimlott, and Levente Littvay. 2010. "Does an EMILY's List Endorsement Predict Electoral Success, or Does EMILY Pick the Winners?" *PS: Political Science and Politics* 43:503–508.

Hannam, June, Mitzi Auchterlonie, and Katherine Holden. 2000. *International Encyclopedia of Women's Suffrage*. Santa Barbara, CA: ABC-CLIO.

Hansen, Karen V. 1994. *A Very Social Time: Crafting Community in Antebellum New England*. Berkeley: University of California Press.

Harris, Kenneth. 1995. "Prime Minister Margaret Thatcher: The Influence of Her Gender on Her Foreign Policy." Pp. 59–70 in *Women in World Politics: An Introduction*, edited by F. D'Amico and P. R. Beckman. London: Burgin and Garvey.

Haskova, Hana and Alena Krizkova. 2008. "The Impact of EU Accession on the Promotion of Women and Gender Equality in the Czech Republic." Pp. 155–173 in *Gender Politics in the Expanding European Union: Mobilization, Inclusion, Exclusion*, edited by Silke Roth. New York: Berghahn Books.

Haub, Carl and Diana Cornelius. 2000. *2000 World Population Data Sheet*. Washington, DC: Population Reference Bureau.

Hawkesworth, Mary, Kathleen J. Casey, Krista Jenkins, and Katherine E. Kleeman. 2001. *Legislating by and for Women: A Comparison of the 103rd and 104th Congresses*. New Brunswick, NJ: Center for the American Woman and Politics.

Hayward, Clarissa R. 2000. *De-Facing Power*. Cambridge, UK: Cambridge University Press.

Heath, Roseanna Michelle, Leslie A. Schwindt-Bayer, and Michelle M. Taylor-Robinson. 2005. "Women on the Sidelines: Women's Representation on

Committees in Latin American Legislatures." *American Journal of Political Science* 49:420–436.

Heckscher, Gunnar. 1984. *The Welfare State and Beyond: Success and Problems in Scandinavia.* Minneapolis: University of Minnesota Press.

Hegel, Georg. [1821] 1977. "The Philosophy of Right." Pp. 161–170 in *History of Ideas on Women: A Source Book,* edited by R. Agonito. New York: G. P. Putnam's Sons.

Heleta, Vanessa. 2008. "Women's Rights in the Backburner?" *FOCUS* 51. Asia-Pacific Human Rights Information Center. Retrieved May 14, 2012 (www.hurights. or.jp/archives/focus/section2/2008/03/womens-rights-in-the-backburner.html).

Helferrich, Barbara and Felix Kolb. 2001. "Multilevel Action Coordination in European Contentious Politics: The Case of the European Women's Lobby." Pp.143–161 in *Contentious Europeans: Protest and Politics in an Emerging Polity,* edited by Doug Imig and Sidney Tarrow. Lanham, MD: Rowman and Littlefield.

Hellmann-Rajanayagam, Dagmar. 2008. "The Living Sacrafice . . . ? Heroes, Victims, and Martyrs." Pp. 206–231 in *Goddesses, Heroes, Sacrifices: Female Political Power in Asia,* edited by Dagmar Hellmann-Rajanayagam and Andrea Fleschenberg. Berlin: LIT.

Henig, Ruth and Simon Henig. 2001. *Women and Political Power: Europe Since 1945.* London: Routledge.

Henley, Jon. 2011. "Angela Merkel: Europe's Savior—or Biggest Problem?" *The Guardian,* November 22. Available online at http://www.guardian.co.uk/world/2011/nov/22/is-angela-merkel-europes-problem.

Hernández Castillo, R. Aída. 2010. "The Emergence of Indigenous Feminism in Latin America." *Signs: Journal of Women in Culture and Society* 35(3):539–545.

Hiers, Cheryl. 2004. "The Nineteenth Amendment and the War of the Roses." Available online at http://www.blueshoenashville.com/suffragehistory.html.

High-Pippert, Angela and John Comer. 1998. "Female Empowerment: The Influence of Women Representing Women." *Women and Politics* 19(4):53–66.

Hill, David B. 1981. "Political Culture and Female Political Representation." *Journal of Politics* 43:159–168.

Hill, Felicity, Mikele Aboitiz, and Sara Poehlman-Doumbouya. 2003. "Nongovernmental Organizations' Role in the Buildup and Implementation of Security Council Resolution 1325." *Signs* 28(4):1255–1269.

Hinojosa, Magda and Susan Franceschet. Forthcoming. "Separate but Not Equal: The Effects of Municipal Electoral Reform on Female Representation in Chile." *Political Research Quarterly.*

Hochschild, Arlie. 1989. *The Second Shift: Working Parents and the Revolution at Home.* New York: Viking.

Hoff, Joan. 1985. "Gallant Warrior for Peace." Paper presented at the dedication of the Jeannette Rankin's Statue May 1, Washington, DC.

Hogan, Robert E. 2001. "Campaign Spending by Men and Women Candidates for the State Legislature." Paper presented at the annual meeting of the American Political Science Association, August 29–September 2, San Francisco, CA.

Holmsten, Stephanie S., Robert G. Moser, and Mary C. Slosar. 2010. "Do Ethnic Parties Exclude Women?" *Comparative Political Studies* 43(10):1179–1201.

Holt, Renee. 1991. "Women's Rights and International Law: The Struggle for Recognition and Enforcement." *Columbia Journal of Gender and Law* 1:117–141.

hooks, bell. 1981. *Ain't I a Woman: Black Women and Feminism.* Boston: South End Press.

hooks, bell. 2000. *Feminist Theory: From Margin to Center.* 2nd ed. Boston: South End Press.

Horton, Susan. 1995. *Women and Industrialization in Asia.* New York: Routledge.

Howell, Jude. 2008. "Gender and Rural Governance in China." Pp. 55–80 in *Women's Political Participation and Representation in Asia,* edited by Kazuki Iwanaga. Copenhagen: Nordic Institute of Asian Studies.

Htun, Mala. 2003. *Sex and the State: Abortion, Divorce, and the Family under Latin American Dictatorships and Democracies.* New York: Cambridge University Press.

Htun, Mala. 2005. "Women, Political Parties and Electoral Systems in Latin America." Pp. 112–121 in *Women in Parliament. Beyond Numbers. A New Edition,* edited by Julie Ballington and Azza Karam. Stockholm: International IDEA.

Htun, Mala. 2012. *Intersectional Disadvantage and Political Inclusion: Getting More Afrodescendant Women Into Elected Office in Latin America.* Washington, DC: Inter-American Development Bank.

Htun, Mala and Mark P. Jones. 2002. "Engendering the Right to Participate in Decision-Making: Electoral Quotas and Women's Leadership in Latin America." Pp. 32–56 in *Gender and the Politics of Rights and Democracy in Latin America,* edited by N. Craske and M. Molyneux. Houndmills, UK: Palgrave.

Htun, Mala and Jennifer M. Piscopo. 2010. "Presence Without Empowerment? Women in Politics in Latin America and the Caribbean." Prepared for the Conflict Prevention and Peace Forum, December 1.

Htun, Mala and Timothy J. Power. 2006. "Gender, Parties, and the Support for Equal Rights in the Brazilian Congress." *Latin American Politics and Society* 48(4): 83–104.

Htun, Mala and S. Laurel Weldon. 2012. "The Civic Origins of Progressive Policy Change: Violence Against Women in Global Perspective." *American Political Science Review* 106(3):548–569.

Hughes, Melanie. 2004. "Armed Conflict, International Linkages, and Women's Parliamentary Representation in Developing Nations." *Social Problems* 56: 174–204.

Hughes, Melanie M. 2005. "The Continuing Importance of History: The Residual Effects of Colonialism on Women's Parliamentary Participation." Paper presented at the 100th American Sociological Association Annual Meeting, August 13–16, Philadelphia, PA.

Hughes, Melanie M. 2007. "Windows of Political Opportunity: Institutional Instability and Gender Inequality in the World's National Legislatures." *International Journal of Sociology* 37(4):26–51.

Hughes, Melanie M. 2009a. "Armed Conflict, International Linkages, and Women's Parliamentary Representation in Developing Nations." *Social Problems* 56(1):174–204.

Hughes, Melanie M. 2009b. "Post-9/11 Politics and Muslim Women's Political Representation in the West." Paper presented at the American Political Science Association Annual Meeting. Toronto, Canada, September 3–6.

Hughes, Melanie M. 2011. "Intersectionality, Quotas, and Minority Women's Political Representation Worldwide." *American Political Science Review* 105(3):604–620.

Hughes, Melanie M. Forthcoming. "The Intersection of Gender and Minority Status in National Legislatures: The Minority Women Legislative Index." *Legislative Studies Quarterly.*

Hughes, Melanie M., Mona Lena Krook, and Pamela Paxton. 2012. "Transnational Women's Activism and the Global Diffusion of Gender Quotas." Working paper.

Hughes, Melanie and Jeffrey Tienes. 2011. "Representing Ethnic Muslim Women." Paper presented at the Political Studies Association Women and Politics Biennial Conference, February 18, Bristol, UK.

Hughes, Melanie M. and Aili Mari Tripp. n.d. "Civil War and Trajectories of Change in Women's Political Representation in Africa, 1985–2010." Unpublished manuscript.

Hunt, Swanee. 2007. "Let Women Rule." *Foreign Affairs* 86(3):109–120.

Hust, Evelin. 2004. *Women's Political Representation and Empowerment in India: A Million Indiras Now?* New Delhi, India: Manohar.

Inglehart, Ronald and Pippa Norris. 2000. "The Developmental Theory of the Gender Gap: Women's and Men's Voting Behavior in Global Perspective." *International Political Science Review* 21:441–463.

Inter-Parliamentary Union. 1995. *Women in Parliaments: 1945–1995: A World Statistical Survey.* Geneva, Switzerland: Inter-Parliamentary Union.

Inter-Parliamentary Union. 2000. *Politics: Women's Insight.* Geneva, Switzerland: Inter-Parliamentary Union.

Inter-Parliamentary Union. 2005a. *Women in National Parliaments* [Webpage]. Retrieved December 7, 2005 (http://www.ipu.org).

Inter-Parliamentary Union. 2005b. "Women's Suffrage: A World Chronology of the Recognition of Women's Rights to Vote and to Stand for Election." Available online at http://www.ipu.org/wmn-e/suffrage.htm.

Inter-Parliamentary Union. 2010. "Women in National Parliament: World and Regional Averages." Available online at http://www.ipu.org/wmn-e/world.htm.

Inter-Parliamentary Union. 2012a. *Parline Database.* Retrieved January 30, 2013 (http://www.ipu.org/parline-e/parlinesearch.asp).

Inter-Parliamentary Union. 2012b. "Women in National Parliament: World and Regional Averages: Situation as of December 31, 2011." Available online at http://www.ipu.org/wmn-e/world.htm.

International Alliance of Women. 2005. "Declaration of Principles." Available online at www.womenalliance.com/declare.html.

International Institute for Democracy and Electoral Assistance. 2005. "Voter Turnout by Gender." Available online at http://www.idea.int/vt/survey/by_gender.cfm.

International Institute for Democracy and Electoral Assistance. 2009. "Women's Political Participation in Colombia: A Challenging Road Ahead." Retrieved May 22, 2012 (http://www.idea.int/americas/colombia/womens_participation.cfm).

International Institute for Democracy and Electoral Assistance. 2012a. *Global Database of Quotas for Women.* Available online at http://www.idea.int/quota.

International Institute for Democracy and Electoral Assistance. 2012b. "Voter Turnout by Gender." *Global Database of Quotas for Women.* Available online at www.idea.int/quota.

International Monetary Fund. 2012. "World Economic Outlook: Coping With High Debt and Sluggish Growth." Retrieved March 20, 2013 (http://www.imf.org/external/pubs/ft/weo/2012/02/index.htm).

International Tibet Network. 2012. "Chinese Leaders." Retrieved May 31, 2012 (http://chinese-leaders.org/).

Ishiyama, John T. 2003. "Women's Parties in Post-Communist Politics." *East European Politics and Societies* 17:266–304.

Iwanaga, Kazuki. 2008a. "Women in Thai Politics." Pp. 173–209 in *Women's Political Participation and Representation in Asia,* edited by Kazuki Iwanaga. Copenhagen: Nordic Institute of Asian Studies.

Iwanaga, Kazuki. 2008b. "Women's Political Representation in Japan." Pp. 101–129 in *Women's Political Participation and Representation in Asia,* edited by Kazuki Iwanaga. Copenhagen: Nordic Institute of Asian Studies.

Jalalzai, Farida. 2004. "Women Political Leaders: Past and Present." *Women and Politics* 26:85–108.

Jalalzai, Farida. 2006. "Women Candidates and the Media: 1992–2000 Elections." *Politics and Policy* 34(3):606–633.

Jalalzai, Farida. 2008. "Women Rule: Shattering the Executive Glass Ceiling." *Politics & Gender* 4(2):205–231.

Jalalzai, Farida. 2009. "Women National Leaders: No Less Prepared to Rule." Paper presented at the annual meeting of the American Political Science Association, September 3–6, Toronto, ON, Canada.

Jalalzai, Farida. 2011. "A Critical Departure for Women Executives or More of the Same: The Powers of Chancellor Merkel." *German Politics* 20(3):428–448.

Janardhan, N. 2005. "In the Gulf Women Are Not Women's Friends." *The Daily Star* (Lebanon). June 20.

Japanese Ministry of Health, Labour, and Welfare. 2005. *Basic Survey on Wage Structure.* Available online at http://web-japan.org/stat/stats/18WME42.html.

Jaquette, Jane S. 1994. "Introduction: From Transition to Participation—Women's Movements and Democratic Politics." Pp. 1–11 in *The Women's Movement in Latin America,* edited by J. S. Jaquette. Boulder, CO: Westview Press.

Jaquette, Jane S. 2009. *Feminist Agendas and Democracy.* Durham, NC: Duke University Press.

Jaquette, Jane S. and Sharon L. Wolchik, eds. 1998. *Women and Democracy: Latin America and Central and Eastern Europe.* Baltimore: Johns Hopkins University Press.

Jayawardena, Kumari. 1986. *Feminism and Nationalism in the Third World.* London: Zed Books.

Jeannette Rankin Peace Center. 2006. "Jeannette Who?" Available online at http://www.jrpc.org/jeannette_who.html.

Jenkins, J. C. 1983. "Resource Mobilization Theory and the Study of Social Movements." *Annual Review of Sociology* 9:527–553.

Jeydel, Alana and Andrew J. Taylor. 2003. "Are Women Legislators Less Effective? Evidence From the U.S. House in the 103rd–105th Congress." *Political Research Quarterly* 56:19–27.

Joachim, Jutta. 2003. "Framing Issues and Seizing Opportunities: The UN, NGOs and Women's Rights." *International Studies Quarterly* 47:247–274.

Johnson, Deb with Hope Kabuchu and Santa Vusiya Kayonga. 2003. "Women in Ugandan Local Government: The Impact of Affirmative Action." *Gender and Development* 11(3):8–18.

Johnson, Helen Kendrick. 1913. *Woman and the Republic.* New York: Guidon Club.

Jones, Mark P. 1998. "Gender Quotas, Electoral Laws, and the Election of Women: Lessons From the Argentine Provinces." *Comparative Political Studies* 31(1):3–21.

Jones, Mark P. 2004. "Quota Legislation and the Election of Women: Learning From the Costa Rican Experience." *Journal of Politics* 66:1203–1223.

Jones, Mark P. 2009. "Gender Quotas, Electoral Laws, and the Election of Women: Evidence From the Latin American Vanguard." *Comparative Political Studies* 42(1):56–81.

Jones, Mark P. and Patricio Navia. 1999. "Assessing the Effectiveness of Gender Quotas in Open-List Proportional Representation Electoral Systems." *Social Science Quarterly* 80(2):341–356.

Jones, Nicola Ann. 2006. *Gender and the Political Opportunities of Democratization in South Korea.* New York. Palgrave MacMillan.

Jorgensen-Earp, Cheryl R., ed. 1999. *Speeches and Trials of the Militant Suffragettes: The Women's Social and Political Union, 1903–1918.* London: Associated University Presses.

Josephson, Hannah. 1974. *Jeannette Rankin: First Lady in Congress.* New York: Bobbs-Merrill.

Kabeer, Naila. 1994. *Reversed Realities: Gender Hierarchies in Development Thought.* London: Verso.

Kabeer, Naila, Ayesha Khan, and Naysan Adlparvar. 2011. "Afghan Values or Women's Rights? Gendered Narratives about Continuity and Change in Urban Afghanistan." IDS Working Paper 387. Institute of Development Studies.

Kabeer, Naila and Simeen Mahmud. 2004. "Globalization, Gender, and Poverty: Bangladeshi Women Workers in Export and Local Markets." *Journal of International Development* 16(1):93–109.

Kaden, Wolfgang. 2012. "All Systems Reverse!" *Spiegel Online,* March 2. Available online at http://www.spiegel.de/international/europe/euro-crisis-debate-all-systems-reverse-a-818807.html.

Kahn, Kim Fridkin. 1996. *The Political Consequences of Being a Woman: How Stereotypes Influence the Conduct and Consequences of Political Campaigns.* New York: Columbia University Press.

Kampwirth, Karen. 2002. *Women & Guerrilla Movements: Nicaragua, El Salvador, Chiapas, Cuba.* University Park, PA: Pennsylvania State University Press.

Kampwirth, Karen. 2003. "Arnoldo Aleman Takes on the NGOs: Antifeminism and the New Populism in Nicaragua." *Latin American Politics and Society* 45(2):133–158.

Kampwirth, Karen. 2004. *Feminism and the Legacy of Revolution: Nicaragua, El Salvador, Chiapas.* Athens: Ohio University Press.

Kampwirth, Karen. 2010. "Gender Politics in Nicaragua: Feminism, Antifeminism, and the Return of Daniel Ortega." Pp. 111–126 in *Women Activism in Latin America and the Caribbean: Engendering Social Justice, Democratizing Citizenship,* edited by Elizabeth Maier and Nathalie Lebon. New Brunswick, NJ: Rutgers University Press.

Kang, Alice. 2009. "Studying Oil, Islam, and Women as if Political Institutions Mattered." *Politics & Gender* 5: 560–568.

Kanter, Rosabeth Moss. 1977. *Men and Women of the Corporation.* New York: Basic Books.

Kantola, Johanna. 2010. *Gender and the European Union.* Basingstoke: Palgrave Macmillan.

Karam, Azza. 1999. "Strengthening the Role of Women Parliamentarians in the Arab Region: Challenges and Options." Available online at http://www.pogar.org/publications/gender/karam2/section5.html.

Karam, Azza. 2000. "Democrats Without Democracy: Challenges to Women in Politics in the Arab World." Pp. 64–82 in *International Perspectives on Gender and Democratisation,* edited by Shirin M. Rai. Houndmills, UK: Macmillan.

Karvonen, Lauri and Per Selle. 1995. "Introduction: Scandinavia: A Case Apart." Pp. 3–23 in *Women in Nordic Politics: Closing the Gap,* edited by L. Karvonen and P. Selle. Aldershot, UK: Dartmouth.

Kathlene, Lyn. 1994. "Power and Influence in State Legislative Policymaking: The Interaction of Gender and Position in Committee Hearing Debates." *American Political Science Review* 88:560–576.

Kathlene, Lyn. 1995. "Alternative Views of Crime: Legislative Policymaking in Gendered Terms." *Journal of Politics* 57:696–723.

Kathlene, Lyn, Susan E. Clarke, and Barbara A. Fox. 1991. "Ways Women Politicians Are Making a Difference." Pp. 31–38 in *Gender and Policymaking: Studies of Women in Office,* edited by D. L. Dodson. New Brunswick, NJ: Center for the American Woman and Politics.

Kawamara-Mishambi, Sheila and Irene Ovonji-Odida. 2003. "The 'Lost Clause': The Campaign to Advance Women's Property Rights in the Uganda 1998 Land Act." Pp. 160–187 in *No Shortcuts to Power: African Women in Politics and Policy-Making,* edited by A. M. Goetz and S. Hassim. London: Zed Books.

Keck, Margaret E. and Kathryn Sikkink. 1998. *Activists Beyond Borders: Advocacy Networks in International Politics.* Ithaca, NY: Cornell University Press.

Kelber, Mim. 1994. *Women and Government: New Ways to Political Power.* Westport, CT: Praeger.

Kelly, Liz. 2000. "Wars Against Women: Sexual Violence, Sexual Politics and the Militarised State." Pp. 45–65 in *States of Conflict: Gender, Violence, and Resistance,* edited by Susie Jacobs, Ruth Jacobson, and Jen Marchbank. London: Zed Books.

Kenworthy, Lane and Melissa Malami. 1999. "Gender Inequality in Political Representation: A Worldwide Comparative Analysis." *Social Forces* 78:235–268.

Kidu, Dame Carol. 2012. "Sex, Women and the 21st Century in Papua New Guinea." Pamela Denoon Lecture, Australian National University. Retrieved May 14, 2012 (www.pameladenoonlecture.net).

Kim, Haingja. 1975. *A Comparative Study of the U.S. House of Representatives and the National Assembly of Korea: A Cross-Cultural Study Focusing on Role Analysis of Female Politicians.* PhD dissertation. Honolulu: University of Hawaii.

King, Brayden G. and Marie Cornwall. 2004. "Specialists and Generalists: Learning Strategies in the Woman Suffrage Movement, 1866–1918." Unpublished manuscript.

King, James D. 2002. "Single-Member Districts and the Representation of Women in American State Legislatures: The Effects of Electoral System Change." *State Politics and Policy Quarterly* 2:161–175.

Kirkpatrick, Jeane. 1974. *Political Women.* New York: Basic Books.

Kishor, Sunita and Kiersten Johnson. 2004. *Profiling Domestic Violence: A Multi-Country Study.* Columbia, MD: ORC Macro.

Kiss, Yudit. 1991. "The Second 'No': Women in Hungary." *Feminist Review* 39 (Autumn):49–57.

Kittilson, Miki Caul. 2006. *Challenging Parties, Changing Parliament: Women and Elected Office in Contemporary Western Europe.* Columbus: The Ohio State University Press.

Kittilson, Miki Caul and Kim Fridkin. 2008. "Gender, Candidate Portrayals and Election Campaigns: A Comparative Perspective." *Politics & Gender* 4(3): 371–392.

Klausen, Jytte. 2001. "When Women Voted for the Right: Lessons for Today From the Conservative Gender Gap." Pp. 209–228 in *Has Liberalism Failed Women: Assuring Equal Representation in Europe and the United States,* edited by J. Klausen and C. S. Maier. New York: Palgrave.

Kling, Kristen C., Janet Hyde, Carolin Showers, and Brenda N. Buswell. 1999. "Gender Differences in Self-Esteem: A Meta-Analysis." *Psychological Bulletin* 125(4):470–500.

Knight, Louise W. 2004. "Educating Women Worldwide." *International Higher Education* 37(Fall):15–16.

Koch, Jeffrey. 1997. "Candidate Gender and Women's Psychological Engagement in Politics." *American Politics Quarterly* 25:118–133.

Koester, David. 1995. "Gender Ideology and Nationalism in the Culture and Politics of Iceland." *American Ethnologist* 22:572–588.

Kostova, Dobrinka. 1998. "Women in Bulgaria: Changes in Employment and Political Involvement." Pp. 203–221 in *Women and Democracy: Latin America and Central and Eastern Europe,* edited by J. S. Jaquette and S. L. Wolchik. Baltimore: Johns Hopkins University Press.

Kraynanski, Joan M. 2007. *Women Walking Silently: The Emergence of Cambodian Women in the Public Sphere.* Master's thesis. Center for International Studies, Ohio University.

Kristof, Nicholas. 2004. "Sentenced to Be Raped," *The New York Times,* September 29, p. A25.

Kristof, Nicholas. 2005. "Raped, Kidnapped, and Silenced," *The New York Times,* June 14, p. A23.

Kristof, Nicholas D. and Sheryl WuDunn. 2009. *Half the Sky.* New York: Vintage.

Krook, Mona Lena. 2003. "Not All Quotas Are Created Equal: Trajectories of Reform to Increase Women's Political Representation." Paper presented at the European Consortium for Political Research, Joint Sessions of Workshops, March 28–April 2, Edinburgh, Scotland.

Krook, Mona Lena. 2004. "Promoting Gender-Balanced Decision-Making: The Role of International Fora and Transnational Networks." Pp. 205–220 in *Crossing Borders: Re-mapping Women's Movements at the Turn of the 21st Century,* edited by H. R. Christensen, B. Halsaa, and A. Saarinen. Odense, Denmark: University Press of South Denmark.

Krook, Mona Lena. 2009. *Quotas for Women in Politics: Gender and Candidate Selection Reform Worldwide.* New York: Oxford University Press.

Krook, Mona Lena and Diana Z. O'Brien. 2010. "The Politics of Group Representation: Quotas for Women and Minorities Worldwide." *Comparative Politics* 42(3):253–272.

Krook, Mona Lena and Diana Z. O'Brien. 2011. "All the President's Men? The Appointment of Female Cabinet Ministers Worldwide." Paper presented at the Midwest Political Science Association National Conference, Chicago, IL, April 22–25, 2010. Revised version presented at the Midwest Political Science Association National Conference, Chicago, IL, March 31–April 3, 2011.

Krook, Mona Lena, Diana Z. O'Brien, and Krista Swip. 2010. "Military Invasion and Women's Political Representation: Gender Quotas in Post-Conflict Afghanistan and Iraq." *International Feminist Journal of Politics* 12(1):66–79.

Krupavičius, Algis and Irmina Matonytė. 2003. "Women in Lithuanian Politics: From Nomenklatura Selection to Representation." Pp. 81–104 in *Women's Access to Political Power in Post-Communist Europe,* edited by R. E. Matland and K. A. Montgomery. Oxford, UK: Oxford University Press.

Krupskaya, Nadezhda K. 1938. "Introduction." Pp. 5–10 in *Women and Society,* edited by V. I. Lenin. New York: International Publishers.

Kukathas, Chandran. 2001. "Is Feminism Bad for Multiculturalism?" *Public Affairs Quarterly* 15(2):83–98.

Kunovich, Sheri. 2003. "The Representation of Polish and Czech Women in National Politics: Predicting Electoral List Position." *Comparative Politics* 35:273–291.

Kunovich, Sheri. 2012. "Voting Rates 1989 to 2007: Is There a Gender Gap?" *International Journal of Sociology* 42(1):60–77.

Kunovich, Sheri and Pamela Paxton. 2005. "Pathways to Power: The Role of Political Parties in Women's National Political Representation." *The American Journal of Sociology* 111:505–552.

Kvennalistinn. 1987. *Aims of the Women's Alliance.* Available online at http://www .mith2.umd.edu/WomensStudies/GovernmentPolitics/InternationalDirectory/ Europe/iceland.

Kymlicka, Will. 1999. "Liberal Complacencies." Pp. 31–34 in *Is Multiculturalism Bad for Women? Susan Moller Okin With Respondents,* edited by J. Cohen, M. Howard, and M. C. Nussbaum. Princeton, NJ: Princeton University Press.

LaFraniere, Sharon. 2005. "Entrenched Epidemic: Wife-Beatings in Africa," *The New York Times,* August 11, p. A1.

Lane, Amanda. 2001. "Promoting Voter Awareness among Jordanian Women and Youth." *The Network Newsletter* 23:6–7.

Larson, Taft A. 1965. "Woman Suffrage in Wyoming." *Pacific Northwest Quarterly* 56(2):57–66.

Lauti, Alamanda and Jon Fraenkel. 2006. "Report 5: Advancing Women's Representation in Tuvalu." Pp. 209–255 in *A Woman's Place Is in the House.* Suva, Fiji: Pacific Islands Forum Secretariat.

Lavrin, Asuncion. 1994. "Suffrage in South America: Arguing a Difficult Case." Pp. 184–209 in *Suffrage and Beyond: International Feminist Perspectives,* edited by C. Daley and M. Nolan. New York: New York University Press.

Lawless, Jennifer L. and Richard L. Fox. 2010. *It Still Takes a Candidate: Why Women Don't Run for Office.* New York: Cambridge University Press.

Lee, Sun-Hee. 2009. "Women in Politics (Fiji, the Solomon Islands and Vanuatu)." Center for Democratic Institutions. Retrieved May 14, 2012 (http://www.cdi .anu.edu.au/).

Lerner, Gerda. 1986. *The Creation of Patriarchy.* New York: Oxford University Press.

Liddell, James. 2009. "Gender Quotas in Clientelist Systems: The Case of Morocco's National List." *al-raida* 126–127:79–86.

Lilja. Mona. 2008. *Power, Resistance and Women Politicians in Cambodia: Discourses of Emancipation.* Copenhagen: Nordic Institute of Asian Studies.

Lindberg Falk, Monica. 2002. *Making Fields of Merit: Buddhist Nuns Challenge Gendered Orders in Thailand.* Doctoral Dissertation. Department of Social Anthropology, Göteborg University.

Lindberg, Staffen. 2004. "Women's Empowerment and Democratization: The Effects of Electoral Systems, Participation, and Experience in Africa." *Studies in Comparative International Development* 39:28–53.

Lipman-Blumen, Jean. 1973. "Role De-Differentiations as a System Response to Crisis: Occupational and Political Roles of Women." *Sociological Inquiry* 43:105–129.

Lipset, Seymour M. 1960. *Political Man.* London: Heinemann.

Liswood, Laura A. 1995. *Women World Leaders: Fifteen Great Politicians Tell Their Stories.* New York: HarperCollins.

Lithwick, Dahlia. 2001. "Double Dipping at the Waffle House." Available online at http://www.slate.com/id/117140/.

Little, Thomas H., Dana Dunn, and Rebecca E. Deen. 2001. "A View From the Top: Gender Differences in Legislative Priorities Among State Legislative Leaders." *Women and Politics* 22:29–49.

Lloyd, Trevor Owen. 1971. *Suffragettes International: The World Wide Campaign for Women's Rights.* New York: American Heritage Press.

Longman, Timothy. 2006. "Rwanda: Achieving Equality or Serving an Authoritarian State?" Pp. 133–150 in *Women in African Parliaments*, edited by G. Bauer and H. Britton. London: Lynne Rienner.

Lorber, Judith. 2003. "'Night To His Day': The Social Construction of Gender." Pp. 33–47 in *Feminist Frontiers*, 6th ed., edited by L. Richardson, V. Taylor, and N. Whittier. New York: McGraw-Hill.

Lough, Oliver. 2012. "Equal Rights, Unequal Opportunities Women's Participation in Afghanistan's Parliamentary and Provincial Council Elections." Afghanistan Research and Evaluation Unit. United Nations. Retrieved May 22, 2012 (www .areu.org.af).

Lovenduski, Joni. 1993. "Introduction: The Dynamics of Gender and Party." Pp. 1–15 in *Gender and Party Politics*, edited by J. Lovenduski and P. Norris. Newbury Park, CA: Sage.

Lovenduski, Joni and Pippa Norris. 2003. "Westminster Women: The Politics of Presence." *Political Studies* 51:84–102.

Luciak, Ilja A. 2001. *After the Revolution: Gender and Democracy in El Salvador, Nicaragua, and Guatemala*. Baltimore: Johns Hopkins University Press.

Lukes, Steven. 1974. *Power: A Radical View*. London: Macmillan.

MacDonald, Jason A. and Erin E. O'Brien. 2011. "Quasi-Experimental Design, Constituency, and Advancing Women's Interests: Reexamining the Influence of Gender on Substantive Representation. *Political Research Quarterly* 64(June):472–486.

Mackay, Fiona, Meryl Kenny M., and Louise Chappell. 2010. "New Institutionalism Through a Gender Lens: Towards a Feminist Institutionalism?" *International Political Science Review* 31(5):573–588.

MacKinnon, Catharine. 1989. *Toward a Feminist Theory of the State*. Cambridge, MA: Harvard University Press.

Madrid, Raúl L. 2005. *Indigenous* Parties and Democracy in Latin America. *Latin American Politics & Society* 47(4):161–179.

Maffii, Margherita A. 2010. "Political Participation of Indigenous Women in Cambodia." *Asien* 114–115:16–32.

Magin, Raphael. 2011. "Women in Local Assemblies—Rare Guests or (Almost) Equal Partners? An Analysis of the Causes of Women's Under-representation in the German County Councils." Pp. 37–55 in *Women and Representation in Local Government: International Case Studies*, edited by Barbara Pini and Paula McDonald. New York: Routledge.

Maier, Elizabeth and Nathalie Lebon, eds. 2010. *Women's Activism in Latin America and the Caribbean: Engendering Social Justice, Democratizing Citizenship*. New Brunswick, NJ: Rutgers University Press.

Mair, Lucille. 1991. "Religion as Catalyst for Female Activism." Pp. 155–159 in *Women, Politics, and Religion*, edited by H. L. Swarup and S. Bisaria. Etawah, India: A. C. Brothers.

Mann, Michael. 1986. "A Crisis in Stratification Theory? Persons, Households/Families/Lineages, Genders, Classes and Nations. Pp. 40–56 in *Gender and Stratification*, edited by R. Crompton and M. Mann. Cambridge, UK: Polity.

Manninen, Merja. 2004. "Women's Status in Finland." Available online at http://virtual.finland.fi/netcomm/news/showarticle.asp?intNWSAID=25736.

Mansbridge, Jane J. 1999. "Should Blacks Represent Blacks and Women Represent Women? A Contingent 'Yes.'" *Journal of Politics* 61:628–657.

Mansbridge, Jane and Katherine Tate. 1992. "Race Trumps Gender: The Thomas Nomination in the Black Community." *PS: Political Science and Politics* 25: 488–492.

Manza, Jeff and Clem Brooks. 1998. "The Gender Gap in U.S. Presidential Elections: When? Why? Implications?" *American Journal of Sociology* 103(5): 1235–1266.

Margolis, Diane Rothbard. 1993. "Women's Movements Around the World: Cross-Cultural Comparisons." *Gender and Society* 7:379–399.

Martin, Patricia Yancy. 2004. "Gender as a Social Institution." *Social Forces* 82: 1249–1273.

Matland, Richard E. 1993. "Institutional Variables Affecting Female Representation in National Legislatures: The Case of Norway." *Journal of Politics* 55: 737–755.

Matland, Richard E. 1998. "Women's Representation in National Legislatures: Developed and Developing Countries." *Legislative Studies Quarterly* 23: 109–125.

Matland, Richard E. 2002. "Enhancing Women's Political Participation: Legislative Recruitment and Electoral Systems." Pp. 65–90 in *Women in Parliament: Beyond Numbers,* edited by A. Karam. Stockholm, Sweden: IDEA.

Matland, Richard E. 2003. "Women's Representation in Post-Communist Europe." Pp. 321–342 in *Women's Access to Political Power in Post-Communist Europe,* edited by R. E. Matland and K. A. Montgomery. Oxford, UK: Oxford University Press.

Matland, Richard E. 2005. "Enhancing Women's Political Participation: Legislative Recruitment and Electoral Systems." Pp. 93–111 in *Women in Parliament: Beyond Numbers: A Revised Edition,* edited by A. Karam. Stockholm, Sweden: IDEA.

Matland, Richard E. and Deborah D. Brown. 1992. "District Magnitude's Effect on Female Representation in U.S. State Legislatures." Legislative Studies Quarterly 17:469–492.

Matland, Richard E. and Kathleen A. Montgomery, eds. 2003. *Women's Access to Political Power in Post-Communist Europe.* Oxford, UK: Oxford University Press.

Matland, Richard E. and Donley T. Studlar. 1996. "The Contagion of Women Candidates in Single-Member District and Proportional Representation Systems: Canada and Norway." Journal of Politics 58:707–733.

Mazur, Amy G. and Mark A. Pollack. 2009. "Gender and Public Policy in Europe: An Introduction." *Comparative European Politics* 7:1–11.

McAdam, Doug. 1982. *Political Process and the Development of Black Insurgency, 1930–1970.* Chicago: University of Chicago Press.

McAdam, Doug. 1983. "Tactical Innovation and the Pace of Insurgency." *American Sociological Review* 48:735–754.

McAdam, Doug, John D. McCarthy, and Mayer N. Zald. 1996. *Comparative Perspectives on Social Movements*. Cambridge, UK: Cambridge University Press.

McCammon, Holly J. 2001. "Stirring Up Suffrage Sentiment: The Formation of the State Woman Suffrage Organizations, 1866–1914." *Social Forces* 80:449–480.

McCammon, Holly J. 2003. "'Out of the Parlors and Into the Streets': The Changing Tactical Repertoire of the U.S. Women's Suffrage Movements." *Social Forces* 81:787–818.

McCammon, Holly J. and Karen E. Campbell. 2001. "Winning the Vote in the West: The Political Successes of the Women's Suffrage Movement, 1866–1919." *Gender and Society* 15:55–82.

McCammon, Holly J., Karen E. Campbell, Ellen M. Granberg, and Christine Mowery. 2001. "How Movements Win: Gendered Opportunity Structures and U.S. Women's Suffrage Movements, 1866 to 1919." *American Sociological Review* 66(1):49–70.

McDonagh, Eileen L. and H. Douglas Price. 1985. "Woman Suffrage in the Progressive Era: Patterns of Opposition and Support in Referenda Voting, 1910–1918." *The American Political Science Review* 79:415–435.

McDonald, Paula and Barbara Pini. 2004. "A Good Job for a Woman? The Myth of Local Government as Family Friendly." *Local Governance* 30:144–151.

McGrew, Jaura, Kate Frieson, and Sambath Chan. 2004. "Good Governance From the Ground Up: Women's Roles in Post-Conflict Cambodia." Women Waging Peace Policy Series. Retrieved June 1, 2012 (http://www.womenwagingpeace.net).

Meier, Petra. 2000. "From Theory to Practice and Back Again: Gender Quotas and the Politics of Presence in Belgium." Pp. 106–116 in *Deliberation, Representation and Association*, edited by M. Saward. London: Routledge.

Meintjes, Sheila. 2002. "War and Post-War Shifts in Gender Relations," Pp. 63–77 in *The Aftermath: Women in Post-conflict Transformation*, edited by S. Meintjes, A. Pillay and M. Turshen. London: Zed Books.

Metoyer, C. 2000. *Women and the State in Post-Sandinista Nicaragua*. Boulder, CO: Lynne Rienner.

Meyer, John W., John Boli, George M. Thomas, and Francisco O. Ramirez. 1997. "World Society and the Nation State." *The American Journal of Sociology* 103(1):144–181.

Meznaric, Silva. 1994. "Gender and an Ethno-Marker: Rape, War, and Identity Politics in the Former Yugoslavia." Pp. 76–97 in *Identity Politics and Women: Cultural Reassertions and Feminisms in International Perspective*, edited by V. M. Moghadam. Boulder, CO: Westview Press.

Miguel, Luis F. 2008. "Political Representation and Gender in Brazil: Quotas for Women and Their Impact." *Bulletin of Latin American Research* 27(2): 197–214.

Mill, John Stuart. 1859. *On Liberty*. London: J. W. Parker.

Mill, John Stuart. 1861. *Considerations on Representative Government*. London: Parker, Son and Bourn.

Mill, John Stuart. 1869. *The Subjugation of Women*. London: Dent.

Miller, Melissa K., Jeffrey S. Peake, and Brittany Anne Boulton. 2010. "Testing the Saturday Night Live Hypothesis: Fairness and Bias in Newspaper Coverage of Hillary Clinton's Presidential Campaign." *Politics & Gender* 6(2):169–198.

Minor v. Happersett, 21 Wallace, U.S. Reports. (1835).

Mission, Gina. 1998. "Their Own Worst Enemies: Gender Politics in the Philippines." Available online at http://www.geocities.com/Wellesley/3321/win8d.htm.

Moghadam, Valentine M. 1994. *Gender and National Identity: Women and Politics in Muslim Societies*. London: Zed Books.

Moghadam, Valentine M. 1997. "Gender and Revolutions." Pp. 137–167 in *Theorizing Revolutions,* edited by J. Foran. New York: Routledge.

Moghadam, Valentine M. 1999. "Revolution, Religion and Gender Politics: Iran and Afghanistan Compared" *Journal of Women's History* 10(4):172–195.

Moghadam, Valentine M. 2003. "Engendering Citizenship, Feminizing Civil Society: The Case of the Middle East and North Africa." *Women and Politics* 25(1/2): 63–88.

Moghadam, Valentine M. 2005. *Globalizing Women: Transnational Feminist Networks*. Baltimore: Johns Hopkins University Press.

Molyneux, Maxine. 1985a. "Legal Reforms and Socialist Revolution in Democratic Yemen: Women and the Family." *International Journal of the Sociology of Law* 133:147–172.

Molyneux, Maxine. 1985b. "Mobilization Without Emancipation? Women's Interests, the State, and Revolution." *Feminist Studies* 11:227–254.

Mondak, Jeffery J., and Mary R. Anderson. 2004. "The Knowledge Gap: A Reexamination of Gender-Based Differences in Political Knowledge." *Journal of Politics* 66(2):492–512.

Mong, Adrienne. 2011. "China's Leadership: Where Are the Women?" *MSNBC News,* March 7. Retrieved May 31, 2012 (http://behindthewall.msnbc.msn.com/_news/2011/03/07/6206108-chinas-leadership-where-are-the-women?lite).

Monjib, Maati. 2009. "A Legislated Victory for Moroccan Women." Carnegie Endowment for International Peace. Retrieved May 30, 2012 (http://www.carnegieendowment.org/sada/2009/10/06/legislated-victory-for-moroccan-women/6bjc).

Montgomery, Kathleen A. 2003. "Introduction." Pp. 1–18 in *Women's Access to Political Power in Post-Communist Europe,* edited by R. E. Matland and K. A. Montgomery. Oxford, UK: Oxford University Press.

Montoya, Lisa J., Carol Hardy-Fanta, and Sonia Garcia. 2000. "Latina Politics: Gender, Participation, and Leadership." *PS: Political Science and Politics* 33(3):555–561.

Moore, Gwen and Gene Shackman. 1996. "Gender and Authority: A Cross-National Study." *Social Science Quarterly* 77:273–288.

Moraes, Dom. 1980. *Indira Gandhi*. Boston: Little, Brown.

Morgan, Robin. 1984. Sisterhood Is Powerful: An Anthology of Writings From the Women's Liberation Movement. New York: Random House.

Morna, Colleen Lowe and Loveness Jambaya Nyakujarah, Eds. 2011. SADC Gender Protocol 2011 Barometer. Johannesburg, South Africa: SADC Gender Protocol 2011. Available online at blogs.uct.ac.za/blog/gender_studies/2012/08/06/sadc-gender-protocol-2011-barometer.

Moser, Robert G. 2003. "Electoral Systems and Women's Representation: The Strange Case of Russia." Pp. 153–172 in Women's Access to Political Power in Post-Communist Europe, edited by R. E. Matland and K. A. Montgomery. Oxford, UK: Oxford University Press.

Moser, Robert G. and Stephanie S. Holmsten. 2008. "The Paradox of Descriptive Representation: Can PR Simultaneously Elect Women and Ethnic Minorities?" Paper presented at the annual meeting of the Midwest Political Science Association, April 3–6, Chicago, IL.

Moses, Claire G. 1984. French Feminism in the Nineteenth Century. Albany: State University of New York Press.

Murdock, George P. 1967. "Ethnographic Atlas: A Summary." Ethnology 7: 109–236.

Murray, Rainbow. 2010. Parties, Gender Quotas and Candidate Selection in France. London: Palgrave.

Murray, Rainbow, Mona Lena Krook, and Katherine A. R. Opello. 2011. "Why Are Gender Quotas Adopted? Party Pragmatism and Parity in France." Political Research Quarterly 65(3):529–543.

Najibullah, Farangis. 2010. "Do Central Asia's Gender Quotas Help or Hurt Women?" Radio Free Europe. March 8. Retrieved June 9, 2012 (http://www.rferl.org/content/Do_Central_Asias_Gender_Quotas_Help_Or_Hurt_Women/1977535.html).

Nash, Jennifer C. 2008. "Re-thinking Intersectionality." Feminist Review 89:1–15.

National Center for Education Statistics. 2006. Number of Bachelor's Degrees Earned by Women, by Field of Study. Available online at http://nces.ed.gov/.

National Committee on Pay Equity. 2013. "The Wage Gap Over Time: In Real Dollars, Women See a Continuing Gap." Retrieved March 20, 2013 (http://pay-equity.org/info-time.html).

National Democratic Institute. 2009. "Gender Quota in Burkina Faso Marks Feats Accomplished, Challenges Ahead." Retrieved May 22, 2012 (http://www.ndi.org/node/15289).

Nechemias, Carol. 1987. "Changes in the Election of Women to U.S. State Legislative Seats." Legislative Studies Quarterly 12(1):125–142.

Neyland, M. and D. Tucker. 1996. "Women in Local Government." In Gender Politics and Citizenship in the 1990s, edited by B. Sullivan and G. Whitehouse. Sydney: University of New South Wales Press.

Noftsinger, Kate. 2010. "Gender Quotas for African Parliaments—Do They Work?" Ms. Magazine, August 2. Available online at http://msmagazine.com/blog/blog/2010/08/02/gender-quotas-for-african-parliaments-do-they-work/.

Noftsinger, Kate. 2011. "Gender Quotas for African Parliaments–Do They Work?" Ms. Magazine. Retrieved June 6, 2012 (http://msmagazine.com/blog/blog/2010/08/02/gender-quotas-for-african-parliaments-do-they-work/).

Noonan, Rita K. 1995. "Women Against the State: Political Opportunities and Collective Action Frames in Chile's Transition to Democracy." *Sociological Forum* 10(1):81–111.

Norderval, Ingunn. 1985. "Party and Legislative Participation Among Scandinavian Women." *Women and Politics in Western Europe* 18(4):71–89.

Nordlund, Anja Taarup. 2004. "Demands for Electoral Gender Quotas in Afghanistan and Iraq." Working Paper Series 2004:2. Available online at http://www.statsvet.su.se/quotas/a_nordlund_wps_2004_2.pdf.

Norrander, Barbara and Clyde Wilcox. 2005. "Change and Continuity in the Geography of Women State Legislators." Pp. 176–196 in *Women and Elective Office: Past, Present, and Future,* 2nd ed., edited by S. Thomas and C. Wilcox. Oxford, UK: Oxford University Press.

Norris, Pippa. 1985. "Women's Legislative Participation in Western Europe." *West European Politics* 8:90–101.

Norris, Pippa. 1987. *Politics and Sexual Equality: The Comparative Position of Women in Western Democracies.* Boulder, CO: Lynne Rienner.

Norris, Pippa. 1993. "Conclusions: Comparing Legislative Recruitment." Pp. 309–330 in *Gender and Party Politics,* edited by J. Lovenduski and P. Norris. Newbury Park, CA: Sage.

Norris, Pippa. 1997. *Passages to Power: Legislative Recruitment in Advanced Democracies.* Cambridge, UK: Cambridge University Press.

Norris, Pippa. 2006. "The Impact of Electoral Reform on Women's Representation." *Acta Politica* 41:197–213.

Norris, Pippa. 2009. "Petroleum Patriarchy? A Response to Ross." *Politics & Gender* 5(4):553–560.

Norris, Pippa and Ronald Inglehart. 2001. "Cultural Obstacles to Equal Representation." *Journal of Democracy* 12:126–140.

Nussbaum, Martha C. 1999. *Sex and Social Justice.* Oxford, UK: Oxford University Press.

Odunjinrin, O. 1993. "Wife Battering in Nigeria." *International Journal of Gynaecology and Obstetrics* 41:159–164.

Office of International Women's Issues. 2003. "Women's Participation in the Constitution-Making Process in Afghanistan." Retrieved June 4, 2012 (http://2002–2009-usawc.state.gov/news/24277.htm).

Office of the President of the Republic of Lithuania. 2011. "Presidential Functions." Available online at http://www.lrp.lt/en/institution/presidential_functions_318.html.

Office of the Prime Minister and Department of Women's Affairs. 2004. *Vanuatu: Combined Initial, Second, and Third Reports on the Convention on the Elimination of All Forms of Discrimination Against Women.* United Nations.

Ohman, Magnus. 2011. "Global trends in the Regulation of Political Finance." Prepared for the IPSA-ECPR Joint Conference, February, 16–19, Sao Paulo, Brazil.

Okin, Susan Moller. 1979. *Women in Western Political Thought.* Princeton, NJ: Princeton University Press.

Okin, Susan Moller. 1999. "Is Multiculturalism Bad for Women?" Pp. 7–26 in *Is Multiculturalism Bad for Women?* edited by J. Cohen, M. Howard, and M. C. Nussbaum. Princeton, NJ: Princeton University Press.

Okin, Susan Moller. 2005. "Multiculturalism and Feminism: No Simple Question, No Simple Answers." Pp. 67–89 in *Minorities Within Minorities: Equality, Rights and Diversity,* edited by A. Eisenberg and J. Spinner-Halev. Cambridge, UK: Cambridge University Press.

Okonjo, Kamene. 1994. "Women and the Evolution of a Ghanaian Political Synthesis." Pp. 286–297 in *Women in Politics Worldwide,* edited by B. J. Nelson and N. Chowdhury. New Haven, CT: Yale University Press.

Olafsdottir Bjornsson, Anna. 2001. "Homepage: The Women's Alliance." Available online at http://www.itn.is/~annari/kveensk.htm.

Opello, Katherine A. R. 2004. "Explaining the Timing of the French Socialist Party's Gender-Based Quota." *French Politics, Culture & Society* 22(3):25–50.

Opfell, Olga. 1993. *Women Prime Ministers and Presidents.* London: McFarland.

Oxley, Zoe M. and Richard L. Fox. 2004. "Women in Executive Office: Variation Across American States." *Political Research Quarterly* 57(1):113–120.

Oyewumi, Oyeronke. 1997. *The Invention of Women: Making an African Sense of Western Gender Discourses.* Minneapolis: University of Minnesota Press.

Paixão, Marcelo, and Luis M Carvano. 2008. *Relatório Anual das Desigualdades Raciais no Brasil, 2007–2008* (Annual Report on Racial Inequality in Brazil, 2007–2008). Rio de Janeiro: Laboratório de Analise Econômicas, Sociais e Estatísticas em Relações Raciais (LAESER) at the Federal University of Rio de Janeiro.

Pankhurst, Donna. 2002. "Women and Politics in Africa: The Case of Uganda." *Parliamentary Affairs* 55(1):119–128.

Pankhurst, Donna. 2003. "The 'Sex War' and Other Wars: Towards a Feminist Approach to Peace Building." *Development in Practice* 13 (2/3):154–177.

Papadimitriou, Dimitri B. and L. Randall Wray. 2011. "Euroland in Crisis as the Global Meltdown Picks Up Speed." Working Paper No. 693, The Levy Economics Institute, Annandale-on-Hudson, NY.

Parpart, Jane L., Shirin M. Rai, and Kathleen Staudt. 2002. "Rethinking Em(power)ment, Gender and Development: An Introduction." Pp. 3–21 in *Rethinking Empowerment: Gender and Development in a Global/Local World,* edited by J. L. Parpart, S. M. Rai, and K. Staudt. London: Routledge.

Pateman, Carole. 1988. *The Sexual Contract.* Cambridge, UK: Polity.

Pateman, Carole. 1989. *The Disorder of Women: Democracy, Feminism, and Political Theory.* Cambridge, UK: Polity.

Pathways of Women's Empowerment. 2011. "Case Study: Women and Politics in Bangladesh." Retrieved June 1, 2012 (http://www.pathwaysofempowerment.org/Women_and_Politics_in_Bangladesh_case_study.pdf).

Paxton, Pamela. 1997. "Women in National Legislatures: A Cross-National Analysis." *Social Science Research* 26:442–464.

Paxton, Pamela, Jennifer Green, and Melanie M. Hughes. 2008. *Women in Parliament Dataset, 1893–2003.* [Computer file]. ICPSR24340-v1. Ann Arbor, MI: Inter-university Consortium for Political and Social Research [distributor], 2008-12-22.

Paxton, Pamela, Melanie M. Hughes, and Jennifer Green. 2006. "The International Women's Movement and Women's Political Representation, 1893–2003." *American Sociological Review* 71(6):898–920.

Paxton, Pamela, Melanie M. Hughes, and Matthew Painter. 2010. "The Difference Time Makes: Latent Growth Curve Models of Women's Political Representation." *European Journal of Political Research* 49(1):25–52.

Paxton, Pamela and Sheri Kunovich. 2003. "Women's Political Representation: The Importance of Ideology." *Social Forces* 81(5):87–114.

Pesonen, Pertti. 1968. *An Election in Finland: Party Activists and Voter Reactions.* New Haven, CT: Yale University Press.

Pettman, Jan J. 1996. *Worlding Women: A Feminist International Politics.* London: Routledge.

Phillips, Anne. 1991. *Engendering Democracy.* University Park: Pennsylvania State University Press.

Phillips, Anne. 1995. *The Politics of Presence: The Political Representation of Gender, Ethnicity and Race.* Oxford, UK: Clarendon Press.

Pinto-Duschinsky, Michael. 2002. "Financing Politics: A Global View." *Journal of Democracy* 13(4):69–86.

Pinto-Duschinsky, Michael and Alexander Postnikov, in collaboration with Christian Nadeau and Robert Dahl. 1999. "Campaign Finance in Foreign Countries: Legal Regulation and Political Practices (A Comparative Legal Survey and Analysis)." Washington, DC: International Foundation for Election Systems.

Pinto, Vânia Carvalho. 2011. "Arab States." Pp. 10–22 in *Women in Executive Power: A Global Overview,* edited by Gretchen Bauer and Manon Tremblay. London: Routledge.

Pintor, Rafael L. and Maria Gratschew. 2002. *Voter Turnout Since 1945: A Global Report.* Stockholm, Sweden: International IDEA.

Pitkin, Hanna F. 1972. *The Concept of Representation.* Berkeley: University of California Press.

Povey, Elaheh Rostami. 2003. "Women in Afghanistan: Passive Victims of the borga or Active Social Participants?" *Development in Practice* 13(2/3):266–277.

Powley, Elizabeth. 2003. *Strengthening Governance: The Role of Women in Rwanda's Transition.* Available online at http://www.un.org/womenwatch/osagi/meetings/2004/EGMelectoral/EP5Powley.PDF#search=%22%22elizabeth%20powley%22%22.

Przeworski, Adam. 2009. "Conquered or Granted? A History of Suffrage Extensions." *British Journal of Political Science* 39:291–321.

Pulzer, P. G. J. 1967. *Political Representation and Elections in Britain.* London: Allen and Unwin.

Putnam, Robert D. 1976. *The Comparative Study of Political Elites.* Englewood Cliffs, NJ: Prentice Hall.

Putnam, Robert D. 1994. *Making Democracy Work: Civic Traditions in Modern Italy.* Princeton, NJ: Princeton University Press.

Quesada, Ana I. G. 2003. "Putting the Mandate Into Practice: Legal Reform in Costa Rica." Paper presented at the workshop for the International Institute for Democracy and Electoral Assistance, February 23–24, Lima, Peru.

"Quote of the Day." 2005. *The Independent,* May 17, p. 25.

Qusti, Raid. 2004. "Women Driving Cars Is a Sinful Thing: Al-Qarni." *Arab News,* January 25. Available online at http://www.arabnews.com/?page=1&section=0& article=38586 &d=25&m=1&y=2004.

Radio New Zealand International. 2011. "Samoa PM Seeks Legislation to Guarantee 10% of Parliament is Women." October 4. Retrieved November 10, 2011 (http://www.rnzi.com/pages/news.php?op=read&id=63532).

Radsch, Courtney C. 2012. *Unveiling the Revolutionaries: Cyberactivism and the Role of Women in the Arab Uprisings.* James A. Baker III Institute for Public Policy, Rice University.

Rai, Shirin M. 2002. "Class, Caste, and Gender—Women in Parliament in India." Pp. 115–123 in *Women in Parliament: Beyond Numbers,* edited by A. Karam. Stockholm, Sweden: International IDEA.

Rai, Shirin M. 2005. "Reserved Seats in South Asia: A Regional Perspective." Pp. xx–xx in *Women in Parliament: Beyond Numbers—A Revised Edition,* edited by Julie Ballington and Azza Kazam. Stockholm: International IDEA.

Rakowski, C. 2003. "Women as Political Actors: The Move From Maternalism to Citizenship, Rights, and Power." *Latin American Research Review* 38(2):180–194.

Raman, Vasanthi. 2002. "The Implementation of Quotas for Women: The Indian Experience." Paper presented at regional workshop The Implementation of Quotas: Asian Experiences, September 25, Jakarta, Indonesia.

Ramirez, Francisco O., Yasemin Soysal, and Suzanne Shanahan. 1997. "The Changing Logic of Political Citizenship: Cross-National Acquisition of Women's Suffrage Rights, 1890 to 1990." *American Sociological Review* 62(5):735–45.

Randall, Margaret. 1981. *Sandino's Daughters: Testimonies of Nicaraguan Women in Struggle.* Vancouver, Canada: New Star Books.

Randall, Vicky. 1987. *Women and Politics: An International Perspective.* 2nd ed. Chicago: University of Chicago Press.

Ransford, Paige and Meryl Thomson 2011. "Moving Through the Pipeline: Women's Representation in Municipal Government in the New England Region of the United States." In *Women Voice and Representation in Local Government,* edited by Barbara Pini and Paula McDonald. New York & London: Routledge.

Ray, Raka and A.C. Korteweg. 1999. "Women's Movements in the Third World: Identity, Mobilization, and Autonomy." *Annual Review of Sociology* 25:47–71.

Redlund, Johan. 2004. "Women in the Panchayats—A Study of Gender Structures and the Impact of the 73rd Amendment to the Indian Constitution." Master's thesis. Department of Political Science, Lund University.

Rehn, Elisabeth and Ellen Johnson Sirleaf, eds. 2002. *Women War Peace: The Independent Experts' Assessment. Progress of the World's Women, Vol. I.* Available online at http://www.parliament.gov.za/pls/porta130/docs/folder/parliamentary_information/publications/unifem/index.htm.

Reingold, Beth. 1992. "Concepts of Representation Among Female and Male State Legislators." *Legislative Studies Quarterly* 14(4):509–537.

Reingold, Beth and Adrienne R. Smith. 2012. "Welfare Policymaking and Intersections of Race, Ethnicity, and Gender in U.S. State Legislators." *American Journal of Political Science* 56(1):131–147.

Remmert, Consuelo. 2003. "Rwanda Promotes Women Decision-makers." *UN Chronicle* 4:25.

Reskin, Barbara and Heidi I. Hartmann. 1986. *Women's Work, Men's Work: Sex Segregation on the Job.* Washington, DC: National Academy Press.

Reskin, Barbara and Patricia Roos. 1993. "Sex Segregation in the Workplace." *Annual Review of Sociology* 19(1):271–300.

Reynolds, Andrew. 1999. "Women in the Legislatures and Executives of the World: Knocking at the Highest Glass Ceiling." *World Politics* 51(July): 547–572.

Reynolds, Andrew. 2006. "The Curious Case of Afghanistan." *Journal of Democracy* 17(2):104–117.

Reynolds, Andrew. Forthcoming. "Representation and Rights: The Impact of LGBT Legislators in Comparative Perspective." *American Political Science Review.*

Reynolds, Andrew, Ben Reilly, and Andrew Ellis. 2005. *Electoral System Design: The New International IDEA Handbook.* Stockholm, Sweden: International Institute for Democracy and Electoral Assistance.

Reyntjens, Filip. 2010. "Constructing the Truth, Dealing With Dissent, Domesticating the World: Governance in Post-Genocide Rwanda." *African Affairs* 110(438):1–34.

Richards, Patricia. 2004. *Pobladoras, Indígenas, and the State: Conflicts Over Women's Rights in Chile.* New Brunswick, NJ: Rutgers University Press.

Ridgeway, Cecilia L. 2001. "Gender, Status, and Leadership." *Journal of Social Issues* 57:637–655.

Ridgeway, Cecilia and Lynn Smith-Lovin. 1999. "The Gender System and Interaction." *Annual Review of Sociology* 25:191–216.

Risman, Barbara J. 2004. "Gender as a Social Structure: Theory Wrestling With Activism." *Gender and Society* 18:429–450.

Robbins, Sarah J. 2011. "Esraa Abdel Fattah, 'Facebook Girl' The World Changer." *Glamour Magazine.* Retrieved May 30, 2012 (http://www.glamour.com/inspired/women-of-the-year/2011/esraa-abdel-fattah).

Robertson, Claire. 1986. "Women's Education and Class Formation in Africa, 1950–1980." Pp. 92–113 in *Women and Class in Africa,* edited by C. Robertson and I. Berger. New York: Africana.

Rosenthal, Cindy Simon. 1998a. "Determinants of Collective Leadership: Civic Engagement, Gender or Organizational Norms?" *Political Research Quarterly* 51:847–868.

Rosenthal, Cindy Simon. 1998b. *When Women Lead: Integrative Leadership in State Legislatures.* Oxford, UK: Oxford University Press.

Rosenthal, Cindy Simon. 2005. "Women Leading Legislatures: Getting There and Getting Things Done." Pp. 197–212 in *Women and Elective Office: Past, Present, and Future,* 2nd ed. Oxford, UK: Oxford University Press.

Roshan, Benazeer. 2004. "The More Things Change, the More They Stay the Same: The Plight of Afghan Women Two Years After the Overthrow of the Taliban." *Berkeley Women's Law Journal* 19(1):270–286.

Ross, Michael. 2008. "Oil, Islam, and Women." *American Political Science Review* 102:107–123.

Roth, Silke. 2007. "Sisterhood and Solidarity? Women's Organizations in the Expanded European Union." *Social Politics: International Studies in Gender, State, and Society* 14:460–487.

Roth, Silke. 2008. "Introduction: Gender Politics in the Expanding European Union: Mobilization, Inclusion, Exclusion." Pp. 1–16 in *Gender Politics in the Expanding European Union: Mobilization, Inclusion, Exclusion,* edited by Silke Roth. New York: Berghahn Books.

Rousseau, Stéphanie. 2009. *Women's Citizenship in Peru: The Paradoxes of Neopopulism in Latin America.* New York: Palgrave-Macmillan.

Rowlands, Jo. 1997. *Questioning Empowerment: Working With Women in Honduras.* Oxford, UK: Oxfam Publications.

Rueschemeyer, Marilyn. 1994. "Difficulties and Opportunities in the Transition Period: Concluding Observations." Pp. 225–237 in *Women in the Politics of Postcommunist Eastern Europe,* edited by M. Rueschemeyer. Armonk, NY: M. E. Sharpe.

Rule, Wilma. 1981. "Why Women Don't Run: The Critical Contextual Factors in Women's Legislative Recruitment." *Western Political Quarterly* 34:60–77.

Rule, Wilma. 1987. "Electoral Systems, Contextual Factors and Women's Opportunity for Election to Parliament in Twenty Three Democracies." *Western Political Quarterly* 20:477–498.

Rule, Wilma. 1994. "Parliaments of, by, and for the People: Except for Women?" Pp. 15–31 in *Electoral Systems in Comparative Perspective: Their Impact on Women and Minorities,* edited by W. Rule and J. F. Zimmerman. Westport, CT: Greenwood Press.

Rupp, Leila J. and Verta Taylor. 1999. "Forging Feminist Identity in an International Movement: A Collective Identity Approach to Twentieth-Century Feminism." *Signs* 24:363–386.

Ruppert, Uta. 2002. "Global Women's Politics: Towards the 'Globalizing' of Women's Human Rights." Pp. 147–159 in *Common Ground or Mutual Exclusion? Women's Movements and International Relations,* edited by M. Braig and S. Wolte. London: Zed Books.

Ruthven, Amanda. 2005. "Women in Washington: Will Women Ever Be Adequately Represented in Congress?" *Feminist Uproar.* Available online at http://www.democracy matters.org/press/spring2005feministuproar.php.

Ryan, Michelle K., S. Alexander Haslam, and Clara Kulich. 2010. "Politics and the Glass Cliff: Evidence That Women Are Preferentially Selected to Contest Hard-to-Win Seats." *Psychology of Women Quarterly* 34:56–64.

Sabbagh, Amal. 2007. "Overview of Women's Political Representation in the Arab Region: Opportunities and Challenges." Pp. 7–18 in *The Arab Quota Report: Selected Case Studies.* Stockholm, Sweden: International IDEA.

Sacchet, Teresa. 2008 "Beyond Numbers: The Impact of Gender Quotas in Latin America." International *Feminist Journal of Politics* 10(3):369–386.

Sagot, Montserrat. 2010. "Does the Political Participation of Women Matter? Democratic Representation, Affirmative Action, and Quotas in Costa Rica." *IDS Bulletin* 41(5):25–34.

Saint-Germain, Michelle. 1989. "Does Their Difference Make a Difference? The Impact of Women on Public Policy in Arizona Legislature." *Social Science Quarterly* 70:956–958.

Saint-Germain, Michelle. 1993. "Women in Power in Nicaragua: Myth and Reality." Pp. 70–102 in *Women Heads of State,* edited by Michael Genovese. Newbury Park, CA: Sage.

Saint-Germain, Michelle A. and Cynthia Chávez Metoyer. 2008. *Women Legislators in Central America.* Austin, TX: University of Texas Press.

Sambanis, Nicholas. 2002. "A Review of Recent Advances and Future Directions in the Literature on Civil War." *Defense and Peace Economics* 13:215–243.

Sanbonmatsu, Kira. 2002a. *Democrats, Republicans, and the Politics of Women's Place.* Ann Arbor: University of Michigan Press.

Sanbonmatsu, Kira. 2002b. "Political Parties and the Recruitment of Women to State Legislators." *Journal of Politics* 64:791–809.

Sanbonmatsu, Kira. 2003. "Gender-Related Political Knowledge and the Descriptive Representation of Women." *Political Behavior* 25:367–388.

Sapiro, Virginia. 1982. "Private Costs of Public Commitments or Public Costs of Private Commitments? Family Roles Versus Political Ambition." *American Journal of Political Science* 26:265–279.

Sauer, Lauren. 2012. "A Worthy Fight: Helping Increase Gender Equality in Papua New Guinea." International Foundation for Electoral Systems. Retrieved March 20, 2013 (http://www.ifes.org/Content/Publications/Interviews/2012/A-Worthy-Fight-Helping-Increase-Gender-Equality-in-Papua-New-Guinea.aspx).

Sawer, Marian. 1990. *Sisters in Suits: Women and Public Policy in Australia.* Sydney, Australia: Allen and Unwin.

Sawer, Marian. 2000. "Parliamentary Representation of Women: From Discourses of Justice to Strategies of Accountability." *International Political Science Review* 21:361–380.

Saxonberg, Steven. 2000. "Women in East European Parliaments." *Journal of Democracy* 11:145–158.

Scammell, Margaretand and Holli Semetko, eds. 2000. *The Media, Journalism and Democracy.* Aldershot: Ashgate.

Schlozman, Kay Lehman, Nancy Burns, and Sidney Verba. 1994. "Gender and the Pathways to Participation: The Role of Resources." *Journal of Politics* 56(4): 963–990.

Schmidt, Gregory D. and Kyle L. Saunders. 2004. "Effective Quotas, Relative Party Magnitude and the Success of Female Candidates: Peruvian Municipal Elections in Comparative Perspective." *Comparative Political Studies* 37:704–734.

Schreiber, Ronnee and Brian Adams. 2008. "Women's Political Fortunes in Local Elections: A Study of Three Cities." Paper presented at the annual meeting of the Western Political Science Association, San Diego, CA. March 2008.

Schroeder, Patricia. 1998. *24 Years of Housework . . . and the Place Is Still a Mess: My Life in Politics*. New York: Andrews Mcmeel.

Schwindt-Bayer, Leslie A. 2006. "Still Supermadres? Gender and the Policy Priorities of Latin American Legislators." *American Journal of Political Science* 50: 570–585.

Schwindt-Bayer, Leslie A. 2009. "Making Quotas Work: The Effect of Gender Quota Laws on the Election of Women." *Legislative Studies Quarterly* 34(1):5–28.

Schwindt-Bayer, Leslie A. 2010. *Political Power and Women's Representation in Latin America*. Oxford, UK: Oxford University Press.

Scola, Becki. 2006. "Women of Color in State Legislatures: Gender, Race, Ethnicity and Legislative Office Holding." *Journal of Women, Politics & Policy* 28(3/4): 43–70.

Seitz, Barbara. 1991. "Songs, Identity, and Women's Liberation in Nicaragua." *Latin American Music Review* 12(1):21–41.

Seltzer, Richard A., Jody Newman, and Melissa Voorhees Leighton. 1997. *Sex as a Political Variable: Women as Candidates and Voters in U.S. Elections*. Boulder, CO: Lynne Rienner.

Shapiro, Robert Y. and Harpreet Mahajan. 1986. "Gender Differences in Policy Preferences: A Summary of Trends From the 1960s to the 1980s." *Public Opinion Quarterly* 50:42–61.

Shaul, Marnie S. 1982. "The Status of Women in Local Governments: International Assessment." *Public Administration Review* Nov./Dec.:491–500.

Shayne, Julie D. 2004. *The Revolution Question: Feminisms in El Salvador, Chile, and Cuba*. New Brunswick, NJ: Rutgers University Press.

Shehadeh, Lamia. 1998. "The Legal Status of Married Women in Lebanon." *International Journal of Middle East Studies* 30:501–519.

Shella, Kimberly. 2011. "Choosing Between Electing Women or Ethnic Candidates? Ethnic Concentration and Electoral Rules in African States." Paper presented at the annual meeting of the American Political Science Association, Seattle, WA.

Shelton, Beth Anne. 1990. "The Distribution of Household Tasks: Does a Wife's Employment Status Make a Difference?" *Journal of Family Issues* 11: 115–135.

Shin, Youngtae. 2004. *Women and Politics in Japan and Korea*. Lewiston, NY: Edwin Mellen Press.

Sideris, Tina. 2001. "Rape in War and Peace: Social Context, Gender, Power, and Identity." Pp. 142–158 in *The Aftermath: Women in Post-Conflict Transformation*, edited by S. Meintjes, A. Pillay, and M. Turshen. London: Zed Books.

Siemienska, Renata. 2003. "Women in the Polish Sejm: Political Culture and Party Politics Versus Electoral Rules." Pp. 217–244 in *Women's Access to Political Power in Post-Communist Europe*, edited by R. E. Matland and K. A. Montgomery. Oxford, UK: Oxford University Press.

Siemienska, Renata. 2004. "Gender Party Quotas in Poland." Paper presented at the workshop of the International Institute for Democracy and Electoral Assistance, October 22–23, Budapest, Hungary.

Sierra, María Teresa. 2001. "Human Rights, Gender and Ethnicity: Legal Claims and Anthropological Challenges in Mexico." *PoLAR* 24(2):76–93.

Sierra, María Teresa. 2007. *La renovación de la justicia indígena en tiempos de derechos: Etnicidad, género y diversidad.* Retrieved June 8, 2012 (http://lanic.utexas.edu/project/etext/llilas/vrp/sierra.pdf).

Silber, Irina Carlota. 2011. *Everyday Revolutionaries: Gender, Violence, and Disillusionment in Postwar El Salvador.* New Brunswick, NJ: Rutgers University Press.

Simmons Levin, Leah. 1999. "Setting the Agenda: The Impact of the 1977 Israel Women's Party." *Israel Studies* 4(2):40–63.

Singla, Pamela. 2007. *Women's Participation in Panchayati Raj: Nature and Effectiveness.* Jaipur, India: Rawat Publications.

"The Single Victim at the Border Sacrifices." 1885. *The Book of Rites. Part I. Book IX. Sacred Books of the East, Vol. 27.* Translated by James Legge. Available online at http://www.sacred-texts.com/cfu/liki/liki09.htm.

Sirleaf, Ellen Johnson. 2006. "Inaugural Address." Retrieved May 19, 2012 (http://www.emansion.gov.lr/doc.inaugural_add_1.pdf).

Skjeie, Hege. 1991. "The Rhetoric of Difference: On Women's Inclusion Into Political Elites." *Politics and Society* 19:233–263.

Skjeie, Hege. 2002. "Credo on Difference—Women in Parliament in Norway." Pp. 183–189 in *Women in Parliament: Beyond Numbers,* edited by A. Karam. Stockholm, Sweden: International IDEA.

Slater, Julia. 2011. "Women Recall How Men Voted 'Yes.'" January 21. Retrieved January 31, 2011 (http://www.swissinfo.ch/eng/Specials/Votes_for_women!/Women_in_politics/Women_recall_how_men_voted_Yes.html?cid=29379110).

Smith, Eric R. A. N. and Richard L. Fox. 2001. "The Electoral Fortunes of Women Candidates for Congress." *Political Research Quarterly* 54(1):205–221.

Smith, Kevin B. 1997. "When All's Fair: Signs of Parity in Media Coverage of Female Candidates." *Political Communication* 14(1):71–82.

Smooth, Wendy. 2001. Perceptions of Influence in State Legislatures: A Focus on the Experiences of African American Women Legislators. PhD dissertation. University of Maryland.

Smooth, Wendy. 2011. "Standing for Women? Which Women? The Substantive Representation of Women's Interests and the Research Imperative of Intersectionality." *Politics & Gender* 7(3):436–441.

Sobritchea, Carolyn I. 1990. "Gender Inequality and Its Supporting Ideologies in Philippine Society." Pp. 8–17 in *And She Said No! Human Rights, Women's Identities and Struggles,* edited by L. Bautista and E. Rifareal. Caloocan City: National Council of Churches in the Philippines.

Solheim, Bruce O. 2000. *On Top of the World: Women's Political Leadership in Scandinavia and Beyond.* Westport, CT: Greenwood Press.

Sorush, Lisa. 2005. "Women's Leadership and Religion." Paper presented at the Afghan Women Leaders Speak Conference, November 16–19, Columbus, OH.

Sperling, Valerie. 1998. "Gender Politics and the State During Russia's Transition Period." Pp. 143–165 in *Gender, Politics, and the State,* edited by V. Randall and G. Waylen. London: Routledge.

Spinner-Halev, Jeff. 2001. "Feminism, Multiculturalism, Oppression, and the State." *Ethics* 112(1):84–113.

Squires, Judith. 1996. "Quotas for Women: Fair Representation?" Pp. 73–90 in *Women and Politics,* edited by J. Lovenduski and P. Norris. Oxford, UK: Oxford University Press.

Squires, Judith. 2004. "Gender Quotas: Comparative and Contextual Analyses." *European Political Science* 3(3):51–58.

Squires, Judith. 2005. "The Implementation of Gender Quotas in Britain." Available online at http://www.quotaproject.org/CS/CS_Britain_Squires.pdf.

Stanton, Elizabeth Cady. 1848. *Declaration of Sentiments and Resolutions.* Seneca Falls, NY. Available online at http://ecssba.rutgers.edu/docs/seneca.html.

Stanton, Elizabeth C., Susan B. Anthony, and Matilda Joslyn Gage, eds. 1887. *History of Woman Suffrage, Volume I.* Rochester, NY: Susan B. Anthony.

Staudt, Kathleen. 1986. "Stratification: Implications for Women's Politics." Pp. 197–215 in *Women and Class in Africa,* edited by C. Robertson and I. Berger. New York: Africana.

Staudt, Kathleen. 1998. *Policy, Politics, and Gender: Women Gaining Ground.* Bloomfield, CT: Kumarian.

Sternbach, Nancy Saporta, Marysa Navarro-Aranguren, Patricia Chuchryk, and Sonia E. Álvarez. 1992. "Feminisms in Latin America: From Bogotá to San Bernardo" *Signs* 17:393–434.

Stetson, Dorothy McBride. 1995. "The Oldest Women's Policy Agency: The Women's Bureau in the United States." Pp. 254–271 in *Comparative State Feminism,* edited by D. M. Stetson and A. G. Mazur. Thousand Oaks, CA: Sage.

Stetson, Dorothy McBride and Amy G. Mazur, eds. 1995. *Comparative State Feminism.* Thousand Oaks, CA: Sage.

Stockemer, Daniel. 2009. "Women's Parliamentary Representation: Are Women More Highly Represented in (Consolidated) Democracies Than in Non-Democracies?" *Contemporary Politics* 15(4):429–443.

Stockemer, Daniel and Maeve Byrne. 2011. "Women's Representation Around the World: The Importance of Women's Participation in the Workforce." *Parliamentary Affairs* 65(4):802–821.

Stokes, Wendy. 2005. *Women in Contemporary Politics.* Oxford, UK: Polity.

Sumbul, Aysha. 2004. "Women's Reservation Bill—A Critique." *PUCL Bulletin.* Available online at http://www.pucl.org/Topics/Gender/2004/womens-reserva tion-bill.htm.

Susan B. Anthony List. 2006. "What's New?" Available online at http://www .sba-list.org/.

Swers, Michele L. 1998. "Are Women More Likely to Vote for Women's Issue Bills Than Their Male Colleagues?" *Legislative Studies Quarterly* 23:435–448.

Swers, Michele L. 2002a. *The Difference Women Make: The Policy Impact of Women in Congress.* Chicago: University of Chicago Press.

Swers, Michele L. 2002b. "Transforming the Agenda: Analyzing Gender Differences in Women's Issue Bill Sponsorship." Pp. 260–283 in *Women*

Transforming Congress, edited by C. S. Rosenthal. Norman: University of Oklahoma Press.

Tahri, Rachida. 2003. "Women's Political Participation: The Case of Morocco." Paper presented at the conference Implementation of Quotas: African Experiences, November 11–12, Pretoria, South Africa.

Takash, Paule C. 1993. "Breaking Barriers to Representation: Chicana/Latina Elected Officials in California." *Urban Anthropology* 22(3–4):325–360.

Tamale, Sylvia. 1999. *When Hens Begin to Crow: Gender and Parliamentary Politics in Uganda.* Boulder, CO: Westview Press.

Tavaana. 2010. "Moudawana: A Peaceful Revolution for Women." November 23. Retrieved May 31, 2012 (http://www.tavaana.org/archive.jsp?restrictids=nu_rep eatitemid&restrictvalues=2071502000341283364790954&lang=en).

Taylor-Robinson, Michelle M. and Roseanna Michelle Heath. 2003. "Do Women Legislators Have Different Policy Priorities Than Their Male Colleagues? A Critical Case Test." *Women and Politics* 24:77–101.

The Telegraph. 2004. "The New Amazons." *The Telegraph,* August 15. Retrieved January 17, 2013 (http://www.telegraphindia.com/1040815/asp/look/story_3622999.asp).

Thirani, Neha. 2012. "In India, a Surge in Female Voters," *The New York Times.* Retrieved June 7, 2012 (http://india.blogs.nytimes.com/2012/03/07/women-voters-flock-to-polls-in-indias-latest-elections/).

Thomas, Gwynn and Melinda Adams. 2010. "Breaking the Final Glass Ceiling: The Influence of Gender in the Elections of Ellen Johnson-Sirleaf and Michelle Bachelet." *Journal of Women, Politics and Policy* 31(2):105–131.

Thomas, Shibu. 2011. "HC: Why Bar Women From Working at Night?" *The Times of India,* July 5. Retrieved May 21, 2012 (www.articles.timesofindia.indiatimes.com/2011–07–05/mumbai/29737938_1_bar-women-waitress-womanist-party).

Thomas, Sue. 1991. "The Impact of Women on State Legislative Priorities." *Journal of Politics* 53:958–976.

Thomas, Sue. 1994. *How Women Legislate.* Oxford, UK: Oxford University Press.

Thomas, Sue. 1998. "Introduction: Women and Elective Office: Past, Present, and Future." Pp. 1–14 in *Women and Elective Office: Past, Present, and Future,* edited by S. Thomas and C. Wilcox. Oxford, UK: Oxford University Press.

Thomas, Sue. 2003. "Scenes in the Writing of 'Constance Lytton and Jane Warton, Spinster: Contextualising a Cross-Class Dresser." *Women's History Review* 12(1):51–71.

Thomas, Sue and Susan Welch. 1991. "The Impact of Gender on Activities and Priorities of State Legislators." *The Western Political Quarterly* 44:445–456.

Thornton, Arland, Duane F. Alwin, and Donald Camburn. 1983. "Causes and Consequences of Sex-Role Attitudes and Attitude Change." American Sociological Review 48(2):211–227.

Tiltnes, Uga, 2000. 'Women and Political Participation in Jordan." In *Arab Women and Political Participation,* edited by Hussein Abu Rumman. Amman: al-Urdon al-Jadid Research Centre.

Tinker, Irene and Jane Jaquette. 1987. "The UN Decade for Women—Its Impact and Legacy." *World Development* 15:419–427.

Togeby, L. 1994. "Political Implications of Increasing Numbers of Women in the Labour Force." *Comparative Political Studies* 27:211–240.

Towns, Ann E. 2004. *Norms and Inequality in International Society: Global Politics of Women and the State.* PhD dissertation, University of Minnesota, Minneapolis.

Towns, Ann E. 2010. *Women and States: Norms and Hierarchies in International Society.* New York: Cambridge University Press.

Tremaine, M. 2000. "Women Mayors Say What It Takes to Lead: Setting Theory Against Live Experience." *Women in Leadership Review* 15:246–252.

Tremblay, Manon. 1993. "Political Party, Political Philosophy and Feminism: A Case Study of the Female and Male Candidates in the 1989 Quebec General Election." *Canadian Journal of Political Science* 26:507–522.

Tremblay, Manon and Rejean Pelletier. 2000. "More Feminists or More Women? Descriptive and Substantive Representations of Women in the 1997 Canadian Federal Elections." *International Political Science Review* 21:381–405.

Tripp, Aili Mari. 1994. "Gender, Political Participation, and the Transformation of Associational Life in Uganda and Tanzania." *African Studies Review* 37:107–131.

Tripp, Aili Mari. 2000. *Women and Politics in Uganda.* Madison: University of Wisconsin Press.

Tripp, Aili Mari. 2002. "Conflicting Visions of Community and Citizenship: The Politics of Women's Rights and Cultural Diversity in Uganda." Pp. 413–440 in *Gender Justice, Democracy, and Rights,* Vol. 25, edited by M. Molyneaux and S. Razavi. Oxford, UK: Oxford University Press.

Tripp, Aili Mari. 2003. "The Changing Face of Africa's Legislatures: Women and Quotas." Paper presented at the workshop of the International Institute for Democracy and Electoral Assistance, November 11–12, Pretoria, South Africa.

Tripp, Aili Mari. 2005. "Regional Networking as Transnational Feminism: African Experiences." *Feminist Africa* 4.

Tripp, Aili Mari. 2006. "Uganda: Agents of Change for Women's Advancement?" Pp. 111–132 in *Women in African Parliaments,* edited by G. Bauer and H. E. Britton. Boulder, CO: Lynne Rienner.

Tripp, Aili Mari. 2009. "Debate: Does Oil Wealth Hurt Women?" *Politics & Gender* 5(4):545–75.

Tripp, Aili, Isabel Casimiro, Joy Kwesiga, and Alice Mungwa. 2009. *African Women's Movements: Transforming Political Landscapes.* New York: Cambridge University Press.

Tripp, Aili M. and Alice Kang. 2006. "Quotas: The Fast Track to Increasing Female Legislative Representation around the World." Working paper.

Tripp, Aili M. and Alice Kang. 2008. "The Global Impact of Quotas: The Fast Track to Female Representation." *Comparative Political Studies* 41(3):338–361.

Tripp, Aili, Colleen Lowe Morna, and Dior Konaté. 2006. "Electoral Gender Quotas—Sub-Saharan Africa." In *Women, Quotas and Politics,* edited by D. Dahlerup. London: Routledge.

Truth, Sojourner. 1851. "Ain't I a Woman?" Available online at http://www.suffragist .com/docs.htm#truth.

Tucker, Judith E. 1993. *Arab Women: Old Boundaries, New Frontiers*. Bloomington: Indiana University Press.

Tusi, Nizamu'l-Mulk. 1977. In *Studies in Muslim Political Thought and Administration*, edited by H. K. Sherwani. Philadelphia: Porcupine Press.

Tymoshenko, Yulia. 2005. "Biography of Yulia Tymoshenko." Retrieved August 29, 2005 (http://ww2.tymoshenko.com.ua/eng/about/).

U.S. Census Bureau. 2010. *Race and Hispanic or Latino Origin: 2010*. 2010 Census Summary File 1. Retrieved May 10, 2012 (http://factfinder2.census.gov/).

U.S. Department of State. 2005. "Background Note: Uganda." Retrieved January 17, 2013 (http://www.state.gov/r/pa/ei/bgn/2963.htm).

U.S. Government Printing Office. 2000. *Public Papers of the Presidents of the United States: William J. Clinton* (1998, Book I). Washington, DC: U.S. Government Printing Office.

United Nations. 1946. "Political Rights of Women." *General Assembly Resolution* 56(1).

United Nations. 1979. "Convention on the Elimination of All Forms of Discrimination against Women." Retrieved January 17, 2013 (http://www.un.org/womenwatch/ daw/cedaw/text/econvention.htm).

United Nations. 1995. "Fourth World Conference on Women Beijing Declaration." Retrieved December 20, 2012 (http://www.un.org/womenwatch/daw/beijing/ platform/declar.htm).

United Nations. 2000a. *Women Go Global* [CD-ROM]. New York: United Nations.

United Nations. 2000b. *Women in Asia and the Pacific: High-Level Intergovernmental Meeting to Review Regional Implementation of the Beijing Platform for Action, 26–29 October 1999*. New York: United Nations.

United Nations. 2004. *World Population Prospects: The 2004 Revision and World Urbanization Prospects: The 2003 Revision*. New York: United Nations.

United Nations. 2011. *World Population Prospects: The 2010 Revision*. Department of Economic and Social Affairs. Retrieved May 14, 2012 (www.esa.un.org/unpp).

United Nations Development Fund for Women. 2005. "Fiji." Retrieved January 17, 2013 (http://www.womenwarpeace.org/fiji/fiji.htm).

United Nations Development Programme. 1995. *Human Development Report*. New York: Oxford University Press.

United Nations Development Programme. 2000. *Women's Political Participation and Good Governance: 21st Century Challenges*. New York: United Nations Development Programme.

United Nations Development Programme. 2004. *Human Development Report 2004: Cultural Liberty in Today's Diverse World*. New York: United Nations Development Programme.

United Nations Development Programme. 2011. *Human Development Report*. New York: Oxford University Press.

United Nations Educational, Scientific, and Cultural Organization. 2005. *Education for All Global Monitoring Report.* Paris: United Nations Educational, Scientific, and Cultural Organization.

United Nations Population Fund. 2005a. "The Promise of Equality: Gender Equality, Reproductive Health and the MDGs." Available online at www.unfpa.org/swp/2005/english/ch1/index.htm

United Nations Population Fund. 2005b. "State of the World's Population 2005, The Promise of Equality." Available online at www.unfpa.org/public/home/publications/pid/1343

United Nations Statistics Division. 2012. "Table 1a—Population Size." Retrieved June 8, 2012. (http://unstats.un.org/unsd/demographic/products/socind/default.htm).

United Nations Women. 2012. "Women in Politics: 2012." January 1. Available online at http://www.ipu.org/pdf/publications/wmnmap12_en.pdf

Urdang, Stephanie. 1989. *And Still They Dance: Women, War, and the Struggle for Change in Mozambique.* New York: Monthly Review.

Van Cott, Donna Lee. 2005. *From Movements to Parties in Latin America: The Evolution of Ethnic Politics.* New York: Cambridge University Press.

Van Cott, Donna Lee and Jóhanna Kristín Birnir. 2007. *Latin American Research Review* 42(1):97–123.

Van Cott, Donna Lee and Roberta Rice. 2006. "The Emergence and Formation of Ethnic Parties in Latin America: A Sub-national Statistical Analysis." *Comparative Political Studies* 40(6):709–732.

Verba, Sidney, Nancy Burns, and Kay Lehman Schlozman. 1997. "Knowing and Caring About Politics: Gender and Political Engagement." *Journal of Politics* 59:1051–1072.

Verge, Tània. 2011. "Women and Local Politics in Spain: Exploring Gender Regimes and Biased Party Candidate Selection Processes." Pp. 59–75 in *Women and Representation in Local Government: International Case Studies,* edited by Barbara Pini and Paula McDonald. Oxford, UK: Routledge.

Vetter, A. 2007. *Local Politics: A Resource for Democracy in Western Europe? Local Autonomy, Local Integrative Capacity, and Citizens' Attitudes Toward Politics.* Lanham, MD: Lexington.

Vichit-Vadakan, Juree. 2008. "A Glimpse of Women Leaders in Thai Local Politics." Pp. 125–167 in *Women and Politics in Thailand: Continuity and Change,* edited by Kazuki Iwanaga. Copenhagen: Nordic Institute of Asian Studies.

Victor, Kirk. 2005. "Still an Old Boys Club?" *National Journal* 37:748.

Viterna, Jocelyn. Forthcoming. *Women in War: The Micro-processes of Mobilization in El Salvador.* New York: Oxford University Press.

Viterna, Jocelyn and Kathleen M. Fallon 2008. "Democratization, Women's Movements, and Gender-Equitable States: A Framework for Comparison." *American Sociological Review* 73(4):668–689.

von Hippel, Theodor Gottlieb. 1792. *On Improving the Status of Women.* Translated by T. F. Sellner. Detroit, MI: Wayne State University Press.

von Wahl, Angelika. 2008. "The EU and Enlargement: Conceptualizing Beyond 'East' and 'West.'" Pp. 19–36 in *Gender Politics in the Expanding European Union:*

Mobilization, Inclusion, Exclusion, edited by Silke Roth. New York: Berghahn Books.

Wakoko, Florence and Linda Labao. 1996. "Reconceptualizing Gender and Reconstructing Social Life: Ugandan Women and Path to National Development." *Africa Today* 43:307–322.

Walby, Sylvia. 1996. "The 'Declining Significance' or the 'Changing Forms' of Patriarchy?" Pp. 19–33 in *Patriarchy and Economic Development: Women's Positions at the End of the Twentieth Century,* edited by V. M. Moghadam. Oxford, UK: Clarendon Press.

Walby, Sylvia. 2004. "The European Union and Gender Equality: Emergent Varieties of Gender Regime." *Social Politics* 11:4–29.

Walecki, Marcin. 2005. "Political Money and Corruption." International Foundation for Election Systems Political Finance, White Paper Series. Available online at http://www.ifes.org/~/media/Files/Publications/White%20PaperReport/2004/91/IFES_WhitePaper_III.pdf.

Wängnerud, Lena. 2000. "Testing the Politics of Presence: Women's Representation in the Swedish Riksdag." *Scandinavian Political Studies* 23:67–91.

Wängnerud, Lena. 2006. "Sweden: A Step-Wise Development." Pp. 238–248 in *Women in Parliament: Beyond Numbers, A Revised Edition,* edited by Julie Ballington and Azza Karam. Stockholm: IDEA Handbook.

Ward, Kathryn B. 1984. *Women in the World-System: Its Impact on Status and Fertility.* New York: Praeger.

Wartenberg, Thomas E. 1990. *The Forms of Power: From Domination to Transformation.* Philadelphia, PA: Temple University Press.

Wartenberg, Thomas E. 1992. *Rethinking Power.* Albany: State University of New York.

Waylen, Georgina. 1994. "Women and Democratization: Conceptualizing Gender Relations in Transition Politics." *World Politics* 46(3):327–354.

Waylen, Georgina. 1996. *Gender in Third World Politics.* Boulder, CO: Lynne Rienner.

Waylen, Georgina. 2007a. *Engendering Transitions: Women's Mobilization, Institutions, and Gender Outcomes.* New York: Oxford University Press.

Waylen, Georgina. 2007b. "Women's Mobilization and Gender Outcomes in Transitions to Democracy—The Case of South Africa." *Comparative Political Studies* 40(5):521–546.

Weber, Lynn. 2001. *Understanding Race, Class, Gender, and Sexuality: A Conceptual Framework.* Boston: McGraw-Hill.

Weber, Max. 1978. *Economy and Society: An Outline of Interpretive Sociology.* Translated by E. Fischoff. Berkeley: University of California Press.

Weiner, Elaine. 2009. "Eastern Houses, Western Bricks? (Re)Constructing Gender Sensibilities in the European Unions Eastward Enlargement." *Social Politics* 16:303–326.

Weir, Sara J. 1999. "The Feminist Face of State Executive Leadership: Women as Governors." Pp. 248–259 in *Women in Politics: Outsiders or Insiders?* 3rd ed., edited by L. D. Whitaker. Upper Saddle River, NJ: Prentice Hall.

Wejnert, Barbara. 1996. "Introduction: The Dynamics of Societal Macro Changes: Implications for the Life of Women." Pp. xiii–xvii in *Research on Women in Russia and Eastern Europe, Volume 2: Women in Post Communism,* edited by B. Wejnert and M. Spencer. Greenwich, CT: JAI Press.

Welborne, Bozena Christina. 2010. *The Strategic Use of Gender Quotas in the Arab World.* Washington, DC: IFES.

Welch, Susan. 1978. "Recruitment of Women to Public Office." *Western Political Quarterly* 31:372–380.

Weldon, S. Laurel. 2002a. "Beyond Bodies: Institutional Sources of Representation for Women in Democratic Policymaking." *Journal of Politics* 64:1153–1174.

Weldon, S. Laurel. 2002b. *Protest, Policy and the Problem of Violence Against Women: A Cross-National Comparison.* Pittsburgh, PA: University of Pittsburgh Press.

Welter, Barbara. 1966. "The Cult of True Womanhood: 1820–1860." *American Quarterly* 18:151–174.

West, Candace and Sarah Fenstermaker. 1997. "Doing Difference." Pp. 55–81 in *Doing Gender, Doing Difference,* edited Sarah Fenstermaker and Candace West. New York, NY: Routledge.

West, Candace and Don H. Zimmerman. 1987. "Doing Gender." *Gender and Society* 1:125–151.

Whitford, Andrew B., Vicky M. Wilkins, and Mercedes G. Ball. 2007. "Descriptive Representation and Policymaking Authority: Evidence From Women in Cabinets and Bureaucracies." *Governance* 20(4):559–580.

Whitney, Catherine. 2000. *Nine and Counting: The Women of the Senate.* New York: HarperCollins.

Wigfield, Allan, Jacquelynne S. Eccles, and Paul R. Pintrich. 1996. "Development Between the Ages of 11 and 25." Pp. 148–185 in *Handbook of Educational Psychology,* edited by D. C. Berliner and R. C. Calfee. New York: Macmillan.

Wilcox, Clyde, Beth Stark, and Sue Thomas. 2003. "Popular Support for Electing Women in Eastern Europe." Pp. 43–62 in *Women's Access to Political Power in Post-Communist Europe,* edited by R. E. Matland and K. A. Montgomery. Oxford, UK: Oxford University Press.

Wilford, Rick. 1998. "Women, Ethnicity and Nationalism: Surveying the Ground." Pp. 1–22 in *Women, Ethnicity and Nationalism: The Politics of Transition,* edited by R. Wilford and R. L. Miller. Oxford, UK: Routledge.

Williams, Melissa S. 1998. *Voice, Trust, and Memory: Marginalized Groups and the Failings of Liberal Representation.* Princeton, NJ: Princeton University Press.

Willsher, Kim. 2012. "French Elections: Record Number of Female MPs Not Enough, Says Feminists." *The Guardian.* June 18, 2012. Retrieved February 2, 2013 (http://www.guardian.co.uk/world/2012/jun/18/french-elections-record-female-mps).

Winess, Michael. 1991. "How the Senators Handled the Professor's Accusations," *The New York Times,* October 8, p. A22.

The WISH List. 2012. "Women in the Senate and House." Retrieved January 17, 2013 (www.thewishlist.org).

Wolbrecht, Christina and David Campbell. 2007. "Leading By Example: Female

Members of Parliament as Political Role Models." *American Journal of Political Science* 51:921–939.

Wolchik, Sharon. 1981. "Eastern Europe." Pp. 252–277 in *The Politics of the Second Electorate: Women and Public Participation*, edited by J. Lovenduski and J. Hills. London: Routledge and Kegan Paul.

Wolchik, Sharon. 1994. "Women and the Politics of Transition in the Czech and Slovak Republics." Pp. 3–27 in *Women in the Politics of Postcommunist Eastern Europe*, edited by M. Rueschemeyer. Armonk, NY: M. E. Sharpe.

Wollstonecraft, Mary. 1999 (Original work published 1792). *A Vindication of the Rights of Woman*. New York: Bartleby.com. Retrieved January 17, 2013 (http://www.bartleby.com/144/).

Women for Women International. 2004. "Women Taking a Lead: Progress Toward Empowerment and Gender Equity in Rwanda." Women for Women International Briefing Paper, September. Retrieved July 27, 2005 (http://womenforwomen.org/nrrwpap.html)

Women in World History. 2006. *Women and Confucianism*. Retrieved January 17, 2013 (http://www.womeninworldhistory.com/lesson3.html).

Women of Uganda Network. 2005. "Search WOUGNET." Retrieved July 27, 2005 (http://www.wougnet.org/search.html).

Women's Environment and Development Organization. 2007. "Factsheet: Getting the Balance Right in National Cabinets." October 21. Available online at http://www.wedo.org/library/5050-campaign-getting-the-balance-right-in-national-cabinets.

Wong, Pansy. 1997. "Maiden Statement." Retrieved May 20, 2012 (http://www.pansywong.co.nz/eng).

World Values Survey Association. 2005. *World Values Surveys and European Values Surveys, 1981–1984, 1990–1993, and 1995–1997* [Computer file]. ICPSR version. Ann Arbor, MI: Institute for Social Research and Inter-university Consortium for Political and Social Research.

Wright, Erik Olin, Janeen Baxter, and Gunn Elizabeth Birkelund. 1995. "The Gender Gap in Workplace Authority: A Cross-National Study." *American Sociological Review* 60:407–35.

Yarr, Linda F. 1996. "Gender and the Allocation on Time: Impact on the Household Economy." Pp. 110–122 in *Vietnam's Women in Transition*, edited by K. Barry. New York: St. Martin's Press.

Yashar, Deborah. 2005. *Contesting Citizenship in Latin America: The Rise of Indigenous Movements and the Postliberal Challenge*. New York: Cambridge University Press.

Yeatman, Anna. 1993. "Voice and Representation in the Politics of Difference." Pp. 228–245 in *Feminism and the Politics of Difference*, edited by S. Gunew and A. Yeatman. Boulder, CO: Westview Press.

Yoder, Janice D. 1991. "Rethinking Tokenism: Looking Beyond Numbers." *Gender and Society* 5:178–192.

Yoon, Mi Yung. 2001. "Democratization and Women's Legislative Representation in Sub-Saharan Africa." *Democratization* 8(2):169–190.

Yoon, Mi Yung. 2004. "Explaining Women's Legislative Representation in Sub-Saharan Africa." *Legislative Studies Quarterly* 29(3):447–468.

Yoon, Mi Yung. 2011a. "Factors Hindering 'Larger' Representation of Women in Parliament: The Case of Seychelles," *Commonwealth & Comparative Politics* 49(1):98–114.

Yoon, Mi Yung. 2011b. "More Women in the Tanzanian Legislature: Do Numbers Matter?" *Journal of Contemporary African Studies* 29(1):83–98.

Yoon, Mi Yung and Sheila Bunwaree. 2008. "Is a Minority Truly Powerless? Female Legislators in Mauritius." *Asian Women* 24(3):83–102.

Young, Iris M. 1990. *Justice and the Politics of Difference*. Princeton, NJ: Princeton University Press.

Yuval-Davis, Nira. 1997. *Gender and Nation*. Thousand Oaks, CA: Sage.

Yuval-Davis, Nira. 2006. "Intersectionality and Feminist Politics." *European Journal of Women's Studies* 13(3):193–209.

Yuval-Davis, Nira and Pnina Werbner, eds. 1999. *Women, Citizenship and Difference*. London: Zed Books.

Zarakhovich, Yuri. 2005. "Ukraine's Iron Lady: Yuliya Tymoshenko Still Has to Convince Doubters That She's the Right Choice to Be the New Prime Minister," *Time Europe*. January 30.

Zetkin, Clara. 1920. "Lenin on the Women Question." Transcribed by S. Ryan. Available online at http://www.marxists.org/archive/zetkin/1920/lenin/zetkin1.htm.

Zetterberg, Par. 2008. "Do Gender Quotas Foster Women's Political Engagement?: Lessons From Latin America." *Political Research Quarterly* 62(4):715–730.

Zinsser, Judith P. 1990. "The United Nations Decade for Women: A Quiet Revolution." *The History Teacher* 24(1):19–29.

Zubaida, Sami. 1987. "The Quest for the Islamic State: Islamic Fundamentalism in Egypt and Iran." Pp. 25–50 in *Studies in Religious Fundamentalism*, edited by L. Caplin. Albany: State University of New York Press.

Zuckerman, Elaine and Marcia Greenberg. 2004. "The Gender Dimensions Of Post-Conflict Reconstruction: An Analytical Framework for Policymakers." *Gender and Development* 12(3):70–82.

Glossary

19th Amendment—U.S. amendment to the Constitution granting women the right to vote.

Allocation of surplus—control over how excess money, goods, land, and/or labor are to be used.

Authoritarian regime—government, including a dictatorship and military regime, that is unconstrained by the will of the governed and often uses oppressive tactics to maintain power.

Balance—party attempts to include a range of candidates in order to appeal to different subsets of voters.

Boomerang effect—the process by which domestic individuals or organizations seek international support for a cause to pressure governments to act.

Cabinet—a body of governmental officials that advises government leaders, oversees government activities, and in some countries decides the direction the government should take.

Candidate quota—types of **gender quota** that requires all **political parties** in a country to field a certain percentage of female candidates; in contrast to **reserved seat** or **political party quota**.

Civil society—voluntary associations and connections between citizens apart from the state and outside the economy.

Clientelist system—political structure in which power operates through informal and unequal networks of exchange between patrons (politicians) who distribute resources to clients (citizens) in return for loyalty, support, and votes.

Closed party list—a type of **proportional representation system** where parties create lists of candidates and voters have no influence on the order in which candidates on party lists are elected; in contrast to **open party list**.

Congressional delegation—a group of representatives from a U.S. state.

Contagion effect—when the adoption of a policy or practice by one political party generates pressure on other parties in the political system to change as well.

Context—surrounding circumstances, places, or events.

Critical acts—initiatives undertaken that benefit women and lead to further changes on behalf of women, regardless of women's numerical presence.

Critical mass—a theory that, when women or other minority groups are represented in great enough numbers, often 15% or 30%, they will be better able to pursue their distinct policy priorities and legislative styles.

Cross-national—including two or more countries or nations.

Culture—a society's way of life: traditions and systems of belief that define individual behavior.

Demand factors—characteristics of countries, electoral systems, or **political parties** that make it more likely that women will be pulled into office from the supply of willing candidates.

Democracy—a political system with the central tenet of rule by the people where certain freedoms, such as the freedom to associate, are typically guaranteed in law and practice.

Descriptive representation—numeric similarity between legislative bodies and the electorate they represent in terms of gender, race, ethnicity, or other demographic characteristics.

Diffusion—the process by which a new idea or policy is introduced and spread across time and place.

Direct democracy—a form of **democracy** in which the people hold the power to initiate and vote on laws directly, rather than operating through elected representatives.

District magnitude—the number of representatives an electoral district sends to the national legislature.

Double barriers—the multiple obstacles often faced by those occupying more than one marginalized status in a society.

Economic power—a term used by gender stratification theorists to describe when certain groups or classes of individuals exert control over the **means of production** and **allocation of surplus**.

Equal Rights Amendment (ERA)—proposed as the 27th Amendment to the U.S. Constitution to establish that "Equality of rights under the law shall not be denied or abridged by the United States or by any State on account of sex."

Essentialism—the assumption that all women (or all members of another group) share a common set of characteristics, attributes, and/or interests.

Expediency—a strategy used by the women's movement to pursue **suffrage** by any means necessary, including the compromising of other movement goals or values.

Expediency frames—arguments for female **suffrage** based in women's difference or special skills, such as their higher levels of morality; in contrast to **justice frames.**

Export-oriented economies—economies in which the strategy for growth and prosperity is the export of resources rather than the creation and maintenance of domestic markets.

Family laws—laws regulating marriage, divorce, child custody, and inheritance, often disproportionately affecting women.

Feminist/feminism(s)—individuals, theories, or social movements that, although diverse, are similar in advocating for equality between men and women.

First-wave feminism—period of feminist activity during the 19th and early 20th centuries that focused on gaining women's **suffrage** as a primary goal; in contrast to second-wave feminism.

Formal representation—the legal right to participate in politics: women having the right to vote and stand for office.

Framing processes—a term in the study of social movements to describe how movement participants shape movement messages to generate support or motivate action.

Free—a category created by Freedom House to describe countries that have extensive civil and political liberties.

Gender gap—differences between men and women in their rates of voting, policy preferences, party affiliations, vote choices, and forms of political participation.

Gender mainstreaming—the systematic incorporation of gender into all government institutions and policies.

Gender quotas—constitutional regulations, electoral laws, or political party rules that require a certain percentage of candidates or legislators to be women.

Gerrymandering—when legislators draw electoral district boundaries to maximize the chances of election of their own party.

Global south—countries and regions that are less developed or industrialized; sometimes referred to as the Third World.

Head of government—a national leader with ruling authority over the executive cabinet and/or parliament, typically carrying the title of president or prime minister.

Incumbents—the current holders of political office.

Industrialized—regions, countries, or regions of countries that have transformed socially, economically, and technologically to rely on industrial production rather than agriculture or small-scale production; also referred to as "developed."

Intersectionality—a term used to describe how multiple sources of identity (gender, race, ethnicity, class, sexuality, age, etc.) interrelate to affect experience.

Justice frames—arguments that the right to vote should be available to women because they deserve the same rights and privileges as men; in contrast to **expediency frames.**

Land tenure—the system of laws that governs who may own land and how ownership or control over land may be transferred from person to person.

Legislative committees—groups of legislators who meet to prepare or review legislation in a particular area or to oversee legislative functioning; for example, the Rules Committee.

Lower house—one of two chambers in a bicameral legislature, often called the House of Representatives or Chamber of Deputies; usually the chamber with greater power.

Machinery of government—the agencies, departments, and ministries that develop and implement policy within government.

Machismo—a term historically used in Latin America to describe an ideology that exaggerates masculinity, asserts male superiority over women, and links cultural standards, such as large families and women staying home, to male virility; see also **marianismo.**

Majoritarian electoral systems—type of voting systems where the candidate who gains the most votes wins the election, even if he or she does not obtain an absolute majority of votes. Sometimes called a "first past the post" system.

Majority–minority districts—electoral districts in which the majority of constituents are members of racial or ethnic minority groups.

Marianismo—a term used in Latin America to describe an ideology that idealizes women as morally superior, strong, and selfless mothers while also dependent on and submissive to men; see also **machismo.**

Means of production—the land, power, tools, and other materials used to make products.

Military authoritarianism—a form of government in which the military rules, typically unconstrained by the will of the governed and using oppressive tactics to maintain power.

Mixed systems—electoral systems that elect legislatures through a combination of proportional representation and plurality–majority methods.

Modernization—a process of economic and cultural development often linked to industrialization.

Modernizing revolutions—revolutions where the movement leaders advance ideas that serve to emancipate women or challenge women's traditional roles; this is in contrast to **patriarchal revolutions.**

Multimember districts—voting districts represented by multiple elected officials.

Nationalism—a political belief that groups bound by common ethnicity, language, or values have the right to govern themselves within an independent territory.

National legislature—a legislature; internationally elected legislative bodies may be referred to as parliaments or national legislatures.

Not free—a category created by Freedom House to describe countries that lack basic civil and political liberties.

Open party lists—a type of proportional representation system where parties create lists of candidates but voters have at least some influence on the order in which a party's candidates are elected; in contrast to **closed party lists.**

Open seats—seats in which the current officeholder has resigned, died, or is otherwise not running for reelection.

Opposition leader—head of the largest party that is not in the legislative majority.

Optional Protocol—a supplemental treaty to the Convention on the Elimination of All Forms of Discrimination Against Women (CEDAW) designed to improve enforcement by establishing an oversight committee.

Parity quota—a type of **gender quota** requiring that women and men hold equal shares of seats in national legislatures.

Parliament—a legislature; internationally elected legislative bodies may be referred to as parliaments or national legislatures.

Partly free—a category created by Freedom House to describe countries that have moderate levels of civil and political liberties.

Patriarchal revolutions—revolutions that connect national liberation or revolutionary success to women's traditional familial roles; this is in contrast to **modernizing revolutions.**

Patriarchy—the social system of male domination over females, where males hold positions of power and authority in social, political, and economic domains.

Placement mandates—rules about the order of male and female candidates on electoral lists.

Plurality–majority systems—electoral systems where voters typically vote for a single candidate and the candidate with the most votes wins.

Politburo—the executive body that governs the Communist Party.

Political culture—a common set of political ideals or beliefs held by a country or group of individuals regarding how government should be run.

Political Left—ideas, policies, and **political parties** closer to the progressive, socialist, or social democratic part of the political spectrum; it is in contrast to the **political Right.**

Political opportunity structure/political opportunities—the broader political environment, and changes therein, confronting social movements and enhancing or constraining their growth and success.

Political parties—organizations with a common set of political beliefs that seek to attain political power and pursue.

Political party quota—**gender quota** that is regulated by **political parties** and not mandated by a country's laws; in contrast to constitutional quotas or **electoral law quotas**.

Political recruitment model—a model of how individual citizens become politicians as they move from eligible to aspirant to candidate to legislator.

Political Right—ideas, policies, and **political parties** closer to the conservative or classic liberal part of the political spectrum; it is in contrast to the **political Left**.

Political socialization—the process by which young people learn about the political environment and their place in it.

Private sphere—areas of life dealing with the family and home; this is in contrast to the public sphere.

Proportional representation (PR) systems—electoral systems in which citizens vote for parties and seats in the legislature, and they are distributed according to the percentage of the vote received by each party.

Public sphere—areas of life where one interacts with others in the outside world or greater society, including work, politics, schools, and the community; this is in contrast to the private sphere.

Puzzle of success—when women from racial and ethnic minority groups occupy a greater share of their group's legislative seats than do women from majority groups.

Radical flank effects—when the presence of more radical or extremist groups in a social movement helps encourage support of more moderate groups.

Ratification—when a state adopts an international treaty, agreeing to follow the principles and practices enshrined therein.

Reserved seats—parliamentary seats that may only be filled by women regardless of the number of female candidates or nominees.

Resource mobilization—the ability of social movement participants to organize and effectively use financial and human resources to their benefit.

Resource model of political participation—a model that links differences in men's and women's political participation to individual-level inequalities in political resources, such as money, free time, and civic skills.

Safe position—a position on a party list that is expected to win a seat in the legislature.

Sanctions for noncompliance—penalties assessed to **political parties** that do not comply with a **gender quota.**

Second shift—a sociological term for women's continuing responsibility for domestic tasks, such as cooking and cleaning, despite working full-time in the labor force.

Semidemocracy—a political system with elements of both **democracy** and authoritarianism; for example, a system where citizens can elect government representatives but have few freedoms.

Seneca Falls Convention—a convention in 1848 where the first formal demand was made for women's right to vote in the United States.

Social democratic ideology—a politically Left ideology that stresses democratic reform of the capitalist system to reduce social inequalities.

Social movements—groups of people or organizations acting together to generate or resist social.

Social structure—enduring features of social life such as education and work that shape the behavior of individuals and groups.

Standard deviation—a common statistical measure that indicates the dispersion or spread of data points; if data points are close to the average value, the statistic is low, but if data points vary widely, the statistic is high.

Strategic opportunities—the chances and/or benefits that result from occupying more than one marginalized status in a society.

Substantive representation—advocating the interests and issues of a group; for women, ensuring that politicians speak for and act to support women's issues.

Suffrage—the right to vote.

Suffragettes—members of the movement for women's **suffrage,** originally used in the United Kingdom to single out more radical or militant movement participants; in contrast to **suffragist.**

Suffragists—a general term used to identify members of the women's **suffrage** movement, including radical and moderate members and both men and women.

Supply factors—factors that increase the pool of women with the will and experience to compete against men for political office.

Term limits—a legislative or constitutional rule that an individual may only hold a political office for a limited number of terms.

Tokens—small numbers of women or minorities included in organizations or legislatures and assumed to be unable to affect change.

Transgender—individuals who do not identify with and/or present as the sex they were assigned at birth.

Transsexual—a person who lives his or her life as the opposite sex they were assigned at birth and in many cases has taken steps to reassign his or her sex through hormones and/or surgery.

Triple burden—the responsibility to participate fully in the labor force, take care of the home and family, and participate in politics.

Upper house—one of two chambers in a bicameral legislature, often called the Senate; usually the chamber with lesser power.

Women's international nongovernmental organizations (WINGOs)—international nongovernmental groups or associations that serve the interests of women.

Women Power Index—a measure of women's political power; calculated as the percentage of women in parliament in a country, multiplied by the proportion of the world's population that lives in that country, and added across all of the countries of interest.

Women's policy machinery—a government body or bodies devoted to promoting the status of women.

Index

⑤SAGE researchmethods

The essential online tool for researchers from the world's leading methods publisher

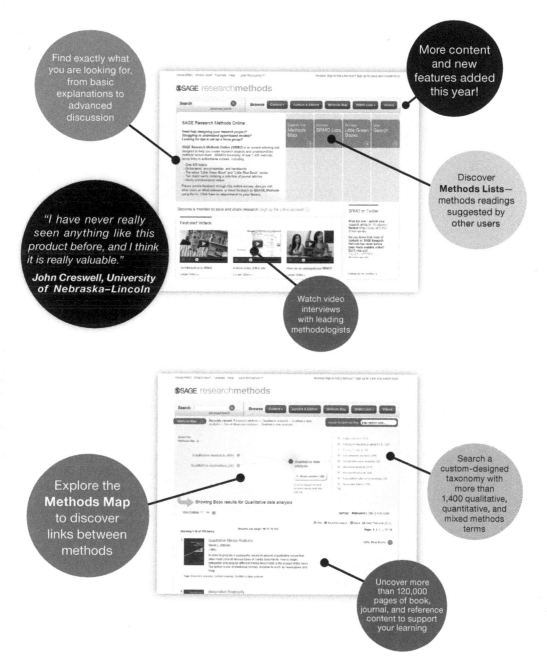

Find exactly what you are looking for, from basic explanations to advanced discussion

More content and new features added this year!

"I have never really seen anything like this product before, and I think it is really valuable."

John Creswell, University of Nebraska–Lincoln

Discover **Methods Lists**— methods readings suggested by other users

Watch video interviews with leading methodologists

Explore the **Methods Map** to discover links between methods

Search a custom-designed taxonomy with more than 1,400 qualitative, quantitative, and mixed methods terms

Uncover more than 120,000 pages of book, journal, and reference content to support your learning

Find out more at
www.sageresearchmethods.com